BIRCHERS

Also by Matthew Dallek

*Defenseless Under the Night: The Roosevelt Years
and the Origins of Homeland Security*

*The Right Moment: Ronald Reagan's First Victory and
the Decisive Turning Point in American Politics*

BIRCHERS

How the John Birch Society Radicalized the American Right

MATTHEW DALLEK

BASIC BOOKS

New York

Basic Books
Hachette Book Group
1290 Avenue of the Americas, New York, NY 10104
www.basicbooks.com

Printed in the United States of America

First Edition: March 2023

Published by Basic Books, an imprint of Perseus Books, LLC, a subsidiary of Hachette Book Group, Inc. The Basic Books name and logo is a trademark of the Hachette Book Group.

The Hachette Speakers Bureau provides a wide range of authors for speaking events. To find out more, go to www.hachettespeakersbureau.com or call (866) 376-6591.

The publisher is not responsible for websites (or their content) that are not owned by the publisher.

Print book interior design by Amy Quinn.

Library of Congress Cataloging-in-Publication Data
Names: Dallek, Matthew, 1969- author.
Title: Birchers: how the John Birch society radicalized the American right / Matthew Dallek.
Description: New York: Basic Books, [2023] | Includes bibliographical references and index.
Identifiers: LCCN 2022049307 | ISBN 9781541673564 (hardcover) | ISBN 9781541673571 (ebook)
Subjects: LCSH: Conservatism—United States—History. | John Birch Society—History. | Right-wing extremists—United States—History. | Welch, Robert, 1899-1985. | United States—Politics and government.
Classification: LCC JC573.2.U6 D35 2023 | DDC 320.520973—dc23/eng/20221115
LC record available at https://lccn.loc.gov/2022049307

ISBNs: 9781541673564 (hardcover), 9781541673571 (ebook)

LSC-C

Printing 1, 2023

To Robert Dallek
a great historian—but an even better dad

CONTENTS

Introduction

FRINGE TO CENTER

IN 1962, A SECRETIVE, FAR-RIGHT GROUP CALLED THE JOHN BIRCH Society was scheming to stop the California Republican Party's preferred
candidate in a bitter electoral contest—one of many such campaigns it
was waging in local and state elections. Just four years old at the time, the
Birch Society was already the country's most notorious far-right movement, and it had become known for its brutal tactics and extremist ideas
concerning hidden communist conspiracies within the United States. It
tended to harass its foes and paint them as rank traitors. Its opponent
in this particular battle, Patricia Hitt, was a member of the Republican
National Committee, a top ally of Richard Nixon, and a rare woman
in a position of party leadership. At the time, Birchers were running for
seats on Orange County school boards and plotting to wrest power from
moderates in GOP women's clubs. Hitt was one of the establishment Republicans who stood squarely in their path. When she ran for a seat on
her party's county committee, the society unloaded on her.

Letters, many using the same stock phrases, started arriving at her
home. The tone, she said, was "nasty," and "considerable hate" was rain-
ing down on her and her family. Worse still was the phone harassment.

1

At all hours, Hitt received calls from anonymous speakers with essentially the same message: "You'll rue this day." When she and her husband switched to an unlisted number, the Birchers shifted to calling registered Republicans throughout her district and denouncing her as a "communist," a "socialist," and a "pinko." "That kind of slander" was effective, Hitt recalled. "People who didn't know who I was defeated me."

Tangling with the John Birch Society was an unforgettable ordeal for opponents like Hitt who endured it. More than the loss itself, what scarred Hitt was the Birchers' zealotry. "They were wild," she later reflected. "They were haters beyond anything I've ever seen in my life." They were "an enormously destructive force. In my opinion, they're more destructive than the other extreme. Maybe it's because they're ours. The Birch Society," she underscored, "is ours."[1]

Hitt assumed that such a loathsome faction would stay at the margins of her party. Birchers might harass her and her GOP colleagues, win an election here and there, or launch a few quixotic primary campaigns to topple incumbents. But, she reasoned, they were destined to hover at the far-right edge of the political spectrum. Hitt figured that the mid-century consensus, in which citizens were thought to abhor extremists on the left and the right, would keep Birchers on the defensive and ensure that mainstream sensibilities prevailed. Her colleagues in the Republican establishment—even on the right-wing edge of that establishment—agreed. They were convinced that there was simply no realistic way for the fringe to assemble an electoral coalition that could vault them to power. And for a long time they were correct.

But in recent years, especially with the ascent of Donald Trump to the presidency and to leadership of the American right, what it means to be a conservative or a member of the Republican Party has changed—and the newly dominant political ideas and attitudes bear the imprint of the John Birch Society. The extremist takeover of the American right required more than six decades and was by no means inevitable. In fact, for a while the John Birch Society receded from influence, but over time its ideas—or the lineal descendants of its ideas—solidified their place in the conservative coalition and eventually, in the second decade of the twenty-first century, enjoyed a revival. *Birchers* depicts the life and afterlife of an organization that did more than any other conservative entity to propel this extremist takeover: the John Birch Society, which mobilized a loyal army of activists and forged ideas that ultimately upended American politics.

Even long after its membership waned and its time in the spotlight faded, the Birch Society influenced the ideas and the style of far-right activists and groups, eventually enabling the fringe to engulf the GOP. Drawing on thousands of documents from a variety of archives, this story encompasses the voices of activists, many of them women, as well as those of the movement's allies and critics. It shows the extraordinary steps that a liberal Cold War coalition took to constrain the society, including a massive and previously undisclosed spy operation that targeted Birchers over many years, penetrating its inner sanctum and contributing to the society's downfall. Yet the ideas and tactics of Birchism continued to inspire the far right and today have made a stunning comeback.

The political right in the United States has always encompassed a variety of factions or dispositions, including chamber of commerce conservatives and Wall Street conservatives, libertarians and fundamentalist Christians, those reconciled to the New Deal and those bent on repealing it. Historians have typically distinguished between the more moderate Republicans like Dwight Eisenhower, who dominated the party for years, and the more ideological "movement conservatives," who burst on the scene first with Barry Goldwater in the early 1960s and then, more enduringly, with Ronald Reagan's election as president in 1980.[2] But this story makes clear that another dividing line also existed within the conservative coalition—with *all* the mainstream, electorally successful figures, from Eisenhower to Reagan, on one side and a more extreme, ultraconservative faction, including the Birchers, on the other. It also makes clear that the differences between these ultraconservatives and what I will call the mainstream right were real and substantive.

Many issues separated the Birch fringe from the Reagan-Goldwater right, but major distinctions centered on explicit racism, anti-interventionism versus internationalism, conspiracy theories, and a more apocalyptic, violent, antiestablishment mode of politics. While

the mainstream and fringe wings of conservatism aligned on discrete issues and in particular moments, the Birch Society and the mainstream
conservative movement frequently had sharp differences of opinion that
pulled them in opposing directions. For years, the two were more antagonists than partners, each side working to check the other and seeing
each other as the enemy within. More than mainstream conservatives,
Birchers trafficked in conspiracy theories and advocated aggressive resistance to the civil rights movement. After NAACP leader Medgar Evers
was assassinated by a white supremacist, a Birch film blamed him for
his own death—a contention that didn't sit well with the mainstream
right. Birchers charged that President Eisenhower abetted the communists, distributed flyers calling President John F. Kennedy a traitor, and
repudiated NATO. Their criticisms of government ("one worlders") and
media ("Spanish Inquisition!") helped spark a revolt against America's
institutions and its elites at a time when trust in both was diminishing
across the ideological spectrum. Birchers lobbied school boards to ban
supposedly communist teachings such as sex education (a "filthy communist plot"), shouted down speakers in public forums ("commie-symp!"),
formed front groups to push their causes in secret, and deployed fear
and intimidation as political weapons, threatening to inflict unspecified
harms on their foes.[3]

Conservative GOP leaders like Richard Nixon, Ronald Reagan, and
Barry Goldwater—politicians who, despite their differences with one another, all fit within the Republican conservative mainstream—sometimes
invoked Bircher language and copied these extremist tactics. But their
oratory and ideas were consistently less violent, conspiratorial, and apocalyptic, and when pressed they made clear that they wished to separate
themselves from at least some elements of their far-right flank. This was
true even of Goldwater, seen by many at the time as the epitome of right-
wing Republicanism. Birchers declared that communists controlled the
civil rights movement, but Goldwater, despite voting against the Civil
Rights Act of 1964 as a US senator, avoided such talk. While Birchers
spun out scenarios of communist plots in government, equating liberals
with left-wingers and both with communists, Goldwater merely claimed
that the Democratic Party "was captured by Socialist ideologues in and

about the labor movement."⁴ When Birchers agitated to impeach Chief Justice Earl Warren, Goldwater agreed that Warren and the Supreme Court had abused their power without going so far as to call for his removal. Whereas Birchers occasionally flirted with third parties, ran for office as states' rights candidates, and challenged mainstream conservatives in long-shot GOP primary bids, Goldwater urged conservatives to "grow up" and take over the Republican Party. The handful of Birchers who held seats in Congress during the 1960s and 1970s bucked the Republican Party's support for military interventions and immigration reform, instead clamoring for the United States to withdraw from the United Nations and viewing international alliances as a socialist one-world plot to destroy America's sovereignty.⁵

The far right's role and impact within the broader conservative movement from roughly 1974 to 2010 was a mixed bag. At times, fringe individuals and groups successfully pushed their ideas into the heart of national politics and a position of power within the Republican Party, especially on questions of morality, gender, and sexuality. But on some of the weightiest issues of those decades—immigration, internationalism, military interventions, the size of the welfare state, civil rights, and taxes—the far right also experienced numerous setbacks. The right-wing fringe was part of the conservative GOP's coalition but only intermittently came out on top, and its constellation of ideas—explicit racism, anti-interventionism, conspiracism, an apocalyptic mindset, and culture wars—haltingly, over many decades, exerted more and more authority within the broader GOP conservative coalition.

In the late 1970s and 1980s, the society's culture-war legacy combined with its radical brand of economic libertarianism to become more central to conservative Republicans. In the 1990s, a strain of isolationism began to creep more forcefully into GOP rhetoric and legislative policy, and conspiracy theories in response to Bill Clinton's presidency ensconced themselves in the broader American right. Around 2008 to 2010, with the election of Barack Obama, some Republicans turned to more explicit racism and intensified the Birch-like, apocalyptic approach to politics and policy. In the 2010s, the far right, inheritors of the Birch tradition, finally came out on top. Though it is tempting to lump the mainstream right and the right-wing fringe together, especially in light of where they ended up, the right became radicalized because conservative leaders had courted the fringe (especially during their election campaigns) over five decades; large-scale changes sweeping the economy, culture, and world popularized the far right's ideas; and the fringe's decades-long quest to gain power came to maturation.

Republican conservative candidates for high office also made a series of bets that backfired. They wooed far-right activists on the theory that their political support was essential to winning elections and that their more outlandish ideas could be kept at bay. Conservatives vying for office attended rallies sponsored by the far right, endorsed some of their causes, and spoke in their idiom. But when these GOP leaders took office, they governed to the far right's satisfaction only intermittently. Republican leaders figured that they could do just enough to keep the culture warriors, conspiracy theorists, extreme free marketeers, and anti–civil rights radicals in their camp while also maintaining support from mainstream conservatives, especially suburban women. Their bet paid off for a time, until control over the process ultimately slipped from their grasp. Especially in the final years of George W. Bush's presidency, with the administration losing credibility in both foreign and economic policy, the far right's ideas grew more popular. On the big issues—America's role in the world, the nation's stance toward immigrants, race relations, and views of major institutions and elites—Republican voters started to shift in the far right's favor. The internet made it harder for Republican leaders to check the fringe members of their coalition, and the far right effectively weaponized the primary process. From GOP-backed tax hikes in the 1980s and early 1990s to the GOP-led wars in Iraq, from failure to curb immigration in the 2000s to the financial crash of 2008, the far right's frustration with the conservative establishment intensified, and a narrative among the activists took root: Republican leaders had betrayed them. Bitterness and resentments deepened.

Beyond the internecine warfare, the nation's changing economy and culture enabled Birch successors to gain adherents and ascend to power. In the last two decades of the twentieth century, economic and demographic shifts intensified the far right's sense of alienation and disempowerment. A steady influx of Asian, African, and Latin American immigrants (and fewer white European immigrants) unnerved many whites, who feared that the interlopers threatened their values and their belief that the United States was a white Christian country. The decades-long process of deindustrialization, 1970s-era inflation, and the combination of a fraying safety net, declining public investment, and widening income and wealth disparities in the 1980s seemed to make the American dream increasingly unattainable. The severing of white working-class voters from unions (over many decades) helped break those voters' connection with the Democratic Party and New Deal liberalism. These were forces in the rise of Reagan, of course, but they also played into the agenda of the Birch Society's successors on the movement's fringe, who exploited the cultural shifts and economic shocks, stoking white citizens' resentments. Such broad changes in politics and culture amplified fears that immigrants were flooding the borders and taking people's jobs. Structural shifts—including popular revulsion with the federal government—blocked Democrats' attempts to mitigate economic pain. Right-wing press and politicians constantly told voters that snooty liberal elites were laughing at them, disrespecting them. The culture—Hollywood actors, Harvard professors, Beltway pundits—now seemed stacked against many white citizens, rigged to mock their habits, their faith, their families. After failing to win majorities at the ballot box, some heirs to the Birchers increasingly turned to violent and anti-democratic means of wielding power.

The end of the Cold War also shook the foundations of American politics and imbued the anti-interventionist successors to the Birchers with political authority and moral zeal. The fall of the Berlin Wall in 1989 gave isolationists a chance to critique the broad bipartisan commitment to America's liberal internationalist leadership. With the implosion of the Soviet Union, the conservative belief in militarism abroad started to waver. Pat Buchanan, Ron Paul, and other proponents of anti-intervention argued that America's alliances, treaties, wars, and free-trade pacts eroded US sovereignty. They urged Americans to revive the 1920s-era traditions of avoiding entangling alliances, closing America's borders, and celebrating the nation's Anglo-Saxon heritage.[6]

The September 11, 2001, terrorist attacks initially undercut these America First sentiments. But the quagmires in Afghanistan and Iraq, followed by civil war in Syria, the rise of the Islamic State, and the refugee crisis in Europe, triggered still more doubts about the wisdom of globalization, immigration, and trade as tools to spread democracy overseas.

Economic and social developments internal to the United States also led a resurgent far right to capitalize on the shifting debate late in George W. Bush's administration. By 2008, economic conditions had grown increasingly dire in the eyes of many Americans, and the collapse of Bush's electoral coalition rattled the Republican Party and helped the fringe clamber atop the GOP. The financial crisis and the Great Recession sharpened income inequality and exposed the fragility and unfairness of the nation's economic system. Bush's decision to bail out the banks and the automotive industry triggered a rebellion from the more populist elements within his own party and fomented discontent on the far right. Republicans were abandoning him during the worst financial crisis since the 1930s. Something profound was reshaping the Republican Party and what conservatives believed and wanted. Activists and donors soured on Bush as another exponent of the establishment, a Judas to their cause, and seized on the crisis to challenge conservative Republican orthodoxy. Only pure antigovernment activists could save the United States from a corrupt ruling elite. The election of the nation's first African American president combined with the enactment of sweeping health care reform and the halting economic recovery to produce the Tea Party, and a more explicit racism and nativism took root. Powered by thousands of activists fighting to take back what they said was their country (with support from far-right foundations and donors, some of which had ties to the Birch movement), the Tea Party drew on Birchite conspiracy theories and tapped its white supremacist, anti-interventionist, and antiestablishment themes. These ideas gained more and more sway within the Republican Party during Obama's presidency.

BIRCHERS IS IN PART THE STORY OF A SMALL BAND OF ANTI–NEW DEAL businessmen who founded an organization named after an evangelist turned warrior who was killed by Chinese communists. It is also a chronicle of how, from 1958 till the early 1970s, these defenders of radical individualism mobilized an estimated sixty thousand to one hundred thousand white, upwardly mobile, change-fearing, mostly Christian, often suburban men and women, who united to defeat a set of common threats and reclaim a moral universe that they believed underpinned their own social, spiritual, and economic well-being. Finally, this book is an exploration of how Birch ideas and practices outlasted the organization itself and came to influence today's Republican Party in unexpected ways.[7]

During its heyday in the early and mid-1960s, the Birch Society was hardly seen as the avatar of a new brand of dominant politics. Critics, including Republicans, ridiculed the Birchers, derided them as fanatics and a "lunatic fringe," and condemned them as representative of a "paranoid style in American politics" that rebelled against modernity.[8] But time and again, the group's leaders weaponized such dismissals, stoking members' resentment and intensifying their desire to fight for their beliefs. The elite slights also ignored the innovations that Birchers, among other groups, brought to politics—causes and strategies that established an alternative to the *National Review*-Goldwater-Reagan model, proving that the supercharged activism of thousands of diehards could outmatch the votes of millions of citizens and over time transform the GOP. While Birchers promoted baseless conspiracy theories as fact (fluoridation in the water represented "a massive wedge for socialized medicine," "extremely dangerous . . . to the public water supplies"), they also understood how allegations of a plot against the United States rallied activists in opposition to a common foe and motivated citizens to participate in the struggle for power. They used modern technology, understood contemporary culture, and functioned as largely rational political beings. They were one of the groups on the right that demonstrated how mass mobilization around single issues could reap dividends far beyond the particular issue at hand, showing subsequent generations of conservatives how to campaign against the likes of abortion rights, gun control, and Obamacare and how to win multitudes of converts in the process.[9]

Beyond the potent influence of Birch Society leaders lay the tectonic-shifting power of tens of thousands of activist homeowners, housewives, and middle-class professionals, whose zeal initially posed a problem for conservative Republicans but soon made the GOP a more robust antigovernment party.[10] Birch activists won seats on local school boards, traded ideas in their neighborhood bookstores, and volunteered for like-minded candidates. They filtered a conspiratorial brand of single-minded anticommunism through the perceived needs of their towns and suburbs. At times they trafficked in racist or antisemitic stereotypes and succeeded in braiding these strains of hate into a broader culture war, integrating bigots into a larger coalition. They rejected virtually the entire post–World War II, US-led international order, urging the United States to get out of the United Nations, denouncing the foreign policy establishment as a communistic cabal, and telling leaders to focus on the gravest threat to the country: the internal plot to destroy Americans' liberties.

Although conservative political leaders denounced Birch Society founder Robert Welch, they benefited from his followers' work. Birchers enthusiastically voted in local elections, publicized issues of law and order and anticommunism at the community level, volunteered in and donated to Republican campaigns, and got out the vote on Election Day. Even during the organization's period of relative dormancy after 1974, Birch successors—hard-right conservatives who kept the society's legacy alive, adopting its ideas and tactics—continued to fuel grassroots mobilization, popularize conspiracy theories, promote isolationism, elevate public morality, and police values in the culture at large. All these Birch-tinged efforts helped the GOP and conservative political leaders, even those who would have been uncomfortable with card-carrying Birchers in their ranks.

In its time, the Birch Society helped forge a coalition of super-wealthy industrialists and upwardly mobile professionals with white working-class conservatives and evangelicals, many of them Southern and many of them sometime Democrats. The society united conservatives geographically as well. While its brand of far-right politics found many adherents in the Sunbelt, its appeal was considerably broader, resonating with a subset of voters and activists in every region of the United States. The society's national footprint augured an underappreciated breadth of cross-sectional popular support for the far right. In the Midwest and the Northeast, Birchers were surprisingly energetic, belying the long-held assumption that California, Arizona, and Texas were bellwethers where the fringe road-tested plans and erected infrastructure. From Helena and Indianapolis to Milwaukee and Boston, Welch and his followers ignited a nationwide movement.

The society also embraced a view of freedom that influenced future far-right activists. Birchers defined freedom not through access to the ballot box for all, nor as the freedom to act in accord with one's own precepts, and certainly not as the freedom from want. They claimed, "We're a republic, not a democracy," holding that a relatively small group of Americans who looked and acted like Birchers should be in charge of the United States. Their conception of the republic demanded the dismantling of the welfare state and dreamed of imposing their own version of Christian values on American schools and culture.[11] The society was also an early adopter of a strain of right-wing culture-war politics that became increasingly important to conservatives. Birchers inspired the religious right, thrust wedge issues of sex, gender, race, and education into a dominant place in American politics, and helped embed in the culture a set of traditional values around which supporters could rally.

THE QUESTION OF HOW THE FAR RIGHT CAME TO DOMINATE CONSERVATISM and overtake the GOP has been a focus of a great deal of analysis. Some historians have depicted the Birch Society as "the 'mainstream' right's vanguard." Trump's election as president revealed the surprising (and, to many, disturbing) resonance of certain ideas and tendencies, from outlandish conspiracism to naked racism, that most analysts had assumed would always remain confined to the fringes. Some now argued that the Republican Party or the conservative movement had all along been awash in these extreme views, that Bircher ideas had always been central, not merely peripheral—we just hadn't seen or acknowledged it.

But in the rush to explain Trump, these accounts understated how much he directly took on the movement conservatism that had held sway, more or less, through the George W. Bush presidency. The process of radicalization of the Republican Party was in fact contingent, halting, and gradual, not foreordained and inevitable. There was not a clear split between the "addled, racist fringe" and the mainstream conservative

movement, but nor was the fringe "the base" of the conservative movement, fundamental to its worldview. The distinctions, in other words,
were as significant as any commonalities. Drawing too straight a line
from the past to the present elides the tensions, conflicts, and contra-
dictions within the modern conservative coalition and gives more power
to proponents of the far right than they actually deserve. Birchers and
their successors were not in the vanguard of the mainstream right but
were fringe actors who hovered around the margins of politics and policy.
Rather than driving the American right, ultraconservatives amounted
to one element in a set of shifting and unstable Republican conservative
electoral coalitions. Less pragmatic than the establishment right, the far
right had an agenda that was rarely enacted into law (unless it dovetailed
with positions shared by the Republican mainstream), and the GOP's
coalitions, for the most part, were vaster and more consumed by internal
strife than some accounts have implied.[12]

Still, some recent scholarship on the far right has yielded useful insights into the overlap between the establishment and extreme wings of
the GOP. Perhaps the most trenchant corrective has concerned the role
of William F. Buckley, the intellectual founder of modern conservatism
and publisher of *National Review*, who was said to have cordoned off the
Birchers and expelled them through editorials in his magazine. Mainstream political raconteurs long assumed that Buckley was successful in
cutting off the far right, acting as his movement's de facto boundary enforcer and keeping true conservatism clean and free of its seedier aspects.
But the lines between mainstream and fringe were murkier than these
portraits suggest. As two astute political scientists have shown, "However
mythologized by movement conservatives since, Buckley's halting project
of excommunication was more notable for its ineffectuality and tardiness
than its impact in drawing a cordon sanitaire."[13] Throughout the 1950s
Buckley published writers whose work also appeared in *American Mercury*, which had become an antisemitic magazine with ties to the Birch
Society. In 1957 he anticipated the society's anti–civil rights stance when
he called white people "the advanced race" and defended the legitimacy
of Jim Crow. He deplored critics of the red-baiting senator Joseph Mc-
Carthy, a Bircher hero.[14] In short, in light of these and other extreme

positions, Buckley's gesture toward kicking out the Birchers was far more concerned with cordoning off Robert Welch while retaining the support of the rank-and-file members.

The Birch Society's founders tapped traditions with deep roots in the Old Right, the conservative faction that had sought to thwart the progressive and New Deal–era political order. Like the Old Right, Welch and his colleagues believed that the growth of the federal government was a grave betrayal, that labor rights were an offense to individual rights, and that white Christians had repeatedly been forced to accept changes that negated their identity. Women's suffrage and fights for racial equality and labor rights seemed like pieces of the same sinister puzzle.

Finding inspiration from their predecessors, Birch leaders looked to activists who had fought for immigration restriction, opposed the teaching of evolution in schools, and promoted the Ku Klux Klan's anti-Catholic, anti-Jewish, and anti-Black activism. On foreign affairs they drew on the legacy of anti-interventionists and Midwestern isolationists who had opposed America's entry in the First World War and abhorred the Treaty of Versailles as a sop to internationalists and progressives. This older generation of conservatives had argued that the war's true aim was to line the pockets of arms manufacturers and bankers, and that President Woodrow Wilson's League of Nations proposal would destroy America's rights as a sovereign nation. Both arguments of larger forces twisting the nation's creed later informed the Birchers' platform.[15]

To the dozen men who launched the John Birch Society in December 1958, few politicians embodied socialist evil more than the architect of the New Deal, Franklin Delano Roosevelt. Roosevelt's ideas had triumphed; theirs had been mocked. One of the Birch founders described FDR's decision to recognize the Soviet Union in 1933 as "a monumental mistake" and blamed "our government's psychopathic sympathy and support of Russia during World War II" for all the country's problems.[16]

For many Americans across political persuasions, the end of World War II vindicated the ideas and policies of the United States. Spared a land invasion and air raids, the country emerged as the greatest economic and military power in the world. The victory over fascism validated US faith in democracy and free enterprise under a mixed and regulated economy. In the words of the popular liberal columnist Walter Lippmann, "What Rome was to the ancient world, what Great Britain has been to the modern world, America is to be to the world of tomorrow."[17]

But the war's aftermath left the Birch Society's future founders dismayed rather than triumphant. They saw their country abandoning its free-market system and traditional individualistic values. As the Soviet Union grabbed control of Poland, Romania, Bulgaria, and Czechoslovakia and developed atomic weaponry, the men who would found the society came to see President Harry Truman as an effete commander unwilling to halt communist expansion. Although the GOP won majorities in Congress in 1946, Truman's Fair Deal agenda—premised on national health care, civil rights, a progressive income tax, and federal aid to education—showed that FDR's New Deal and wartime government expansion would not be easily repealed. As Welch warned in 1948, "We are throwing away" the country's past achievements "for a phony 'security' and a creeping collectivism."[18]

The Republican Party's ascent to the White House in 1952 was no salve for the Birch Society's founders, who saw 1958 as a particularly dark year. Dwight Eisenhower had been in office for six years, and his administration had produced a string of defeats, including the Korean War stalemate, the Soviet *Sputnik* launch, and acceptance of the New Deal. Conservative groups and organs like *National Review* lacked the kind of direct action and mass educational appeal that the founders felt was necessary to reverse these setbacks. Welch and his cohort believed that mainstream conservatives who focused on military interventions abroad had failed to see the more urgent threat of internal conspiracies at home. These conservatives also struck some Birch founders as unwilling to stomach the kind of in-your-face actions that would alert the country to the enemy within: the destruction of their liberties and religious faith at the hands of their own fellow citizens.

If anything, the Republican Party appeared to be moving in the opposite direction, leaving the Birch founders profoundly disillusioned. After McCarthy's death in 1957, William Proxmire, a Democrat, assumed his seat in the US Senate, and in the 1958 midterm elections Democrats

Eugene McCarthy of Minnesota, Harrison Williams of New Jersey, Stephen Young of Ohio, Clair Engle of California, and Vance Hartke of Indiana won Senate seats previously held by Republicans. (The latter three wins especially pained the society's founders, as the departing GOP incumbents, John Bricker, William Knowland, who in 1958 was running for California governor, and William E. Jenner, had been among the few GOP officials who shared their ideas.) Democrats rejoiced ("Little remains of the reactionary wing of the Senate elected in 1946 and 1952," cheered Americans for Democratic Action in a press release), while Republicans sulked.[19] What the American people needed, Welch and his allies believed, was a national education program to spread the word that communists had taken control of the nation's institutions and that Armageddon was at hand. In December 1958 they created it.

From roughly 1958 to 1974, the Birch Society evolved into a mass movement that influenced political debates about the meaning of conservatism, garnered reams of media coverage in national, local, and international outlets, generated fresh fears of a surge in homegrown fascist politics, and brought an energetic far-right presence to local schools, libraries, and theaters. Birchers became known for their confrontational tactics and seemingly bizarre ideas—that fluoride in drinking water was a communist plot to poison citizens, to cite one example. As the leading symbol of the excesses of the far right, the Birch Society also drew thousands of supporters and adherents—donors, card-carrying members, and nonmember sympathizers. The group became a Rorschach test for where one stood on the nation's political spectrum.

THOUGH THE SOCIETY DECLINED IN THE MID-1970S, BIRCHISM HELPED seed Trumpism. For decades Birchers (and their successors) remained a mostly fringe movement, not regaining strength until the 2010s. Historically Birchers distrusted Richard Nixon, loathed Gerald Ford, and occasionally denounced Ronald Reagan, who had appointed numerous hard-liners but few who subscribed to Birch ideas. The far right regarded George H. W. Bush as a sinister architect of what he called a "new world order" and an emblem of the decrepit Republican Party establishment. And George W. Bush championed some causes that were anathema to

Birch ideology, from immigration reform to the educational platform known as No Child Left Behind, the wars in Afghanistan and Iraq, a massive new homeland security apparatus, and bank bailouts.

The Birch Society did not equal the conservative movement as a whole; the fringe was not, for the most part, the biggest driver of the GOP—until very recently. And it's not bound to remain so indefinitely. The Birchers mattered because they bequeathed a usable past and forged an alternative political tradition, and because GOP mandarins accommodated the Birchers, wooed them for money and votes, and gave them a political home. Such encouragement enabled Michele Bachmann, Sarah Palin, Donald Trump, Marjorie Taylor Greene, and far-right media personalities like Glenn Beck and Alex Jones to thrive and gain power within the conservative movement and the GOP electoral coalition.

Ultimately, as the social and political contexts changed, the far right capitalized on the multiplicity of crises. In the twenty-first century the movement drew on Birch ideas and the Birch conspiratorial style and found a model in the Birch movement.

If you look, then, you will see, in COVID denialism, vaccine disinformation, America First nationalism, school board wars, QAnon plots, and allegations of electoral cheating, a movement from the 1960s, long thought dead, casting its shadow across the United States.

Chapter 1

"GOD'S ANGRY MEN"

IN LATE OCTOBER 1958, ROBERT WELCH, A WEALTHY RETIRED CANDY manufacturer from Belmont, Massachusetts, invited seventeen friends to a "completely 'off the record'" meeting in Indianapolis that would start at 9:00 a.m. on Monday, December 8, and end at 6:00 p.m. the next day. He wished to discuss a topic so sensitive that he refused to set it to paper.

Security measures, Welch believed, were needed. He advised that if anyone asked the participants why they had come to Indiana, they should simply say they were there "on business." He instructed them to book their own hotels to reduce the chance that they would be seen together in public. Still, Welch assured them, there was "nothing even remotely conspiratorial about this gathering."[1]

Welch hoped to launch an organization that could educate the public about the communist conspiracy that allegedly was stripping Americans of their God-given freedoms. He and his allies hoped that if they exposed the threat, citizens would come to appreciate its multidimensional and existential character.

Eleven men ultimately joined Welch for the meeting. The invitees, Welch assured them, were "all A-1 men" who had "unshakable integrity, proved ability, and fervent patriotism." Welch's choice of venue, a Tudor-style home owned by Marguerite Dice, also proved shrewd. While not officially invited to the meeting, Dice was sympathetic to the cause at its center. As national vice-chair of the anticommunist Minute Women, Welch explained, she, too, evinced "fervent patriotism, guided by a sound sense of propriety unpierced by the 'lunatic fringe,'" though what he meant by the last phrase wasn't clear. In 1953 Dice had appeared on Edward R. Murrow's CBS news program *See It Now* wearing a pillbox hat and wire-framed glasses, a study in middle-American rectitude. But her message was bracing. She declared that it would be a "travesty" to permit the American Civil Liberties Union to use the War Memorial Building in Indianapolis to establish a local chapter there. The ACLU's "open and avowed purpose," she warned, was "to overthrow our government by force and violence, as well as by infiltration."[2]

The meeting organized by Welch went well. Between lengthy monologues detailing the nature of the communist threat, the men took time for lunch, coffee breaks, and snippets of conversation.[3] They trusted Welch and generally shared his politics. Over the past decade, the eleven men had heard some of his lectures, seen his books and articles. Some knew him from when they had served together on the board of the National Association of Manufacturers (NAM). They liked him. His view of conditions in the United States aligned with theirs.

The men who had come to Indianapolis held what were widely regarded as extremist views while also appearing on the surface to be respectable participants in partisan politics and leaders of vital civic and government institutions. They subscribed to the notion that a communist plot posed an existential internal threat to the United States, a view that stood apart from the two-party system and was generally considered fringe. At the same time, they embraced pragmatism, negotiations, and institution building. It was a seeming contradiction that stood at the core of who they were. But holding the first mindset was not at odds with engagement in mainstream civic life.

In the context of mid-twentieth-century politics and culture, some Americans promulgated unconventional beliefs and yet inhabited esteemed institutions. The interpretation of the world held by the Birch

Society's founders marked them as lying outside the bounds of respectable discourse, but in fields ranging from manufacturing to architecture, the military to oil, these men had acquired positions of wealth, status, and respectability. They wielded knowledge and expertise to advance their institutions and navigate the precarities of their professions.

Though many Americans abhorred their belief system, the Birch founders still swam in the warm currents of a kind of centrist cultural life. Some of them led wholesome organizations such as the YMCA. Others delivered talks before equally mainstream institutions such as Rotary Clubs, churches, and synagogues. Some fundraised and campaigned for Republican candidates. In 1953 the *Milwaukee Sentinel* named one of them its "man of the year." Several of the men had held leadership posts with NAM, and one of them had served in Eisenhower's administration. They were rich, white, and almost uniformly Christian. They were still in their prime, colossi bestriding the world's most dynamic economy. They had cause to celebrate the rules and arrangements that had undergirded their achievements. Looked at from one perspective, they could be considered charter members of the American establishment.[4]

Nonetheless, their conspiratorial politics clashed with any pragmatic tendencies they may have harbored. They scorned the democratic political system and the welfare state even as they benefited from them and felt at home in the mainstream of American life. The men who came to Indianapolis believed that wealthy business executives should lead the United States and that popular democratic representation could easily slip into mob rule, tyranny of the majority. This bent, a skepticism of democracy, functioned as an ideological bond, providing the men with purpose and a shared sense of defiance.

Their primary concern, while sitting in Dice's living room sipping coffee, was not about their own livelihoods or fears for their own status or physical safety. Much as they worried that government obstruction of free enterprise threatened their businesses, what had brought them to Welch's meeting was a common belief in a far greater danger. They feared that left-wing ideas had gripped US institutions and defiled American ideals, imperiling the capitalist system and the moral values they cherished. Against that backdrop, the dozen men, in spite of their wealth and power, felt abandoned. They had been exiled to the margins and saw themselves as heretics. Powerful elites had betrayed them time after time, in their judgment, and their frustration with the drift in society had been building over many decades. It was time for them to take their country back.

THE ATTENDEES IN INDIANA SHARED IDEOLOGICAL TENETS AND PROFESsional interests but also an interpretation of history. They believed that their conception of the real America—a nation defined by small government, maximum freedom, and a white, Christian populace—was receding into the past. They regarded the growth of government in the first half of the twentieth century, US participation in World Wars I and II, and the unrelenting expansion of welfare programs as steps toward living under communist rule. They shared a rage at what they considered a string of failures and deceptions that had brought the United States to its knees.

Their motivations for coming to Indianapolis, and their willingness to entertain Welch's idea of forging a new kind of anticommunist movement, were rooted in similar impulses. Some of them had tried to find a home in the GOP but by 1958 had grown disillusioned in the party. This group included President Eisenhower's former Internal Revenue commissioner T. Coleman Andrews, who was enraged by taxes—and racial integration. He had called for the abolition of the federal income tax, which, he once warned, was "conceived in class hatred" and "plays right into the hands of the communists," and in 1956 he ran for president on a pro–Jim Crow platform as the candidate of the States' Rights Party.[5] Robert W. Stoddard, president of the Worcester, Massachusetts–based Wyman-Gordon Company, Ernest Swigert, head of Portland, Oregon's Hyster Company, and Laurence E. Bunker, former personal aide to General Douglas MacArthur, had similarly served as leaders of major institutions, yet had accepted Welch's invitation after concluding that the culture at large was rotting from within.

Half the men in the meeting were Midwesterners who combined marginal ideas with a knack for politics. Fred Koch, president of Rock Island Oil and Refining, promoted the notion of a communist conspiracy overrunning the United States and would become a zealous purveyor of anticommunist literature.[6] Other Midwesterners embraced an uneasy mix of radical views on issues like labor unions and foreign affairs. W. B. Mc-Millan served as president of the St. Louis–based Hussmann Refrigerator Co. and became a generous funder of Birch Society causes, while Milwaukee's William J. Grede—the *Sentinel*'s "man of the year"—had led his state's Republican Party, fundraised for Dwight Eisenhower, backed hard-right senators Robert Taft and Joseph McCarthy, and successfully fended off efforts to unionize his factories. Milwaukee architect Fitzhugh Scott helped found the Vail Ski Resort in Colorado. Revilo P. Oliver, the sole academic in the group, was a tenured professor of literature and classical languages at the University of Illinois, Champaign-Urbana. He, too, toggled between seemingly reputable institutions and far-out ideas, contributing articles to William F. Buckley's *National Review* while espousing antisemitic conspiracy theories in other forums.[7]

The lone Indiana-based member of this club, Louis Ruthenburg, was a retired president of Servel Inc., a manufacturer of gas refrigerators in Evansville. Like his fellow founders, he held radical views of dark conditions afflicting the United States while enjoying the status of leading major civic institutions valued within his community. He had served as president of the state's chamber of commerce, a plum post. Still, he viewed politics and policy since World War II as a string of "suicidal" concessions to communist regimes and believed that the world's most powerful nation was on the verge of annihilation. In Evansville, Ruthenburg announced in a speech in 1946 that "Communism against Americanism" was the quintessence of the struggle, and he later established a Council for Community Service to tutor neighbors in the evils of the conspiracy. Welch, he wrote after reading some of his articles, was "amazingly well informed and articulate in the area that had claimed my own interest for so many years," and the two of them struck up a correspondence and became friends.[8]

The men who came to Indianapolis proved amenable to building a movement that would work outside the two-party system and whose main purpose would be to teach citizens about the scale and nature of the communist threat. They left the two-day listening session at Dice's house determined to crusade on behalf of a righteous cause. As Welch outlined his program of education and direct anticommunist action, the men understood that he would be the brains behind the organization, while his cofounders would help fund it, find recruits, and give advice. In December 1958 the group resolved to build a new kind of movement, powered by an organization that they called the John Birch Society, naming it after the first American killed by Chinese communists, by the first shots fired in a holy war. Education, they concluded, would save Christianity, capitalism, and individual freedom from a vast communist conspiracy. Working together, they would rise, organize, smash communism, and save Americans from Armageddon.

WELCH WAS THE UNQUESTIONED LEADER OF THE DOZEN MEN WHO CONvened in Indiana. A blue-eyed, balding business owner living in a staid, wealthy Boston suburb, he would become America's most visible rightwing extremist of the 1960s.

Born in 1899 on a farm in Chowan County, North Carolina, Welch came from a family of Baptist preachers and farmers. His father tilled the land while his mother, a former elementary school teacher, homeschooled Welch. He was a prodigy who seemed bound from an early age to do something special with his life. Later he claimed to have memorized long passages of classic poems, read Goethe's entire body of work in the original German, dallied in mathematician Pierre de Fermat's Last Theorem, and competed against several chess masters.

Welch's early years foretold his conflicted stance toward revered American institutions. He graduated from the University of North Carolina at age sixteen and entered the Naval Academy hoping to see action in World War I. But when the war ended, he left the academy and took an altogether different path: Harvard Law School. Just six months before graduation, however, he dropped out. He had clashed in class with future Supreme Court justice Felix Frankfurter, whom he considered a Marxist, and bristled at the liberal confines of Harvard Yard.

Having abandoned careers in both the navy and law, Welch decided to go into business, launching a fudge-making company in Cambridge, Massachusetts. When he became mired in debt during the Great Depression, his company folded, and he joined his brother's already established

candy-making business, the James O. Welch Company, as a sales manager. He spent decades selling Pom Poms and helped turn the company
into a multimillion-dollar operation. "Bob Welch was one hell of a mar-
keting man in the candy business," a Birch Society colleague recalled.
Welch became rich, soured on the New Deal, and developed a hatred of
federal business regulations such as price controls.[9]

Welch looked to history to find the roots of the problem. He pinned the
blame on Woodrow Wilson's progressive agenda, which he believed had
put "this nation on its present road to totalitarianism." He fingered federal
agencies, global financiers, and elite-run international institutions such as
the Council on Foreign Relations as "the insiders" that were conspiring to
destroy the nation's founding virtues of free enterprise and citizens' liberty.

The New Deal further disillusioned Welch toward the dominant trends
in American politics. In an unpublished article written in the 1930s, he
warned that the unchecked growth of federal power marked the passing
of "the glory that is . . . the America that I was born in" and lamented
that "my America is being made over into a carbon copy of thousands of
despotisms that have gone before."[10]

He began to write books. His first, *The Road to Salesmanship*, published
in 1941, offered primers on the art of the sale and broadsides against
federal intrusions into private commerce. Invoking the late-nineteenth-
century utopian novel *Looking Backward*, by Edward Bellamy, Welch
cautioned that "paternal government" sought to satisfy all human needs
but ultimately would lead the nation to evisceration of the "profit mo-
tive." He maintained that Karl Marx's "hazy conceptions of a government which provides everything for its citizens, and which would leave
no room nor occasion for competing creators and competing organizers
to try to sell their wares to the public" were on the ascent. "Such conceptions," he added, "have become the mirage towards which super-liberals,
misguided zealots, and hypocritical self-seeking demagogues alike, have
tried to steer our course."[11]

Welch viewed World War I as an abject blunder that had aided Russia's communists and wasted America's resources, and the outbreak of a
second war in Europe, in 1939, only confirmed his distaste for any kind
of US immersion in the folly of European conflict. Led by antisemitic

aviator Charles Lindbergh, the America First Committee recruited hundreds of thousands of Americans to lobby on behalf of keeping the United States out of the war. Passionately antiwar, Welch took a relatively benign view of Adolf Hitler, opposed any alliance with Joseph Stalin's Soviet Union, feared that a wartime government would inevitably drift toward tyranny, and believed the Franklin D. Roosevelt administration was using totalitarian tactics to suppress antiwar dissent. Like other prominent future members of the John Birch Society, Welch joined America First. He also praised Lindbergh's leadership and allied himself with those "who had known anti-Semitic tendencies or were suspected of being sympathetic to Nazi Germany," his biographer Edward Miller writes. Anti-interventionism became a touchstone of his orientation toward America's place in the world.[12]

To Welch's thinking, America's victory in World War II more closely resembled an epic setback and malevolent capitulation, and the Cold War only deepened Welch's radicalism. Truman's expansion of the welfare state was destroying the individualistic ethic that had once made the United States a beacon of freedom, he concluded. Caught up in the anticommunist tide washing over postwar politics, Welch used his status as a successful candy executive to give public talks on the Red Menace. On visits to England in the late 1940s, he recoiled at the "state socialism" he saw there and upon his return cautioned American audiences against "let[ting] ourselves be infected by such diseases . . . as socialism and communism and other ideological cancers."

As Welch's anticommunist fervor intensified, his wealth and public profile grew. Political candidates in Massachusetts began to solicit his endorsement. He delivered rousing speeches and recruited volunteers to aid his chosen candidates. In 1950 Welch ran for lieutenant governor of Massachusetts as a Republican, his lone try for elective office. He remarked that socialists were already testing their ideas in Massachusetts, a laboratory soon to spread to the rest of the country. "The forces on the socialist side amount to a vast conspiracy to change our political and economic system," he warned shortly before Election Day. He finished a distant second. His conspiratorial bent intensified, and his aching sense of grievance and betrayal by "the establishment" began to harden, spurring him to speak out and write more. Although he never fully renounced electoral politics, he soon abandoned hope that the GOP could be saved from the clutches of socialism. When the Republican establishment denied his bid to become a delegate to the 1952 national convention and then handed the presidential nomination not to Senator Robert Taft but to the moderate Dwight Eisenhower, Welch decried "the dirtiest deal in American political history."[13]

The string of military setbacks in Asia concerned him greatly and solidified his conviction that communists were pulling the strings of US foreign policy. From the "loss of China" to the stalemate in Korea to Truman's decision to fire General Douglas MacArthur, the failures in the Pacific were as unthinkable and distressing as they were acute. Welch was hardly alone in his increasingly hard-line views. He joined senators such as Joe McCarthy, John Bricker, and William Knowland, and other anticommunist leaders such as Alfred Kolhberg and General A. C. Wedemeyer, in concluding that government officials were to blame for the string of debacles in the Far East. "Either consciously or unwittingly," the State Department had conceded China to Mao Tse-Tung, one dogged anticommunist charged.[14] Former president Herbert Hoover warned that recognizing the Chinese government would turn its US-based consulates into "nests of communist conspiracies." Knowland assailed "the appeasement clique in New York and Washington" that clamored for China's admission to the United Nations.[15]

Welch had the mindset of a crusader. He sought to open people's eyes to the forces that sought "the destruction of our own liberty," as the *New York Times* characterized one of his early arguments. "That there are more communists and communist sympathizers in our government today than ever before seems to me almost a certainty," Welch declared. Yet Welch was no Don Quixote tilting his lance at windmills. Taking advantage of his social connections to men of wealth and power, he produced a string of hard-hitting and high-profile articles, letters, books, and lectures. After persuading conservative publisher Henry Regnery to publish a thirty-thousand-word letter he had written as a short book, *May God Forgive Us*, in 1952, he formed the American Mailing Committee to urge potential readers to buy the book and learn from its revelations. Based in

Belmont, the nonprofit, volunteer-led committee relied on outside contributions as it sought "to enlighten our fellow citizens concerning socialism and Communism." Welch enlisted conservative notables such as libertarian economist Ludwig von Mises and oil magnate J. Howard Pew to endorse books that promoted limited government and "traditional" values. His committee sent a thousand copies of future Bircher Leonard Read's *Government: An Ideal Concept* (a "little masterpiece," Welch called it) to select figures in the business world and directors of chambers of commerce across the country, to promote "thinking about the fundamental principles of government."[16] He would draw on these experiences when he set up the Birch Society later in the decade.

At least one mainstream reviewer appeared unimpressed with Welch's book. A *New York Times* book critic summed it up as a "savage indictment" of US foreign policy as a communist plot. "The trouble with this oversimplified thesis," the critic wrote, "is that it takes no account of human fallibility and the possibility of honest, if lamentable, mistakes."[17]

Even so, Welch's writings and lectures made him a rising star on the anticommunist right. Adherents flocked to his cause, enticed by his way of articulating the heart of the matter. "Either the chains of Communist slavery will be thrown off by that third of the peoples of the world who are now enslaved," he told the New Hampshire Federation of Women's Clubs in 1953, "or we ourselves in time will be shackled with them."[18]

Around the time Welch published *May God Forgive Us*, his friend Bill Knowland, a US senator from California, learned about a man named John Birch, a twenty-seven-year-old Baptist missionary and army intelligence officer who was killed by Mao's communist forces in 1945, ten days after V-J Day, which celebrated the Allied victory over Japan in World War II. Knowland obtained classified files on the circumstances surrounding Birch's death and gave Welch access to the documents.

Birch's life and death resonated with Welch. Both men were Southern evangelicals, and Birch's virtues and suffering offered the kind of Manichaean tale that moved Welch to action. Birch seemed an almost Christlike figure whose sacrifice could lead Americans out of the darkness and help them recognize and escape the evil conspiring to snuff out their lives and their freedoms. If Welch could publicize Birch's martyrdom, he could alert his countrymen to the awful truth. Welch decided to write a short biography of Birch to distill "the difference between the civilization for which he gave his life and the pseudo-civilization by which he was murdered." As the society later explained, Birch's "heroism, accomplishments and nobility of character made him a legend which the Communists could not allow to live."[19]

The Life of John Birch, published in 1954, depicts Birch as the first victim of the Cold War. The initial murderous shots were fired by ruthless enemies in a war to the death that continued to rage with no end in sight. But Welch was convinced that Mao's communist forces weren't the only ones culpable for the murder of a patriot. The crime, he asserted without citing any real evidence, had been hidden by State Department officials sympathetic to Mao's regime. Welch's conspiratorial understanding of American life had escalated, and he now concluded that the true allegiance of some of America's leaders was to the Communist Party, not to the Constitution. They had sworn a solemn oath to defend the United States against all enemies, but their actions demonstrated that this oath was a fraud. Communists pulled the strings. The murder of Birch was a heinous crime. The cover-up was worse.

Another influence pushing Welch and his colleagues toward the meeting in Indianapolis was their anticommunist activism as board members of the National Association of Manufacturers, the nation's most influential proindustry lobbying group. Welch's time on NAM's board during the 1950s added to his stature and enabled him to find a home with likeminded ultraconservatives. The organization supplied a "shock troop brigade" of the nation's industrialists, in the words of one scholar, and gave several of the Birch Society founders the connections and wherewithal to forge their political movement.[20] It incubated some of the policies and style that would animate Birchism, as historians such as Kim Philips-Fein and Jennifer Delton have shown. Although NAM's staff preferred probusiness pragmatism to the hard-liner brand of antistatism, some of NAM's leaders embraced a conspiratorial view of the New Deal and regarded taxes, unions, and welfare programs as inimical to the nation's heritage. The board members who later established the Birch Society—Swigert, Grede, Stoddard, Koch, Robert Gaylord, and Cola Parker—absorbed the anticollectivist ideas promulgated by libertarian economists Friedrich Hayek and Ludwig von Mises, and sought to sway public opinion in favor of rolling back federal regulations on private enterprise.

NAM's hard-liners also worked to ply their ideas through Leonard Read's Foundation for Economic Education, Robert LeFevre's Colorado-based libertarian Freedom School, and Notre Dame Law School dean Clarence Manion's radio program, where he espoused proisolationist, anti–New Deal opinions. The hard-liners tended to be leaders of relatively large firms (with more than two thousand employees) that manufactured heavy machinery and industrial items: Grede's firms produced iron and steel and farm tractors; Koch produced oil; Parker manufactured Kleenex and other paper products; Stoddard's factories made aircraft engines and missile parts. Three of the early Birch Society leaders served as president of NAM's board—Grede (1952), Parker (1956), and Swigert (1957). To-gether, they helped birth a burgeoning world of far-right mobilization, coupling extreme ideas with a mainstream sensibility, fighting to liberate Americans, as one NAM memo put it, "from regimentation and exploita-tion by government or any group" and to defend "high moral principles based on religious convictions."[21] Many of them had close ties to Grede, who inspired the others with his successful efforts to thwart unionization on his factory floors.

NAM's extremists spent time in the trenches in the early and mid-1950s, which prepared them for the battles they would later wage in the John Birch Society. They opposed the liberal college graduates on the staff of NAM and the business-executive members who were willing to come to terms with a kind of New Deal moral capitalism that afforded some protections and rights to workers, the aged, and other vulnerable citizens. Grede, Welch, and the others fought against NAM's endorse-ment of unemployment insurance and the minimum wage and opposed any negotiations with unions and calls by NAM to lower tariffs. Grede excoriated some of NAM's largest corporate members for bending to "what is popular with the public." Critics denounced the ultraconser-vatives' "reactionary and rigid ideas" and "feudal and futile pronounce-ments," foreshadowing the attacks they would endure after launching the society.

These political clashes taught some of the Birch founders the value of political organizing and reinforced the importance of alternative media channels for speaking directly to potential converts. They gave the NAM hard-liners a taste for political combat, presaging the battles that would come later. American Motors Corporation president George Romney, for example, pulled his company out of NAM due to a "fundamental disagreement" with some of NAM's hard-right antiworker policies. The future Birch leaders developed a feel for who sided with them and how to handle the George Romneys of the world.

Welch spent seven years on NAM's board, including three as a regional vice president and one as chairman of its education committee. Education—a key to the Birch Society's activism—was also a centerpiece of the hard-liners' approach, and the future Birch leaders often served on NAM committees that focused on education, communications, and public relations. These ultraconservatives found ideological kin in conservative housewives who banded together in places such as Pasadena, California, to oppose local school desegregation and reject progressive teaching. Welch urged his NAM allies to lobby universities and colleges to adopt an economics textbook that he thought espoused the conservative viewpoint, and he suggested that parents had a right to stop teachers from indoctrinating children in what he called a "style of socialism."[22]

NAM ultimately enabled the future Birch founders to combine their shared contempt for unions, communists, liberals, and the mainstream news media into a cohesive anticommunist philosophy with pro-free-market undertones. The founders' penchant for conspiratorial thinking coexisted with their faith in commerce, and Welch used his perch with the manufacturers to lay the groundwork for what became the Birch Society's political achievements.[23]

NAM also gave Welch entree to the wider world. On trips overseas, he met with political and military leaders who offered affirmation of his worldview: the conspiracy had numerous tentacles, it extended throughout Asia, and only true anticommunists could save civilization.[24]

On Tuesday, August 9, 1955, Welch boarded a Pan American flight in Seattle that stopped in Honolulu and landed in Tokyo at noon on

Thursday. His friends at NAM had set him up with his own chauffer, interpreter, and touring car (provided by the president of the Nagoya Sugar Refining Company, in Tokyo) and arranged an itinerary fit for a head of state. There was dinner with China's ambassador to Japan; golf with the Philippines' minister to South Korea; a nearly hour-long conversation with South Korean premier Syngman Rhee at Seoul's "White House"; a seat on the dais where Rhee addressed ten thousand South Korean troops; dinner with Japanese notables ("For the first time in my life . . . I successfully manipulated chopsticks"); and audiences with Chiang Kai-shek and Madam Chiang in Taipei. Taiwan's minister of education informed Welch that *May God Forgive Us* had been translated into Mandarin and named to the ministry's recommended reading list to promote "Citizens' Fundamental Education."

Welch spent a day with a distant relative, an army master sergeant "who comes from my corner of North Carolina," and he was thrilled to give "a short speech" to Madam Chiang's Anti-Aggression League and to run "into any number of people who had known John Birch personally."

As exciting as these meetings were, Welch's discomfort with conditions in Asia surfaced during the trip. Korea's situation, he railed, "is frustrating and pathetic." America's policies—presumably its failure to overthrow North Korea's communist regime—"are a disgrace." And "it is only the genius, the courage, and the determination of Syngman Rhee, supported by the almost universal reverence in which he is held by the Korean people, which has kept the Republic of Korea alive."[25]

NAM also afforded Welch the opportunity to deepen his friendships with fervid anticommunists and sharpen his oratorical skills. Just as Ronald Reagan developed his "Speech" (his paean to free enterprise and critique of top-down, communist-controlled societies) during his years-long tour for General Electric in the 1950s, Welch honed his message and his presentation during his time on the stump with NAM.[26] Shortly after his Asia tour, in Hot Springs, Arkansas, he delivered a talk to NAM colleagues that pricked the conscience of a fellow board member. After listening to Welch, F. E. Masland Jr., who had what he called "the crusading urge," decided that the speech was "an offensive action in our battle to defend the Free Enterprise System" that "should be heard by millions of people from coast to coast." Masland urged Welch to take a sabbatical from his business and tour the United States. Although Masland wasn't rich, he promised to contribute $1,000 to a tour should Welch undertake one. Several other NAM members were already developing programs to put Welch before audiences across the country, and NAM president Bill Grede said he would raise the idea of a Welch speaking tour with NAM's leaders in the coming weeks.[27]

Welch's time with the manufacturers planted seeds that would later bear fruit with the founding of the John Birch Society. Losing interest in the candy business, Welch was forming unshakable bonds with like-minded businessmen and immersing himself more fully in political affairs. He marshaled his skills as a marketer and pamphleteer to burnish his image as an anticommunist visionary speaking impolite truths to America's sleepwalking political establishment. He sharpened his conspiracy theories, notions that were also deeply rooted in the history and culture of American life, which Welch had a special talent for exploiting.

Such ideas had existed in the hothouse of US politics since the founding of the republic. They were endemic to the United States, and the nation's freewheeling culture created ideal conditions to host and sustain them. Typically the plots involved fears of immigrants—foreigners settling in the United States with alien values and alien allegiances—infusing politics with a sinister hue. These outsiders, conspiracy theorists claimed, sought to subvert Christianity and twist the Constitution to serve the goals of foreign powers. Eighteenth-century Americans fretted that the Illuminati, a German secret society promoting Enlightenment ideals, would seize control of the government. Catholics in the nineteenth century came under attack for alleged obeisance to the pope rather than to the Constitution. With the nation's democracy perceived as brittle and vulnerable, Americans have entertained the idea of plots to overthrow the government; as historian David Brion Davis has observed, "Americans have been curiously obsessed with the contingency of their experiment with freedom."[28]

In a nation that has tended to elevate individual rights above the common good, fears that these freedoms would be abridged by shady, un-American forces have found enduring appeal. The federal government itself has drawn suspicion, serving as a vector of all kinds of conspiratorial plots allegedly hatched to trample the people's rights and distort the popular will beyond recognition. As the welfare state and wartime governments harvested more power in the twentieth century, the federal leviathan at times engaged in actual conspiracies. These genuine abuses have lent plausibility to baseless claims of conspiracy theorists, as historian Kathryn Olmsted has argued. During World War I, the federal government conspired to harass and jail dissidents, and during the Cold War a sprawling, clandestine network of CIA operatives and National Security Agency spies plotted against foreign governments without informing the American public, in whose name they worked. The FBI also (illegally) spied on civil rights workers and antiwar activists. The periodic exposure of the vast apparatus of security and surveillance has intensified perceptions of an out-of-control state capable of numerous hidden abasements and invasions of privacy.

Welch functioned in a Cold War context suited to the spread of conspiratorial thinking. Mind-bending real-world developments, such as the invention of atomic and hydrogen bombs and their acquisition by the USSR, deepened the notion that what was once unthinkable had actually transpired. Unnamed officials armed with scientific and technological marvels had now acquired weapons of unfathomable destructive power. The existence of a handful of actual Soviet spies in the federal government, such as Alger Hiss and Julius Rosenberg, lent an aura of legitimacy to claims that subversives had penetrated deep into US agencies.[29] Such conditions made conspiracies involving government plots appear believable even to those without a conspiratorial bent. Movies like *The Day the Earth Stood Still* (1951) and TV shows like *The Twilight Zone* (1959–1964) depicted a world of surrealism—involving fourth dimensions and aliens from outer space—where reality and science fiction merged.

Then there were the political and publishing incentives that aligned with the promulgation of conspiracy theories. Welch and his allies, such as Regnery, recognized that alternative modes of communication—whether books, magazines, or recordings beyond the reach of established mass media—could circumvent mainstream news outlets and provide forums for a set of ideas that were resistant to fact checks. Individuals in possession of funds, savvy, and the right bombshell messaging had an opportunity to persuade thousands of people that their version of events was actually the truth, even if it wasn't. And for some, there was money to be made on misinformation—the more sensational, the better.[30]

Welch gravitated to conspiracy theories in part because they explained trends and setbacks—at home and abroad—with tales of apocalyptic battles that set righteous believers against evil infidels, Christian civilization against godless communism.[31] Welch's conspiratorial stance was also grounded in a view that cliques and minority factions could corrode individual rights and tarnish institutions. They could manipulate a somnolent public unaware of the evil.

Even as a board member of the National Association of Manufacturers, Welch distrusted factional politics, complaining that although some board members wished to see reductions in tariffs, the problem with the policy-making process ran deep. Individuals and small groups, he charged, believed "in their own infallibility," and this small number of "self-appointed infallibles" used aggression and wiles to exploit "the usual lethargic attitude of an unperturbed majority." Thus, on the question of tariffs and trade, a tiny unrepresentative elite imposed their antimajoritarian views on the entire organization. This cabal pushed down on "a small lever to activate a larger lever which operates a still larger lever until certain views are established, with the appearance of great prestige, that never did have majority support anywhere along the line except in the first very small group that started the steamroller on its way." It was part of a pattern. "Over recent years we have seen many illustrations of great organizations being thus beguiled into at least ostensible support of positions which a vast majority of the individuals in those organizations did not really approve," he warned, expressing his suspicion of elite misrule. "I, for one, do not want to see the NAM *used* in any such fashion by any person or group, no matter how sure they may be of their righteousness, nor how noble their intentions."[32]

In his analysis of the Cold War, Welch armed himself with a counternarrative to rebuff official explanations of how communism had made so many inroads. Incompetence alone did not, could not, suffice as an explanation. The truth had to lie in the corridors of American power.

Communists were in the driver's seat. They were the authors of the nation's downfall. And this "cabal" was manipulating the majority of the American people, who went about their lives unaware of the evil in their midst.

Ultimately, conspiracy theories that government was rife with communist agents had practical appeal. They became metaphors for what Welch and his followers believed to be a long arc of American decline; their genius lay in their shape-shifting adaptability to almost any issue. Welch's conspiracy theories narrated the toppling of a great nation, the crushing of radical individualism by false idols, and they encompassed the free market, religion, education, and sovereignty. Sticking the communist label on an opponent enabled him to cast people and ideas as poison to the Constitution.

IN 1956, WELCH'S SECOND-TO-LAST YEAR ON NAM'S BOARD, HE DEcided to retire from business and commit himself to political organizing full time. He had been moving toward a decision like this for years. Involved in a feud at work with his brother James, who owned the company, he also felt disrespected and underappreciated. Welch had made enough money to provide a comfortable life for his family and wished to find more meaning in his work than the candy business provided. And it was a natural leap for him to retire during Eisenhower's presidency, when the GOP seemed hopeless (even as he nursed dreams of running for Congress).[33]

It was retirement in name only. Welch stepped up his speechmaking and letter writing and tapped his network of ultraconservative allies, encouraging friends such as Grede, Parker, and Wedemeyer to serve on the editorial advisory board of a new magazine he wished to publish: *One Man's Opinion*, an outlet for his anticommunist beliefs. "There is only one thing which the Kremlin really fears today," he wrote in his recruitment letter to potential donors. "That is, having the American people learn the truth about the nature, the methods, and the frightening progress of the world-wide Communist conspiracy." Welch's requests for help from his allies generated so many positive responses that he called his campaign "the most encouraging and rewarding experience in my life so far. It is wonderful to have such friends."[34]

By late June, twenty-nine men, roughly half of them leaders in heavy industries, had joined the advisory board. The other members were some combination of army officers, lawyers, and authors. Their us-against-the-world mindset was in tension with their deep roots in their communities and their secure status in the upper echelons of American life. As Welch observed in a letter to board members, the men were at the top of their professions, undisputed leaders of businesses and industrial associations who performed good works "on various charitable, educational, and public-service boards and committees." His allies were equally active in battling on behalf of what he called "basic Americanism against the socialist steamroller." And Welch conferred a special name on those who were "devoting all or a major part" of their lives "to anti-collectivist activities": he called them "God's Angry Men!" For all their material achievements, these men were raging against the course of human events, rallying to stop the country's slide further down the path to autocracy.[35]

This network proved crucial to the formation and growth of the John Birch Society. Of the eleven men besides Welch who attended the founding meeting in Indianapolis, five of them had served on his editorial advisory board. Of the twenty-nine on the board, more than half ultimately became members of or contributors to the society. The network also gave Welch a sympathetic forum to air his theories about the nefarious forces that were ruinous to late-fifties America. Welch sent many of the men copies of a private letter that he had first written in 1954 to his circle of friends. In it he described Eisenhower as a "dedicated, conscious agent of the communist conspiracy." He later published the letter as a book and called it *The Politician*. On September 29, 1958, three months prior to the Indianapolis meeting, he sent an "extremely confidential" copy of his book-length missive to T. Coleman Andrews via first-class mail. Urging Andrews to "safeguard the document," Welch promised that "even so well informed a man as yourself" would learn about new aspects of "the conspiracy which we face." Handling the manuscript required "extreme precautions," he instructed Seattle's J. W. Clise a few months later. Welch didn't fear for his own safety but rather "that having the manuscript get into the wrong hands at the present time" could undermine the anticommunist cause in unspecified ways.[36]

By the time he stepped foot in Dice's home in December of that year, Welch had been preparing for the moment for the better part of a decade. He had studied world history, witnessed the fallacies of Marxist economics in Europe, unearthed what he considered communist inroads at home and overseas, befriended the anticommunist leaders of East Asia, and road-tested parts of his conspiratorial message to audiences far and wide.

Welch's vision for the John Birch Society was informed in part by his personal grandiosity. But he also earnestly believed that Armageddon was closing in on the United States. His remarks in Indianapolis juxtaposed formalities with alarmist words and ideas. He began by welcoming the men to Dice's home and thanked them for taking time from their busy schedules. He assured the men that they would be part of "a movement of historical importance" and told them that he was "now spending my whole life spreading bad news, every day, everywhere I can." With a nod to Ralph Waldo Emerson (each mind must "make its choice between truth and repose"), he promised to share a "truth which may shatter a lot of the comfort you already feel."[37]

He would give this talk an estimated twenty-eight times over the next two years. But in Indianapolis on December 9, when the men agreed to establish the John Birch Society, most Americans had not yet heard of its namesake, or of Welch. They had yet to discover what Welch later called "the shape and color of my horns." They would see them soon enough.[38]

Chapter 2

"SOME RATHER FRIGHTENING ASPECTS"

IN MAY 1959, SIX MONTHS AFTER THE JOHN BIRCH SOCIETY WAS BORN, Herbert Philbrick walked into an apartment on the Upper East Side of Manhattan to attend a recruitment meeting. Welch had convened the meeting, and Philbrick joined twenty or so other guests who shared wealth, status, and a conviction that communists posed a grave internal threat to the United States. Among them was Spruille Braden, the former US ambassador to Cuba, Colombia, and Argentina, who had seen communists gain ground in Latin America and now wished to stop their attacks within the United States.[1] Also in the room was lawyer and insurance executive Merwin Hart, who admired Spain's Francisco Franco for his anticommunism and later became the society's first chapter leader in New York City. Talk-radio kingpin Dan Smoot was present as well, having won notoriety for railing at supposed plots to fluoridate the water supply and poison Americans.[2]

Even in this group, Philbrick arguably had the most sterling hardline credentials of all. An ex-communist turned FBI informant, he had written extensively about the threat in his syndicated newspaper column and in his memoir, *I Led Three Lives*. In the 1950s he had become famous after a hit TV series based on his life portrayed him as a hero.

Tension filled the air. Though Philbrick had been a personal acquaintance of Welch's since his time working in advertising in Boston during the Great Depression, the "cloak and dagger atmosphere" of this meeting set him on edge. Each guest had been forced to undergo a security screening, and that type of vetting for a small, private gathering of like-minded people rankled him.[3] Philbrick tried to open the apartment's front door from inside, but someone had locked it from the outside. *Freeman* magazine editor Ed Opitz joked, "We must be a captive audience!" Philbrick wasn't amused.

The gathering was representative of how many of the early recruitment meetings proceeded. Welch led the sessions, and over one, sometimes two, days he delivered a version of the talk nearly identical to what the founders had heard at the meeting in Indianapolis. The lecture Welch gave to the assembled guests in host Harry King's home started out fine from Philbrick's perspective. The first part, on the communist threat around the globe, painted "a rather well-done picture," Philbrick reported. But the last tranche, in which Welch highlighted his vision for the Birch Society, featured "some rather frightening aspects" that unnerved the ex-spy. Welch had announced that the society would require "a tough dictatorial boss" to lead it. This boss would order his soldiers to pick up their "clubs" and "clobber" anyone who "tried to breach the wall." He charged that US officials were guilty of "treason."

Philbrick was far from soft on communism, but the tactics the new society was contemplating gave him pause. Based on Welch's remarks, he concluded that the movement was probably going to "take action outside of the law" and attract "extreme radicals." Welch's demonization of opponents and intimations of violence echoed "the appeal made by Adolph [*sic*] Hitler to the German people" in the 1930s. Philbrick put his concerns to paper and submitted a memo to the FBI.

His fears didn't come out of nowhere. The far right had long tarred opponents as "pink" and used violent means to suppress the left and its perceived enablers. During World War I prowar vigilante leagues had beaten draft resisters, and in the following decade the KKK and its allies had terrorized immigrants, Catholics, Jews, Blacks, and progressive ed-ucators. In the 1950s massive resistance to civil rights had accelerated as white mobs used bats, fists, and rocks to assail nonviolent activists across the Deep South. Those tactics were facts of life in the United States, but in the aftermath of World War II they evoked the specter of fascism for some Americans, including Philbrick.

Despite Philbrick's belief in the evils of communism, there were some steps he refused to take, some lines that he implied were just not crossable. He rebuffed invitations to join the society in the months following the meeting. He even reported on its activities to the FBI. In the end, how-ever, he decided to support the society's agenda. He provided recommen-dations to Welch, using his connections to aid with recruitment, on the grounds that his enemies, communists, were far deadlier than those in his own ranks who might harbor authoritarian aspirations.

Like Philbrick, most of the elite group in the New York City apart-ment who heard Welch's pitch ultimately signed on as members or pro-vided other kinds of assistance, like endorsements. Such high-powered men became the backbone of the early Birchers. They didn't find Welch's lecture frightening. They found it exhilarating, and their association with the movement gave them hope—for American politics, for the anticom-munist cause, and for a future in which they fought for freedom.[4]

THE LATE FIFTIES WAS A GOOD TIME TO LAUNCH A HARD-LINE ANTICOM-munist movement in the United States. By then, Welch's allies felt, they had become trapped in a particularly brutish episode of *The Twilight Zone*. Heroes like Joe McCarthy and Bob Taft were almost all dead or out of power, and the GOP seemed irredeemably liberal in its politics and policies. Where could they turn? Abject betrayals on the home front had piled up since the New Deal, they fretted, while debacles abroad—the loss of Hungary, stalemate in Korea, the launch of *Sputnik*—demonstrated a litany of failure. Communists reigned from Cuba to China and in their eyes were making inroads on America's college campuses and in other institutions in the United States. Hope was hard to keep alive.

Beyond their simmering dismay, the founders and early members had deep pockets and contacts in high places. Uniting behind a leader they trusted, they used their considerable resources to fuel the society's suc-cessful launch in the first months of 1959. Some early meetings—one at the Harvard Club in New York City, another at the Union League Club in Chicago—stamped the founders with a seal of respectability.[5] The leaders' hard-won experience in the nuts and bolts of organization build-ing proved invaluable in the early going. And the initial recruits had become more and more open to the idea of a fresh approach to political mobilization and moral agitation when Welch's Birch Society entered the picture.

Shortly after the founders' meeting in Indianapolis, Welch promised to build his movement "vigorously and promptly." He and his team did just that. A lawyer for the society filed a successful application with the Commonwealth of Massachusetts for nonprofit educational status. The group's headquarters, in a two-story redbrick building near Welch's Bel-mont home, started to hum with life. Its flagship magazine, *American Opinion*, and its prescriptive monthly *Bulletin* began publishing in-house, while a basement storage room stocked far-right books and pamphlets. Welch's corner office looked down on Belmont's post office, and the soci-ety soon became its top customer.[6]

With its infrastructure in place, the movement now needed money and members, both of which Welch generated in the first few months. To start, the founders focused on the familiar—people they knew and felt comfortable around—and launched a campaign to recruit friends and acquaintances. This first wave of recruits came from the top income strata and tended to be white, highly educated elites, both the superrich and upper-middle-class professionals: businessmen and businesswomen along with upwardly mobile doctors, dentists, lawyers, engineers. Some gravitated to the Birch Society because they wished to protect their eco-nomic status and what they considered the beauty of the free-enterprise system. Others felt drawn to a set of hot-button cultural issues that the society also started to hype in its pitches. Above all, the early recruits united in opposition to the dominance of liberalism at home and abroad. They were fed up with the ever-enlarging welfare state in Washington, DC, and regarded the failures to stop communist expansion overseas as a string of deceptions and misrule.

The society gave these elites a way to spend their excess income on what they considered a deeply meaningful pursuit. Early members were singularly receptive to the message of the movement and the promise that their clout and resources could be deployed to change the trajectory of American life. The recruiters also tapped into larger trends and ideas percolating in late-fifties America: the growing resistance to civil rights, a desire to teach "Americanist" ideas in schools, the need to reject any accommodation of the Soviet Union, and a long-mounting fury that the GOP had abjectly failed to stanch and had actually expanded on and enshrined the liberal internationalist visions of FDR's New Deal and Truman's Fair Deal. The brilliance of the society in its first months was its ability to appeal to elites on all these issues at the same time—and to mobilize them in innovative and irresistible ways. The John Birch Society functioned as a third-party shock force within the larger American polity that sought to erode the perceived national consensus and remap the political geography of Eisenhower's America.

Recruitment meetings demonstrated that these ideas had found their audience. A one- or two-day lecture by Welch or a coordinator in front of fifteen to twenty potential members yielded the kinds of dividends that the founders had envisioned. They shrewdly looked to enlist not "tolerant and reasonable" individuals but like-minded ones—as Welch put it to one ally, "top-flight men . . . who think nearly enough the same way you and I do." Freewheeling philosophical and political deliberations were to be avoided; the founders asked that meetings be distraction-free zones, and anyone likely to "bog down the discussions" was barred.[7]

Welch's early ambitions were soon reshaped by the practical experience of recruitment. He had originally hoped that thirty thousand people would join in the first year, with a long-term goal of furnishing the United States with a million-member Birch Society army. He swiftly realized the impossibility of this ambition and abandoned it. "What we can accomplish through small chapters is immensely greater than we thought," he said. Modest-size groups of highly motivated businesspeople and professionals who carried clout in their communities could have a political impact far greater than their numbers suggested. They could win attention for their causes and thrust key ideas into the center of public conversation. And although Welch initially conceived the organization as composed primarily of men, when one of his former colleagues on the board of NAM brought his wife to a session and she expressed eagerness to join, he opened up the society to "the wives" as well.[8]

Two early meetings in Joe McCarthy's home state of Wisconsin demonstrated the promise of elite mobilization on behalf of the Birch cause. The society's first recruitment session was held in the Milwaukee suburbs, which was also home to two Birch founders and many business leaders who loathed communists and unions. Of the fifteen people who showed up for Welch's lecture, only a husband and wife filed membership applications, joining the organization without much prompting, yet Bill Grede acknowledged that he had neglected to follow up and remind the attendees to join following the meeting, as Welch apparently had expected him to do. No one would repeat that mistake.[9]

Fortunately for the society, two wealthy Milwaukee-area businessmen came through. Fred Loock, president of the Allen-Bradley Company, and Harry Bradley, the company's owner and a conservative family scion, contributed $25,000, a sum that amounted to a statement from industrial titans that the young movement had worth and merited investment.[10]

A second recruitment meeting took place at the prestigious Milwaukee Country Club. Elite friends and acquaintances of the founders liked what they heard. One attendee said that he felt inspired by Welch's presentation. Further buoyed by an endorsement from his friend Grede and a positive review from a high-ranking official in the Catholic Church, he opted to donate to the Birch cause. Following this model, Birchers tapped into a network of prestige across the nation. From Boca Raton, Florida, to New York City, from Boston to Santa Barbara, early recruiting flourished among some of the country's wealthiest individuals.[11]

Welch's pitch wasn't for everyone. Even in the context of that era's relatively staid radio, television, and print media environment, it came across to some as windy and monotonous. Ronald Reagan's paean to free enterprise on behalf of General Electric in the 1950s often electrified audiences, and Reagan had magnetism; Welch, not so much. His speech's centerpiece consisted of a conspiracy theory, the internal plot against America, that touched a more extremist chord than Reagan typically struck. Even a close ally of Welch's warned a member in the society's early days that the boss gave his audience "a pretty healthy dose, and it's not easy to sit for two solid days."[12]

Still, this friend concluded that Welch's presentation paid dividends. The speech, which would be immortalized in the society's *Blue Book* and sell for two dollars a copy, was emotional, devout, and, to the men and women of means and station who got to hear it in 1959, revelatory. "If people who see and hear you . . . are not stirred to their very souls, to want to be a part of this great work you are doing, there must be something wrong," a California housewife wrote Welch.[13]

Welch's hours-long tour of the communist threat offered an explanation for current events that had stumped his listeners. He connected the dots for McCarthy- and Taft-supporting conservatives in search of an analysis of what had gone wrong with America and above all gave them a plan to stem the communist infiltration that now imperiled the United States.

The business elites who heard Welch's message that year had been primed for it. They already resented the federal government, scorned the Republican establishment, and loathed unions, regulations, and taxes as anathema to the free-enterprise system that in their opinion had once made America great. In the aftermath of depression and world war, the expansion of government control over their lives felt grotesque, a constitutional violation that inalterably sapped the strength of capitalism. Welch's conspiracy theories landed easily too; rather than being alien to the far right's culture, they were endemic to it. McCarthy, the House Un-American Activities Committee (HUAC), and radio talkers such as Clarence Manion and former FBI agent Dan Smoot had warned of an internal communist plot throughout the decade, making Welch's audience more receptive to his ideas. While not to everyone's taste, the conspiracy theories formed one pillar of the lecture's appeal, acting as a gravitational pull for the true believers.

Welch's contention that the nation's problems started at the top gave his pitch a lurid power. Although not all the early recruits believed his every word, they absorbed the big picture, and there was titillation in the plots he spun. "The peculiar cancer of which Bob Taft died," Welch once wrote, may have been "induced by a radium tube planted in the upholstery of his Senate seat, as has been so widely rumored." He similarly wondered "whether Joe McCarthy met with foul play, either before or after he went to the hospital."[14] Washington, he stated point-blank, could not be trusted with its solemn duty to protect the lives of American citizens, and Eisenhower was so immersed in the conspiracy that he didn't want anyone "even looking at all the clear signs of the enemy closing in on us from every side, and at the beginnings of the police state already at work within our own borders." The influential citizens in these rooms already tended to distrust Eisenhower, and Welch was speaking their language.

He was particularly adroit at weaving together factual tidbits, historical trends, and philosophical references, spinning them into vivid metaphors that explained the swift pace of America's descent into darkness. He acknowledged that some of his assertions lacked documentation; "I shall be saying many things today that I cannot strictly prove," he once admitted. But those caveats felt candid and brave, bolstering his credibility. Welch cast himself as an expert on the communist threat, and his wealthy early audiences liked learning about the enemy's plans from someone who seemed so knowledgeable. He reminded listeners of his years of "experience in analyzing communist methods, purposes, and personnel," and said that his sole aim was to plumb the schemes of "a deadly enemy, who has vowed to destroy us." It was no secret that Welch had given up his life's work in the candy business to organize and snuff out communism on a full-time basis. The sacrifice impressed attendees who valued such notions.

The early recruits also tended to be religious Protestants and Catholics, and they liked the theological implications of Welch's message. The John Birch Society was nothing so much as a righteous instrument to execute God's will—humanity's "last hope." The apocalyptic tilt magnified Welch's appeal to people who chafed at decades of decline and nursed a common faith that the locusts had arrived and their country was enduring a kind of biblical plague. "Either the whole world goes under, with a long stretch of slavery and brutality and darkness ahead of us," he said, "or we turn back the forces of evil before it is too late." Like Welch, they agreed that Christ was in a fight to the death with the devil. They were moved by his insistence that "some Force put us here at this time and place, to play a most important part—perhaps the decisive part—in determining" the fate of the world. One admirer stated that the "destiny" of the United States "lies a great deal in your hands." By the end of the lecture, many listeners were saying amen.[15]

The farsighted aspects of Welch's vision seemed to inspire the most excitement. "We are not a copy of any movement of the past," Welch argued. "We are something new, as befits a moving force for a new age."[16] As the country stood on the cusp of a new decade, as the Eisenhower years receded into a miasma of frustration, Welch's offer to build "a moving force" meant a way for wealthy and powerful people who felt disempowered to regain influence in the public sphere. And anticommunist deeds, supplementing the words, would be paramount. Implicit in his talk was the promise of an alliance uniting wealthy, upper-middle-class, and potentially even working-class white Christians in a vast anticommunist brigade. In rejecting the culture of the 1950s—which Birchers derided as internationalist, pluralist, secular, and complacent—Welch offered an exit from that era and a way to stand in loud defiance of the liberal establishment. In fervor if not in direction, his crusade anticipated the New Left and some of the mass protest movements, such as Students for a Democratic Society and Young Americans for Freedom, that shook the sixties.

By February 1959 the Birch Society had acquired what Welch termed "a surprising amount of steam." Armed with a faith that their cause was just, the group's leaders believed that patriots willing to sacrifice could make a decisive difference in a Cold War that the United States had been losing. Two months after its birth, the society had become a combatant in the fight to remake the lives of millions of citizens.[17]

LIKE A LOT OF EARLY BIRCHERS, FRED KOCH HAD ALREADY SPENT YEARS in the anticommunist trenches. In 1958 he had worked to stymie union organizing by successfully lobbying for an amendment to Kansas's state constitution, making it a so-called right-to-work state. An oil-and-gas magnate from Wichita, Koch was a founding father of the Birch Society who also served on its National Council, a group of roughly two dozen men who acted as sounding boards for Welch and advisers to the organization. He agreed with Welch's focus on educating the public and forging a movement that functioned outside the traditional two-party system. The society's promise to promote both anticommunism and religious faith moved Koch to get active.

Koch's experience in anticommunist organizing, his passion for proselytizing, and his visibility and resources gave him a foothold in the culture at large. Like his brethren, he hated unions, federal regulations, and any other constraints on what he deemed his unfettered rights to pursue his business interests as he saw fit. Free enterprise, he believed, was the greatest of all systems, and it had been under siege for three decades. More than the other founders, Koch had seen the evils of Russian communism firsthand. In the 1930s he had helped build oil refineries, first in Stalin's Soviet Union and then in Hitler's Germany, and his brushes with both regimes shaped his Cold War philosophy. In the USSR, he knew people who had been purged by Stalin, and a Soviet minder was assigned to trail him on his visits. In contrast, he liked what he saw when he inspected his refineries in Nazi Germany. Koch thought the people in fascist nations were better off and more motivated to work hard than in countries where a central government had established a safety net for workers.[18]

His brush with Soviet totalitarianism helped fuel his postwar devotion to a militant brand of anticommunist activism. Although he had long pressed anticommunist literature into the hands of others, his affiliation with the Birch Society intensified his zeal. The society gave Koch direction, imbuing him with an even greater commitment to spread the word that liberals within the United States posed the gravest of all threats.

Koch tapped his local network to spread the society's message. With the zeal of a one-man crusade, he engaged in campaigns that rippled across Kansas and around the country. An avid consumer and purveyor of anticommunist texts and recordings, in 1958 he obtained a tape recording of a speech produced by the HUAC that railed at the internal communist threat and played it for the editor of the *Wichita Beacon*. The editor's face turned ashen. He was persuaded by what he had heard and concluded that his own paper's "damned press bureau in Washington" had lied to him about the scale of the internal communist problem.

Koch was just getting started. He played the HUAC speech at dinner clubs, at a Masonic Lodge, for members of the Kansas Farm Bureau—for "literally thousands of people" in all.[19] He advised his fellow Birch founders to play the speech—the "most effective device for convincing the apathetic that there is a deadly Communist menace"—before any audiences they could corral. Using the pseudonym "An American Businessman," he wrote a thirty-nine-page pamphlet in 1961 and distributed it widely. In it, Koch excoriated union bosses ("a great danger"), the United Nations (Moscow's puppet), and America's colleges and universities ("definitely socialist"). He used his status and wealth to put other anticommunist documents in front of congressional committees, the American Bar Association, and other entities, reaching what he estimated to be a hundred thousand Americans with the society's message that expanding the welfare state meant taking steps toward communist slavery. He appealed to CEOs to join the society and serve on its National Council, and at least one of his company's employees distributed anticommunist tape recordings to firefighters and marines.[20]

Koch cultivated a network of allies who helped spread Bircher dogma and fight for its principles, and his alliances aided the society's cause, making it a force in Wichita politics. Leonard Banowetz, a lawyer for the Kansas State Chamber of Commerce who had worked with Koch to enact their state's right-to-work amendment, became the first leader of the Birch Society's Wichita chapter, which sprang organically from Koch's activism and visibility in the community. In that role, Banowetz waged a campaign to coerce the University of Wichita to fire its allegedly procommunist faculty and hire conservative anticommunists in the political science and economics departments. He prevailed on donors to withhold funding, heralding the power of business-led financial pressure and sending a signal to universities and other institutions to practice anticommunism or else incur the wrath of Birchers. "You can't just kick all the businessmen in the teeth" without reaping the consequences, Banowetz said.[21] His campaign caught the attention of university administrators, although it was not clear if the university seeded its faculty with more conservatives.

Koch also was drawn to the infusion of Christian moralism into the anticommunist movement, and the society appealed to him as a religious struggle to achieve the kind of country he wanted. A sermon from the Reverend Wayne Poucher moved him, and Koch distributed a recording of it to his networks, touting it as one of the most spiritual anticommunist talks he had ever heard. Koch's leadership of the society conferred some key advantages on the early Birch movement. His deep pockets, stature in his community, and zeal for converting nonbelievers to the society's cause helped Birchers spread their ideas through the Midwest, Koch's home base. Koch embodied the talent for publicity, the willingness to spend his own resources on a social cause, and the crusading orientation that characterized many of the early Birch leaders as they sought to recruit members and put their views before the American people. He brought all these attributes to the fledgling organization in 1959. His participation augured well for a movement that was just hitting its stride.[22]

As the society prepared to expand its membership drive to ordinary citizens, news broke that alarmed the early recruits and gave founders a sense of direction. Soviet premier Nikita Khrushchev was visiting the United States, and a summit with Eisenhower was to take place. The prospect of a summit angered conservatives already outraged by Ike's soft foreign policy. Never ones to let a crisis or a controversy go to waste, Birch leaders moved with speed to capitalize on the moment. To the elites starting to join the society, the summit confirmed at a minimum that Eisenhower had capitulated to the Soviet Union in the Cold War. He wasn't interested in victory; he was in hot pursuit of diplomacy, code for accommodation and surrender. Khrushchev, a fiend, now had an invitation to tour the United States and meet with the commander-in-chief of its armed forces, and this abomination demanded a full-throated reaction. The Birch Society seemed to have been built for just this moment.

To turn public opinion against the summit and undermine Khrushchev's propaganda coup, Birchers established one of their first front groups: the Committee Against Summit Entanglements (CASE). The committee was 100 percent a Birch operation disguised as an independent, spontaneous assemblage of outraged citizens. Just as Welch wished to keep the Birch Society itself secret from the communists to give it room to launch without opposition, he set up front groups and gave them names that would grant them freedom to operate without unduly alerting detractors.

CASE enjoyed the support of a wide swath of the American right, from the Daughters of the American Revolution to much of the conservative movement's political and intellectual leadership. When the committee circulated a letter decrying the summit as a moral surrender to the personification of evil in the modern world, its signatories included William Buckley, Barry Goldwater, libertarian economist Ludwig von Mises, Birch funders such as Olive Simes (who also supported white supremacist causes) and Pierre S. du Pont, and movement leaders such as Welch, Grede, Koch, Hart, and Braden. Tom Anderson, a member of the society's National Council, denounced the summit, writing, "We've decided we'd rather live on our belly than die on our feet."[23]

In late August 1959, after raising some $58,000 plus an additional $29,000 through CASE-specific benefactors, the committee ran ads in more than a hundred newspapers, including a full-pager in the *New York Times.* The text urged the cancellation of the summit and reminded readers that the Cold War was "a war to the death." Negotiation was impossible; the enemy had to be destroyed once and for all. CASE mailed more than half a million postcards bearing the message "Stay Away—U.S.A.," reaching an estimated three million citizens, and deluged the White House with antisummit telegrams and letters.[24]

In the end the summit wasn't canceled, but CASE was a success as a form of propaganda and recruiting. Welch wrote that it had generated "moral backing" from conservatives across the country. The petition circulated by the committee had been entered into the *Congressional Record*. "Scores of outstanding American patriots" had praised its efforts. And this brave band of true anticommunists had forced what had been planned as a "tour of triumph" to become an icy debacle, he trumpeted. Welch credited the campaign with delivering "to millions of our fellow citizens . . . realization of the real character of this monster."[25]

Above all, the society's first big campaign using a front group illustrated the power that political and business elites wielded to draw publicity and excitement to the Bircher cause. And through attention-grabbing efforts in the media, it could potentially reach wider audiences lower down the income scale. The antisummit front underscored the society's potential as a force within the broader constellation of American conservatism, a coalition that spanned the range of right-wing anticommunist thought. The Committee Against Summit Entanglements also confirmed that the society had enough funds to deliver its message to the American public and to pressure political leaders to veer away from procommunist policies. Having so many successful businessmen on board certainly helped.

The use of front groups soon became a Birch Society calling card, a signature of the movement. The fronts had at least two big advantages: They allowed conservatives to support a cause while keeping their distance from the society and its baggage. And they transformed the society's promise of direct action into political reality. This early effort at concealing who was behind a group became a template for conservative advocacy for decades to come. And, importantly, an issue that the far right pushed could gain adherents beyond the circle of Birch members and penetrate public debate.

As 1959 unfolded, the society began to attract support outside the world of senior business leaders, tapping the ranks of doctors, lawyers, dentists, engineers, midlevel executives, other professionals, and retirees. When Wisconsin's *Racine Journal-Times* editorialized that antisummit conservatives represented the "voice of the old gang"—a band of "unreconstructed isolationists, frustrated military officers, war-mongers, anti-taxers, and chronic agin-ers"—J. I. Case Company vice president Harry Barr excoriated the editor for slandering patriots who had "created jobs for thousands of Wisconsin citizens." When Dr. Anna Mathiesen heard retired general (and Birch ally) Albert Wedemeyer on a Baltimore radio station decrying Eisenhower's duplicity regarding the summit, she fumed to Welch that the president had abdicated his oath of office.[26] In response to hearing Birch leaders make their pitch, many professionals outside the upper crust of business executives responded favorably. At less than a year old, the society had shown that it could draw recruits beyond the original circle of elites, and that professionals could make it a potent political force nationwide.

THE BIRCH SOCIETY APPEALED TO UPPER-MIDDLE-CLASS PROFESSIONALS for some of the same reasons that had persuaded wealthy businesspeople. It offered the promise of activism, and to some conservatives who had supported candidates for office it presented a more constructive outlet for their energies than what they viewed as toiling in the bowels of Eisenhower's listless GOP or the perennially liberal Democratic Party.

A Texas businessman who joined the society told the home office as much. Although local groups had urged him to run for Congress, he felt he could do the best work possible as a direct-action volunteer to educate and propagandize in his community. He assured Welch, "The enthusiasm for both you and the Society remains as strong as ever in my heart." Others chimed in: a Catholic priest in Connecticut, a Protestant fundamentalist in Massachusetts, an Arkansas teacher. In Arizona, a businessman explained that he and his wife had drawn more inspiration from the society than from any other recent political development. A "working mother" from Wisconsin announced that it felt "good to belong to an active, directed unit of a growing army in this struggle with the Communists."[27]

As recruitment expanded beyond the founders' circle of friends and acquaintances, the society had to accommodate more and more members spread across a vast geographic area. At first, all members joined the society's "home office," essentially a national chapter. By early 1959, however, Welch permitted the establishment of individual chapters at the local level. Each chapter had a cap of twenty members. If more than twenty conservatives wished to join in a given city or town, they were required to form a separate chapter; the cap enabled the society to hatch plans in relative secrecy and mobilize its members for quick strikes against enemy forces. The organizing approach partly drew on the model of communist cells, operating in small numbers in order to conceal their actions and maximize their capability to react rapidly. "Recruiting . . . and the formation of new chapters, is the order of the day," one Birch publication instructed its members.[28]

Particularly in the early months, the society tasked members with pitching neighbors and coworkers on joining.[29] As the *Bulletin* stated in 1959, "Sponsorship by somebody we trust will be increasingly required."[30]

As the society expanded beyond its early cadre of business executives, the founders wanted reliable conservatives who wouldn't distribute the *Blue Book* to communists, reporters, and other potential critics. Birch leaders wanted to avoid "infiltration" by "traitors."

The society expected members to pledge loyalty to the movement and adhere to the home office's directives. It charged annual dues of $24 for each man and $12 for each woman (on the theory that men had more resources), and it mandated attendance at monthly chapter meetings. It urged members to keep up with *American Opinion*, the *Bulletin*, and a slew of recommended books. Other than yearly dues, these directives were difficult for Welch's team to enforce, but many members apparently followed at least some if not most of them. Inevitably, those who complied had the resources, connections, professional status, education, and leisure time needed to participate. A box-factory worker from Massachusetts captured the class dynamic in some chapters when he noted that his fellow members included a doctor, a piano teacher, an optometrist's wife, "some old maids," and him, "the only ordinary worker."[31]

By February 1959, within three months of the society's birth, it already had ten chapter leaders in Boston, including medical professionals and lawyers. It hired full-time paid coordinators in various regions of the country to aid recruitment, help form chapters, and guide members. A Protestant minister from Michigan became one of the first coordinators, and Medford Evans, a former professor and the editor of the white supremacist newspaper *Citizen's Council*, worked as a coordinator for Louisiana and Mississippi.[32]

To professionals who had longed for a direct-action movement to channel their Cold War political energy, the excitement was infectious. In 1959 Mr. and Mrs. Kent Tewel of Grosse Point, Michigan, a wealthy suburb of Detroit, established John Birch Society Chapter 12 (the chapters were originally numbered, but some would later be lettered) before a coordinator had even been assigned to the region. The Tewels started playing Birch-produced anticommunist tape recordings for friends and acquaintances, and the chapter reached its twenty-member limit so fast that a second one had to be established to satisfy demand.[33]

Professionals also flocked to the society in other Midwestern industrial states. Grede and Bradley helped fuel the movement in Wisconsin, as did several influential Catholic priests with eager congregations. The legacy of McCarthy didn't hurt. But it was a Milwaukee husband-and-wife team of volunteer coordinators who most embodied the passion, idealism, and grit of successful on-the-ground organizing. Just over a year after the society's founding, Don and Mrs. Rueber (her first name was absented from the record, a common practice of the time) attended a weeklong School for Anti-Communism in Wisconsin that was organized by Australian doctor Fred Schwarz and his Christian Anti-Communism Crusade. The Birch Society had supplied much of the literature available to participants, and its volunteers sat at tables selling items like antisummit postcards and *Blue Book*s. The Ruebers quickly sold all twenty-five of their *Blue Book*s. More importantly, working for five straight days from eight in the morning to midnight, they talked with virtually all the 750 participants about joining the Birch Society. The couple's tirelessness and success underscored the potential of immersive face-to-face organizing by a small but hardy band of the brave.

Don Rueber spoke at length, for example, with Harold Tuttle of Eagle River, "a fine American" who wished to immediately set up a chapter in his hometown and promised "that there are excellent prospects for many more in his area," in towns like Rhinelander and Tomahawk. Rueber asked the Belmont, Massachusetts, home office to send Tuttle "a Library" full of Birch literature. The Ruebers assured Dorothy Hughes, of Thiensville, that they would deliver recruiting tapes to her community so that she, too, could establish a chapter, and they received commitments from a "Mrs. Walter Graham" and from Paul Stout, who had crossed state lines to visit from Lombard, Illinois. "All in all it has been a long, hard week," Rueber reflected, "but we enjoyed every minute of it." He left the meeting more convinced than ever "that we have the only <u>real</u> answer to the problem of fighting Communism. . . . I find it most difficult to contain my enthusiasm and optimism for the complete success of the Society in this State. I have no doubt that we will have the finest organization of Chapters in the entire nation." He called his five days of nonstop work "the most useful vacation I have had in recent years."[34]

In Columbus, Ohio, Charles Pavey, a former president of the Association of American Physicians and Surgeons and a leader in one of the nation's most esteemed professions, became another adept recruiter. Part of a surge of doctors who joined in the early months, Pavey displayed images of Ohio River steamboats on the walls of his office. Medical books lined his shelves, betraying no hint of political radicalism. He was a leader of the right-wing group We the People when he started receiving free copies of *American Opinion* from the Birch Society. He liked what he read, responded favorably to Welch's pitch, and decided to subscribe. He traded letters with Welch and traveled to Chicago to hear his two-day presentation, returning to Columbus with the belief that the society was "the answer to every anti-communist's prayer." The question that had haunted him about the Red Menace—"what the hell can I do about it?"—no longer did. The society, he said, "gives you the chance" to fight for freedom, and he seized it.

In May 1960, Pavey started to organize Columbus's first chapter. The city was fertile ground for Birch-style conservatism, with two dailies that were at least somewhat sympathetic to Birch causes. Pavey was close friends with *Citizen-Journal* editor Don Weaver, who had praised the society as "dedicated to the battle against Communism" and a welcome addition to the local fray. The congressman from Columbus, Samuel Devine, a former FBI agent, also hailed the "fine, patriotic" Birchers in his district.[35]

Again, word of mouth proved among the most potent forms of outreach. Pavey invited people he knew to recruitment meetings. Others who might be sympathetic received invitations to home screenings of Birch films such as *Operation Abolition*. An especially effective tool for pushing conservatives to take the plunge, the film portrayed anti-HUAC student protesters on the steps of San Francisco's City Hall as communists staging an attempted coup. Savvy at picking up on a single event as a symbol of what ailed the country, the society capitalized on the San Francisco footage as proof that the threat was internal and growing more dangerous. The protests, Welch said, resembled "communist-inspired student riots" similar to those that had toppled South Korea's anticommunist Rhee and demonstrated that communists inside the United States were making a grab for "the reins of power."[36]

Within two months, the Birch Society was soaring in Columbus, just as it had around Milwaukee. Pavey became the leader of Chapter 224 and recruited sixty-six members, prompting the formation of multiple additional chapters. (By the summer of 1961, the city had the same number of chapters as New York City—twenty, with more on the way.) Signs that the society was more than just a hard-line libertarian group surfaced early in its existence. Patriotism and morals became defining issues for some members. Warring against "anti-American" elements in the culture was paying off. When Pavey learned that no local cinema was screening *The Alamo*, starring John Wayne, he phoned theater managers and asked why. He successfully pressured at least one local theater to put the movie on the schedule. The Columbus chapters lobbied libraries and bookstores to stock the book *Roosevelt's Road to Russia* and other hard-right anticommunist publications.

Like the Midwest, the Northeast became a buzzing hub of early Birch organizing among professionals and others who found it empowering to take direct action against communism rather than just decrying it. Welch had long argued that democracy was a form of "mobocracy"; it enabled small claques, "temporary" majorities, to trample on the constitution and enact un-American policies. A great nation, he said, should not be ruled by "the sudden whims of the electorate." In Wilton, Connecticut, chapter leader John Moore, owner of Johnnie's Auto Clinic, a car repair shop, launched an effort to paste Birch stickers on doors and windows all over town that said, "This is a Republic—not a Democracy. Let's keep it that way."

Born in Brooklyn and active in the Catholic Church, Moore had embraced anticommunism around 1947, at the Cold War's outset. But it was his church that turned him on to the society. His parish priest led a local anticommunist study group, and Moore read the pamphlets and books on offer. His immersion in the literature led him to conclude that "the world [was] slipping away to Communism through liberalism and socialism." In the 1950s he sometimes wrote protest letters and handed out pamphlets, but the groups he had joined "didn't really do anything. . . . You'd go home at night and forget about it." In contrast, the Birch Society stressed the need for action. As a chapter leader he became

energized by this culture of the like-minded with an emphasis on direct intervention. Chapter meetings where they discussed ideas in depth
gave him additional satisfaction, and the explosive growth of the society
across his region—"chapters all around here—Stamford, Dunbury [sic],
Waterbury"—infused the movement with excitement and an acute sense
of common purpose. Moore felt so much pride in his membership that
he pasted society stickers on bills he paid. His membership demonstrated
that small business owners, and not just highly educated doctors, lawyers, and dentists, were attracted to the movement.[37]

The early growth of the John Birch Society was impressive. In 1959,
its first full year of operation, it raised a reported $200,000 in donations,
fees, sales, and dues, enough money to operate comfortably and effectively. Around its one-year anniversary, the home office had signed up
more than three hundred members representing more than twenty-five
states ("the best known, most highly regarded, and most influential conservatives in our country"). The national organization had an estimated
eighty-two chapters, including anywhere between one and twelve chapters each in Iowa, Illinois, Michigan, Wisconsin, Texas, Louisiana, Tennessee, Arkansas, Florida, Virginia, South Carolina, New Hampshire,
New York, Connecticut, Massachusetts, California, and Washington.
Seven full-time, paid coordinators were on staff, covering such states as
Michigan, Tennessee, California, Texas, and Louisiana, and six volunteer
coordinators assisted in recruitment across the South and along the West
Coast (volunteer coordinators were reimbursed only for travel expenses).
An estimated 10 percent of the chapters were considered "weak," but the
rest were booming. The society produced eighteen recordings for chapter
leaders and coordinators to use for recruitment, distributed four thousand *Blue Books* nationwide, and had a "very solid base" on which to
build. "We have barely scratched the surface in building the John Birch
Society," Welch announced in late 1959. "We are just now beginning . . .
to become a force of dependable impact."[38]

Like the society's ideas, its tactics toggled between mainstream conservative and fringe, between acceptable and radical. Its recommendations to
its members fell into at least two overlapping categories. First, on the media front, the society sought to put its "Americanist" books and pamphlets

in as many homes, offices, and libraries as possible, to promote its favorite talk-radio hosts and pundits through word of mouth, and to expand the circulation of its magazines. Birch films were particularly effective at grabbing the attention of more than the elites the movement had identified as its prime recruiting targets. Its first color film—launched with a six-minute introduction by Welch—was a half-hour hosanna to free enterprise, featuring a guided tour of the Milwaukee-based Allen-Bradley factory, which manufactured pioneering electronic equipment, as a shining example of the brilliance of the nation's capitalist system. Films like this, the society's leaders thought, were particularly useful for reaching the less educated. "To the ordinary audience of middle-class or lower economic levels," Welch asserted, "this film is a heartening revelation." Such presentations demonstrated how the society viewed education as a key to spreading knowledge (in this case, the wonders of free enterprise) and to eroding white working-class Americans' support for unions. Education could recruit citizens who hadn't attended college, even forging a cross-class alliance.[39]

Second, and more radically, the society employed petitions, front groups, and "the weapon of letter-writing" to pressure people in power to adopt Birchers' stands on issues. In November 1959 the society asked its members to write to defense industrialist Edgar Kaiser to take him to task for allegedly failing to supply the military with the taxpayer-funded planes he had promised. In December it urged members to buy a postcard, write on it, "Who murdered Bang-Jensen?" (a Danish diplomat from the United Nations), and send it to UN Secretary-General Dag Hammarskjöld. Povl Bang-Jensen had killed himself with a bullet to the head and was found in a park in Queens, New York, on November 26, 1959. He had been fired from the UN, and Birchers considered him a hero who had been trying to protect the names of Hungarian anticommunist dissidents. They suspected foul play. A Senate Internal Subcommittee later questioned the police ruling of death by suicide and accused the Russians of targeting him for "liquidation." Members also pressed public libraries to carry books critical of union leaders and supportive of the society's single-minded anticommunism. They urged American Airlines president C. R. Smith to rectify the lack of Americanist magazines in planes' seat pockets, with the goal, Welch explained, of "breaking through (at any tiny point) the blanket of obfuscation being increasingly spread by the mass media of communications." Although the society considered business boycotts "an un-American weapon," it nonetheless asked its members to complain to local Ford auto dealerships about a scholarship going to an allegedly subversive student named Clinton Jencks and intimated that Ford's bottom line could take a hit.[40]

The prospect of direct action against their enemies drew Americans from different professions and income brackets to feel that they were finally having an impact. Early in 1960 one society founder, A. G. Heinsohn of Tennessee's Cherokee Textile Mills, informed a Hartford businessman active in the anticommunist movement that the society not only had Welch, "the best (for my money) professional, full-time dedicated student of Communism in America," it also was "the only vehicle I know of which provides dedicated patriots a TOOL with which to work in directed UNISON with other patriots . . . to restore moral and spiritual values to America" by reducing the size of government and invigorating personal responsibility, and it was the only movement that gave individuals the chance to act at "the very grass roots level; thus affording an individual sense of accomplishment to all participating members." Its success, he concluded, lay in "its ability to pin-point concerted actions upon specific targets."[41]

Such actions included waging information warfare on anyone who seemed to be supporting the communist line. The language of violence pervaded society publications and rhetoric. Opponents were the personification of evil, anti-Americanism made flesh. The words pulsed with a raw vitriol—"labor bosses" were "tyrannical"; society members were exhorted to fight "the White House-Defense Department clique." The *Bulletin* characterized Birchers, in contrast, as "a phalanx of tens of thousands of spears, which can be hurled simultaneously as one mighty weapon against any vulnerable spot in the Communist line."[42]

In some communities, the message of action and the demonization of liberals ratcheted up right-wing threats, harassment, intolerance, and aggression. It became clear that even two dozen Birchers could shake a community at its foundation. Welch urged his followers to take over

Parent-Teacher Associations on the theory that local offices would be easier to attain than statewide seats.

In communities with robust chapters, the real-life implications of Birch policies began to crystallize. In Dallas, where growth of the society was strong, a group likely comprising at least some Birchers, many of them women, spat at Lyndon and Lady Bird Johnson and ripped a glove out of Lady Bird's hand when they visited the Adolphus Hotel four days before the November 1960 presidential election. In North Dakota, Birchers hurled epithets at Republican senator Milton Young, branding him a "Communist" and "pro-Communist."[43]

The Darby School District in the Bitterroot Valley of Montana showed what was possible when a handful of local members took an idea from the society and put it into practice. When the district's superintendent decided to replace Bibles that were deemed to be in bad condition, a local minister advised that it would be okay to burn them. After approximately two dozen Birchers learned of the bonfire, their outrage sparked a multiyear crusade to remake the school district. A principal grew so concerned that Birchers were "using the local PTA as a springboard to infiltrate" Darby's schools that he asked Montana's Democratic senator, Mike Mansfield, to send the principal any information Mansfield had on the operation. The senator's office reported that a local Birch chapter sought to establish review committees to study the school's humanities textbooks for evidence of subversive teachings and expurgate what it saw as socialist propaganda from the school library. The school board voted down these Birch proposals, but the chapter members largely succeeded in their scorched-earth campaign of aggression and intimidation. They made menacing phone calls to the superintendent, trashed his home, and stalked him, and eventually he resigned. According to historian Kristin Gates, within a few years the Darby School District lost sixteen of its twenty-three teachers, victims of the Birchers' tear-it-all-down assault.[44]

The professionals and other elites who had joined the movement were making the kind of impact they had desired when they first submitted their dues. But the society was also spearheading a new kind of movement that lured extremists to its ranks, deployed novel, inventive forms of propaganda, and bullied its enemies into submission. Its tactics could turn violent, its orientation antidemocratic. Philbrick may have ultimately come around to the goals of the society, but he had been right about its potential to destabilize politics. Time would tell whether the society's strategies would inflict damage on itself and implode or bring down America's fragile Cold War democracy.

Chapter 3

WITCH HUNT

Fᴿᴼᴹ ɪᴛs ꜰᴏᴜɴᴅɪɴɢ ɪɴ Dᴇᴄᴇᴍʙᴇʀ 1958, ᴛʜᴇ Bɪʀᴄʜ Sᴏᴄɪᴇᴛʏ sᴏᴜɢʜᴛ to keep the klieg lights off itself, and for a while it mostly managed to avoid making news. Although the society enjoyed positive coverage from right-wing radio pundits and *L'Intransigeant,* a Paris daily, which applauded its opposition to a French communist movement, Birchers had good reason to shield themselves from the prying eyes of the mainstream press corps. Some members feared that enemies might try to infiltrate the movement once they learned of it. Others figured that if their names surfaced in connection with the society, they might lose customers, alienate neighbors, or even be fired from their jobs. Its well-heeled early boosters and members had much to lose. Reporters had bludgeoned Joe McCarthy, and Birch leaders wished to avoid a similar fate. So rather than try to drum up coverage, the home office in Belmont, Massachusetts, instructed members to keep "general publicity about us to a minimum."[1]

The decision to operate in secret put the society in the same company as the far-left organizations it reviled, but many members of the Birch Society had a reason to hide their ties to the movement. They perceived themselves to hold political views that were so explosive as to put them at risk socially and economically. Birchers considered the consensus of the 1950s, the "vital center," to be so pervasive and powerful that they had to take every imaginable precaution.

In the first year and a half, Birchers largely achieved that goal. They deployed fronts, undertook anonymous letter-writing initiatives, gave chapters inscrutable and nondescript names (e.g., CBEM, a string of letters that apparently was randomly assigned), and refused to disclose their membership lists. When Chapter 26 held a meeting in New York City, the chapter leader encouraged members to "operate through other organizations" and use additional surreptitious means to evade detection.[2]

In the end, though, the society's membership was so prominent, its tactics so aggressive, and its ideas so provocative that it could not remain a secret forever. Press coverage of the society's activities sparked unease and a renewal of a decade-old academic debate. Scholars, many of them on the faculty of Columbia University, had argued in the 1950s and early 1960s that "pseudo-conservatives" prone to authoritarianism, conspiracy theories, and violence stood far outside the American consensus. Historian Richard Hofstadter posited that the far right was engaging in "an underground revolt against all these tormenting manifestations of our modern predicament" such as the Cold War's uncertainties, the growth of liberal government, and values like pluralism and tolerance.[3]

Hofstadter and his colleagues contended that the far right threatened the norms and principles that had enabled the United States to save capitalism during the Depression and save democracy from the Nazis in World War II. Right-wing extremists rejected pluralism, civil liberties, federal economic regulations of private enterprise, and the kind of liberal internationalism and alliance building that had largely contained the spread of communism from Europe to Asia. This grim view of the far right prepped the public and the press to look with suspicion for any sign that Nazi sympathizers and homegrown fascists were making a comeback.

Knowing how far out of the mainstream they swam, the Birch Society had essentially built a dam to hold back public scrutiny, and for the first year and half it held up. But in the summer of 1960 cracks appeared.

The *Chicago Daily News*, the *Chicago Sun-Times*, the *Milwaukee Journal*, and the *Wichita Eagle* reported that the society's leader had branded Eisenhower a "conscious agent of the communist conspiracy." In the *Daily News*, reporter Jack Mabley broke the story after Fred Schwarz, the Australian leader of the Christian Anti-Communism Crusade, appeared before a group of hundreds of people in Illinois and asked Stillwell Conner, a member of the society's National Council, if Welch had accused Ike of being a communist. Mabley justified the exposure on the grounds that the ordinary citizens who were joining the movement ought to know something about Welch's far-fetched ideas.[4] With dozens of copies of *The Politician* in circulation, it was going to be hard for Welch to keep the society under wraps forever.

This initial flurry of press scrutiny gave Birchers a bitter taste of what lay in store for their movement. "Group Branding Ike as Red," a headline announced in the *Journal*. The piece identified three Wisconsin businessmen as leaders of the society and noted that it already had ten chapters in the state and that law enforcement, for reasons unknown, had launched an investigation.

Some leaders of the society sought to control the damage. Welch, implausibly, denied to the *Boston Herald* that he had pinned the communist label on Eisenhower "in print"—speculating that in any case the president "may be too dumb to be a communist."[5] Welch's conspiratorial musings, another Birch leader explained, were merely "a personal matter with Bob" that bore little relation to the society's action-packed agenda.

Criticism continued to rain down on Birch leaders from various quarters. Some leaders of the National Association of Manufacturers expressed shock that Welch, a former colleague, had associated the president with "treason." Welch, one board member concluded, was "a g . . d . . . crackpot." Other acquaintances of Birch officials voiced outrage as well; one described the society as "a subversive group," and another denounced a Birch leader with GOP ties as a "disgrace."[6]

The most explosive reaction to the first wave of news articles came from the top. President Eisenhower was "hopping mad," one of his aides observed. He found the treason charge unhinged, completely unmoored from the evidence of his lifetime of service to the country. Ike had established himself as one of the greatest military commanders of the century. After the war, he had served as president of Columbia University, a major institution of higher education. Now, in his final summer as president of the United States, he looked at his record and believed—with some justification—that he had led the nation through a thicket of nuclear-fraught crises and negotiations in the first full decade of the Cold War. The president had defended freedom at home and abroad with vision, candor, and wisdom.

But to Eisenhower, the most galling element in the news reports wasn't Welch's cockamamie theory. What most offended was the revelation that a member of Eisenhower's own administration, Wisconsin foundry owner Bill Grede, was identified as a Bircher. On the recommendation of Commerce Secretary Fritz Mueller, the president had tapped Grede to serve on the White House Labor-Management Committee. When Ike heard about the Birch connection, he fumed to Mueller that "this is the man you asked me to put on that panel."[7]

The revelation about Grede's role in the society confused and repulsed many in the administration. During the past decade Grede had served as chair of the Wisconsin GOP's fundraising and had persuaded some of Taft's supporters to back Ike after he'd secured the GOP presidential nomination in 1952. Four years later Grede delivered again. His speeches across Wisconsin in support of Eisenhower's reelection made him a highly prized presidential surrogate. For him to serve as a leader of the Birch Society felt like a betrayal.[8]

Grede moved on multiple fronts to assuage the president and defend his reputation as a Republican and the Birchers' reputations as patriots. Mueller and Labor Secretary Jim Mitchell informed Grede that he needed to resign and write a letter of apology to the president. They went back and forth about the language. The final version, sent to Ike, represented an effort to bridge a GOP leader's loyalty to his party with a Birch leader's loyalty to his movement.

Mitchell and Mueller pressed Grede to go further and issue a full-throated denunciation of Robert Welch. They suggested that he describe Welch as "an extremist" who, in a moment of acute "emotional anxiety," had voiced an "absurd opinion" about Ike and "would forever regret" it. Grede took a more equivocal approach. He reminded Ike of his loyal campaign service. He explained that Welch's notions did not represent his own views. Moreover, he said, the typical Bircher knew nothing about Welch's ideas and had joined the movement in order to halt the infiltration of communism in the United States. Birchers, Grede assured the president, were "busily engaged in helping to elect a Republican ticket in 1960."[9]

Grede's fence-mending worked, up to a point. The president replied on White House stationery, "You have removed unfair and unjustified conclusions from my mind." Still, the administration appeared utterly unmoved by Grede's defense of the Birch Society. The president's view of the movement as a fringe and subversive organization remained unchanged.[10]

The first news stories about the Birchers led to another sour note: ten members from Illinois and Indiana submitted their resignations. But the publicity produced some unexpected good news for the society too. On balance, the stories in the summer of 1960 actually appeared to help the group's recruitment efforts. Support started to surge. In Chicago, fifty conservatives applied for membership in response to what they perceived as the media's attacks. Wisconsin retained all its members. One leader met with three different membership groups, and Welch's conspiracy theory never even surfaced as a topic of conversation.[11]

Expressions of support landed at the home office and gave Birch leaders a sense of reassurance and relief. They began to see a pattern: the seeming broadsides from the dailies outraged and emboldened the society's rank and file, who rallied in earnest in shared loathing of the mass media. Fifteen members of a San Diego chapter promised headquarters, "We are with you more solidly than ever." Another supporter rejected the news articles as pure "rubbish." A teacher in Milwaukee contended that the *Journal* had published an article to help John Kennedy win the presidency. Welch took heart at the many "reaffirmations of loyalty and support." His members had brushed off the reports, and their faith in the movement had deepened. One industrialist identified as a Birch leader felt so much anger that he threatened to sue the *Milwaukee Journal* for libel.[12]

In 1960, the news media had the power to make or break political movements, and it did some of both to the Birchers. In the wake of the press accounts, the society's reputation took a hit from some businessmen and GOP officials. But others saw the coverage as biased; many reacted by joining the movement, and many who were already members deepened their devotion to it. The far right found a villain in big-city dailies and the big three television networks, and these common enemies united Birch members and steeled their determination to vanquish liberalism and remake American life.

Still, increasing scrutiny spelled troubles ahead for the Birch movement. A far greater media feeding frenzy swept up the society in early 1961, and this coverage would make aligning with it a political liability. Santa Barbara was fertile recruiting ground for the society, which enlisted hundreds of members there. The *Santa Barbara News-Press* caught wind of the movement and published a series of articles highly critical of the organization. The *Los Angeles Times* followed with its own exposé. Republican senator Milton Young of North Dakota considered himself a fairly conservative member of Congress. But when Birchers in his state targeted him as a "communist," he was livid. On March 8, the sixty-three-year-old, soft-spoken farmer—"he does not court the press or the photographers," journalist Russell Baker wrote in the *New York Times*—delivered a speech on the Senate floor, denouncing Welch's conspiracy theory about Eisenhower as deranged.[13] The press had the power to make Birchers look ridiculous with their own words, and the harsh coverage made it harder for the Birchers to gain power over the Republican Party.

In the spring of 1961 the wall-to-wall news coverage made some Birchers feel as if they were under siege psychologically and physically. Outside the society's Belmont headquarters, news photographers and television crews camped on the grounds and tried to snap pictures of Birchers through office windows; Birchers had to push journalists out of the offices when they entered without permission. Welch informed his colleagues that one New York television station had asked Connecticut's Birch coordinator if it could film a chapter meeting. When the coordinator refused the request, the TV station was said to reply, "Okay, then, we'll simply fake a meeting and get that one on television." Birchers loathed the press with a passion. The mainstream media simply couldn't be trusted to report the truth, in their view. Elite reporters lied, used deceptive tactics, and staged fake events in order to paint anticommunists in the worst possible light. Birchers figured that if they were going to smash communism inside the United States, they also needed to destroy, or at least discredit and circumvent, the corrupt American news media.[14]

IN EARLY 1961, AS THE KENNEDY ADMINISTRATION ASCENDED, THE Birchers attacked another conspicuous Republican. This time they chose a more divisive target than the grandfatherly war hero Ike: chief justice of the Supreme Court Earl Warren, avatar of New Deal liberalism and desegregation in the public schools. The campaign to impeach Warren was impossible for the press to ignore, ending any semblance of secrecy and caution and thrusting the Birch Society from the periphery to the epicenter of national politics. The decision to pick this particular fight was both brilliant and diabolical, and it became perhaps the group's single most effective crusade of the 1960s.

Warren was a prime architect of the liberal order, which to the Birchers was virtually indistinguishable from communism. As a Republican governor of California in the 1940s and early 1950s, he'd led an administration that had expanded the social safety net, embraced the New Deal at the state level, and epitomized the liberal strain that held sway over the Republican Party. Eisenhower appointed him to the Supreme Court as chief justice, and Warren proceeded to lead the court to a string of major decisions that Birchers believed trampled the Constitution and sullied their most cherished moral truths. Warren stood as the embodiment of what the society denounced as "the whims and views of demagogues temporarily in power," and with a lifetime appointment he posed an even graver threat. *Nine Men Against America*, a book promoted by the Birch Society, painted the justices as traitors to the United States.[15]

In the eyes of the society, the Warren court's most offensive decision was *Brown v. Board of Education*, the landmark ruling to mandate racial desegregation in schools. Birchers repudiated Brown as "procommunist." The society also complained that the court had coddled communists by giving them back their jobs, denigrated Christianity by banning prayer in public schools, and undermined law enforcement by protecting suspected criminals with unprecedented rights.[16]

The ingenuity of the impeachment campaign—and one reason it spawned so much publicity—rested on its simplicity. "Impeach Earl Warren" was direct and attention grabbing. It provided an easy-to-grasp shorthand for the need to restore the "respect for the Constitution" that had been lost under what Birchers construed as Warren's dictatorial rule.[17] A justice of the nation's highest court had never been impeached, and Warren enjoyed affection from Americans who considered him a pillar of constitutional wisdom and progressive vision. Assailing such a revered figure carried the kind of shock value that made people take notice.

The ensuing actions were as provocative as the words, and the effect was bracing. In 1961 Birchers gathered signatures on a petition and sent it to Congress to urge lawmakers to advance Warren's impeachment. An essay contest sponsored by the society asked undergraduates to submit three thousand words explaining why the chief justice deserved to be impeached and offered nine prizes with a total value of $2,500.[18] In 1964 Birchers picketed Warren when he delivered a commencement address at the New School for Social Research in New York City.[19] But in 1961 and 1962, what generated the most publicity were billboards, visible from roads, highways, and bridges, in which "Help Impeach Earl Warren" appeared over a head shot of the chief justice.

The billboards galvanized Birchers, their critics, and the press alike, and both the medium and the message caught fire. Members heeded the call to "help," relishing the task of spreading the word, their activism akin to planting a Birch flag in the landscape of American politics. They placed a twenty-by-nine-foot billboard near a bridge connecting Staten Island and New Jersey, and a thirty-six-year-old Bircher named Frank Benning used his own funds to erect twenty-five billboards in his hometown of Atlanta. On February 8, 1961, Clarence Manion, a right-wing radio host and member of the Birchers' National Council, delivered an address to two thousand people packed into Los Angeles's First Congregational Church. When someone in the audience asked Manion if he endorsed Warren's impeachment, he simply replied, "Yes." The applause was so thunderous that the building reportedly shook.[20]

But to some conservative media figures, the effort to oust Warren seemed unrealistic and counterproductive. *Richmond News Leader* editor James J. Kilpatrick, who had ties to the White Citizens' Councils and had criticized civil rights, huffed to William Buckley about "these idiots" who had "set off on a hare-brained campaign to impeach Earl Warren." Kilpatrick had said as much in his paper, and the society struck back hard. Welch urged Birchers to send letters protesting Kilpatrick's editorializing, and a deluge followed. Kilpatrick explained that he wrote individual replies to the first twenty or thirty Birchers, sent form letters to the next hundred, and "the next 400 we simply filed. I am not even sure my Girl Friday is opening the damned things now." It was "the most incredibly disciplined pressure group ever to come my way, and we are frankly a little stunned by it."[21]

The press also evinced alarm at the undertow of physical violence that the impeachment drive had surfaced. One Bircher proposed a twist on the campaign's slogan: "EARL WARREN, MAY HE REST IMPEACHED!" Critics weren't amused. Impeachment tapped "a deep vein of resentment toward Warren and the Warren court," one of his biographers has said, and law enforcement regarded the campaign as a threat to the chief justice's safety. When Warren flew to Atlanta to deliver a speech at Georgia Tech, city and airport police and agents from the Georgia Bureau of Investigation secured the airport for his protection. Two police cruisers trailed Warren's limousine, and plainclothes officers, uniformed police, and Pinkerton guards secured the coliseum where Warren spoke. Warren's wife, Nina, was perturbed by the Birch effort to use impeachment as a weapon against her husband, and even the normally placid chief justice, some of his clerks recalled, winced whenever anyone mentioned the billboards.[22]

In the end, neither Warren's safety nor his place on the court were in serious peril, but the Birchers had succeeded in communicating that they opposed the liberal direction of the nation's highest court. They spread their message that aggressive proclamations of new rights from unelected judges besmirched the nation's heritage and its constitutional traditions. The Birchers' proposed remedy exhilarated its members and shocked the public. Like their protests against the Khrushchev summit less than two years earlier, the impeachment crusade showed that there was more than one way to win. Birch Society members, Welch explained, never expected that "in just three or four months, by writing a few thousand letters to Congressmen," they would succeed in having Earl Warren impeached. Instead, the goal was to gin up conservatives who disliked Warren's rulings and to mobilize the far right in opposition to a hated liberal foe. Welch gloated that although Birch campaigns often failed, "none of them have left the enemy laughing by the time we finished."[23]

THERE WAS A GREAT DEAL OF MOCKERY OF THE SOCIETY ALONGSIDE THE more anxious reports of its toxicity. Journalists depicted Birchers as mentally unhinged; in columnist Al Capp's formulation, they were "nuts" who were frenetically trying to "take over the asylum." *The John Birch Coloring Book* spoofed the *Blue Book*, pegging Birchers as little kids who used crayons. Other portrayals said that Birchers had become infected with a "virus" that had left them dazed and fuzzy headed. What they needed to cure it was "a quick course in American history, a heart-to-heart talk with a trustworthy friend, and then, perhaps, a good long rest." California attorney general Stanley Mosk characterized the Birchers as "pathetic," as "little old ladies in tennis shoes." US Attorney General Robert Kennedy called them "ridiculous"—even as the FBI under his command opened an investigation of the movement with an extensive undercover operation.[24]

Besides targeting Warren, Birchers heckled speakers at town halls, relentlessly pushed school boards and public libraries to offer conservative texts, took over PTAs, and picketed Kennedy events, where they called him a communist. By early 1961 the society had thousands of members, and the sensational news that Welch had once called Eisenhower a communist dupe became an irresistible hook for journalists to once again play up. Stories appeared in virtually every major newspaper and magazine in the United States. The *New York Times*, the *Los Angeles Times*, *Time*, *Newsweek*, and *Life* were among the publications that recounted the Birchers' activities and their disruption of normally tranquil towns and well-functioning cities. Welch became notorious as an aspiring dictator who ruled the movement with an iron fist and pushed his radical ideas on the rest of America. Whether its members were painted as crazy zealots or dangers to democracy, the society could hide its fingerprints no more.

To much of the mainstream media, the news of the society's existence and exploits provided an opportunity for journalists to do their jobs and expose a dangerous mass movement to the American public. The society threatened the peaceful conduct of civic affairs, and the media used its enormous power to shine a bright light on its radicalism and freeze it out of the mainstream. *Santa Barbara News-Press* publisher Thomas Storke ran a series of editorials and reported pieces vilifying the society as secretive, dictatorial, and paranoid. Storke wrote that Birchers represented "a monolithic organization ruled with a dictatorial hand" and considered it his mission as a newsman to stand up and expose the menace. For his efforts he received a Pulitzer Prize and two other major journalism awards.[25]

Divining the meaning of the Birch Society acquired the status of national pastime. Wags of all kinds wanted to interpret the implications of the movement for the future of American democracy, hinting at a return of homegrown fascism. Political scientist Alan Westin warned in *Commentary* that Birchers represented "the most appealing, activist, and efficient movement to appear on the extreme right since the fertile decade of the 1930's." He wrote that they threatened opponents, used baseless conspiracy theories to weaken faith in the country's leadership and major government and educational institutions, and sought to return to a nonexistent halcyon past. In *The Nation*, Hans Engh spoke for many journalists and pundits when he wrote in March 1961 that the Birch Society was out to "whip up a good deal of unrest and suspicion." Birchers, he charged, called citizens "communist at the drop of a hat, and semi-secret meetings create an aura of fear and hate. . . . Together with other 'know nothing' organizations scattered through the country, it represents a basic, continuing phenomenon in American society: that regressive force which, under one guise or another, seems to pop up whenever the country as a whole seems destined to move into a more progressive era."[26]

The society, like a speed bump, slowed Americans as they progressed inexorably toward a more enlightened future. This theme in the national news filtered down to local coverage too. An Amarillo, Texas, newspaper defended citizens who approved of various Bircher bugaboos that the group had labeled communist, like public health (mental health, water fluoridation), internationalism (the UN), and education (federal funding for schools).[27]

Some mainstream media outlets viewed the society more favorably. Despite the assumption that journalists uniformly loathed it, a handful of publications depicted it as a welcome addition to the pantheon of anticommunist activists. The *Pasadena Star-News* praised those who simply wished to eradicate communism. William Loeb, the conservative publisher of the *Manchester Union Leader*, depicted the Birchers as good people and patriotic citizens. Outlets routinely published Birchers' letters to the editor and gave them free airtime on the radio, letting them take an active part in the nation's political debate. But to other conservatives the society's promulgation of baseless conspiracy theories endangered what they considered their more respectable, fact-based conservative philosophy. The *Los Angeles Times* publisher, Otis Chandler, editorialized that his newspaper firmly believed in conservative ideas, "but the Times does not believe the argument for conservatism can be won . . . by smearing as enemies and traitors those with whom we sometimes disagree." Rightwing "subversion," he thundered, "is still subversion." Birchers had employed communist "techniques and rules of conspiracy" so they could do battle with communists, and the means, Chandler implied, could not possibly justify the ends.[28]

JUST AS NEWS OUTLETS FIXATED ON THE SOCIETY AND RAISED ITS VISIbility, the era's relatively consolidated media landscape meant that elites could fairly easily relegate Birchers to the margins. Unlike their counterparts in the twenty-first century, mainstream newspapers, magazines, television, and radio could still counteract the growing number of rightwing outlets. To some Birchers and their allies, the coverage felt like wall-to-wall criticism from sources big and small: a Columbus, Ohio, student newspaper branding them "a threat to our national morale"; an editorial cartoon depicting Birchers standing on a vulture's wing alongside the KKK as the vulture pecked at the Statue of Liberty. The outpouring of condemnation engendered some sympathy among conservatives who thought the victims were martyrs, but it also warned GOP leaders and activists to put some distance between themselves and the most racist, conspiratorial, antisemitic, and nativist members of their coalition.[29]

The media's ongoing project to expose and ultimately marginalize the Birchers came to a head in the case of General Edwin A. Walker of the US Army. In the spring of 1961 the *Overseas Weekly*, a privately owned tabloid read by US soldiers, reported that Walker, who commanded the army's 24th Infantry Division, based in West Germany, had established an education program designed to instruct his men in the teachings of the John Birch Society and the true nature of the communist enemy. Welch's *The Life of John Birch* appeared on Walker's recommended-reading list. Further, the *Weekly* charged, Walker, a Silver Star–awarded World War II and Korean War veteran, had identified Harry Truman and Eleanor Roosevelt as "definitely pink." (Why he singled them out isn't clear.)

The bombshell report prompted the White House press corps to ask the president his views of the Walker scandal. During an April 21 news conference, Kennedy took a shot at the society as a movement based on delusions. "I am not sure that the John Birch Society is wrestling with the real problems which are created by the communists' advance around the world," he told reporters assembled in the briefing room. "I would hope all those who are concerned about the advance of communism would face that problem, and not concern themselves with the loyalty of President Eisenhower, or President Truman, or Mrs. Roosevelt, or myself, or someone else."[30]

By June the Defense Department had completed an investigation of Walker's activities. The army concluded that Walker had made "derogatory remarks of a serious nature about certain prominent Americans, the American Press, and TV industry and certain commentators, which linked the persons and institutions with Communism and Communist influence," and it reassigned him. Rather than accept his reprimand, Walker resigned from the service. He wanted, he explained, "to be free from the power of little men who . . . punish loyal service," and decided to use his platform to promote Birch ideas and educate the like-minded about the sinister threat of internal communism.

The media exposure not only triggered Walker's resignation but also ratcheted up fears that a strongman could seize control of the federal government and establish a dictatorship. The *New Republic* published a series of fictional "news" reports in 1961 imagining Walker leading a military coup and installing a junta in the White House. In the narrative, Walker, the temporary president, appoints Welch as head of a Subversive Activities Control Board and taps a rogues' gallery of right-wing businessmen, media moguls, and arch segregationists to other key posts.[31]

Walker retained pockets of support among Birchers and a few of their allies in the conservative movement, and some in the society considered him a rising star. *Newsweek* put him on its cover in 1961 with the headline "Thunder on the Right" positioned above a description that labeled him a "new crusader."

And yet the society had its defenders at the highest levels of government and in the right-wing establishment. "Since when is it wrong to advance the cause of Americanism?" Edgar Hiestand, a Republican congressman who was a Birch member, asked on the House floor. *National Review* editor William Buckley commiserated with Walker about the "injustices that have been done to you," and about "the Liberals" who "seem to be seizing the opportunity to degut an orientation program necessary for an enlightened military."[32]

As the spotlight grew brighter, Walker's extremism intensified. Like a lot of Birch leaders, Walker believed that communists were behind the drive to topple Jim Crow. In 1962 he was arrested on charges that he had led prosegregationist riots at the University of Mississippi. (The charges—incitement of insurrection—were later dropped.) Upon his return home to Dallas, he was surrounded by cheering supporters who held signs that said, "Welcome Walker" and "Walker for President, '64." One fan hoisted a Confederate flag.

But Walker's tangles with the press and his increasingly erratic behavior made him a liability to the Birch Society and the conservative movement. In April 1962, after delivering rambling congressional testimony denouncing Secretary of State Dean Rusk as part of an "apparatus" devoted to selling out the United States, Walker socked a reporter in the face. The antipress screeds had led to violence against a journalist, and now there was evidence that at least one Bircher was willing to pummel the enemy with not just his words but also his fists. Increasingly belligerent and outwardly racist, Walker found himself frozen out by some Birch leaders, and *National Review* ultimately denounced him as a fanatic.[33]

In other instances the press adopted a muscular approach, unearthing the identities of Birch members who held sensitive positions of public trust that seemed incongruous with serving in the secretive John Birch Society. Media exposure helped to sideline the career of army major Arch Roberts, one of Walker's aides. Gene Grove, a reporter at the *New York Post* and author of one of the first critical books about the society, had penetrated a secret Birch chapter meeting in New York City. There, he discovered that a senior army officer was a member despite the army's reprimand of Walker for indoctrinating his soldiers with Bircher ideas. When columnist Drew Pearson subsequently reported that Roberts had delivered a pro-Birch speech to the Daughters of the American Revolution, the army launched an investigation and suspended him. The press had used the power of the pen to expose a conflict between a far-right political movement and the ideal of a nonpartisan military under civilian control. Roberts was just one person, but the press had also sent a message that being a Bircher could be hazardous; membership risked social embarrassment, reputational damage, and career-altering consequences.[34]

THE TIDAL WAVE OF MEDIA COVERAGE NOT ONLY TURNED MANY CONSER-vative allies into active Birchers but also made it nearly impossible for political leaders of all stripes to avoid talking about the Birch Society. Numerous Republicans and Democrats were now expected to weigh in. "The John Birch movement is certainly causing pain to a great many people on both sides of the fence," *Los Angeles Times* publisher Chandler observed to a Democratic leader in April.[35]

But Republicans bore the brunt of the clashes. The society had re-served a special animus for two members of the GOP, Warren and Ei-senhower. The press reported that two congressmen—Edgar Hiestand and John Rousselot, both Republicans—belonged to the Birch Society. Welch had once sought the GOP nomination for lieutenant governor of Massachusetts and had dreamed of mounting a Republican bid to unseat John Kennedy in the Senate. Grede and T. Coleman Andrews had held posts in Eisenhower's administration. Virtually every Birch inspiration in elective office from the 1950s and 1960s—Taft, McCarthy, Bricker, Knowland, Goldwater—was a member of the GOP. As the Birchers saw it, the Democratic Party had hosted Wilson's New Nationalism, Roosevelt's New Deal, Truman's Fair Deal, and John Kennedy's New Frontier; clearly, Democrats were progovernment. Although the Republican Party encompassed varied factions from liberal and moderate to conservative and far-right, if Birchers were to engage in partisan politics, the GOP was the natural landing pad. On the whole, it was more anticommunist and more anti–New Deal, and Birchers posed a special kind of internal problem for Republican leaders and conservative activists alike.

Southern Democratic segregationists such as Strom Thurmond and James Eastland had praised the Birch Society as a movement of patriots. Dixiecrats, conservative southern Democrats who would eventually change their registration to Republican, formed another base of Birch support. Birchers' denunciation of civil rights as a Red plot synced with the most rabid foes of segregation in the Jim Crow South. If communists controlled the African American and white northern agitators who marched and went on "freedom rides" and "sat in" at lunch counters, then white opponents of civil rights could wave off the movement as alien and un-American, a hotbed of trickery and treason. Thus Kent and Phoebe Courtney, Medford Evans, Lester Maddox, George Wallace, and other southern segregationists either joined the society or later counted Birchers as among their most fervid grassroots enthusiasts.[36]

On the whole the GOP had far closer ties to the movement than the Democrats. And although a New Mexico Democratic Party official fretted that a Birch power grab in the GOP spelled trouble for the stability of the two-party system and democracy itself, some Democrats recognized that internal Republican discord was best left to their opponents to handle. "Finally," California's Democratic Party chair Roger Kent remarked, the GOP was "cursed with something almost as bad as vociferous communists who claimed to be Democrats."[37]

Some GOP conservatives initially jumped to defend the Birch Society. Arizona Republican senator Barry Goldwater ignored Welch's most polemical ideas and instead noted approvingly that "a lot of people in my hometown have been attracted to the society." The Birchers he knew were principled, impressive citizens, "the kind we need in politics." Ohio Republican congressman Gordon Scherer, a member of HUAC, also looked favorably on the movement, praising Birchers as outstanding anticommunists.[38]

Liberals wasted little time concluding that the society posed a lethal threat to democracy, and the Birchers-as-paranoid portrayal sank deep roots in Democratic Party culture. The society's "image of world events and American politics is wholly conspiratorial," Westin, who had read almost every word Welch had written, argued in *Commentary*. But liberals focused so heavily on Welch's overwrought writings that they failed to see that countless Birchers were rational, educated, skilled political operatives for whom the movement had touched a chord.[39] They underestimated the society's depth of support and summarily assumed that the far right was destined for failure.

Many liberals, especially moderate Republicans and nonsouthern Democrats, regarded members of the society as politically useful foils. Above all, Birchers tested the quality of liberals' moral leadership. As California's GOP senator Thomas Kuchel, one of the society's most hated foes, declared on the Senate floor, Welch's Eisenhower charge was appalling. "Good God," he thundered. "Should the American people and the American Government let that kind of spleen be poured upon one who has given his whole life to freedom?" Ohio Democratic senator Stephen Young called on Congress to eliminate the Birch Society's status as a tax-exempt nonprofit, and he eviscerated a pro-Birch New Hampshire judge as "a crackpot."[40]

Liberals tended to highlight the Birchers as a viable, though likely ephemeral, threat to American democracy. Former president Harry Truman called them "the sick among us" and assured his fellow citizens that "they are so volatile they blow themselves out." Taking their cues from the growing body of scholarly literature about the far right (in which books and articles often focused on the society's excesses and platform as indicative of its "paranoid style") and from the explosion of acidic press, liberals contorted themselves to poke fun at the society at the same time they warned gravely that it posed an existential threat. California attorney general Stanley Mosk's 1961 report portrayed Birchers as alternately ineffectual and "totalitarian," as fools and "wealthy businessmen, retired military officers." Above all they were dangerously unhinged: the typical Bircher's "paranoia," the report said, had turned daily life in modern America into an unending "nightmare." Birchers suffered from "systematized delusions" that had vaulted them into "a vortex of fanaticism and despair."[41]

President John Kennedy issued some of the harshest attacks on the society made by any liberal in 1961. The Birchers had harassed him at events, holding aloft signs that tarred him with the brush of communism. In a succession of remarks that year, Kennedy pilloried the movement as a fringe force outside the bounds of respectable discourse and legitimate politics. Picking up on the idea that Birchers were fundamentally irrational and consumed with fantasies untethered to the problems of the real world, the president told attendees of a Democratic fundraiser at the Hollywood Palladium in November that "the basic good sense and stability of the great American consensus has always prevailed" over "the discordant voices of extremism."

History was on his side. Kennedy acknowledged that "there have always been those on the fringes of our society who have sought to escape their own responsibility by finding a simple solution, an appealing slogan or a convenient scapegoat." But these movements tended to have short lifespans and had been deprived of popular support. The Birch Society, he argued, represented irrational reactions to "the strains and frustrations imposed by constant tension and harassment" of modern life. JFK didn't mention the Birchers by name, but everyone knew he was pointing his finger right at them.

Rather than face the true danger to the United States—international communism—the society had instead unearthed "treason in our churches, in our highest court, in our treatment of water," a reference to the antifluoride movement that Birchers helped lead. They "equate the Democratic Party with the welfare state, the welfare state with socialism, socialism with communism."

Kennedy urged the country to reject "these counsels of fear and suspicion." Complex problems required complex solutions. Incremental progress was possible, but only if people responded to hard challenges with pragmatic policies. "Let us concentrate more on keeping enemy bombers and missiles away from our shores, and concentrate less on keeping neighbors away from our [bomb] shelters," he urged. "Let us devote more energy to organizing the free and friendly nations of the world, with common trade and strategic goals, and devote less energy to organizing armed bands of civilian guerrillas that are more likely to supply local vigilantes than national vigilance."

Unity and strength of purpose were essential to meet the challenge of the times, and the Birchers' "crusades of suspicion" only served to divide Americans, Kennedy declared. Even so, the appeal of liberal internationalism and the New Frontier as part of the great national consensus held the hope of a brighter future. As Kennedy said, "The one great irreversible trend in the history of the world is on the side of liberty—and we, for all time to come, are on the same side."[42]

Kennedy's speech capped a remarkable twelve-month run for the Birch Society and its growing legion of critics in media and politics. The society argued that the press attacks had grown "in size, number, and viciousness." Two US presidents had blasted the movement as a scourge and purged its members from federal service. Virtually every major news outlet in the country had condemned the group. Welch had become almost a household name to politically minded Americans. By the summer of 1961, in part thanks to widespread public condemnation that rallied the far right and some conservatives supportive of its ideas, the society occupied a solid spot in the nation's political firmament. It was unlikely to fade away anytime soon.

To the society, the blistering attacks—in the press, in Congress, from the Oval Office—signaled that its opponents were frightened. The Birchers' positions had more popular support than liberals suggested, and their movement was on the move. Soon, a Massachusetts member predicted, the country will return to the days of "sanity and Constitutional government. . . . 'Liberalism' is on the way out."[43]

THE MEDIA'S EXPOSURE YIELDED UNANTICIPATED BENEFITS FOR THE Birchers. Under relentless assault, they became, to some conservatives, sympathetic figures. Conservatives of all stripes disliked the mainstream media as elitist and unfailingly biased against them. In the midst of the controversies of 1961, the media's potential to elicit a universal rallying cry from the right and far right emerged when Robert Welch appeared on NBC's flagship Sunday news program, *Meet the Press*. The interview presented a golden chance to defend the society on national television, to assure Americans that he wasn't a horned devil, and to prove that he led a red-blooded movement of patriotic anticommunists. On May 21 panelist Lawrence Spivak and three other journalists challenged the Birch leader with contentious questions regarding his conspiracy theory about Ike and other suspect aspects of the movement, such as its professed hatred of democracy. "We just furnish an opportunity for a guest to make or break himself," Spivak once said in reference to his reputation as a tough inter-viewer. Welch handled himself with aplomb. In a calm voice and clear words, he distanced himself from his past commentaries, downplaying his earlier assertion that Ike was a communist, and framed his movement as patriotic and nonthreatening.[44]

Still, the most telling aspect of the televised exchange wasn't what any-one said on the show but how viewers responded. Letters and cards from Birch supporters across the United States (roughly double the number *Meet the Press* typically received in response to a show that year) inun-dated NBC's studios to complain that Welch had been treated shabbily. The writers identified themselves as conservatives, a handful said they were society members, and some claimed they were Republicans. A star-tling number of them were women, indicating an intensification of wom-en's affinity for the society. Above all, the letter writers lacerated Spivak as a typically arrogant, anti-American journalist who sided with commu-nists rather than with Americanists. The resentment toward media elites pervaded the barbed missives.

Brooklyn's Jane Wilson saw the show from Florida, where she was at-tending a Republican Women's Convention and had enjoyed a screening of the Birch-backed film *Communism on the Map*. The *Meet the Press* in-terviewers, she wrote, had come across as "One Worlders and appeasers," and as soon as the show ended she and her husband decided to join the Birch Society. One Utah couple was so livid after watching reporters grill

Welch that they mailed a donation to the Birch Society. The interviewers seemed biased in favor of liberalism, New Mexico's Blanche Bell wrote NBC, and she was now tempted to enlist in the Birch movement.[45] Why did "every good patriot" brave enough to assail the communists come under a barrage of "ridicule and smear" from the news media? Lois Hefferman asked. Chicago's C. Jacobson complained that the panelists' questions were "disgusting" and gave off "shades of the Spanish Inquisition!" Clair Linton, an ear, nose, and throat doctor from Phoenix, questioned Spivak's "loyalty" to the United States, while Pearl Stein of Milwaukee charged that NBC had just "harassed a fine American." (She wanted to join the movement but couldn't afford the dues.)[46]

For many conservative viewers, the interview crystallized the idea that the reporters were unpatriotic, while Welch, even if his conspiracy theory was strange, effectively positioned himself as a true anticommunist. It also anticipated a widening tribal rift, a form of identity politics that would intensify through the 1960s and culminate in the countercultural demand to know "which side are you on?" A woman who had lost two sons in World War II took umbrage at the journalists vilifying Welch while they protected the "egg-heads" and Harvard graduates who dominated the Supreme Court and State Department. A member of the Daughters of the American Revolution since 1917 berated Spivak and asserted that Birchers, like members of her group, had originally settled the country and had "cleared the forests to make YOU comfortable HERE."[47]

As the klieg lights shined on the Birch Society, they revealed both fervent support and dark shadows. Welch's appearance on *Meet the Press* gave his conspiracy theories and his organization main-stage exposure, a place in the living rooms of a million-plus viewers, transforming the society from a clandestine, virtually unknown entity into a ubiquitous subject of nightly dinner-table conversations. But the high wattage also turned "Bircher" into an epithet in much of the country, making it harder for members to crack open doors and take power within the GOP.

Still, if liberals and mainstream Republicans thought they had vanquished their nemesis, they severely underestimated the Birch Society. Of all the skills mastered by Welch and the other Birch leaders, perhaps most impressive was their ability to weaponize defeat. There were benefits to nationwide notoriety, and no one was more adept at harnessing them. Birchers discovered that tangling with the mainstream press was balm for their spirits. Attacks on their movement raised members' defenses and infused them with energy and purpose. They thrived when they had an enemy to battle, and this particular enemy—the mainstream press, which minimized the Red Menace and ridiculed them—infuriated less extreme partisans as well, unifying conservative factions and bringing additional recruits to the far right.

Birchers may have numbered in the mere thousands in a nation of nearly two hundred million, but they had more allies than their critics appreciated, and they were louder and far angrier than the typical voter. If the numbers were on one side, the passion was on the other. After Welch's interview, he and his movement became the main protagonists, either heroes or villains, depending on your perspective, in a national debate about extremist threats to the conservative movement—and to the future of two-party politics in the United States.

Chapter 4

SHOCK TROOPS

BIRCHERS WERE CONSERVATIVES, AND MANY OF THEM HAD VOTED RE-publican for years, but as they met and joined forces with their ideological allies in 1959 and 1960, they had to decide whether they should remain Republicans. As Birchers alleged, as they knew in their bones, the GOP establishment had betrayed the United States time after time, expelling the real anticommunists from their ranks. Republicans had stolen the presidential nomination from Robert Taft in 1952, censured Joe McCarthy in 1954, and withheld support from Senator William Knowland, causing him to lose his bid for California governor in 1958. Given this pattern of treachery, in the fall of 1959 Birch leaders seriously considered establishing a third party.

Leaders converged at a conference in Chicago in the fall of 1959. Organized by Kent Courtney, a New Orleans publisher, the conference featured speeches from William Buckley, Robert Welch, and Tom Anderson, a Birch National Council member and the editor of *Farm and Ranch*, who exhorted the one thousand people in the audience to fight for a share of power through the political process and lead the nation to a "spiritual rebirth." The society considered Barry Goldwater, Strom

Thurmond, J. Edgar Hoover, and Clarence Manion as possible leaders of their third party. They also discussed a platform that would abolish the federal income tax, eliminate foreign aid, thwart civil rights, ratify the isolationist Bricker Amendment, and return the United States to the gold standard.[1]

They held off on a definitive decision as the conference dispersed, but those who tried to form third parties didn't fare terribly well. Courtney returned home to Louisiana and ran for governor on the States' Rights ticket in 1960, winning around 2.5 percent of the vote. T. Coleman Andrews, one of the original twelve founders of the Birch Society, had sought the US presidency through the States' Rights Party in 1956, and he also failed badly. In New York, Birchers campaigned for Robert Pell for US Senate on the Conservative Party line, but he abandoned the race. In the end, the third party just had too many drawbacks—it was simply too hard to win elections as a third-party candidate.[2]

Birchers resigned themselves to working within the two-party system to achieve their goal of educating the public about the true nature of the communist danger. If any party was going to crack its doors ajar for the society, it was the GOP, the Birchers' logical home.

Birchers found a lot to like there. Republicans represented the likes of Warren Harding and Herbert Hoover. McCarthy, Taft, and Knowland were heroes to numerous activists. The most promising up-and-comer, Republican senator Barry Goldwater, was a rising star in the society's firmament if not an official member. Welch supported Goldwater for the Republican presidential nomination in 1960. (One Birch leader urged colleagues to endorse Nixon, but most mistrusted him and declined.) By 1961, the society had two of its own in Congress—John Rousselot and Edgar Hiestand—and both of them conferenced with the GOP.[3]

Pro–Jim Crow southern Democrats like Strom Thurmond echoed the Birch philosophy and provided moral support. Like communists, Thurmond once said, big-government liberals had a "mistrust of individual liberty and reliance on State control." Still, Birchers found the party of FDR, Harry Truman, and JFK fundamentally hostile to the society's agenda, and JFK's blazing anti-Birch oratory had hardened their already jaundiced impression of the Democrats.[4]

By the early 1960s Birchers had settled on the course they would follow in the decades to come. They would operate on the fringe of the conservative movement and, episodically and erratically, within the Republican Party. Sometimes Birchers ran for office as Republicans and knocked on doors in campaigns to elect Republicans. In other moments they abandoned the GOP and used third parties to send a message that elites of both parties were corrupt. Blending a disarming style, strategy, and ideology, they waged guerilla warfare in their towns, suburbs, and cities over particular issues that had previously been seen as nonpartisan.

But ultimately, by remaining part of the GOP's coalition, Birchers made sure that their Armageddon-like sensibility couldn't be ignored. The Cold War's debates were already hard-edged, but the alarmism became more entrenched, more routinized, once Birchers joined the fray in earnest in 1961 and 1962. Strategically, the society trod fresh ground by using its own media outlets as well as mainstream television and radio stations to influence public opinion in local communities. Birchers also employed letter writing, phone banking, and other direct-action techniques to pressure CEOs, educators, and nonprofit leaders who had run afoul of the society's mission. By operating both within the party and on its far-right fringes, the society pushed party leaders to acknowledge the Birch position on issues and made leadership pay attention to what the grassroots activists wanted.

Ideologically, the society flaunted its antiestablishment sensibility and pumped hot-button cultural issues—patriotic education, moral library books, an end to teaching sex ed in schools—into local debates over their communities' most valued and nonpartisan institutions.

Yet as much as they claimed to loathe the establishment, on the local level Birchers benefited from party power brokers and structures. Clout flowed to the society partly because influential people and entities provided access. State elected officials, members of Congress, GOP operatives, and allies on the far right endorsed Birch positions and welcomed Birch support for their shared agendas. Groups such as the Daughters of the American Revolution and the American Legion, churches and Rotary clubs, high schools and universities, radio stations and neighborhood organizations also sponsored lectures and seminars and sometimes teamed with Birchers. These institutions provided forums where the society asserted its claims and hectored its opponents, legitimizing it as a voice with a contribution to make to the United States during the Cold War, at least in the eyes of some Americans.

Debates hosted by esteemed institutions afforded Birchers the chance to air their views in front of large community audiences. Members were able to broadcast their message and persuade some non-Birchers that the society wasn't totalitarian but passionately anticommunist and patriotic. In Maine, home to Senator Margaret Chase Smith, an early McCarthy critic, a debate at St. Francis College pitted Republican leader Philip Hussey Jr. against the society's coordinator for three New England states, William Cupples. With his square jaw and colorful tie and sports jacket, Cupples, who had quit a job doing field work with the Red Cross to fight communism on a full-time basis, cut an arresting figure. He denied Hussey's accusation that the society's divisive tactics were unwittingly aiding the communists, and Hussey came off as stodgy. According to one anti-Birch attendee, Cupples seemed sincere, and some audience members found his views reasonable. In a debate at Manchester College in North Manchester, Indiana, one Birch member explained to the society's home office that she was prepared to do battle (she didn't say against whom). She expected the students "to tear us to pieces," but she believed in spreading the word that the society was politically sensible and a worthy cause.[5] In small towns, big cities, suburbs, and rural areas, Birchers vigorously injected contentious issues into local politics. Even when they lost their fights, victory of some sort tended to come their way.

THE LOCAL ORIENTATION OF THE BIRCHERS WAS ENCOURAGED FROM the top of the organization. Having badly lost a lieutenant governor's campaign in 1950, Bob Welch understood that local races were easier to win than statewide runs. He recommended that his members seek election to school boards and other once-undervalued offices. From these posts Birchers would have a chance to influence the culture of a community and launch a revolution from below.

The home office in Belmont, Massachusetts, issued explicit, sometimes minutely specific, instructions to chapter members. Members were urged to vet library books and high school texts to root out socialist influences, and also to investigate allegations that communists had seized power at Vassar College and to lobby their clergy to give more full-throated anti-communist sermons. Birchers should pressure firms that sold any goods "made in Yugoslavia" to remove those products from shelves because they had a communist taint. Chapters often took such home-office commands to heart—one Bircher berated Filene's, a large department store chain, writing that "such a fine old New England store has stooped to the level of buying imports from a country which is 100% Communistic." Yet Birch leadership did not have unlimited control over the type of politics practiced by individual chapters, and some had entrepreneurial streaks, seizing local opportunities as they surfaced in their hometowns. One teenage Bircher named Robert Bragner led a campaign to ban SANE, an anti–nuclear weapons committee, from his high school in Passaic, New Jersey.[6]

Birchers' political ambitions reached far beyond electoral campaigns. They viewed politics as the mobilization of core activists, the recruitment of new members, the swaying of public opinion, and the surfacing of issues that otherwise might lie dormant. They took their case to mainstream and far-right media and voiced their ideas at town halls, school boards, and churches. "We have found a way to get truthful information past the barriers set up by the media . . . to the grassroots," one Birch member wrote in the *Boston Herald*. He was proud to put "truth in the hands of thoughtful, religious, patriotic and courageous citizens."[7]

Chapter members brought special zeal to fights involving their local schools and public libraries. They had a sense of ownership of these institutions, which served as hubs of knowledge and values for parents and children alike, and they thought the fight for freedom could be won or lost on bookshelves and in classrooms. The Supreme Court's ban on communal prayer in schools inflamed some members who saw it as an affront to their Christian heritage. In Middleboro, Massachusetts, Birch member Leo Kahian delivered a thirty-minute broadside at a meeting to protest the school board's decision to adhere to the Supreme Court's prayer ban. Leading a Birch front group called the Committee to Restore Daily Bible Reading and Prayer in Our Public Schools, Kahian urged the board to defy the Warren court and let students pray as an act of civil disobedience.[8]

The struggle over the ideas, values, and books featured in local curricula and programming for children touched a nerve in the Birch universe. In Wellesley, Massachusetts, Laurence Bunker, a Birch founder, Harvard-trained lawyer, and onetime aide-de-camp to General Douglas MacArthur, won a seat as a trustee of the town's public library. His victory raised the prospect that the library might clear its shelves of any books offensive to the society. Bunker's Birch membership so troubled his pastor at the Wellesley Unitarian Church that the pastor mounted a campaign to unseat him from the library board.[9]

Controversies raged on the other side of the country too. In Paradise, California, a conservative town in the Sierra foothills north of Sacramento, Birchers teamed with members of a local American Legion post to make sweeping changes at Paradise High School. The Birch-Legion contingent consisted of veterans, an ex–police officer, and a chewing gum salesman who had children in the school. They came to believe that Virginia Franklin, a popular teacher of American government and a Democratic Party activist, was exposing her students to ideas that smacked of anti-American subversion.

Franklin's goal was to tutor students in democracy and give them an education that helped them become informed citizens of the United States. She organized mock debates, took students on field trips to the state capital, and worked to expose them to varied philosophies and to sharpen their skills as critical thinkers. One assignment even asked students to listen to a lecture by Robert Welch.

When Birchers in town heard that Franklin had taken her students to a political conference on human rights sponsored by the American Friends Service Committee, they revolted. The Quakers promoted the kind of pacifism that Birchers equated with surrender, and the conference had featured a performance by Joan Baez. Worse still, the Birch chapter members learned that Franklin had assigned students an article in *The Nation* that had appeared alongside an ad for a book about sexual intercourse.

Birchers got to work making phone calls and writing letters to school administrators. Franklin, they asserted, was engaged in brainwashing teenagers in progressive-communist values and ideas. A realtor with an eighteen-year-old son in Franklin's class reportedly cut a hole in his son's textbook and hid a tape recorder inside it to catch Franklin in the act of indoctrination. The son asked his teacher if students could have time to pray prior to a mock Senate hearing the class was holding. Franklin took a vote; the noes prevailed. Paradise's principal received a tip that a student was trying to record Franklin's class without her knowledge. The principal informed Franklin, and they discovered the recorder in the student's book.

Having made little headway with the school's administrators, some Birchers decided to run for seats on the town's school board, losing by just a few hundred votes. The school board responded to the uproar by investigating the allegations into Franklin's teaching, and though they cleared her she didn't feel victorious. Testifying before a committee in the State Assembly that was investigating the controversy, Franklin described the effect of the campaign, explaining how she "had this terrible anxiety that I could not allow myself one single mistake."

Franklin found her position untenable in the face of such a sustained attack. She successfully sued some of the Birchers for defamation, winning damages worth $16,500, but ultimately moved to Marin County to take up a new teaching job. She had been driven out of Paradise High. And thanks to the Birch operation, any teacher who wished to expose students to progressive ideas and readings now had to think hard about the consequences.[10]

Such local skirmishes sharpened the society's skills in waging information warfare to sway public opinion and energize its conservative supporters—especially in towns scattered throughout the sparsely populated Mountain West. Most towns in Wyoming, for example, had only one television station and one or two radio stations, enabling deep-pocketed Birchers to "saturate" the airwaves and "produce political results," as Wyoming's Democratic senator Gale McGee explained to the Kennedy White House. On local radio and television, Birch chapters in the state were able to air right-wing programs such as the *Manion Forum*, the *Dan Smoot Report*, Tom Anderson's *Farm Journal* program, and Kent Courtney's Conservative Society of America broadcast. Birch backer H. L. Hunt, the state's largest cattleman, aired his *Lifeline* program on

Wyoming's radio stations. The pro-Birch Reverend Carl McIntire supposedly spent $1,000 a month just in Wyoming on society-friendly pro-
grams in the early 1960s.

The campaign effectively captured the state. McGee described it as
amounting to a Bircher "public brainwashing operation through newspapers, TV, radio, and speakers on civic club programs" that had real
success in shaping opinions and influencing the state's GOP. There
wasn't a single Birch member in the state's legislature, yet most Republicans there promoted a Birch Society agenda. Republicans had urged
the elimination of the federal income tax and wished to get the United
States out of the UN. They endorsed an end to foreign aid and abolition
of the Arms Control and Disarmament Act. A right-to-work law drew
GOP support, and reapportionment in the party's hands became a tool
to empower rural areas. "In my state," McGee said, the GOP "starts
from the John Birch position."[11]

Nineteen sixty-two marked the first time that Birchers consistently engaged with traditional politics in its most recognizable for-
mat: campaigns and elections. Birchers were so active in campaigns that
year that a field organizer cracked, "It almost seemed like the membership took a leave of absence from Society endeavors." McGee called
Birchers "idea people seeking political action," and that analysis explains
in part why they stuck with two-party politics even if they distrusted
both parties.[12]

Perhaps the most rousing force in some of the midterm races was the
society's desire to defeat any Republican (conservative or moderate) perceived as hostile to the Birch agenda. From Eisenhower and Warren to
Kuchel and Nixon, some powerful Republicans appeared as roadblocks
to Birch goals, enemies who had contributed to the nation's demise—
and Birch activism in the midterms represented the logical extension of
its early efforts to discredit Ike and impeach Warren. When Michigan
automotive executive George Romney launched his bid for governor on
February 10, 1962, he took a veiled shot at "any single clique" threatening the people of Michigan. Birchers replied that Romney, whom they
considered a moderate, had mouthed the communist line.[13]

While some Republicans abhorred the society as a small extremist faction contrary to the spirit of good government and rational problem-solving, others came to rely on it for votes and energy. John Rousselot, a representative from the San Gabriel Valley in Southern California and a high-profile Bircher, delivered several speeches to Massachusetts Republican youth groups apparently interested in the society. At one stop on his tour, he addressed the Harvard-Radcliffe Club of Young Republicans and members of the Buckley-backed Young Americans for Freedom. When he finished, an audience member stood up and asked others in the crowd to become active in the Birch Society.[14] But the society's best-known, most visible, and most consequential campaign dramas of 1962 unfolded in Rousselot's home state, where he and three other Birchers were running for Congress and three of the four raised a total of $250,000, making their races the flushest of any in Southern California that year.

Birchers settled on a strategy of supporting candidates who shared their views even if they were not members of the society. With Republicans they saw as apostates, however, they spoiled for confrontations, none more heated than when Richard Nixon ran in California's GOP gubernatorial primary to face Pat Brown, the Democratic incumbent. Still smarting from his loss to Kennedy in the 1960 presidential campaign, Nixon had nonetheless delivered California to the Republicans—a victory that failed to mollify the Birchers. Although he had first drawn national attention in the late 1940s as a HUAC firebrand and antagonist of accused communist spy Alger Hiss, and he had hammered Helen Gahagan Douglas, his 1950 Democratic opponent for Senate, as "the pink lady," Nixon's eight-year stretch as Eisenhower's vice president was sufficient reason for many Birchers to doubt his standing as a true anti-communist. More personally to them, Nixon had made it a point to criticize Welch's baseless conspiracy theories about Ike. If the Birch Society failed to defeat such turncoats, Kent Courtney declared, "we might as well teach our children how to count in rubles."[15]

Nixon's rival for the GOP nomination for governor in 1962 was Joseph Shell, a wealthy oilman, USC football hero, and Republican minority leader of the California State Assembly, who eagerly took up the effort to make Nixon pay for his treachery. Shell wasn't a Birch member, but he might as well have been. Birchers loved him, and the feeling was mutual. He praised the *Blue Book* ("What I found there is anti-communism, and I am for that") and expressed admiration for the society's leaders. At a Doctors for Americanism rally in Pasadena, he shared a stage with Rousselot and said, "I could agree with no one more." Shell concurred that a Nixon administration would push California toward socialism and charged that Nixon's perfidy "has alienated a large bloc of Republicans in this state," warning that "a large number would not vote for Richard Nixon."[16] He and the society also found common ground in their barbed attacks on Nixon's family and on the former vice president's duplicity. Shell's wife, Barbara, reportedly spread a rumor that Nixon's wife, Pat, had had a nervous breakdown, and Shell's team predicted that Nixon might fake being sick so he could leave the race and save himself from a humiliating defeat.[17]

Nixon, meanwhile, pitched his appeal to the center of the electorate and explicitly criticized the Birchers. "I could not look myself in the mirror if I support them," he told his speechwriter Stephen Hess while shaving in a private bathroom next to his office before a dinner engagement. Aide Patricia Hitt, who later became Nixon's assistant secretary of health, education, and welfare, recalled that he considered the Birch movement "a dangerous thing" that he had an obligation to denounce. Nixon's attack on the society "was absolutely necessary," she added. "He had to let it be known that he was not going to be beholden to them."[18]

The Birchers could barely contain their animosity. A Birch-friendly newsletter warned that the loss of their support could easily "cost Nixon the election," and the LA County Board of Young Republicans voted to censure Nixon for attempting to purge Birchers from their party. Some mounted a campaign to send him into retirement, slamming him for endorsing "one-world government," along with the "United Nations, foreign aid without reservations, socialized medicine, and federal aid to schools—and the control that would follow."[19]

Courtney recruited Birchers and other far-right allies to attend more than half a dozen meetings to discuss ways to boost Shell and several other Bircher candidates in California. These included Howard Jarvis, an antitax activist running for US Senate, as well as Rousselot, Hiestand, and

H. L. Richardson, all of whom were seeking congressional seats. The meetings were held at pro-Birch bookstores, including Poor Richard's. Ward Poag, a former field organizer for the society in west Tennessee and eastern Arkansas, was hired to promote this slate of West Coast conservatives, and he hit the road in a Chevy station wagon painted with far-right signs.[20]

For the Birchers, the 1962 California midterm results were mixed. Shell won a respectable one-third of the primary vote against Nixon but not the gubernatorial nomination. Nixon had underestimated the extent of the Birch Society's electoral muscle and the price he would pay for crossing it so directly. His attacks cleaved the GOP, and he lost the general election to Pat Brown by some three hundred thousand votes, in part because Birchers stayed home, apparently unmoved by his taunting Brown for being "soft on communism." The Birchers did achieve their goal of forcing Nixon's retirement from politics—which he memorably announced by asserting that his detractors would no longer "have Nixon to kick around"—though the retirement turned out to be short-lived. All four Birch House candidates in California lost too, although Rousselot had been gerrymandered into a tough district, and each of them won around 45 percent of the vote in their respective elections, a decent showing.

As with so many bruising clashes involving Birchers, even defeat brought victories of a sort. Nationally, around 100 out of 150 candidates endorsed by Americans for Constitutional Action, which developed an "index" to rank lawmakers' votes, won election, and those candidates tended to express support for at least some of the society's agenda. Though Welch called the midterm results "a sweep for the left," his categorical pessimism was overstated, as Birchers had entered the center of local conversations throughout the country. They emerged better positioned than ever to set the tone, spread their tactics, and define the issues for political debate across the United States.

THE SOCIETY TRAINED AN ARMY OF SHOCK TROOPS IN THEIR RUTHLESS brand of political combat, and during the 1962 midterms many of the trainees came into their own. Consider the case of Stuart Morrison, who resigned his post in the Young Republicans in Sutter County, California, to lead his local Birch chapter unencumbered by a GOP affiliation. Soon after, he aimed his wrath at the *Sacramento Bee*, Governor Pat Brown, and a Democrat named Clarence Edmonds, who had written a letter to the editor defending Brown. On March 8, 1962, Morrison sent Edmonds a letter accusing him and other liberals of bringing the United States closer to "The Valley of Death." Then he got personal. "You may have been a good big hero in WWII," Morrison wrote, but "you and your leftist friends which fill the Socialist Bee Staff are living in the past!" He complained that they were ignoring the real threat, communism, and screeched, "Get hep [*sic*] man!!!" (Morrison said he had earned a PhD and majored in business and political science but preferred blunt talk to fancy words.) The Birchers, he warned, were "well organized and well financed, and are ready to politically crush Brown beginning in about mid-April." He envisioned a campaign to "bury" Brown "in his own filthy mire" as part of "one of the most horrid elections for the Democrats you will ever live to see." His letter concluded with another warning: "As for you, Edmonds, I would keep my big mouth shut and refrain from your leftist babble." When Morrison eventually took power in Sacramento, "the Socialist Bee will finally be silenced."[21]

Another California firebrand who found his voice during this period was Max Rafferty, a sometime teacher, principal, and district superintendent who was running in 1962 for the ostensibly nonpartisan position of state superintendent of public instruction. Like Joe Shell, Rafferty was not a member of the Birch Society but fit the mold. His scorching oratory and strident policies dovetailed with the society's, and as much as Birchers admired Shell, their ardor for Rafferty was even more intense.

After giving a speech to the La Cañada school board in 1961, Rafferty surged into the collective conscience of a lot of Birch members. The speech, which he titled "The Passing of the Patriot," limned a hot topic among the Birch faithful: the evils of a progressive education. Rafferty claimed that although public schools were supposed to teach young minds about the need to "preserve the nation," under three decades of liberal leadership public education had seeded a crisis among the youngest generation. Teens had learned how to act like "booted, side-burned, ducktailed, unwashed, leather-jacketed slobs, whose favorite sport is ravaging little girls and stomping polio victims to death; youth coming into maturity for all the world like the best of our young people fresh from a dizzying rollercoaster ride, with everything blurred, with nothing clear, with no positive standards, with everything in doubt. No wonder so many of them welsh out and squeal and turn traitor when confronted with the grim reality of Red military force and the crafty cunning of Red psychological warfare." If he won the election, he vowed to make "our young people informed and disciplined and alert—militant for freedom, clear-eyed to the filthy menace of Communist corruption . . . , [and] happy in their love of country."[22]

Reader's Digest reprinted Rafferty's address, which was also distributed as a pamphlet. The *New York Times* reported that it had transformed the educator and administrator into a right-wing political star. Rafferty recalled that "the rise of the John Birch Society . . . and other pro-American groups had created a tinderbox and I unwittingly dropped a lightning bolt in the middle of it." Soon afterward, his campaign received lavish financial backing from at least three wealthy businessmen with Birch ties: Frank Adams, who had endorsed the society; Knott's Berry Farm's Walter Knott, who promoted its ideas; and Dr. Ross's Dog Food executive D. B. Lewis, who advertised only in newspapers that espoused the society's views. Rafferty appeared at rallies with Birch publisher Paul Drake and Representatives Rousselot and Hiestand (the latter at a "Yankee Doodle Days" event). Soon his campaign for state superintendent of education attracted national attention, observed syndicated columnist Drew Pearson, "because for the first time, the extreme right-wing represented by the John Birch Society and kindred thinkers, are trying to take over the educational system of an important state. Their drive is to put California schools back in the McGuffey's Reader [a moralistic nineteenth-century textbook] era and make education a matter of indoctrination rather than a search for the truth."[23]

Unlike Shell and the Birch-allied congressional candidates in California, Rafferty won his race, and when he arrived in Sacramento he used his position to advance the sort of education policies that Birchers were fighting to enact in their hometowns. He advocated prayer in public schools, government funding for Christian academies, private-school vouchers, parental veto power over sex education programs, and bans on textbooks that Birchers deemed insufficiently patriotic. He opposed the teaching of evolution and busing to achieve racial desegregation.[24]

Education policy aside, Rafferty proved a formidable ally in the fight against the Birchers' most reviled enemies: moderate Republicans. He charged that Senator Thomas Kuchel, a leading anti-Birch voice in California, had failed the state's conservative movement. In the fall of 1964, when foes surfaced a sworn affidavit from an ex-policeman saying that he had arrested Kuchel for being gay in 1949, the network of Birch-backed bookstores, called American Opinion Bookstores and Libraries, put the affidavit in the hands of readers. Four people associated with the baseless smear were indicted for criminal conspiracy to commit libel, and three took pleas, but the incident damaged Kuchel.[25] Rafferty later defeated Kuchel in a GOP Senate primary and sounded the death knell for his political career.

Some American Opinion Bookstores had been opened in the early 1960s and were already paying dividends by 1962. Birchers owned and ran the stores, knew their clientele, and worked with the society's home office to make a profit and, above all, spread key texts and foundational ideas to the brothers and sisters in the movement. Owners were expected to raise at least $2,000 in capital for start-up costs, and they did so through bake sales and garage sales, auctions, and contributions solicited from business leaders in their communities. Ideally the stores were located in suburbs (where they would be free of harassment from gangs); they had to have a "professional," "clean" appearance and feature books approved by the home office, according to a manual the society sent to store owners and managers. They served as "the physical symbol of a resurgent American spirit," a "great morale-builder for all conservative-minded Americans." As the society observed, "The multiplied strength and cumulative effect of hundreds of identically named bookstores has a significant influence on publishers, writers, community leaders, and on politicians," and these "respected and sought-after enterprises all across the country" made it easier for Birchers to reach beyond their immediate circles and foster a common understanding of the nation's greatest problems. Birchers became invested in a shared culture that was insulated from the moral rot infecting the rest of the United States. The books the society promoted included *Murder to Order, Apostles of Deceit, Why Johnny Can't Read, Your Church—Their Target, What They Are Doing to Your Children, Black and Conservative,* and *Open Occupancy vs Forced Housing Under the Fourteenth Amendment: A Symposium on Anti-Discrimination Legislation, Freedom of Choice, and Property Rights in Housing.*[26]

When an American Opinion Bookstore in Baltimore incurred hundreds of dollars of debt (its location and the "extremist" label affixed to it by local critics had hurt sales), the Birchers running it decided to act. They went door-to-door "selling the best product in the world—individual freedom." In fact, they sold American flags, eagle door knockers, and colonial-print dish towels—and raised enough money to move the store to a better location and turn it into a prosperous business and a thriving venue for Birch chapter meetings and other gatherings. The society innovated, setting up "mobile libraries" on the East Coast that attracted customers "like magnets in a box of paper clips," according to Sally Riley, who ran the society's bookstore operations.[27]

In California and beyond, the Birchers and their allies achieved something else. American politics has never suffered a shortage of acid rhetoric and barbed darts aimed at opposing candidates. Since the nation's founding, politicians of all stripes have demeaned and denounced their rivals as unpatriotic and a peril to the people's livelihoods and personal safety. And yet in the early 1960s the Birchers injected politics with a level of rancor toward liberal opponents that further coarsened the atmosphere in the public square and set the stage for more.[28]

THE 1962 MIDTERMS PROVIDED ANOTHER STEP FORWARD IN THE SOCIety's effort to solidify its status as an organization with the financial might and grassroots army to change the country. Despite the electoral losses, Birchers had a plan to establish at least one chapter for every five voting precincts in the country, and thus, a White House aide observed, they had connected "the problem of membership growth and organization to the political structure of the country." In this regard, far from hurting the cause, the elections propelled the society as an electoral force in select communities.

Financially, its future looked bright. According to filings with the Massachusetts attorney general's office, the society generated revenues of nearly $750,000 in 1962, $200,000 more than in 1961. Donations accounted for more than $300,000, membership dues contributed $296,000, and assorted business revenues (paid speeches, magazine ads) generated an additional $100,000-plus. The society had plenty of expenses, but most of them went to strengthening the organization at the national, state, and local levels. Approximately half its income paid for employee wages, $139,000 was spent on travel and other recruitment expenses, $55,000 on printing, and $33,000 on postage.

As the movement looked ahead, it sets its sights high. Goals for 1963 included doubling the field staff (and outfitting them with films, books, tapes, and video equipment), tripling the number of libraries, and expanding public relations to feature weekly news releases and raise media visibility. For an allegedly extremist organization that hovered at the margins and faced doom in the long run, the society operated a highly effective business, and its growth showed no sign of slowing.[29]

Although most of their candidates had lost, Birchers could taste the momentum. The society's headquarters bustled with sixty-four employees. Nine staffers occupied offices in the West Coast headquarters, in San Marino, California. Seven people worked at the American Opinion Speakers Bureau, in Brookfield, Massachusetts. Run by general manager Douglas Morse, the bureau drew from a list of hundreds of volunteer speakers who delivered remarks to women's clubs, PTAs, and civic groups, and it organized lecture tours for some of its marquee speakers. The talks generated fees for the society, drew extensive press coverage, exposed Americans to its message, and bound members closer to their leadership.[30] Approximately two hundred volunteer section leaders, who typically took responsibility for a few chapters with guidance from a regional coordinator responsible for several states, helped recruit new members, supervise chapter activities, and establish new chapters.

The society also benefited from a robust research department. Headed by Dr. Francis Gannon, the research arm furnished members with information about the society's activities and stands on issues, and replied to members' questions and monthly messages to the home office. In addition to the periodicals *American Opinion* and *Bulletin*, there were two book-publishing divisions, one that reprinted paperbacks by right-wing authors, and another, Western Islands, that released original books.

ALTHOUGH STILL SEEN BY SOME IN 1963 AS AN ISLAND OF FAR-RIGHT MIS-fits, the movement slipped into the culture and politics of the country in underappreciated ways. A host of individuals and organizations helped sustain the society as it headed into the off-election year. Ties to numerous conservative organizations helped it amplify its message beyond its membership, and the lines separating the fringe from the mainstream were getting harder to pin down. After losing his reelection bid in November 1962, Rousselot became a paid public relations director of the society—a Republican congressman turned Birch spokesman—while his brother-in-law served as chairman of the Young Republican Club in Pittsfield, Massachusetts. Birchers drew sustenance from Fred Schwarz's Christian Anti-Communism Crusade schools, where they set up tables to sell literature and recruit new members. (After Schwarz accused the Birchers of stealing the crusade's membership, he and Welch became rivals.)[31]

Other conservatives boosted some of the society's favorite causes and echoed its messages. Willis Stone, founder of the National Committee for Economic Freedom, promoted the Liberty Amendment, a proposal to repeal the Sixteenth Amendment to the Constitution and prohibit federal income taxes. Walter Knott also endorsed this antitax amendment as a step on the road to a free society.[32]

Civil rights became a galvanizing issue as Birchers came to see politics as a necessary means to defend white supremacy and thwart federal intervention. Some of the South's leading segregationists provided their own brand of institutional cover for the society's anti–civil rights agenda. In the fall of 1963, the chairman of a committee supporting the presidential candidacy of Governor Ross Barnett, a Mississippi segregationist, asked the society for political assistance. Barnett's campaign, an aide informed the society, was "competing for some of the same personal contributions and personal effort as the IMPEACH WARREN campaign."[33]

Welch's anti–civil rights activism—and his tacit support for massive resistance—helped bind the society to whites who repudiated the burgeoning movement. Welch had argued that civil rights protests stemmed from a communist plot to establish "a Negro-Soviet Republic," and that if the communists had stayed out of the South, African Americans would never have favored desegregation. Welch also blamed communists for the Birmingham church bombing that murdered four black girls (false) and claimed that federal marshals had instigated the 1962 white riots at Ole Miss (false). He asserted that a Black member of the Birch Society could document his theories. And, he explained, the society had two all-Black chapters (one estimate said thirty members total) and "no mixed chapters," and left the integration question up to individual members.[34]

The Birchers also built on their midterm political work by showing off their organizing muscle in support of the Edwin Walker–Billy James Hargis speaking tour, a seventeen-state, twenty-seven-city campaign that started on February 27 in Miami and ended on April 3 in Los Angeles. Dubbed Operation Midnight Ride, it sought to rally the true believers in the fight against Satan and enjoyed help from Birchers in each city. There were Walker-Hargis press conferences, radio and TV interviews, and items in local newspapers to stimulate "ample advance publicity." Members formed "telephone squads" to build crowds at every stop. The tour was considered a success by the far right, and Walker's stemwinder, clocking in at around ninety minutes, often received standing ovations.[35]

Critics tended to miss the extent of tacit support that Birchers received from at least some mainline organizations. The society had an armada of far-right media programs, but it also found mainstream media platforms willing to air its views despite Birchers' claims of unalterable hostility. In the fall of 1963 Leo Kahian appeared as a guest speaker before the Duxbury, Massachusetts, Holy Name Society. Eight days later, he participated in an open mic forum on New Bedford radio station WBSM and took questions on the Birch Society.[36] Trusted sources within a community sometimes affirmed that Birchers were at odds with the caricature popularized in the news media. The cumulative effect was to give Birchers an aura of respectability. In the years to come they would expect to make use of it.

IN THE AFTERMATH OF THE MIDTERMS, THE FEARS THAT BIRCHERS posed a fresh authoritarian threat to the smooth functioning of democracy intensified. As New Frontiersmen looked toward Kennedy's 1964 reelection campaign, at least some of them concluded that weaponizing the backlash against the far right was key to JFK's chances. "The right-wing problem may well turn out to be a/or the winning issue for 1964," Wyoming senator Gale McGee wrote to White House aide Myer "Mike" Feldman in August 1963. "There is popular revulsion against the extremism of the right wing," he added, and the administration should "keep the villain alive and kicking for a year from now" by delaying congressional hearings targeting far-right extremism. "I may be overly optimistic on how long it may take to blow these fellows out of the water, but I suspect that a disclosure of their financial operations and their tactics on a nationwide scale would be more devastating than the scattered assaults upon them at the present time." Any attack, McGee concluded, must be timed to achieve "maximum national attention and impact."[37]

Feldman, who had dug up opposition research on Nixon for Kennedy's 1960 presidential campaign and whom the *New York Post* called "the White House's anonymous man," echoed McGee's advice in his own eighty-plus-page report to the president on the far right as both national threat and political opportunity.[38] He reported that since 1959, hundreds of far-right groups had been established, and "the radical right-wing constitutes a formidable force in American life today." The John Birch Society stood as the most influential among them. Feldman assumed that Goldwater would be the Republican nominee and that his strategy was to sweep the white South and win the West and Midwest, "where Right-Wing Radicals and conservatives are strongest."

To stop the GOP in 1964, Feldman urged the president to turn the far right into the Republican Party's albatross. In 1961 Kennedy had successfully framed the debate as a fight between unhinged extremists and pragmatic, hardheaded liberals, and now Feldman wanted him to take the next step and use the levers of federal power to investigate, hound, and discredit the Birchers. The society had "harass[ed] local school boards, local libraries, and local government bodies," and now was the time for the White House to return fire. Feldman recommended federal investigations into whether right-wing nonprofit groups were "using tax-exempt funds for political purposes." The Federal Communications Commission also needed to determine whether the society had misused media outlets in violation of the Federal Communications Act, which mandated "a fair presentation of both sides of a question." Kennedy should also investigate the sources of right-wing candidates' contributions and examine the US Post Office's discounted prices for right-wing publications such as *Human Events*.[39]

The White House believed that a suitable attack could badly wound the Birch Society and leave it writhing and feeble. Unlike those who had ridiculed it and underestimated its strength early on, the Kennedy administration recognized that the Birch-led coalition on the right had built a structure that made it politically potent. Feldman estimated that the radical right spent between $15 million and $25 million annually and raised funds from seventy foundations, at least 250 individuals, and more than a hundred corporations. Some one thousand radio stations carried right-wing programs, and speeches, newspaper ads, and mailers brought the messages to even more Americans.

The society's most dramatic impact came from its members' zeal to advance the right-wing agenda and from its leaders' ability to make common cause with a variety of like-minded groups. "Right-Wing conservatives . . . view American domestic policy since the New Deal as Socialistic and dangerous, and foreign policy of the last 30 years as prone to 'softness' and appeasement in dealing with the Communist threat," Feldman wrote. The Birchers and other conservatives agreed "on the nature of the evils they fight—Federal taxes, Federal social welfare programs, Federal spending, and Federal government interference with private business, as well as foreign aid, all or many of the activities of the U.N., and American efforts to reach agreements with the Kremlin through negotiation."

He continued, "This basic agreement has led to an ideological blur between Radicals and conservatives of the Right that often makes it difficult to classify Right-Wing groups as one or the other. The similarities are, in fact, far more compelling than the differences. . . . The Conservative Right and the Radical Right, in short, often make common cause, and if the conservatives are not card-carrying Birchers and do not—for instance—advocate the impeachment of the Chief Justice, they deplore the same Supreme Court decisions as those who do." Even if conservatives denounced Welch's Eisenhower-as-communist depiction as a step too far, Feldman wrote, they "do not reject" the Birch rank and file.[40]

And yet, if the Birch movement had more support on the right and was more mainstream than critics had understood, Birch ideas were hardly dominant in the Republican Party. The society had grown more powerful and better organized and had become more attuned to electoral politics at the local level. In some communities, the society was very much in the ascendant. Its influence in the GOP in 1963 was also greater than at any time since its inception. But most Birchers had lost their elections, they failed to stop candidates such as Romney from winning their races, and numerous Republicans from the Northeast to the Midwest to the West Coast remained vigorously opposed to their ideology and political style. Unbeknownst to the society, in the summer of 1963 the White House was preparing to launch an all-out assault that had the potential to knock the Birch movement to the ground. The society's prospects remained uncertain and contingent. The struggle for power in the Republican Party—and in the United States—was heating up. Birchers warned of Armageddon, cast critics as traitors and degenerates, disrupted civic meetings, harassed teachers and principals, and hinted at physical violence. More than any other movement of the 1960s, the Birch Society ignited what they described as an end-times contest for the very soul of the United States.

Chapter 5

"A DIRTY WAR"

O N NOVEMBER 22, 1963, WHEN PRESIDENT JOHN F. KENNEDY WAS assassinated while riding in a motorcade in Dallas, suspicion immediately fell on the Birch Society. Kennedy had spent his presidency warning the country that right-wing extremism was possibly the single greatest internal threat to democracy, and now he had been shot in the head. Dallas was well known as a hotbed of the far right, where Birchers such as talk-radio host Dan Smoot were a loud and divisive presence. The city's Birchers had already garnered a reputation for their propensity for political violence. Just that October, Birchers had picketed UN Ambassador Adlai Stevenson outside Dallas Memorial Auditorium; when he departed, a woman hit him in the head with a sign, another picketer spat on him, and two members of the mob were arrested.[1] Birchers had protested Kennedy's visit to the city, holding aloft signs, chanting slogans, and demonizing the president as a traitor. Even if Birchers had not pulled the trigger, they had seemingly put the president in the crosshairs.

Some members of the Birch Society initially feared that one of their own—or, plausibly, a segregationist allied with them—had killed Kennedy. In the wake of the shooting, a Tufts University government

professor—"short, wore glasses, and described himself as a 'conservative,'"
according to a memo from the society describing the encounter—visited
the headquarters in nearby Belmont and unloaded on Robert Welch,
blaming the society's ideological venom for JFK's murder. He "spoke so
harsh to you," Welch's assistant later told his boss. A section leader warned
that the backlash to Kennedy's assassination spelled "the end of the John
Birch Society." Perhaps Kennedy had been right all along: the Birchers had
whipped up so much hate and fear that blood had flowed on the streets of
Dallas. Now the society would reap the consequences and self-destruct.[2]

The group went into damage-control mode. In the days immediately
following the shooting, its leaders decided to delay publication of its *Bulletin* and halt publication of *American Opinion*'s December issue, which
was set to feature articles sharply critical of the Kennedy administration.
Welch even sent Jacqueline Kennedy a condolence card. The society canceled its New England Rally for God, Family, and Country in Boston
and scheduled an emergency meeting for its National Council to discuss
the fallout.[3]

Yet what initially appeared disastrous for the society actually became
an opportunity. As law enforcement identified and arrested Lee Harvey
Oswald—a self-proclaimed Marxist—and charged him with murder,
Birchers were quick to capitalize on the news. Always adept at exploiting
angst and dread, they stoked the public's fear of extremism and used it
as a recruiting and fundraising tool. In mid-December, they reportedly
spent $35,000 on a national advertising campaign blaming a communist
plot for the assassination. Full-page ads in the *New York Times*, the *Washington Post*, the *Los Angeles Times*, the *St. Louis Globe-Democrat*, and the
Salt Lake City Tribune urged "every red-blooded American" to request
literature from the society and send donations to support its anticommunist agenda. Though some pushed back against the campaign—the *Wall
Street Journal* and the *Dallas Morning News* refused to run the ad, and
newspaper columnist Drew Pearson called the ad's sponsors "a roll call of
disgruntled tycoons and out-of-step NAM executives"—the Birch worldview came through the crisis validated, even strengthened.

The unimaginable had happened, and with Kennedy dead the notion
of what was possible had shifted. Conspiracy theories became a tad less

surreal, a bit more believable. The American public had grave doubts that a lone gunman could have killed the most powerful man on earth. One Gallup poll from early December reported that a mere 29 percent of Americans thought Oswald had acted alone, while 52 percent blamed "some group or element" for Kennedy's murder. More ominously, the National Opinion Research Center found that a substantial minority of citizens believed that Kennedy's pro–civil rights stance meant that he "had it coming to him."[4]

The government had failed; the Secret Service, CIA, FBI, and Dallas police had failed. And one consequence that flowed from the catastrophe was the diminishment of faith in the ability of America's institutions to protect its citizens and do the right thing. In the long run, that loss of trust served Birchism.

To Birchers, Oswald's Marxist ties confirmed the scale of the communist menace operating within American society. If a communist plot could kill a president, the Birch line about communists as the preeminent domestic threat seemed less irrational and even prophetic. A few Birchers glimpsed a diabolical plot in which the assassination was part of a plan to discredit the Birch Society, the most effective anticommunist organization in the world.[5]

Some Birch leaders thrived on conspiracy theories—the weirder, the better. To an organization already inclined to far-out beliefs, Kennedy's assassination spawned a firehose of convoluted explanations from Birch leaders. One leader charged that family patriarch Joseph Kennedy had "discovered that you had to play ball with the [communist] conspiracy" in order to make his son president, and his son, in a speech in 1957 criticizing Western colonialism, "adopted the communist line . . . for the first time in his career" to repay the communists for their aid.[6]

The appointment of Earl Warren to lead the investigation into the assassination was something of a boon to the far right. Samuel Blumenfeld, a lecturer with the American Opinion Speakers Bureau, charged that the chief justice was a man the communists could trust with the inquiry. "They had to be sure it was in safe hands," he told one audience. The American Nazi Party picketed the White House over Warren's leadership, an alignment that tainted the Birchers, but Warren was such a lightning rod on the right that his involvement inspired a nationwide Birch membership drive. Dr. Slobodan Draskovich, a National Council member, told a secret meeting on Long Island that this recruitment campaign was based on the idea that the Warren Commission would work to cover up the communist plot to kill Kennedy.[7]

Such insinuations strained credulity among most Americans but fired up the Birch faithful. Blumenfeld speculated that Oswald might also have been responsible for slaying civil rights worker Medgar Evers, because New Orleans, where Oswald had lived, wasn't far from Mississippi, where Evers had been murdered. Another National Council member, Eisenhower's former secretary of agriculture Ezra Taft Benson, claimed that "communism killed Kennedy" because it had planted "seeds of treason in [Oswald's] mind." He also implicated "American liberals," a "highly organized, hard-core establishment in the United States" that had abetted the communist cause. Any calls for unity, Benson added, were "blind, senseless, [and] irresponsible" in the wake of Kennedy's death. Rather, he argued, Americans should return to sound moral and constitutional principles and wage "a war with the devil—Christ versus anti-Christ. And I am willing to fight it."[8]

If the assassination boosted the society politically, it also revealed some of the ugliness and divisions hiding within it. There were reports that in the aftermath, Birchers in Southern California bedroom communities had removed American flags from their homes as a protest against the communist infiltration in the country. Birch favorite Joe Shell alleged that both Oswald and Jack Ruby, who assassinated Oswald, had a decade-long affiliation with a communist organization, and he questioned Earl Warren's integrity.[9]

Critics fretted that the assassination would further inflame the already smoldering conspiratorialism of the Birchers, and then, in the words of one liberal organization, "the anti-Semites will add the usual Jewish fillip to the alleged Communist conspiracy." Such fears weren't groundless. Observers chronicled an uptick in antisemitic violence and symbols nationwide. "Jews are Commies—Jews smell" was painted on the walls of a synagogue in California, and five swastikas desecrated the door to the Minneapolis office of the Anti-Defamation League. A well digger in upstate New York faulted a "Jewish conspiracy" for JFK's assassination and fired shots at tin cans on which he had scrawled Jewish names.[10]

Birchers turned on one another, too, as they debated where to draw the line. Some rank-and-file members wondered if their leaders had gone too far. David Eisenberg, a self-described "loyal patriotic member" from Tucson, Arizona, listened to a talk by classics professor and Birch spokesman Revilo Oliver titled "Marxmanship in Dallas," and it made him sick. Oliver's lecture, Eisenberg said, "was delivered in a slovenly manner and loaded with a nastiest type of sarcasm." He worried that Oliver's description of civil rights workers as "cockroaches" would reinforce stereotypes that the society was a bona fide "'hate' group."[11] A local newspaper editor said the speech essentially "drug a dead man around the room."

"It will take the Birch Society of Tucson ten years to live this one down," attendee Edna Shumaker predicted. "There is no honor in making ourselves stink!" When Oliver delivered similar bombshells in Glendale, Arizona, Birch member Robert Miland recoiled in disgust. He informed headquarters that the talk—in which Oliver alleged that a week prior to the assassination, "funeral rehearsals were held in Washington"—was so off-the-wall offensive it drove away potential recruits. The baseless insinuation of a federal government plot to kill JFK, he said, was "indefensible," and such "unfounded innuendo makes it very difficult to defend the Society."[12]

Nonetheless, as 1963 came to an end, it seemed increasingly clear that Kennedy's assassination had strengthened the hand of the Birch Society. The revelation of Oswald's left-wing ties gave members and leadership alike a psychological boost, a sense that their ideas had become more resonant and persuasive than ever. The society's name recognition boomed. It had a firm organizational foundation, and its ideas had seemed to seep ever more slowly into the center of national political debate. The Birch Society thrived in the hothouse of media controversy, and its activities brought it international recognition. Nikita Khrushchev and Fidel Castro denounced the society as a fascist movement, heightening its anticommunist credentials. And it seemed that one of the society's favorite sons was ascending the ranks of the Republican Party and preparing to bring Birch ideas into the Oval Office.[13]

NINETEEN SIXTY-FOUR BROUGHT A MOMENT OF HOPE FOR THE BIRCH Society. Members considered Arizona senator Barry Goldwater a patriot who spoke truth to liberals holding the reins of power, and he was running for president that year. With his candidacy, rather than tilting at windmills Birchers could start to win and achieve real power to change the things they hated.

Goldwater wasn't the favorite of every Birch member. Segregationists Kent Courtney and Medford Evans found him impure and too liberal, and they pined for a third-party candidate. But most Birchers, as field director Thomas Hill said after touring chapters nationwide, "are devoting much of their time to political work" and pinning their hopes on Goldwater.[14] To the vast majority of members, he spoke in moral terms about what it meant to be American. He didn't hide his views to assuage the establishment. He battled Republicans on the coasts with zeal and had a serious shot at deposing the GOP's liberal wing after decades of setbacks and disappointments.

Moreover, Goldwater's life story resonated with many rank-and-file Birchers. Like a lot of Bircher leaders he was a businessman; he ran a department store in downtown Phoenix, experiencing firsthand how the government hampered free enterprise and interfered with a person's rights to run businesses as he desired. Like Birchers, Goldwater despised the federal income tax, regulations on businesses, and laws protecting workers' rights to organize. Although he rejected some far-out conspiracy theories, he also excoriated the "fuzzywuzzy" minds of the men in government who had brought the country closer to socialism. He had branded Eisenhower's domestic agenda "a dime-store New Deal," echoing the Birch attack on Ike's record, spoke of the need to make Social Security voluntary, and decried spending federal dollars to fund education. Years before, Goldwater had written in his 1960 bestseller *The Conscience of a Conservative* that the Democratic Party had been "captured by the Socialist ideologues in and about the labor movement," and the GOP had an "unmistakable tendency . . . to adopt the same course." Although he rejected the society's official theory that communists were manipulating the civil rights movement, he also spoke the Birchers' language when decrying the *Brown* decision as the Supreme

Court ("a rule of men") substituting its own beliefs for the Constitution. During the Senate floor debate over the landmark Civil Rights Act of 1964, Goldwater warned of a police state if the bill passed, and called the "attempted usurpation of such power to be a grave threat to the very essence of our basic system of government."[15]

On foreign policy, too, Goldwater was simpatico with a few aspects of Bircher orthodoxy. He endorsed cutting off funds for the UN should Red China be admitted and proposed an end to all foreign aid. Back in 1959, Birchers recalled, he had put his name on a list of sponsors of the society's Committee Against Summit Entanglements. Spokesman John Rousselot praised him for agreeing to support the committee after Goldwater spoke with Welch on a phone in the Senate cloakroom.[16] In 1961 Birch member and former ambassador Spruille Braden wrote a memo criticizing the Kennedy White House's Latin America policies as soft on communism. Braden shared the memo with Goldwater, who liked Braden's arguments and praised his wise analysis. Further, the senator complained to Braden, the press had done a "hatchet job" on Goldwater's own views of US policy in the region. Braden suggested that the two men get together when Goldwater was next in New York and offered to host a dinner for him with CEOs at the Metropolitan Club, a private gentlemen's club founded by J. P. Morgan.[17]

The ties between Goldwater and Birch leaders were abundant. National Council member Ralph Davis joined other Birchers in donating to Goldwater's campaign while also hosting a dinner in honor of Welch.[18] Rousselot praised the candidate's "conservative constitutional position" and said that Goldwater posed a graver threat to the communist movement than any candidate in the past thirty years. As society ally Phyllis Schlafly indicated in the title of her self-published 1964 bestseller, *A Choice Not an Echo*, Goldwater represented a true alternative, not just another liberal Republican. The Birchers were prepared to back him to the max.

This support was not always overt. As an educational nonprofit the society was prohibited from issuing endorsements, and it didn't officially endorse anyone that year. Headquarters urged members to work in politics as individuals—and many members worked for Goldwater, often with no prodding.[19]

The Goldwater campaign and conservative leaders were just as cautious in their approach to the Birchers. In April 1961, as Birchers became the personification of radical-right excess, William Buckley wrote a carefully parsed editorial in *National Review* depicting Welch as a man whose worldview rested on false assumptions, namely, that Eisenhower was a communist.[20] Even that faint rebuke came about after a great deal of handwringing and internal debate at the magazine.

The Birchers' rising profile had forced Buckley and his colleagues to figure out what to say about the movement. They groped for a response. In essence, Buckley and his team agreed that Welch's theories were absurd and impolitic, but they also knew that some Birch leaders wrote for *National Review* and that Birch members were devoted anticommunist conservatives and a crucial constituency for their magazine.

Proposals surfaced. Editor Frank Meyer recommended that they write an article criticizing Welch's "extravagances" but cautioned against attacking the rank and file. "Some of the solidest conservatives in the country are members of the John Birch Society," he reasoned, "and we should act in such a way as to alienate them no more than is strictly necessary from a moral, political, or tactical point of view." Another Buckley ally reminded him in a letter, "As Senator Goldwater told you: The members appear to be high type, educated and dedicated anti-communist conservatives," including "some important businessmen."[21]

The top editors concurred. Welch was fair game. But, as publisher William Rusher wrote in a memo, "We are going to have to open our minds to the possibility that the society is going to be around for quite a while and that its membership—as distinguished from its founder—has not yet earned our condemnation, by any means."[22]

Prominent Birchers applied fierce pressure on Buckley to steer clear of the controversy and say nothing negative at all. Clarence Manion, a Birch leader and *National Review* contributor, pointedly warned Buckley that criticism from his magazine would enable the dreaded liberals to "drive a hole through the wall of conservative opposition," splitting their ranks and allowing their opponents to seize the political advantage. He added that "the origins of this drive against John Birch are so foul and disreputable that I cannot describe them in a telegram."

Any Birch–*National Review* showdown, one correspondent wrote, "could be apocalyptic." Paul Talbert, a member of the society's National Council, warned Buckley that Birchers might react negatively to any criticisms, causing them to withhold their support from the magazine. "I want to see the National Review succeed," he wrote, "but I hope you can see you are putting me on a permanent 'hot seat.'" Talbert was already taking heat from his local press in California and urged Buckley not to join the pile-on. He had been called "a satrap, fascist, neo-fascist, silver shirt, brown shirt, black shirt, red shirt, etc."[23]

Buckley vowed "to make it absolutely clear that National Review approves of the John Birch Society, while disapproving [of] Bob's tendency to frame his entire position on the presumption of endemic disloyalty." In a letter to Goldwater, Buckley was blunter: "Bob Welch is of course nuts on the Eisenhower-Dulles business. But the society has some very good people in it. . . . It is a pity W. didn't restrain himself. I fear he will do our cause much damage."[24] In January 1962 Buckley and Goldwater agreed during a meeting at the Breakers in Palm Beach to visibly divorce themselves and the conservative movement from the Birch Society's wildest conspiracy theories by casting Welch as the crackpot his critics had alleged while at the same time defending Birch members, whom Goldwater called "nice people."

In February 1962 Buckley wrote a second editorial that called Welch's "views on current affairs . . . far removed from common sense." Goldwater affirmed Buckley's attack and added that in his opinion, Welch's views did not "represent the feelings of most members of the John Birch Society." In other forums, Goldwater denounced Welch as an "extremist," called his ideas about Ike "stupid," and said, "I don't recall speaking to Bob Welch other than 'hello' and 'goodbye' over the last nine years or so." (He claimed that Buckley, not Welch, had asked him to serve on the antisummit committee.) In a surreal echo of 1950s liberals explaining their youthful flirtation with communism in the 1930s, Goldwater issued a roundabout mea culpa when he said, "All of us in public life sometimes lend our names to movements that later we wished we'd taken a little more time to find out about."[25]

When a Birch acolyte criticized *National Review* for its anti-Birch stands, Rusher responded by sending a copy of the February 1962 editorial and inviting him "to point out to me, anywhere in its first five pages, a single word of criticism of the John Birch Society." Buckley sounded similarly defensive a few months later when he wrote to Birch founder T. Coleman Andrews, "I don't think in my life I have made a single unfavorable reference to any members of the John Birch Society."[26]

For decades, conservatives and liberals have praised Buckley for those two (and subsequent) editorials. They celebrated him as a model of sobriety and rationality for panning the Birch Society and expunging the far-right fringe from conservative ranks. Over the past decade, however, the legend has come under scrutiny. Historians now argue that Buckley's vaunted excommunication of the fringe is a myth. They are not impressed by his supposedly Solomonic decision to repudiate the low-hanging fruit of Welch and his conspiracy theories while sparing the society's rank and file. By welcoming them into the fold both before and after *National Review*'s supposed break with the society, Buckley and his magazine continued to benefit from Birchers' political activism, funding, and engagement.

Ideologically, Buckley was not as far from the Birchers as has been claimed. He wrote a book defending McCarthy, supported massive resistance to civil rights in the late 1950s, and gave the cranks intellectual cover. Moreover, there was significant overlap between his supporters and the Birchers: many *National Review* subscribers also subscribed to *American Opinion*; Buckley's 1965 Conservative Party campaign for mayor of New York drew Birch and fringe support; and Buckley maintained professional and personal relationships with some of the most extreme Birch leaders, such as Revilo Oliver, who promoted antisemitic conspiracy theories.[27]

Nevertheless, by late 1965, Buckley's broadsides had infuriated some Birch leaders. Louis Ruthenburg, for example, excoriated Buckley for his "defamation of the John Birch Society." Overtly engaging with the Birchers remained an even thornier issue for a presidential candidate. By the time the presidential campaign of 1964 was underway, Goldwater continued his awkward pas de deux with the society. At times he sought to put space between himself and some of the Birchers' best-known positions. Asked about Earl Warren's "loyalty" at a February campaign rally in Claypool, Arizona, he told a crowd of seven hundred supporters that "he's a very loyal man" and that calling him "un-American" was just wrong. Silence fell over the attendees. When he fielded another question with Birch overtones about the "problem" of communists inside American government, he said he wasn't "overly concerned" and thought the problem was minor at best.[28]

While renouncing some of the views and incendiary rhetoric of Welch and other Birch leaders, he gingerly tried to avoid alienating the membership. As numerous historians have recently argued, Goldwater and other prominent conservatives more often than not welcomed the society's rank and file and many of their ideas to the fold. The candidate referred to the Birchers he knew from Arizona as "fine citizens" and expressed hope that they would become active in electoral politics. The balance wasn't easy to strike. The society's leadership and full-time staff in the home office said and wrote much that conflicted with the ideas that Goldwater wished to discuss. In response to a query from a member in North Carolina, for example, the research department in Belmont explained that Franklin Roosevelt, rather than Japan, had "triggered the attack upon Pearl Harbor."[29]

Goldwater couldn't say that there were fine people in the society while escaping all association with their more extreme expressions of radicalism. In the summer of 1964, Revilo Oliver addressed about thirteen hundred affluent residents of Orange County, California. Standing on a brightly lit stage with a massive American flag behind him, the classics professor decried "the bipeds who are too lazy, too stupid, too savage to work for themselves" and had no right to sponge off the hard work of good patriots like those in the audience. Oliver spoke of "profound biological differences between human races"; at one point, according to *Washington Post* reporter Julius Duscha, he read a letter from a critic using a "mocking Jewish accent." The audience apparently laughed and cheered.[30]

Having it both ways—benefiting from the passion of the rank-and-file activists but shearing off the racism, antisemitism, and conspiracy theories—was going to be extremely difficult for the Goldwater campaign. Birchers had a well-established, off-putting reputation for being highly aggressive and partial to intimidating tactics. They placed late-night calls, pinned labels like "com symp" on opponents, shouted down speakers, threatened lawsuits, and warned of unspecified consequences for those who crossed them. They—and by extension Goldwater—couldn't entirely avoid being tainted by some members' associations with more violent offshoots of the American right.

The society's part in Goldwater's White House run deepened fears that a homegrown fascist movement would sow violence, pitting citizen against citizen in a war for the soul of America. In a small town in Illinois, police broke up a Minutemen group armed with 81mm mortars and machine guns and planning to wage war on communists inside the United States. Founder Robert DePugh had been a member of the Birch Society, and his loose network of militarized Minutemen sought to keep tabs on alleged subversives in their hometowns, theorizing that they knew their friends and neighbors better than the FBI did. The *Bulletin* once called the Minutemen "good patriots." Now the society mildly rebuked their "innocuous tangents" and advised its own members not to follow them on missions into "the hills with groceries and rifles."[31]

THE REPUBLICAN ESTABLISHMENT'S EFFORTS TO DISTANCE ITSELF FROM the movement aside, there was no denying that the Birchers had helped lay the groundwork for Goldwater's 1964 White House run. One of their core conceits was equating morality with an absolutist stand in support of police. By featuring their brand of public morality—criminals versus law-abiders, craven revolutionary leftists versus the men in blue—as a theme in their activism, the society and the candidate aligned on a key emergent issue. A Goldwater television spot opened with gangs of hooligans punching each other as a voice-over narrated, "Immorality surrounds us as never before." Most Birchers agreed with that premise. One member denounced the movement for trying to play "nursemaid to our country's morals," but Reverend D. A. Waite, Welch's assistant, replied that "principles of morality" and fighting "moral pollution" were among the society's highest callings.[32]

Birchers crystallized the issue of public morality with one of their most successful single-issue causes: a movement called Support Your Local Police. The animating idea was that police had come under attack from communists, inner-city riots, and other immoral forces that sowed disorder in the land. Most galling to Birchers, civilian review boards had been formed to monitor the conduct of frontline officers and scour cities for what they saw as nonexistent examples of abuse. Birchers argued that these boards handcuffed law enforcement and, like the Warren court's decisions, gave criminals the upper hand. During his campaign Goldwater trumpeted the idea that city streets were awash in crime. "The leadership of this nation has a clear and immediate challenge . . . to restore law and order in the land," he said in one televised campaign ad. Brochures passed out at Goldwater rallies assured voters that a Goldwater administration would "restore law and order in the streets, protect your home, your family, your job—and bring moral leadership back to the White House."[33]

The Birchers' pro-police campaign turned the civil rights issue on its head. Where African American leaders and their allies urged cities to curb racist police brutality, the society claimed that the real problem was the left-wing agitators and callous ruffians who committed horrific crimes and got off scot-free. As a political movement, Support Your Local Police helped win over police officers to the Birch Society and pushed the issue of public morality, in which police stood as a bulwark against communist evil, to the center of the 1964 political debate, shaping the landscape on which Goldwater had to campaign for his party's nomination.

As they had on all their issues, the society turned to well-placed allies to bring this issue to the fore. FBI director J. Edgar Hoover hated the review boards, which he cast as "ill-advised" and appalling usurpations of the authority of police departments to supervise their own officers. Outside reviewers, he argued, ridiculed the men in blue and were indifferent to morality and public safety. The inspector general for the CIA likewise warned a Senate subcommittee that the "guardians of freedom" who served on police forces had become "a major target of the Communists" who controlled the civilian review boards.[34]

Birchers' pro-police activism helped frame some of Goldwater's morality-tinged campaign themes. It tapped into latent fears felt by mostly white urbanites and suburbanites and spotlighted provocative efforts to buck the tide of liberalism. "Why do we see a flood of obscene literature?" the candidate asked the nation. If elected, he vowed "to make it safe to live by the law" because "enough has been done to make it safe to live life outside the law." Birchers echoed and amplified these issues by flooding the streets with their own brand of activism. An especially dramatic demonstration unfolded in downtown Manhattan, the Bronx, Brooklyn, and western Long Island at two in the afternoon on Saturday, August 8: an estimated 150 Birchers worked in groups of ten to twelve at malls and in groups of four on busy street corners to distribute an estimated eighty thousand pieces of literature, fliers, and stickers. Although at least one store owner shooed away a Birch group, for the most part the reception was extremely positive and invigorated the pro-police campaign. Birchers had informed the police of their plans ahead of time, and the police gave the society "overwhelming cooperation." Field director Hill triumphantly declared that the police were "in love" with Support Your Local Police, especially the push to abolish the dreaded civilian oversight boards.[35]

The alliance between the society and police departments intensified—and the issue of public morality gained more salience—when stories surfaced that some officers were also Birchers. Questions followed: Was a policeman allowed to belong to a controversial political movement like the society? Didn't officers have First Amendment rights to free speech and free association? No one had a good answer. In the big cities on the East Coast, political leaders struggled. To the society the answer was apparent, and Birchers lobbied cities to permit officers to keep their membership without putting their jobs in jeopardy. Birch PR director Thomas Davis visited Newark and beseeched the city's police chief, deputy chief, captains, and lieutenants to allow Newark's Birch coordinator, Jim Fitzgerald, to hold on to his job as a cop. Police Chief Dominick Spina had some sympathy for the society (it was pro-blue, after all), so he decided to declare that "membership in the John Birch Society does not conflict with police regulations." The decision, Davis reported back to headquarters, represented "a victory of some significance."[36]

The Goldwater campaign took notice: big-city liberals appeared to be on the opposite side of the issue from their own police departments. One Goldwater poster charged that "government officials make millions while in public service. They let crime run riot in the streets." In Philadelphia, the contrast between the pro-police conservatives and procivilian review-board liberals was stark. Birchers launched a fight to discredit a civilian review board with a political sophistication that belied their reputation for bumble-headed paranoia. Birchers urged city council members, ward leaders, and state legislators to disband the oversight board, and some members delivered speeches and bombarded local newspapers, unions, and veterans' groups with letters in support of abolition. In teams of four, activists went to churches and gathered signatures supporting their petition to scrap civilian oversight. Some Birchers forged alliances with local business owners, who gave customers literature that bore the title *Why the Philadelphia Police Advisory Board Should Be Abolished*.[37]

In the heat of the presidential campaign, the Democratic mayor of Philadelphia, James Tate, announced that more than a dozen Birchers served on the police force. Like most of his fellow liberals, Tate denounced the society as the "extreme right wing." He added that "the way the Nazis got started in Germany, and the way the Communists operated in the 1930's and 1940's," was not unlike the radical right's foothold in his city's police department. He announced a policy of zero tolerance: all Bircher cops would lose their jobs or be reassigned and put on "limited duty."[38]

Birchers were unfazed by such threats. As Thomas Hill warned of the "danger that we face," he encouraged the society's coordinators to deploy ripped-from-the-headlines films and literature that accentuated Goldwater's message. Railing against disorder and depravity, Hill cited three "alarming incidents which take place each day and which vividly portray the horrible truths of our time": the unruly behavior of teenagers (exemplified by the "cries and shouts" that had greeted the Beatles at Kennedy airport), the terrible allegation that neighbors in Queens did nothing while they heard a man stab a woman to death, and a society coordinator's sighting, on a visit to upstate New York, of "smut type magazines" displayed on a newsstand. The Birch commitment to "freedom" was restricted to the freedom to run a business in any way they wished; other "freedoms"—whether the freedom to sit anywhere on a bus or the freedom to buy pornography—were abhorrent to most Birchers.[39]

Birchers weren't the only ones pushing to insert a morality plank in the heart of Goldwater's campaign. His team helped establish Mothers for Moral America, a group that had William F. Buckley's mother and Nancy Reagan on its national committee and urged members to get behind what they called a "moral crusade," claiming that liberals were responsible for a host of scourges including crime, urban riots, and pornography. The Pasadena-based Watchdogs of the Republican Party, established shortly before the Republican National Convention in the summer of 1964 and led by Birchers Jane Crosby, Bea Ziegler, and Marjorie Jensen, kept the society apprised of its activities and enlisted its members to volunteer on Goldwater's behalf, stressing the need to save civilization from the collapse of moral values at the hands of liberals.[40]

EVERY TIME A SEEMINGLY INSURMOUNTABLE SETBACK MATERIALIZED, Birchers were consistently able to expand the reach of the movement. The Khrushchev Summit, Supreme Court rulings, election losses, and Kennedy assassination all seemed to spell doom for the society and its overarching agenda, yet the disapproval of the society's detractors and the sting of defeat served to embolden its members, strengthen its infrastructure, and gain adherents. By the summer of 1964, as Goldwater was poised to take the Republican nomination for president, the mood felt different. A politician they liked and endorsed was about to win the top spot in one of the nation's two major parties. No longer underdogs or outsiders, Birchers might finally get a say in the direction of the GOP. Goldwater might inch the United States closer to their worldview.

Meanwhile, the society had become thoroughly professionalized. Forty-nine paid full-time field staff—including forty-six coordinators (one focused on setting up college chapters), one district governor, and two full-time bookstore specialists—worked to meet the needs of ninety-three American Opinion Bookstores and Libraries nationwide and helped build an impressive infrastructure. In Belmont, seventy-five employees, including Welch's personal aides, were busy connecting members to the national movement's departments—research, accounting, *American Opinion* magazine, the American Opinion Bookstores and Libraries, the American Opinion Speakers Bureau, and the Member's Monthly Message Department.[41]

The sophisticated network of American Opinion Bookstores played a crucial role. Historians have increasingly chronicled the rise of post–World War II conservative media as a kind of origin story for Fox News

In 1966, Birch Society founder Robert Welch was photographed in the offices of *American Opinion*. He had come under withering fire for calling Eisenhower a "communist agent," and joked with one audience that he wouldn't blame them for speculating about "the shape and color of my horns."
Getty images/Bettmann

During one of Welch's appearances around 1960, picketers held signs that read "Don't be a Welcher on civil liberties" and described him as "the would be dictator." The society's insistence that the United States wasn't a democracy dismayed, infuriated, and frightened liberals, many of whom saw Birchers as a quasi-fascist movement imperiling the stability of the nation's democratic and capitalist systems.
American Stock Archive/Archive Photos/ Hulton Archive/Getty Images

Although the society's most iconic billboard called on Congress to "impeach Earl Warren," this billboard, from 1964, captured the society's anti-internationalist streak—an ideological legacy Birchers bequeathed to their twenty-first-century descendants.
Charles O. Cecil/Alamy Stock Photo

On June 21, 1961, police stood watch across from an auditorium where protesters had gathered outside a Birch Society speech in Denver, Colorado. The society's insistence on the existence of a communist plot aimed at destroying the American way of life fueled concerns that the far right would substitute violence for politics. One Birch leader later warned colleagues, "World War III has begun."

Denver Post (Denver Post via Getty Images)

This Birch Society billboard falsely charged that Martin Luther King Jr. had attended a "communist training school" (it was the Highlander Folk School for labor organizing, in fact). Erected on the road where King's 1965 Selma-to-Montgomery march took place, the sign implied that marchers were communist puppets. Mississippi Bircher Ingrid Cowan informed the society's home office that "the KKK is such a strong competitor to the Society at least when it comes to recruiting members." Looking at this billboard, it's not hard to see why.

William Lovelace/Getty Images

At the Birch Society's 1972 New England Rally for God, Family and Country, held in Boston, a boy stands behind a rack of conspiracy-tinged Birch literature. Such tracts transcended their time, influencing the ideas, politics, and style of successors to the movement, including Glenn Beck, Alex Jones, Michele Bachmann, and Sarah Palin.

Photo by Spencer Grant/Getty Images

"Sorry, Old Boy, But Your Wife And I Feel You're Becoming An Embarrassment"

In 1962, the cartoonist Herblock depicted "Birchism" as a young, cigarette-smoking wife abandoning the founder and forging an intimate alliance with the "G.O.P. right wing." The cartoon reflected liberals' fears that Birchers had embedded themselves within the party of Lincoln.

A 1962 Herblock Cartoon, © The Herb Block Foundation

and Breitbart. The Birch Society's bookstores accelerated this cultural development, providing some of the infrastructure that enabled activists to meet, plan, and bring passion to the debate about ideas and to the Goldwater campaign. The stores became a hub for alternative sources of news and information, a cocoon-like structure where members traded thoughts, wooed recruits, and viewed Birch-produced films such as *Operation Abolition* and *Anarchy, USA*, both of which had echoes in the Goldwater campaign film *Choice*. (Estimates said that a thousand Americans each night watched a Birch-produced film.) Amplifying the ideas circulating in far-right outlets like the *Dan Smoot Report*, *Human Events*, the *Manion Forum*, the *American Mercury*, and *American Opinion*, the society provided a buffet of titles that conveyed the fever pitch of the Goldwater campaign and supplemented the growing right-wing alternatives to mainstream media institutions. The books on offer similarly fed ideas that suffused the Birch movement, conservative thought in general, and Goldwater's White House run in particular. The society's best-selling books that year—John Stormer's *None Dare Call It Treason*, Phyllis Schlafly's *A Choice Not an Echo*, and J. Evetts Haley's *A Texan Looks at Lyndon*—hailed Goldwater as a hero and promoted the Bircher-Goldwater notion that socialist ideas had captured the traditional leadership of both political parties. (According to one historian, the books sold a combined eighteen million copies prior to Election Day.)[42]

The cumulative effect was to give Birchers a sense that they belonged to a cause larger than themselves. "If ever we lose this closeness of association within, our feeling of unified purpose and closely knit strength will disappear, and with it, much of our effectiveness and potential," field director Hill, who toured chapters in the Midwest and West, informed coordinators in mid-1964. This "cement" bound the organization into a whole and made it a formidable political force.

Just as the society helped shape the climate in which Goldwater ran for president, his campaign—and the controversies it sparked about his and the society's extremism—piqued conservatives' interest in the movement. "People heard so much about us they were curious" and "they wanted to find out the truth," Rousselot explained. Before 1964 a typical chapter meeting drew eight to fifteen members, but during that year's political campaigns, he estimated that forty members and recruits often crammed into living rooms. Some members reportedly undertook home renovations on their own dime to accommodate all the people flocking to presentations and chapter meetings.[43] The axiom that a small group of relentless agitators pounding pavement can have far more impact than hordes of voters applied to the society. As historians have long noted, Birchers boosted Goldwater through the intensity of their activism. They gave speeches on his behalf, knocked on doors, stuffed envelopes, donated funds, attended his rallies, and got out the vote by urging neighbors and friends to back the conservative icon.

Some defended him from a chorus depicting him as a madman who lacked the mental fitness to have his finger on the nuclear trigger. When *Life* published a cover story based on surveys of psychiatrists and psychologists implicating Goldwater as a nutcase, Bircher Mary Curry, of Chapter 243, notified the home office that an acquaintance of hers who wished to remain anonymous had searched an unnamed psychiatry department and found letters from psychiatrists evaluating Goldwater's acuity and his fitness to serve. "One would get the impression from some [letters] that Goldwater is actually a raving maniac," Curry told Birch leaders. She offered to send the letters to the home office, but whether the society accepted is lost to history.[44]

The enthusiasm was infectious. The number of Birch candidates seeking office surged in 1964, especially in California. Nine members mounted races in the Republican primary for a variety of state and federal offices, and five ultimately won their nominations. Coupled with Goldwater's primary victory in the state, which helped seal his nomination, Rousselot judged the primary results in California a win for conservatives. Former congressman and Birch leader Edgar Hiestand was reportedly "elated." He had backed six candidates in the primary; all of them won. The *New York Times* observed that California GOP candidates refused to "denounce the Birch Society, even though they are not members, because of their obligation and loyalty to Mr. Hiestand and his associates."[45]

But the Kennedy White House's strategy of tying the far right around the neck of the GOP turned out to be extremely effective. The Birch Society became an exquisite foil. Its visibility in electoral politics made it easy to stick the extremist label on the Republican presidential nominee, who made missteps and couldn't evade his own fiery record and past statements. Democrats found plenty of fodder in the Republican Party's national convention proceedings at the Cow Palace in San Francisco. When Eisenhower criticized "sensation-seeking columnists and commentators" for sowing divisions in the GOP, some of Goldwater's supporters shook their fists at the broadcasters in the glass booths above them, and one mass of delegates surged menacingly in the journalists' direction before order was restored in the hall. When Goldwater's forces spotted NBC's John Chancellor on the convention floor, they asked the police for help, and the journalist was pushed out of the hall as he said, camera rolling, "This is a disgrace."[46]

In the wake of this spectacle, liberals eviscerated Goldwater's party as a safehouse for the right-wing fringe. The Democratic governor of California, Pat Brown, charged that the convention carried the "stench of fascism." Some GOP conservatives and moderates partially echoed these criticisms. Joe Shell's campaign manager (and Goldwater supporter) Rus Walton had watched as Birchers seized power in United Republicans of California, a group he had founded, yet denounced members as impolitic militants who tended to make "extreme statements."[47] Liberal Republicans were more withering. Pennsylvania governor William Scranton called Birchers "this weird presence in America," while Connecticut representative Abner Sibal impugned the society, the KKK, and communists as uniformly hostile to the "beliefs of American democracy." Another said that Birchers sought "the subversion of liberty" and were "alien to our shores."[48]

But in truth they were far from alien. Birchers were neither an export from Nazi Germany nor out of step with America's political traditions. The sentiments that undergirded the movement—a defense of white rights, the use of government to enforce Christian tenets and morality in public spaces, the veneration of inviolate freedom for the individual to do as he wished economically, free from government intervention—had deep roots in the nation's historical development. Birchers' use of conspiracy theories to tar their foes as anti-American was native to the United States, too, as was their contempt for multiracial democracy.

The televised images from the Cow Palace gave these traditions a fresh gloss and morphed them overnight into a cautionary tale for what happens when the fringe takes over one of the nation's political parties. The images were ugly, vile, and vicious—a threat to democracy flashing on screens, unfolding in living rooms. New York's Republican governor, Nelson Rockefeller, appeared at the podium. He urged delegates to vote for a plank that moderates had proposed in condemnation of the KKK, the Birch Society, and other extremists. He fumed about "these people who have nothing in common with Americanism. . . . The Republican Party must repudiate these people."

"You goddamned Socialist!"—get that "fink," one Goldwater delegate shouted from the floor. The boos and hisses made Rockefeller's words hard to hear. The governor whom Welch had once slammed as Red lacerated the society and white supremacists for "anonymous midnight and early morning phone calls. That's right . . . smear and hate literature, strong-arm tactics, bomb threats and bombings. Infiltration and takeover of established political organizations by Communist and Nazi methods!"

Amid the growing uproar, he continued, "Some of you don't like to hear it, ladies and gentlemen, but it's the truth."

The effort to pass an antiextremist motion didn't pass. Its failure satisfied the Birch Society but also handed Goldwater's opponents a mass of ammunition for the autumn. For a Republican candidate struggling to shed the "fringe" label, the vote on the plank, combined with televised images of delegates berating and warring with fellow Republicans, dealt heavy blows.[49]

Goldwater's proud invocation of Birch language in his convention address—the part where he declared that "extremism in defense of liberty is no vice"—came off as an unmistakable proclamation that Birchers were a legitimate political force with a place in the Republican Party. When Democrats gathered at their convention in Atlantic City, they did what the GOP couldn't: put a plank in their platform that condemned the John Birch Society as a danger to democracy. Birchers then clarified the contrast between the two parties as Goldwater and the Democratic nominee, President Lyndon Johnson, barreled toward Election Day.[50]

INCREASINGLY, THE SOCIETY ITSELF BECAME *THE* ISSUE. WHERE YOU stood on the Birchers—for or against—revealed your political and social identity, acting as a kind of shorthand for your position on topics ranging from morality and religion to preferred news sources and whether the New Deal was a lifeline for ordinary citizens or a biblical affliction on free peoples. In liberal quarters, the society became something of a sick joke during the campaign. Johnson understood that appending the Birch name to any conservative stung. When a right-wing friend from Texas visited the White House, the president said, "I want you to meet my friend Louis Shanks. He's the only John Bircher friend I have." Shanks, a furniture-store salesman and conservative member of the Austin City Council, wasn't in the society. But to liberals the Birchers were uncouth, a dirty, not-so-hidden tentacle of modern conservatism, and LBJ enjoyed sticking in the knife.[51]

And it wasn't just liberals who assailed the Birch phenomenon in the fall of 1964. Conservatives at times rallied in opposition to a group they considered a threat to democracy, and some felt an obligation to stop it from metastasizing through their own movement. On September 22, a group of friends who were intrigued by what they had heard of the society attended a chapter presentation in Flushing, Queens. Twelve people agreed to join the society that night. Ana Steele wasn't among them.

The meeting calcified Steele's distrust. She and others put tough questions to the New York regional director and chapter leader: Why did so many Americans consider the Birch movement extremist? Why had it worked to undermine "people's faith" in elected officials? "Every objection I and my friends raised was treated as the product of either ignorance or naivete or worse," Steele later explained in a letter to Bill Buckley, whose *National Review* editorial attacking Welch had left an impression on her.

Despite Steele's doubts, two of her friends signed up as members, and one of them, she observed, "was ripe" for the plucking, as he wasn't "quick enough to pick up all the mess of misinformation, and indeed, lies, spread." Steele added that she had grown "tired of assuming that 'the overwhelming majority' [of the society] is well-meaning; and even if it were, the leadership is surely as deceitful and dangerous as can be."[52]

Other aspects of the session gnawed at her. Birch leaders distributed "smear literature," they twisted facts and history, and seeing a copy of Welch's *The Politician* gave her "the creeps." Carmen Steele, presumably a relative of Ana's who had also attended, excoriated the Birch leaders' presentations as the "insidious blending of fact and fiction" and termed their baseless claims "terrifying." The society, she complained, distrusted "almost all the major news media, newspapers, wire services, radio and television" as "either Communist-run or so liberal as to be aids to Communism. Thus, they alone speak the truth. Just what is their pipeline to the truth was left unanswered." Ana Steele asked if Buckley could publish another attack on the society that might help her friends see the light and liberate them from its cultish grip.[53]

IN NOVEMBER 1964, GOLDWATER CARRIED HIS NATIVE ARIZONA AND five states in the Deep South, but he lost the rest of the nation in a rout that pushed the Birch Society in contrasting directions. Some Birchers emerged emboldened, as they had from prior defeats. Others felt under siege in the face of a culture that viewed their movement as a danger to civic life and treated them as a menace to American democracy. Still others consoled themselves with the belief that the election had given the society a legitimacy in the Republican Party and within electoral politics that it had previously lacked.

The pulsing excitement for tasks yet undone, for an organization poised to achieve fresh triumphs, surfaced in many messages sent to the home office. Member Bob Dunim wrote, "I have in the past had moments where I was reluctant to openly announce that I am a Bircher, but [I] will never be so again." Oliver Kelso Jr. marveled at how even in the wake of Goldwater's loss, "we're gaining many new JBS members!!" Eugene Rodgers said that although "we did not get a good man to head the nation . . . with God [*sic*] help and our own bootstrap, we may be saved." Another member observed that "every precinct a JB'er worked" outperformed the precincts where only Republicans had boots on the ground. The mood at headquarters was ebullient. "What wonderful members we have!" a staff member wrote. "They all spent the night of the election being discouraged and downhearted and the next day bounced right back saying we just have to work harder." The Member's Monthly Message Department informed another Bircher that "members are working harder than ever" despite the Election Day setback.[54]

Field director Hill told regional coordinators that his New Year's wish was to build a movement "filled with solid chapters, new chapters, and so many applications that you continue to bury us all with an ever-expanding work load." By January 5, 1965, the home office told a Bircher that "we have just been buried by new members." Connecticut nearly doubled its membership over the next eight months. The sense of an alternative culture that had propelled the society and kept it intact was also heightened. A couple of weeks after Election Day, firebrand writer W. Cleon Skousen, author of *The Communist Attack on the John Birch Society*, delivered a speech sponsored by American Opinion Libraries at Flick-Reedy Corporation, in Bensenville, Illinois. The snowy, record-cold night didn't deter two hundred activists, who traveled to "a way-out location" to hear Skousen's remarks. A sea of literature awaited attendees; pamphlets and stickers blared "Support Your Local Police," copies of Skousen's book were for sale, and recruitment materials abounded.[55]

But Birchers sometimes underestimated their critics' determination to prevent them from holding political power. In 1962 in Milford, Massachusetts, Thomas DePalo, a Bircher and a doctor, rode support from fellow Catholics to win a seat on the Milford School Committee. Once in office, DePalo earned a reputation as a flamethrower. When six of his fellow committee members voted down his resolution to permit school prayer and Bible reading, he threatened, "We will bring [Attorney General Edward] Brooke to trial." Asked who the "we" referred to, he replied, "A group of patriots." By 1964, Protestant clergy found a candidate to mount a bid against the Bircher, and the challenger won an upset victory.[56]

By fighting back, the mainstream could put the Birchers where they belonged—on the outer margins of American life. "The fact is clear, you can't talk with a Bircher," editorialized the *Southwest Jewish Press*, highlighting lessons learned from the brush with Birchism in Milford. The typical Bircher "is so aggressive in defense of the card he carries that he seems to lose sight of country and human dignity. So the best way to beat him is at the polls. Every time he raises his paranoid head, we will be there after him. Sometimes we will win, sometimes we will lose. But, he will know that we are watching."[57]

Some Birchers felt tugged toward a place where hope had faded and the future had darkened. The controversies lit by Goldwater's run made the society even more toxic in the eyes of its critics, a showcase for the true scope of the far-right threat. In response, a conviction that Birchers had been betrayed took hold, leaving members feeling defensive and bitter, though sometimes more motivated than ever. Member Marie Howard lamented that "Republicans cost us this election." A Birch couple expressed dismay that so many "uninformed people" feared "us." They told the home office that "the J.B.S. is no Ku Klux Clan [sic] or Red," but Birchers had now been boxed in and had no choice but to wage "a dirty war."[58]

The heightened scrutiny that accompanied the presidential campaign of 1964 ratcheted up Birchers' suspicions, and some came to believe that the government was planning to destroy the society. California chapter member Vivian Reiswig speculated that postal workers tracked Birch labels affixed to envelopes so the government could identify members and target the movement. "In a small community it's the height of folly to mark the Birch member in such an open way," she wrote, urging headquarters to excise "identifying name and address" from all mailings. "In case of a gov't crack down the postal employees would be the ones to point the finger at us," she warned. "Let's make it a truly 'secret society.'" Another Bircher predicted that in the election's aftermath, "persecution of the Society will assume a new aura of respectability." Pennsylvania member Dr. Eric Zetterberg Jr. speculated, "We may find ourselves on the subversive list." Contemplating the next four years of a Johnson White House, a member who lived in Mexico warned headquarters that "we may have to go underground" and do battle as a far-right remnant in order to save the soul of the country.[59]

Welch fanned these embers as he had done from the very first, secret meeting in Indiana. He once urged members never to carry their Birch membership cards on their persons, and fears that a leviathan state was out to eliminate the movement now surfaced with greater intensity.[60] For the most part, such fears were neither the product of a paranoid style nor the result of irrational minds and schizophrenic personalities. Birchers had plenty of real enemies, many of whom were out to get them. The preceding five years had put them in the crosshairs of numerous investigations. Attorneys general, liberal activists, two presidential administrations, the Defense Department, members of Congress, the news media, and the FBI at various times had studied and analyzed and interpreted the movement for the American public. Some officials called Birchers subversive; others dismissed them as bizarre and pathetic. In recent years, the military brass had reprimanded Birch-preaching officers (the society's supporters criticized the practice as "muzzling"), while some mayors and police chiefs had forbidden police officers to be members. Because many liberals viewed the society as hostile to democracy, Birchers feared that they would be subjected to extraordinary countermeasures, that they would be targeted for retribution, and that their movement would be destroyed.

Members also fretted that their affiliations made it impossible to live a life of freedom, able to pursue their careers unencumbered by suspicion and enmity from their coworkers. Reports circulated that some Birchers actually were being hounded at work. One member in Delaware said that a Lockheed aircraft plant in New Jersey was requiring employees to sign affidavits stating that they weren't Birchers or members of other extremist groups. In New Orleans, a Saturn rocket plant allegedly fired employees when management learned of their Birch affiliations. Other members believed that their livelihoods hung in the balance. One asked headquarters, "What good is a dead hero?"[61]

The national outpouring of sorrow in response to Kennedy's assassination, combined with LBJ's electoral thrashing of a Birch-backed nominee, gave a lot of liberals faith that the consensus had crushed the fringe. The center had held firm. Yet they were hardly content to drop their vigilance. Birchers had gained power within the Republican Party. They had come within striking distance of the Oval Office. Even if the far right was ultimately doomed, Birchers still posed a grave threat. They had eroded the capacity of the nation's democracy to tolerate dissent and find common solutions based on a set of widely accepted facts. If liberals were to build the world they wanted—a world where pluralism trumped hate, science trounced unreason, and democracy conquered fascism—they had to fight harder.

Birchers might occasionally eke out a victory here and there, but liberals could never allow them to find a home in the American center. A coalition of Cold War liberals who believed in a consensus brand of politics as well as in the power of government to improve people's lives sought to wall off the society and confine it to a tiny corner of the political landscape for the rest of the 1960s and beyond. Many believed the fate of democracy itself rested on the success of this endeavor.

Chapter 6

BIRCH WATCHERS

A T 2:00 P.M. ON SATURDAY, MARCH 28, 1964, AN ANTI-DEFAMATION League (ADL) spy code-named Bos #4 knocked on the locked front door of the two-story redbrick headquarters of the John Birch Society in Belmont, Massachusetts. Bos #4 looked through a window and saw a man sitting at a desk. The man looked up, came to the door, and invited the stranger in. The man who opened the door to Bos #4 was Robert Welch.[1]

Bos #4 introduced himself as a Birch Society chapter leader from New Jersey who was in town to visit relatives. He had come to headquarters on the spur of the moment, he said, hoping to pick up literature to take back to his members. Welch "readily accepted my explanation," Bos #4 later recorded in a memo to ADL leadership, and was eager to be of assistance. The men struck up a friendly conversation. Welch searched his office for keys to the mail room in the adjacent building, where the society stored its publications.

Bos #4's visit had been set in motion a few weeks earlier, when Arnold Forster, the ADL's general counsel, received a tip that puzzled him. Welch had allegedly rejected an article that Westbrook Pegler, a prominent conservative columnist, submitted to the society's flagship magazine, *American Opinion*. Forster wanted to know why. He reasoned that the explanation of the rejection might reveal a bit of dirt that the ADL could exploit to embarrass the society in what had become a kind of covert ideological and tactical war between the two organizations. To find out what had happened with Pegler's article, Forster turned to Isadore Zack, director of "fact-finding and public relations" for the ADL's New England region and a master sleuth during World War II who now supervised a cadre of ADL spies, including Bos #4.

As Bos #4 chatted amiably in Welch's immaculate office, he had a natural opening to ask the Birch founder why *American Opinion* had not recently published any of Pegler's pieces. Forster had suspected that antisemitism was a factor (Pegler had at least once referred to Jews as "kikes"), but that wasn't what had caused the rift. Pegler, Welch replied, "hates Chief Justice Warren" and "wishes that Warren would break both of his legs." He told Bos #4 that he'd tried to soften Pegler's violent-sounding screed, but Pegler wouldn't budge. Welch, who said that Pegler's article was unacceptable for the magazine, was furious that he still had to pay Pegler for his unprintable work. "We don't hate anybody," Welch told Bos #4. "We just hate what they stand for."[2]

The informant came away with a good impression of the mastermind of the movement. In his report Bos #4 described Welch as a mentally agile, physically fit workaholic who walked "without any apparent strain," "seemed alert and confident," and used "an economy of words." His affect was neither overbearing nor paranoid, as numerous of his critics had implied; rather, he came across as "folksy."

"Welch understands and has mastered most of the nuances of effective executive leadership," Bos #4 informed Zack, cautioning that Welch and his society should not be taken lightly. Bos #4's visit was just one brief incident in a lengthy, multidimensional, and previously undisclosed counterintelligence operation waged by the ADL to infiltrate and dig up damaging information about the John Birch Society. And his report was just one of thousands of documents created in the process and stored in the ADL's files.[3] The ADL christened its espionage program the "Birch Watchers" and sometimes referred to it by its more pedestrian name, "the counterreaction." Beginning around 1959 and continuing through at least the early 1970s, the ADL's Birch Watchers were part of a sprawling, informal coalition seeking to discredit the Birchers, who were widely seen as a major threat to democracy. The coalition's goal was to stop the far right from gaining power in American politics and popularity in the culture. Birchers, Columbia University law professor Alan Westin wrote, fostered "hate propaganda and calculated violence." The Birch Watchers hoped to extirpate these evils from American soil.[4]

Alongside human rights, labor, and political watchdog groups such as the NAACP and Americans for Democratic Action, the ADL issued press releases, held meetings, and sought to excise Birchers from civic institutions. The ADL's campaign was representative of the liberal response to Birchism and a mainstay in the liberal coalition's efforts to defend democracy inside the United States. Its activism unfolded in conjunction with the civil rights movement, which was using boycotts to change Jim Crow laws and check the power of white supremacy. The United Auto Workers tapped Wesley McCune, a former reporter for *Time*, *Life*, and *Newsweek*, to run Group Research Inc., an organization created to expose the far right's subterranean assault on democratic institutions. McCune's small staff collected correspondence, leaflets, and news reports on Birchers and published a bimonthly newsletter tracing the far right's activities. A few individuals, such as Harry and Bonaro Overstreet, Grace Hoag, and Gordon Hall, kept tabs on the society, published polemics, and delivered anti-Birch lectures. Hall once observed, "No one loves America more than the John Birch Society and no one understands it less."[5]

WHY DID A VENERABLE ORGANIZATION DEVOTED TO CIVIL RIGHTS AND civil liberties deploy subterfuge tactics that seemingly contradicted some of its core values? In 1952 the ADL's general counsel, Arnold Forster, and national director, Benjamin Epstein, hinted at an answer to this question. The ADL, they wrote, felt a duty to expose "a vast enterprise" of hate and to disrupt the "works of professional hatemongers" operating in the United States. Meier Steinbrink, the national chairman, spoke of the need for "ammunition for the war to make our land a more perfect democracy." To the ADL, these righteous ends justified the morally questionable means, which included outright spying. As the Birch Society

emerged and gained strength, it became an ADL bête noire. Epstein
and Forster described it as the "backbone" and the "bellwether" of the
"Radical Right"—a movement that "sees the United States in the grip
of a deeply entrenched, well-advanced internal Communist conspiracy
that maintains a stranglehold on the Federal Government, the local town
council, the school board, the press, the public library, and the pulpit."
By shining a bright, intense light on the far right's dark side, through
whatever means, the ADL hoped to strike a blow for tolerance, progress,
and democracy.[6]

The political climate helped legitimize the spying in the minds of ADL
leaders. Both the right and the left believed that politics carried existential stakes that justified extreme tactics. The conspiracies spread by Birchers about subversive and alarmingly powerful liberals and communists
inspired the ADL's own aggressive approach. Few organizations perceived
the threat to democracy as acutely as the ADL, and none used more drastic methods to expose the far right as a dire threat to democracy. Some
of the ADL's financial investigations, from using third parties for credit
checks to fishing for data about individuals' trusts, may even have been
illegal.

The searing lessons of World War II also galvanized the Birch Watchers. Inaction and silence in the face of fascism had enabled the Holocaust
and brought dictatorship close to American shores. To the watchers,
Birch criticisms of the civil rights movement as a communist plot and of
the US foreign policy establishment as the pawns of international elites
evoked Hitler's scapegoating and persecution of Jews and racial minorities. And the ADL had a history of foiling Nazi plots. In the 1930s a spy
ring in Los Angeles led by ADL and its parent organization, B'nai B'rith,
stopped Nazis from assassinating Jewish Hollywood studio moguls and
from bombing West Coast munitions factories.

The ADL's postwar leaders took this inheritance and built on it. They
grasped the axiom that things could always get worse. Epstein, Forster,
and Zack had had firsthand brushes with Nazism that moved them to
join the ADL and ultimately prosecute what they saw as a war on hate.
In 1934 Epstein was studying history in Berlin as he watched Hitler seize
total power from close up. In 1938 Forster recruited a team of pro bono

lawyers to help the ADL with legal efforts to combat Nazi plots against America.[7] And beginning in 1941 Zack served as a counterespionage expert for the US Army.

During the war Zack ran the army's Subversive Squad and later commanded ten men in the Counter Intelligence Group of the Security and Intelligence Division, based in Boston. He led his team in tracking communists and German, Japanese, and Italian fascists, as well as other individuals and groups who were suspected of subversive activities in New England. He also investigated and reported on labor disputes, racial unrest, sabotage, and riots, yielding information that informed the army's Weekly Intelligence Summaries, which were distributed to the region's law enforcement agencies.

Wearing civilian clothes and carrying fake dishonorable discharge papers, Zack pretended to be a disgruntled former soldier as he roamed the bars, ports, and army bases of a key security zone off the Atlantic seaboard, hunting for intelligence. His team worked out of offices in Brookline, Massachusetts, that had once sold Hoover vacuum cleaners. "For 15 months," he recalled decades later, "no one knew we were there, not even the Brookline police." His wartime actions earned him the Army Commendation Ribbon and three citations for meritorious service. After the war, in 1946, he transitioned to using his spy craft for a different entity but in pursuit of what he saw as the same purpose: to counteract the kinds of extremism that had led to the murder of six million Jews in Nazi death camps.[8]

Having witnessed the tepid initial response to Joe McCarthy's assault on civil liberties in the early 1950s, the ADL's leaders viewed the Birch Watchers' spy effort as urgent, logical, and morally just. President Kennedy praised the ADL's "distinguished contribution to the enrichment of America's democratic legacy" and "tireless pursuit of equality of treatment for all Americans," and Birch Watchers operated with these ideas in the forefront of their minds. Following Kennedy's murder, LBJ captured the ADL's raison d'être when he implored citizens to "turn away from the fanatics of the far left and the far right, from the apostles of bitterness and bigotry." The ADL saw its campaign as a natural outgrowth of this concept.[9]

As the sixties unfolded, growing unrest fortified the ADL's resolve to fight the Birch Society through underhanded methods. Kennedy's assassination shook liberals' faith in the stability of democracy, and Goldwater's White House run deepened their angst.[10] Cold-blooded murders of civil rights workers in Mississippi and of African American girls in Alabama, along with police violence targeting Blacks in inner cities and a raft of urban uprisings, created a sense of racial pandemonium. The Vietnam War and student protests intensified worries that the country was coming unglued. Like many liberals, the ADL's leaders feared that an extremist reaction to the upheaval—a Bircher-led movement fueled by antigovernment zeal and easy access to firearms—could explode into violence against racial and religious minorities, and they felt a moral obligation to stamp it out. The ADL was well aware of the potential hazards of intervention but calculated that timidity had failed catastrophically in the recent past and the risks were worth it.

THE ADL WENT TO GREAT LENGTHS TO KEEP ITS SPY PROGRAM SECRET. The clandestine war on the society was so sensitive that Zack kept his agents' identities hidden from most of his supervisors at the ADL's Manhattan headquarters. Birch Watchers were assigned code names, and although most of their real names have been lost to history, we can glean a few things about their identities. They tended to be rank-and-file ADL members and individuals sympathetic to the league's agenda of rooting out antisemitism and racism in the United States. Some of them worked full-time at the ADL, while others moonlighted.

Hundreds of internal reports reveal that the Birch Watchers came from all walks of life, a motley crew bound together by a shared faith in the goal of making America a safe haven for Jewry and racial progress. They were accountants who fed financial information about Bircher clients to headquarters. They were law enforcement agents who provided tips on local residents who may have been Birchers. They included a gun store proprietor who chased away Birchers seeking to buy firearms, and a banker who conducted credit checks on generous Birch donors to learn how much money they had and the origins of the trusts they owned. They were members of local synagogues who informed on Birch activities in their towns. And they were freelancers who took it upon themselves to drop by American Opinion Bookstores to chat with members and pick up any information they could.[11]

Just as some civil rights activists risked their lives by organizing, marching, and boycotting, ADL operatives imperiled their safety by spying. Roberta Galler was a journalism student at Northwestern University in the early 1950s when she was forced to room with another Jewish student on a Christians-only floor in a campus dormitory. Black students, she realized, had segregated dorms. Her experience with discrimination inspired her to join a small African American student group on campus and become active in student government. Some of her peers branded her a radical, and she decided to transfer to the University of Chicago. Financial hardship ultimately forced her to leave college altogether, but a new path beckoned. She had a professor who used his ADL connections to help her find an entry-level job in the organization's bland-sounding Fact-Finding Department.

The work turned out to be more exciting than the office's name. The Fact-Finding Department, she acknowledged years later, "was really their spying department on the far right wing." At first she just clipped news stories. But her supervisors recognized her skills and brains, began training her as a spy, and eventually gave her a cover. She was told to infiltrate far-right groups by posing as a racist. Her espionage reflected "part of my youthful grandiosity that I could do anything" and involved "playacting and a certain degree of danger." After leaving the ADL, she worked for civil rights in the South, a step that she felt flowed naturally from her previous spy craft. But she did have one regret: she later learned that her reports were forwarded by the ADL to Hoover's FBI, which was harassing and intimidating civil rights leaders, and the collaboration appalled her.[12]

GALLER AND THE OTHER SPIES CAST A WIDE NET. IN ADDITION TO FOLlowing up on tips like the one about Welch rejecting Pegler's article, Zack's team members set out on missions to befriend Birch leaders, track members in small towns and big cities, and hunt for any shred of evidence of antisemitic, racist, violent, or totalitarian inclinations. Quietly, the ADL spies cultivated relationships not just with Birchers but also with G-men, religious leaders, reporters, editors, and broadcasters. They obtained chapter membership lists, ran credit reports on individual Birchers, ferreted out their employment records, traced their financial transactions, wrote down their license plate numbers, obtained a codicil to a Birch donor's will, stumped them with tough questions during call-in radio shows, set up a Birch chapter meeting on false pretenses so an ADL target could be "interviewed," and studied their personal and professional associations. Some of the scariest or most unflattering bits ended up in the press.[13]

The ADL was likely the first organization to start spying on the Birch Society. By early 1959, within weeks of the society's birth, Zack realized that some of the right-wingers he was pursuing had gotten involved with a new organization based in Belmont, Massachusetts. In February he asked a doctor friend to hunt for information about the background of Dr. Harold McKinney, who was "opening his home for meetings of a group in which we are interested." Zack's spies found themselves in a target-rich environment. Birch Watchers investigated the leaders of the Committee Against Summit Entanglements, the Birch front group, with Jerry Bakst, the ADL's director of research and evaluation, urging Zack in September 1959 to "have a volunteer or volunteers, possibly non-Jewish, join both C.A.S.E. and the John Birch Society, attend meetings, get literature, and keep us continually informed." During the first year of the society's existence, Zack directed one of his spies to find a trusted person sympathetic to the ADL who could "run a credit check on B.A. Prince," a suspected Bircher. He advised the spy to use a "friendly source in a large department store" to learn more about Prince's finances—and to do it confidentially.[14]

Birch Watchers adopted a comprehensive approach that encompassed mundane investigations as well as riskier infiltration of the society's headquarters. They visited the Massachusetts secretary of state's office and perused the society's articles of incorporation. Some agents attended Birch-sponsored events and recorded the speakers' comments, noted their identities, and listened for any antisemitic or racist remarks. Birch Watchers tried to assess the society's appeal to the citizenry, and what they found concerned the ADL. One report estimated that nine hundred people, most of them Birchers, had trekked to a downtown Detroit auditorium on a hot summer night, "an outstanding indication of the growing strength and number of the Birch Society in Michigan."[15]

The spies also aimed to drive a wedge between the far right and the GOP. In early 1962 Zack asked a colleague to pass an ADL report on the Birchers to "responsible Republican leaders in your community" to alert them to the menace in their midst. At the same time, Birch Watchers searched for connections between the society and respectable individuals and institutions, to embarrass them into renouncing the right-wing radicals. When agents infiltrated a Birch lecture with 120 attendees at a junior high school in New Bedford, Massachusetts, they found a bonanza. The sympathetic audience included an insurance professional, a priest, three nuns, several students from a nearby parochial school whose government teacher had sent them, and clerks from a New Bedford court and a nearby town hall. Zack wrote a colleague, "We secured the license number of the car in which [the priests and nuns] left the scene of the meeting and we hope to identify them later on."[16]

The Birch Watcher program sometimes applied economic pressure on such individuals. After a 1962 ADL report named Massachusetts-based Philip Jenkins, who worked in the leather industry, as an incorporator of the John Birch Society, he told the group that he wanted his name expunged from the report because Jews in his industry were alarmed by his associations.[17]

The Birch Watchers employed techniques that were on par with government-backed clandestine operations. The group's professionalism and planning reflected Zack's background as a leader in wartime counterintelligence. They set up mail drops to pass information up the chain of command. One operative changed his name—from Fegan to Feygan—to evade detection when registering for a Birch rally in Boston. At another event Birchers spotted an ADL agent in the crowd, politely asked him to leave, and he did so. But Zack had planted a second agent in the audience, and this pinch hitter remained undetected and took copious notes.[18]

Birch Watchers were particularly attuned to the potential for the society's incendiary ideas to spur violence, and they kept a keen lookout for any hints of possible bloodshed. Their reports implicated the society in nefarious undertakings and uncovered ample evidence of a movement that went beyond the bounds of civil discourse. One hour after Kennedy's murder, an anonymous caller warned the ADL's West Coast offices, "You bastards will be next." Two of Zack's covert agents (both of them code-named "Ben Brith," a play on B'nai B'rith) unearthed "what appears to be John Birch Society involvement in the purchase of weapons and infiltration of gun clubs" in Connecticut. These findings "deeply troubled" one of the agents, who called for further investigation. Another Birch Watcher infiltrated a Birch front group (Connecticut Conservatives Inc.) and heard Birchers praise Adolf Hitler and complain that "U.S. television won't let him rest in peace."[19]

Menacing episodes abounded. At a 1963 anticommunist rally at the Shrine Auditorium in Los Angeles—the last stop of the exhaustively hyped coast-to-coast Midnight Ride speaking tour featuring Bircher favorites Edwin Walker and Billy James Hargis—an ADL operative reported that the mood of the estimated forty-five hundred people in the crowd turned "sour and ugly" when civil rights picketers showed up. "Give me a machine-gun," a Birch Watcher quoted one attendee saying, "and I'll mow those bastards down."[20]

When a spy, code-named Bos-7, attended a lecture by Birch PR director John Rousselot, he sat next to a member named Kenneth Robertson, a stockbroker he had befriended during his undercover sleuthing. Bos-7 reported that whenever "someone in the audience asked a question or made a statement which was anti–John Birch," Robertson yelled, "Comsymp." Robertson was drunk, and the ADL agent was clearly concerned about a possible escalation to more than just verbal lashings.[21]

Looking for any dirt that could smear the movement in the public eye, Birch Watchers sifted for evidence of criminal behavior in the pasts of Birch members. An African American police officer in Stamford, Connecticut, who was moonlighting for Zack's operation, reported that he had checked department files for traces of a criminal past for resident Thomas Davis, a Birch PR director covering the northeastern United States, but came up empty.

Birch Watchers went so far as to bait the society's leadership into making mistakes by, for instance, expressing racist ideas themselves or appearing to aid the Birch cause. On the night of March 24, 1965, Zack met one of his agents, BS #2, who had written three reports on his recent infiltration of the headquarters in Belmont. Zack "took BS #2 for a ride in the country so that we could have a talk." They discussed the way Welch and his wife were trying to persuade BS #2 to become a full-fledged proselytizer for the society. Pretending to be a convert to their cause, BS #2 discovered that Welch was hoping to recruit an African American leader to establish a "Birch front made up of Negroes who would operate as a Negro backlash to the civil rights movement." The agent gave Welch a copy of the Muslim Businessmen's Association constitution. Welch held on to the document for two weeks, then informed BS #2 that the association's rules and regulations could serve as a template for an African American chapter within the Birch Society.[22]

Birch Watchers also posed as disgruntled Birchers to infiltrate white supremacist groups and assess the society's existing ties to them. One agent pretended to have left the society to join a more explicitly racist group. On March 29, 1967, he attended a meeting of eighty-seven people at the new basement headquarters of a white supremacist group called the Western Front, at 1515 Sunset Boulevard in Los Angeles. The group had gathered to hear a talk by "the fireman from down under." Eric Butler, an Australian, had long since left firefighting to become a professional white supremacist and had given talks to South Africa's Security Police that helped it enforce apartheid. He wrote for *American Opinion* using a pseudonym. This operation was deemed so sensitive that the Birch Watcher's three-page, single-spaced memo about the event did not even include a code name; the only words scrawled across the top read: "not to be shown."

Like many Birch Watchers, this one was no amateur. He knew the white supremacist movement in LA well enough to report that the only attendees who didn't usually show up at such events were "Houston Myers and Mr. Trump of the Citizens Council." (Alas, ADL and other records offer no further clues to the identity or activities of this "Mr. Trump.")

The Western Front's antisemitism came into focus when a speaker introduced a resolution calling for war "against the forces of international Jewry," drawing vigorous applause. The ADL agent spotted "a number of openly anti-Semitic books" on display, along with "Birch prints." But echoing Birchers' tendency to save some of their harshest criticism for Republicans who were insufficiently right wing, the Western Front expressed disappointment that Birchers had refused "to call a spade a spade." Walter White, the Western Front's leader, declared that it was ineffective "to deodorize the room with a spray disinfectant while ignoring the skunk in the basement"—a dig at the Birch Society for not blaming the Jews enough. (White postponed announcing details for the next meeting "because of the possible presence of 'some ADL agent.'")

When the meeting broke up, "several people clustered around Butler," who spoke about the Birch Society's relationship with the Western Front and with the international white supremacy movement. Describing Butler, the agent wrote, "As he answered questions he munched on cookies and sipped a cup of coffee which he overloaded with PREAM. As he sputtered out replies cookie crumbs fell over the front of his suit or, mixed with saliva, showered those about him. Occasionally he smiled, displaying a set of gold-capped teeth. His face is a massive ruin of sagging flesh; only the dark pinpoint eyes show animation. When he speaks, he looks directly at you."

The agent's cover helped him hunt for scraps of information that could aid the ADL's efforts to tarnish the society.

Poising [sic] as a disheartened Bircher, I asked Butler what he knew of the Draskovich-Oliver resignation and what pressures he, himself, was feeling. I pointed out that all the articles in American Opinion except his carried the author's name. He opened by replying that if they wanted him out they would have to ask him to resign as he would not do it voluntarily.

After the ADL book "Danger on the Right" was published, [American Opinion managing editor] Scott Stanley wrote Butler a letter asking for material to refute the League's accusations. Butler did not say how he replied. But he noticed shortly thereafter that his articles no longer carried his name. Still, Welch considers him an indispensable authority on Communism.

Fishing for signs of internal dissent, the agent quoted Butler extensively, providing a window into the white supremacist's view of Welch and tensions within the movement.

> "As to [the establishment of a] Jewish group within the Society, it struck me odd that such a thing should exist. If as Bob maintains, the Jews are just like everybody else except they have a different religion, then why should they have a separate organization within the Society. In that case, why not have an Episcopalian Society . . . or something else?"
>
> Welch, he said, had made two fundamental errors: he has expanded operations before "establishing a firm base" and he has "overextended his lines of communications." Butler did not elaborate on this military metaphor. But he added that Welch was capable of believing the "wildest delusions and then rationalizing them to himself."

The agent also reported what members of the crowd were saying about the ADL: "A couple standing near chimed in. The man, a regular member of the WF meetings, asked whether anyone had heard that the Society had turned over its entire membership list to the ADL. He had received assurances that such was true from Robert DePugh."[23]

MANY OF THE BIRCH WATCHERS' DISCOVERIES WENT INTO RESEARCH files, thousands of pages that gave ADL leaders insights into the personalities of Birch leaders and the activities of chapters and members. This information amounted to one of the country's most comprehensive assessments of the Birch Society, painting a detailed picture of Birchers as agents of hate and serving as source material for countless ADL books, press releases, and pamphlets. But the voluminous data had another, more secretive purpose: the ADL fed choice bits of it to the nation's press corps, which in turn helped shape much of the media portrayal of the society as an enemy of fact, reason, and democracy.

The program led to some unlikely collaborations. While the FBI and the Birchers might seem like natural allies, with their shared hatred of the left and fervor for law and order, Hoover saw the Birch Society as a destabilizing force with the potential for stoking violence against top US officials. He refused to endorse the Bircher contention that Eisenhower was a communist, and under his leadership the FBI investigated Birch activities and recorded thousands of pages of material as part of a campaign called the Subversive Trends of Current Interest Program.[24]

Although the ADL and FBI disagreed about the civil rights movement, their common antipathy for the Birch Society led to a productive relationship, and Zack's team contributed intelligence to this alliance. In the mid-sixties, the ADL's Pennsylvania director passed along a tip to an FBI agent in an effort to defuse an inflammatory assertion: a likely Bircher named John Noble had told "an American Opinion meeting" that bones found at the Buchenwald concentration camp were the remains not of Holocaust victims but of US soldiers murdered by the Soviet Army. The ADL and the FBI apparently feared that such a baseless claim might incite violence against Jews. In 1965 Zack gave FBI agent John Noonan a tidbit that he thought might someday prove useful. "Our mutual friend," he wrote, "has identified a Negro woman who is probably the most active member of her race in support of the John Birch Society."[25] What the FBI did with the tips isn't clear, but the agency amassed thousands of pages of documents about the society, and the Birch Watchers were just one source that informed the FBI's own countersubversive investigations.

Zack's team cultivated liberals in the Catholic Church too. To counteract a Bridgeport, Connecticut, priest who had praised the society as patriotic, the ADL sought to recruit a national Catholic leader to publish a column attacking the Birch movement. This aggressive media strategy risked amplifying the voices of the society by drawing attention to it, but ADL leaders reasoned that staying silent was an even greater risk. Zack implied that the press represented an extension of the ADL's mission when he confided to a colleague that "Bob Creamer of the *Boston Traveler* was again used effectively to expose a local radical right operation." Creamer's story credited the ADL with identifying the individuals operating a pro-Birch "Let Freedom Ring" phone campaign that was harassing some Boston residents. The writer, Zack explained, notified readers that they could call the phone company, "identify the source responsible for these messages," and file a complaint.[26]

The ADL knew which reporters and editors were sympathetic to their views and tried to lobby them like an athlete jawboning a referee. ADL operative Harvey Schechter informed his colleagues that an A1 story in the *Orange Coast Daily Pilot* about Birch lecturer Lola Belle Holmes illustrated that its editor had become "a good friend of ADL." The *Pilot* had "checked with us late Friday afternoon just before they put the paper to bed," enabling Schechter to insert a bit of dirt (the nature of which was unclear) that cast Holmes in a poor light.[27]

Birch Watchers notched other victories in the local press, slowly and deliberately advancing their campaign and offsetting right-wing efforts. The Vermont news media, an ADL leader wrote a colleague, had run pieces that "effectively counteracted" speeches given in the area by Birchers. After Epstein and Forster published *Danger on the Right*, an exposé of far-right groups that drew on agents' findings, the ADL spun off a thirty-minute tape recording and placed it on local radio stations to compete with Birch propaganda. When a Bircher gave a talk to a group of New Hampshire high school students, Zack asked his contacts to help him find "a counterreaction speaker on the John Birch Society and extremism [to address] this student audience."[28]

Not all news outlets were receptive to the ADL's entreaties, contradicting the Bircher belief that mass media was uniformly hostile to conservatives as well as the stereotype that Jews controlled the media. Some papers sympathized at least somewhat with the society. The pro-Birch slant of "the headline in the [Bridgeport] Post troubles me to no end," one Birch Watcher huffed. Another pressed a New England newspaper to report on a secret Birch meeting held in a private home, but the article failed to materialize, and the agent figured the editor was in the tank for the society. Yet another Birch Watcher complained, "This New Bedford rag maintains a total radical right bias," and its story on the society "aggravates me."[29]

Sometimes Birchers wished to host events without the prying eyes of the press corps, but Birch Watchers lived by Louis Brandeis's creed that sunlight was the best disinfectant. Zack once worked with a Massachusetts doctor to alert newspapers in Boston and Providence to an upcoming appearance that was intended to be secret, a speech by Bircher priest Francis Fenton before an expected audience of 150 to 200 Birchers.[30]

Birchers who faced unfavorable stories in venues ranging from local papers to the ADL's numerous publications to large mainstream outlets sometimes found their careers in jeopardy. Some who were embarrassed by unsavory revelations sued the ADL for libel or defamation, unintentionally attracting more press attention. The Birch Society loathed the ADL as its chief nemesis and most vexing critic. Rousselot complained at a 1964 Harvard Medical School forum that "they're on our backs all the time." The following year Zack observed that Birchers were increasingly assailing the ADL in their publications and in letters to the editor, another sign that the Birch Watcher program had gotten under their skin and put them on the defensive.[31]

To fend off Birch Watcher attacks, the society took up a series of defensive rhetorical moves. Birchers repeatedly felt the need to declare that it welcomed "all races, colors, and creeds" and that it categorically rejected the ADL's charges that it was an engine of hate. Officially, the Birch leadership often took the high road: Birchers, they proclaimed, must be "men and women of good character, humane consciences, and religious ideals." The membership included "Catholics, Protestants, Jews, Negroes, Puerto Ricans and Indians" representing "all social, economic, and educational levels." Further, the society thought it was important to emphatically deny that it had ever "knowingly" admitted a member of the KKK, and its Houston coordinator went so far as to claim that eighty-five antisemites had been expelled from the ranks.[32]

Even some Birch Watchers knew that not every Bircher was a fire-breathing racial arsonist. National Council member Laurence Bunker bore scant resemblance to "a fascist type extremist," one ADL agent reported, and was merely a "reactionary conservative." Some members were similarly pleased to find a movement at odds with their initial impression of a band of rabid hate-mongers. One Salt Lake City Bircher had expected "to find bears, dragons, and such" but was "shocked" to "find no secret rites, no oath-signing in blood, just good hard work and good hard sense."

A Jewish member, Walter Kaufman of the Bronx, had heard rumors of antisemitism in the society, but after six months of membership, three of them as a chapter leader, he called it "the greatest organization ever," adding, "I am proud to show my JBS membership card."[33]

Welch was especially sensitive to charges of bigotry, which he called "vicious nonsense." He expended much energy attempting to refute such smears as part of a dirty communist plot to destroy the left's most effective enemy. "Our defamers do not even try to refute the facts on which we focus attention," he once declared. "They merely call us names for bringing these facts to light." The society's most oft-cited evidence of its tolerance was the composition of its members. Roughly 40 percent of members were Catholic, the society claimed, and in 1965 Welch said that the society had two all-Black chapters. The next year it announced that a few hundred members, including some chapter leaders, were Jewish, and that "Negro speakers" were spearheading the society's campaign to depict the civil rights movement as a communist-directed plot against America.[34] The organization asserted that the memberships of Samuel Blumenfeld of the Jewish Society of Americanists and of African Americans Lola Belle Holmes and Robert Dresser were living proof that the society harbored no bias.

There were at least a few genuine efforts to win support from racial and ethnic minorities. In Fontana, California, a Birch couple informed headquarters that they were seeking to recruit Black members and persuade Black ministers to promote the society to their parishioners. The couple lamented that numerous African Americans were "misinformed especially in the area, Los Angeles, where they are employed as domestics in the homes of JBS members." As part of this recruitment campaign, an African American reverend named Fred Martin showed fifteen Black ministers two Birch films. Another California couple thought that the society had "overlooked" Latinos and urged it to aim "a program of Spanish-language speakers at the large cities . . . with sizable Latin populations" to counteract liberal appeals.[35]

Nonetheless, the society was overwhelmingly composed of white Protestants and Catholics, and the presence of a handful of exceptions hardly constituted persuasive evidence that it was free of animus. Meanwhile, its own words and actions—most glaringly its crusade to impeach the antisegregationist Chief Justice Earl Warren and its official and insistent anti–civil rights stance—undermined its message of brotherhood. Although some Birchers and conservative politicians like Goldwater claimed to personally support racial integration while opposing federal civil rights law because of its supposed unconstitutionality, such convictions were more than drowned out by Birchers' seeming obsession with communist plots infringing on the rights of white citizens. Even some Black Birchers trafficked in such stereotypes. Having spent seven years with the FBI infiltrating the Communist Party, Holmes delivered a lecture that she titled "Is the Civil Rights Movement Directed from the Kremlin?" The notion that subversives were manipulating African Americans with anti-American ideas harked back to slaveowners' criticisms of abolitionists and aligned with the views of the KKK and other elements of the violent massive resistance to civil rights. The Birchers' somewhat sanitized version of this analysis gave succor to the sort of bigotry that its leadership claimed to abhor. "The KKK is such a strong competitor to the Society at least when it comes to recruiting members," Mississippi Bircher Ingrid Cowan informed headquarters.[36]

THE ACTIVITIES UNEARTHED BY THE BIRCH WATCHERS WERE GENERALLY neither as nefarious as the society's critics alleged nor as innocent as its defenders claimed. At the very least the society provided a safe harbor to antisemites and became a natural draw for racists. Birch Watchers succeeded in uncovering countless examples of antisemitic and racist rhetoric, questionable behavior, and conspiracy theories from both the leadership and the rank and file. The conspiracies evoked long-standing antisemitic canards—that sinister forces (code for Jews) controlled the money supply, the news media, and the global order—while white supremacists saw the society as an ally and linked arms with it in support of massive resistance.

Welch may have been able to exclude notions of "leg-breaking" from his magazine, but at the chapter level efforts to patrol the society's public image and purge bigots from the membership rolls were inconsistent. Ronald Carnes, a proud member of Chapter 899 in Gardena, California, wrote Welch in February 1962 that some of his fellow chapter members had raised "the Zionist question" at their meetings and distributed tracts written by Gerald L. K. Smith, who had railed against "Jew Communism" and "black savages ruining our cities." Carnes fretted that "this question will arise" again and felt uneasy inviting friends who were potential recruits to any future meetings. The society's leaders, wrote field director Thomas Hill, "were deeply disturbed to hear about the trend in Chapter 899." Yet in the next breath he downgraded it to "a ticklish situation for we do not know how serious the problem is." He suggested that a section leader attend the next chapter meeting and "see if the members get off on this particular issue."[37]

Birch member John Baker Jr., of Gridley, California, excoriated Welch for his relative tolerance. "I am sure that you are wrong in your evaluation of the Jews," he wrote. "This business of financing other peoples [sic] wars, partly for profit, partly to get rid of the other people . . . goes as far back as the crusades." The reply fell to Welch's assistant, D. A. Waite, who explained to Baker that "the Jewish aspect of this diabolical [communist] force . . . is only one part of the entire picture, rather than the whole of it as some falsely advocate." But Waite added that Israel was "run by Communists" and never forcefully denounced Baker's antisemitism or demanded his resignation. A note appeared on Baker's letter—"file under 'ANTI-SEMITISM'"—suggesting that the problem was common enough to warrant its own folder.[38]

Again and again, the home office responded to its members' hardcore bigotry with mixed signals. When a woman from Salt Lake City (a self-described "AMERICA FIRSTER") sent Welch a ten-page letter saying that only white Christians should enjoy constitutional rights, Waite replied that the "Constitution simply does not support your concept." But once more, he did not ask her to resign, nor did he forbid her to preach racism in her capacity as a Bircher. A member from Dobbs Ferry, New York, sent a handwritten note urging the abolition of "the Anti-Defamation League, B'Nai Brith, [and the] American Jewish Congress" and claiming that his "extensive study of this [communist] evil . . . point [sic] to one root—Jewry." Upon receipt, the Member's Monthly Message Department asked in an interoffice memo, "Is this guy . . . anti-Semitic or what???" A colleague replied, "He's a wild man!" and instructed the membership department to drop him. Sometimes, though, those who were expelled continued to maintain an informal association with the society. The home office ousted Wilma Oswalt, a representative of the white supremacist States' Rights Party in Michigan, but an ADL agent reported that despite the ban she had attended a large Birch event in Detroit.[39]

As these equivocal responses imply, Birch antibigotry stemmed more from a desire to avoid public opprobrium than from a heartfelt passion for racial and religious equality. Some of the society's hard-core proponents of segregation and communist conspiracy theories were fairly restrained in their rhetoric. During a convention to promote his far-right views in 1961, Kent Courtney, whose relatively buttoned-up style belied his strident views and distinguished him from more fire-breathing Birchers, barred an outwardly antisemitic group from the hall. Birch Watchers scoured every session of the convention for signs of antisemitism but found none.[40]

YET IN THE MAIN, DESPITE THE PRESENCE OF A HANDFUL OF JEWISH AND Black members in the organization, antisemitic and racist ideas and language were endemic to the society from the beginning. Almost as early, Birch Watchers helped expose these strains. In the fall of 1959, they noted, the *Bulletin* advertised gift subscriptions to the antisemitic *American Mercury* magazine and promoted the National Economic Council Letter published by Merwin Hart, a Bircher with ties to prominent antisemites who in 1948 had called the notorious *Protocols of the Learned Elders of Zion*, which purported to show a Jewish plot to control the world, "exactly what is being worked out in the present time."[41]

Before it started attracting the wrong kind of attention, the society made no attempt to hide its clear ties to out-and-out white supremacists. Kent Courtney and his wife, Phoebe, were ardent defenders of Jim Crow, while Birch coordinator Medford Evans edited a magazine for the White Citizens' Councils. Robert DePugh was a Bircher before he founded the Minutemen, a white-power militia. Westbrook Pegler, who had a history of using antisemitic slurs and had drafted the violent anti–Earl Warren screed that had been rejected by *American Opinion*, wrote other articles for the magazine.

As the Birch Watchers documented, the racism flourished at the top, receiving an official sanction that helped legitimize the very notions that the society claimed it detested. The society's highest-profile bigot, University of Illinois classics professor Revilo Oliver, had trucked in antisemitic conspiracy theories for years, and the society gave him a bullhorn to air them. He delivered a speech to a Birch audience alleging a "conspiracy of the Jews" filled with "degenerates, scum, dregs, [and] savages" and charged that LSD imported from Israel was fomenting chaos on college campuses. He once served on the "faculty" of a summer youth camp sponsored by Holocaust denier Kenneth Goff. ("I hope we can arrange for someone to attend this camp," an ADL operative wrote a colleague.) At the July 2, 1966, New England Rally for God, Family and Country at a Boston Hilton, Oliver blamed Jews for the erosion of moral verities in Western civilization. A thousand attendees reportedly greeted Oliver's antisemitic diatribe with a loud standing ovation.[42]

Some Birch leaders also sided with apartheid. National Council member Tom Anderson traveled to South Africa with other Birchers and praised the government as "stable, peaceful, prosperous, Christian"—"our real friends." Anderson defended the apartheid system and its leaders, asserting that "separate development of the races is not based on superiority versus inferiority, but on the fact that people are different." The purpose of apartheid, he said, "is to help these natives," and he urged that Americans give South Africa "time to prove that separate development, separate ownership, separate cultures, is not only right, but is the most feasible solution for them." In 1965, speaking to about a thousand well-dressed supporters at a Birch forum in Stratford, Connecticut, Anderson made what an ADL observer called "subtle anti-Negro" remarks, including "constant use of the term cannibal."[43]

Around 1964 the ADL discovered that Bircher James Oviatt, one of the most prominent haberdashers in Los Angeles, had mailed three thousand clients copies of the antisemitic newspaper *Common Sense*, a "rehash of the discredited 'Protocols of the Learned Elders of Zion.'" Oviatt also displayed a full-page advertisement for the Birch Society in one of his store windows. In a letter to him, the ADL wrote, "Your . . . conduct makes it crystal clear that you have committed yourself to a program of disseminating some of the most vicious and vile anti-Jewish propaganda ever concocted by sick minds." The ADL warned him that unless he ceased distribution of antisemitic literature, the organization "would do all in our power to spread his record of activities before the people of the community." Oviatt had engaged in other transgressions, like renting a storefront to the Christian Defense League, whose leader, Wesley Swift, was a protégé of Nazi sympathizer Gerald L. K. Smith.[44]

Oviatt denied the charges and fought back. He claimed through his attorney that his stores had had "several Jewish employees for nearly 50 years," and he sued the director of the ADL's Pacific Southwest regional office, the Southern California B'nai B'rith Council, local editors and publishers, and the national ADL for "libel and invasion of privacy."[45] Invoking antisemitic tropes in his brief, he decried "the Jewish press" and alleged that "the investigative and inquisitorial arm of B'nai B'rith, an international secret Jewish fraternal society," had paid thousands of operatives to compile "dossiers on the political, religious, and philosophical views of millions of American citizens." The defendants' allegations, he said, had caused him "severe and continuing nervous shock and strain." He wrote to his supporters, "I feel it is my duty to have it legally decided, once and for all time, whether or not a private secret gestapo organization shall be permitted to destroy an American's prerogative to freely exercise his right of free speech and press by a conspiracy of abuse, libel, economic pressure, and intimidation."[46]

The Birch Watchers also detected occasional instances of a Birch affinity for eugenics. In 1962 a few members in Los Angeles paired the distribution of society literature with copies of *Race, Heredity, and Civilization*, a book promoting biological racial supremacy written by W. C. George, the chair of the anatomy department at the University of North Carolina Medical School. Birch leaders vowed "to discourage, or stop, the distribution of any such extraneous literature—especially of a 'racist' variety—with our own pamphlets or publications," but they didn't publicly repudiate eugenics, and there's no evidence that officials moved to expel the offenders.[47]

In fact, the society drew energy from bigots, even as it tried to separate itself from their ideas. When a Bircher from Winslow, Arizona, complained that the society was insufficiently supportive of anti–civil rights insurrectionist General Edwin Walker, Waite retorted that the society had actually helped organize Walker's speaking tour with the Reverend Billy Hargis. But Waite jotted a note for his files: Walker, he wrote, was "now getting himself associated with and supported by extreme racists and Anti-Semites, so future developments must be weighed separately." Defending a white supremacist in one breath while denouncing white supremacy in the next underscored the dilemma: the society didn't want to alienate more tolerant conservative members *or* hard-liners. It feared that critics would use charges of racism to discredit the movement, but it wasn't always able to hide its darker impulses and associations. Sometimes it was those darker forces that revolted. In July 1966 Oliver, who had spent more than half a decade espousing antisemitism in his official capacity as a Birch founding father and whom even some members found repellant, resigned from the society. He claimed that he had investigated the matter and discovered that Jews ("the boss's bosses!") had grabbed control of the Birch Society.[48]

Even so, the stereotypes and raw hate kept leaking out from the top and bubbling up from below. By the mid-sixties the society had gained, rather than shed, institutional connections to white supremacists. It joined the White Citizens' Councils and the Ku Klux Klan in a successful effort to unseat Representative Carl Elliott, a liberal Democrat from Alabama, for being what one Birch ally termed "soft on the nigger question."[49]

THE LUMPING OF THE SOCIETY WITH THE KLAN AND NEO-NAZIS RANkled Birchers to no end, and they expended a great deal of time and focus defending it from what they considered scurrilous charges. In July 1964, when the *Los Angeles Herald Examiner* ran a column comparing Birchers to the Klan and communists, Rousselot offered to answer any questions from publisher William Randolph Hearst and urged him to attend a Birch meeting to "see first-hand how we function." On Las Vegas radio, when an ADL supporter denounced the society, Birchers lobbied the station for equal time to rebut the charges, as the FCC's fairness doctrine required. (The station proposed a debate between the society's leader in southern Nevada and the ADL representative, though whether it occurred isn't clear.)[50]

Each side took aim at the other, and the war between the society and the ADL spilled out in the open. Birch PR director Thomas Davis accused ADL's New England director of organizing anti-Birch protests and applying pressure that had ousted him from the Masonic Hall in Hamden, Connecticut, where he was supposed to speak. Davis was furious. Arguing that the hosts had caved to the ADL, he complained of "wide spread rumor mongering" that had caused "serious public embarrassment to both myself and my family as well as the Society I represent." He called charges of antisemitism "the worst kind of defamation" and demanded a public apology. Speaking on the topic of "the Jewish Community and the John Birch Society" at the Knights of Columbus Hall in nearby Milford, he won a standing ovation from some two hundred attendees.[51]

"The Anti-Defamation League is a 'Himmler' agency," one Birch leader argued. "It spies on other Americans and compiles information with which to attack them. . . . The ADL engages in private espionage against politicians, business and professional men and other individuals who are subject to economic or social pressure." When Epstein and Forster published *Report on the John Birch Society, 1966*, Birchers decried it as a "smear book." The society quoted a sympathetic Massachusetts rabbi saying, "In this declaration of war on The John Birch Society, the ADL has gone berserk."[52]

The ADL's Birch Watcher program triumphed, unearthing a trove of information about the society, ginning up negative press that painted Birchers as firmly on the fringe, and exposing the society's dark side to the world. At the apex of an antiextremist coalition that encompassed the White House, the FBI, the national media, and civic groups, the Birch Watchers made the far right toxic in the eyes of most Americans and neutered the ability of violent, conspiratorial, white supremacist elements to win elective office or dominate either party. Birchers were put on the defensive. They were forced to expend time, energy, and resources fending off the ADL's charges of racism and antisemitism, and the incessant public conversation about Birchers as a hate-filled group generated the impression that the organization must be tainted and ought to be shunned.

The ADL's aggressive espionage was one reason the Birch Society ul-timately withered organizationally in the late 1960s and early 1970s, but the society's ideology has endured even so. As calls for racial and gender equality intensified, resistance also grew more vehement. As pluralism and multiracial democracy became more embedded in the political cul-ture, the antipathy toward these developments drew more adherents. The society found itself under siege from the ADL and other coalition mem-bers, and being under siege by liberals fed the Birchers' impulses. That was one reason why a defeat turned into a kind of slow-motion victory for the society. Its promorality, antigovernment agenda flourished partly due to the resiliency and effectiveness of its activists and the growing popularity of their ideas, a gradual, decades-in-the-making development. Birch Watchers constrained the society and the far right for a time, but the ideas, activism, and style that Birchers helped pioneer has continued to thrive well into the twenty-first century.

Chapter 7

"LITTLE OLD LADIES IN TENNIS SHOES"

F ROM THE TIME THE FIRST NEWS STORIES ABOUT THE JOHN BIRCH SO-
ciety hit, around 1960, the organization has often been regarded as the
embodiment of a single man. Robert Welch, the most prominent far-right
figure of the 1960s, was the society's supreme leader, numerous observers
say. He published four books, delivered hundreds of lectures, and wrote
countless articles. Tens of thousands of Americans knew his name. By
1962 he had become an emblem of paranoid conspiracy theories to his
critics and an anticommunist hero to his proponents. He was so deeply
polarizing that a writer recalled his liberal mother forbidding him to buy
the Welch-brand candy called Sugar Babies because of the company's
ties to the Birch founder. Yet Welch's fans encountered him as if meeting the Beatles. A Bircher doctor from Indiana and his thirteen-year-old
son chatted with Welch in an exhibit hall at a Birch rally in New England. The doctor later wrote Welch to tell him, "It meant much to me,
and . . . to my son, to meet you and shake your hand." Another member
wrote to Welch, "I think you are the greatest man in *history*."[1]

Welch set the society's tone and agenda. Yet viewing him as the sun around which the Birch movement revolved has obscured a chapter-level dynamic in which women often moved his proposals from ideas to action; at other times Birch women acted on their own ideas without his input.

At one of the earliest gatherings of the Birch Society, in January 1959, Welch recognized women's potential power as activists for the cause. NAM leader Cola Parker had brought his wife, Martha, to a Welch lecture, and she found herself so engrossed, so eager to join the society, that Welch had to rethink his initial decision to focus on recruiting men only. He reasoned that since "the wives" were "extremely interested" in advancing the cause, they should be welcomed to future meetings. Founders should extend invitations to their wives, daughters, sisters, and other women they knew, as their presence could be "most helpful." By 1965, despite a leadership roster awash in testosterone, approximately half of all Birchers were women, according to one estimate. In California women reportedly constituted a majority of members.[2]

These women were underestimated, even insulted. A 1961 report from the California attorney general's office referred to Birch women as "little old ladies in tennis shoes." Decades later, report author Stanley Mosk recalled the origins of the moniker: "I really saw those little old ladies in political meetings," he explained. "They were the first to arrive and the last to leave and they were always making motions—and their feet hurt, so they wore tennis shoes." The epithet suggests ageist and sexist condescension as much as door-knocking fanatics pursuing communists under every rock. The label stuck.

Other critics viewed women in the society through a more nuanced, albeit darker, prism. These detractors depicted women Birchers as a serious threat who combined diligence, focus, and passion and infused the organization with élan and a sense of grievance. Beat writer Herbert Gold portrayed Birch women as having a serene exterior overlying a formidable interior. On a visit to the society's West Coast headquarters in San Marino, California, Gold observed women working the switchboards, running the in-house bookstore, leading tours for guests. While their industriousness lent the operation the "familiar feeling of an insurance agency," the matchbooks ("Impeach Earl Warren"), bumper stickers

("Support Your Local Police"), and pamphlets on offer carried an air of menace. At a chapter meeting in San Francisco, a woman with the last name of Lenox told Gold that she respected the Hell's Angels, who had violently broken up a march of antiwar protestors.[3]

But if contemporaries saw Birch women as manifesting what Richard Hofstadter described as "a degree of prejudice and social tension not customarily found among the affluent and the educated," they also exemplified resourcefulness and fervor for the cause.[4] And if at heart the society was, as it claimed, an educational organization, women were its shrewdest, most effective, and least heralded teachers.

THE SOCIETY'S NATIONAL LEADERSHIP LAY ALMOST EXCLUSIVELY IN THE beefy hands of stolid Birch men. From spokesman G. Edward Griffin and Washington liaison Reed Benson to Welch and Rousselot, virtually every top official was a man, and almost all of them were white. Throughout the 1960s the society's National Council listed more than two dozen men and zero women. Full-time paid coordinators, public relations officials, field operatives, and other high-ranking staff were similarly male dominated. In the society's earliest days Welch focused on recruiting brothers-in-arms for his membership.[5] The masculine skew reflected the era's cultural norms as well as Welch's belief that wealthy men had the stuff of leadership while women were useful appendages.

Exceptions were rare but notable. By around 1964 women held two of five seats on the American Opinion Library's board of directors. By 1966 Anne Dennison worked as a coordinator tending to members' needs. The speaker's bureau sent Black Americans Lola Belle Holmes and Julia Brown on national lecture tours, where they cast civil rights as a Moscow-directed plot. Occasionally a female Bircher gave public talks: in 1962, a member of the board of selectmen on Cape Cod asked Dedham, Massachusetts, chapter leader Anna McKinney, whose husband and son were also Birch leaders, to address a local workshop on the subject of "Americanism."[6]

The society's leadership was hardly different from the nation's corporate boardrooms and university faculty clubs of the era. For most of the 1960s women in the paid work force remained in subordinate positions. Their jobs were in historically female fields such as teaching, nursing, and secretarial work. They were also expected to volunteer in domains reserved for them, such as the Daughters of the American Revolution and the Red Cross. The realm of politics was nearly devoid of female representation; in 1965 women held a mere 13 of 435 congressional seats, some having taken office after their husbands' deaths (the so-called widow's mandate).[7]

Nonetheless, changes were afoot that swept up the Birch Society. Women's workforce participation had been rising every decade since the beginnings of industrialization in the nineteenth century, and by the 1960s women increasingly worked in paid jobs outside the home. In 1963 Betty Friedan published *The Feminine Mystique*, Congress passed the Equal Pay Act, and the President's Commission on the Status of Women released a report that called for greater gender equality. Three years later, with the establishment of the National Organization for Women, feminism's "second wave" became a movement. The conversation about where women belonged grew in volume and breadth.

The Birch Society and women's liberation emerged simultaneously, and the debate about a woman's place had two contrasting effects on Birch women. On one hand they viewed the push for equality as a threat to the traditional family structure and gender roles. Feminism's rise motivated them to join the society and defend women's rights as homemakers and caregivers. On the other hand Birch women capitalized on the second wave's emphasis on liberation, which made it more acceptable for all women, including conservatives, to get out and run for elective office, lead political campaigns, and rally fellow activists.

Women had a long history of playing major roles in conservative political movements, as documented in books such as *Women of the Klan*, *Mothers of Conservatism*, and *Mothers of Massive Resistance*. In the first half of the twentieth century, reacting to wartime mobilization, industrialization, and urbanization, conservative women in the United States combated ideas that ran counter to what they perceived as the nation's cultural heritage. They pushed schools to teach creationism over evolution, lobbied to ban alcohol, and fought to shut out immigrants arriving from southern and eastern Europe.[8] They sought to use the power of government to enforce white Christian identity in American culture while repudiating allegedly alien values like pluralism and tolerance.

Around the time of World War I, the Daughters of the American Revolution, the American Legion Auxiliary, and antisuffragist groups promoted the notion of "100 percent Americanism." The language would resurface among Birch women in the 1960s. During the 1910s and 1920s right-wing women seized on ideas in circulation that Russian Bolsheviks were degenerates and socially depraved. One US Senate committee investigating the Russian Revolution charged that the new communist regime had embraced a program of "free love," divorce, abortion, and other social ills. The group Daughters of the American Revolution was so outraged that it encouraged members to spy on suspected communists in the United States and plied "the art of guilt by association," as historian Michelle Nickerson writes. Right-wing women also viewed progressive government action as threats to the family unit; the protective Child Labor Amendment of 1924 would "substitute national control, directed from Washington, for local and parental control."[9]

Birch women updated this historical tradition to confront what they considered a surge in morally scurrilous trends ruining the verities they wished to impart to their children. They reached far beyond the household to defend traditional domesticity. Many participated in historically female realms like school boards and PTAs. Nonetheless, these were crucial arenas, and Birch women began to shape them. Still other Birch women ranged farther afield; above all, they refused to stay home. Their activism anticipated Phyllis Schlafly's *The Power of the Positive Woman*, which held that wives and mothers had a moral duty to defend the laws of nature and centuries of wisdom about gender roles and women's purpose. At the same time Schlafly implied that women had to be in the ring—and had to go for broke to save civilization.

Birch women's values and patriotism often inspired them to become leaders in their local chapters. In their view America's liberal elites had twisted the definition of Americanism beyond recognition, persecuting conservatives who honored traditional families, property rights, God, and country. Like the men, they saw the New Deal as an assault on free enterprise, but also as social experimentation run amok, breeding reliance on government and kneecapping men's ability to be the breadwinner. Rather than allowing liberals to corrupt citizens' minds, Birch women wished to define patriotism on their terms. Bircher Grace Terk-horn wrote in 1964 that "many good and talented people are unemployed because they're too American"; she saw patriots as martyrs shut out from the job market due to their beliefs. Another Bircher, Katie Voss, was aghast that Christ had been "taken out of schools" and that Christmas ("His Birthday") had become an orgy of consumption and profiteering. Mildred McGill believed that Christians should showcase their religion by proudly flying "One Nation Under God" flags on their car antennas. An Arizona rancher and society member—only her last name, Fulmer, appeared in her missive—argued that the American government promoted the wrong values such as sloth and dependence. "I am pretty tired of paying taxes to support a bunch of lazy people," she wrote. "This country was made great on *thrift* and *hard work*." The Reverend D. A. Waite, Welch's aide, once wrote that the Birch Society's mission was "to restore . . . the luster and freedoms that made [the country] great," and Birch women couldn't have agreed more.[10]

Many women were able to immerse themselves in the cause because, as one Bircher observed, the "men were at work all the time and women had the freedom." They took advantage of their affluence and their leisure time to demonstrate how a relative handful of core activists could influence politics far more than millions of less engaged citizens. Despite the Birch Society's patriarchal upper management, its structure empowered women at the local level, giving them an organizational edge. The twenty-person cap on chapter membership gave them a fair amount of autonomy within each chapter, and they gladly accepted leadership roles at this rung of the organization and used their networks to become expert recruiters. They lent out their living rooms, garages, and sun porches to show Birch films and hold meetings where state coordinators pitched recruits on the society's mission (one likened membership to joining a church). Non-Birch conservative women also employed word of mouth to laud the society and build the movement. William Buckley's mother, Aloise Josephine Antonia, urged one of her North Carolina acquaintances ("Mrs. C.W. Sauser") to establish one or more chapters in Southern Pines, her hometown, prompting praise from Welch for her "moral support and active encouragement." A sense of sisterhood mobilized women like Dolores Baird of Seattle, who hailed the kinship gained by "so many dedicated people . . . working so hard."[11]

Birch women possessed what the German sociologist Max Weber identified as a key leadership trait: devotion to a cause. They believed that the United States was careening toward moral destruction and that this impending societal apocalypse would reach their own neighborhoods if they failed to act. They united especially behind the field of education, taking their children to rallies to give them a crash course in Birch ideology.[12] They sought to legalize prayer in schools, ban sex education, and prohibit mandatory integration, a purported pathway to totalitarianism. They touted books and films depicting America as the greatest country on earth and in general sought to purify the seemingly toxic wasteland of American culture that polluted their children's minds.[13]

COMMUNIST MOUTHPIECES, BIRCH WOMEN FEARED, CONTROLLED THE nation's newspapers, schools, libraries, film studios, and network television news, erecting a wall of hostility to their own venerated ideals. They saw their wide-ranging educational activism as waging a war to tear down that wall. They created chapters, knocked on doors, distributed pamphlets, operated mobile libraries, swarmed PTA meetings, ran for school boards, wrote letters, made phone calls. They saw books, magazines, and leaflets as a mainstay of their campaign, a way to sate the right's hunger for alternative news and information, and they used Birch tracts to spread their anticommunist message to friends, family, and neighbors.

Women became active as leaders of the American Opinion Bookstores, which fed the entire far-right movement and which one historian likened to coffee houses on the left. The bookstores functioned for many Birch women as classrooms where they filled the roles of principals, teachers, and students. There, they drew up battle plans, taught, lectured, learned, traded ideas, gave advice, held chapter meetings, recommended books, answered browsers' questions, and fostered solidarity. They often managed and owned the stores; in Los Angeles County alone, according to historian Michelle Nickerson, conservative (many of them Birch) women helped run thirty-six right-wing bookstores during the 1960s. Jane Crosby, one of the city's first Birch chapter leaders, explained that in the

1950s conservative women often lent books to one another; by the 1960s they wanted "to come out from behind the bushes and get right out on the main street." A Bircher in Glenview, Illinois, clamored for more *Bulletins* to display on sales racks in the bookstore she helped run, while a volunteer at a Baltimore American Opinion store contributed funds, worked there every day, and urged the society to ask chapter leaders to better support the stores to keep them afloat.[14]

Education also meant shaping the ideas that public schools taught their students and the books that public libraries stocked on their shelves. One Birch couple exhorted citizens to "wake up" to the brainwashing of young minds with anti-American curricula. A woman from Pasadena, California, fretted that the books at her local libraries encouraged "rebellion against parental authority . . . , indifference to cruelty, and . . . pornography," and that the dearth of "patriotic books . . . available for children" needed to be rectified. Another female member denounced the distribution of anti-Birch literature in Catholic schools in St. Augustine, Florida, and urged the home office to counter this propaganda foisted on the teachers and nuns.[15]

In the battle for public opinion, Birch women took aim at the mainstream news media as well. Jane Wilson of Brooklyn considered the coverage of Republicans in the early 1960s "a national disgrace" and declared that the society needed to combat "the designs of the One Worlders and appeasers who are not patriotic Americans and would sell the U.S.A. down the drain." Galled by liberals' putative control of the airwaves, another Birch woman lobbied the home office to step up its dissemination of society literature. A woman in Dallas proposed that "in order to get enough people educated fast enough, there should be a daily newspaper in each city that prints the truth! It should be a real newspaper, with comics, sports, women's news," and full of "facts and not fiction." The women (and men) of Chapter 763 in Savannah, Georgia, started calling in to a two-hour radio program every evening to promote their messages about cultural decay and the far-left media establishment. "They are having great success," one Birch official happily reported.[16]

Hollywood's alleged promotion of smut and anti-Americanism became another frequent target. Pennsylvania resident and Birch member Mabel

Moffat urged the society to stop publishing an *American Opinion* columnist whose film reviews were overly generous to leftist entertainment-industry propaganda. Women watched and distributed Birch-produced films with particular relish. Superfan Sylvia Nobel of Cave Creek, Arizona, wrote that she had attended eight such screenings and "enjoyed them more each time I've seen them."[17]

Time and again, Birch women returned the focus to children and their susceptibility to noxious cultural influences. A Birch woman whose last name was Schubeck urged the society to run pro-Birch advertisements and organize more meetings focused on youth recruitment and messaging. Bircher Catherine Kloppenburg wanted to put what she called "Politica Americana," essentially patriotic books, in more homes. And Kathryn Vogel proposed that headquarters do more to urge members to take their children to pro-Birch events, to expose more young minds to patriotic ideals.[18]

Birch women's educational mission extended to the battle to preserve school segregation. In the Deep South and beyond, they confronted public school districts, leading the fight against court-ordered integration. In Jackson, Mississippi, they helped support Patriotic American Youth, an organization that taught young white people that communists were behind the civil rights protests and that freedom meant states' rights, which in turn meant the perpetuation of segregated schools. The organization shared office space with a local Birch chapter and a Birch bookstore. It also had ties to the local White Citizens' Council.[19]

But Birch women exerted the most influence on schools outside the South. They spread white supremacist ideas throughout the country and kept alive the notion that values of local control and individual autonomy trumped any mandates by the Supreme Court or Congress. They asserted that civil rights represented a frontal assault on the norms of individualism as they defined them. Idaho member Marilyn Miller expressed gratitude that J. Edgar Hoover, pro-Birch writer W. Cleon Skousen, and Robert Welch had helped her see the left-wing role in the civil rights plot. Undergirding her view was a faith in white supremacy. After reading an article written by Malcolm X in the *Saturday Evening Post*,

Miller decided that "negros as a race are loose morally and very highly emotional" and called integration "forcibly pushed by federal powers" a "horrible" communist program. Birch women and defenders of Jim Crow in Mississippi and across the Deep South shared a language and a worldview. Although they may not have belonged to the same organizations, Birch women swam in similar ideological waters, absorbing segregationists' arguments and pushing causes that Dixiecrats also endorsed. Like segregationists, Birchers fought to ensure an Americanist education, targeted school textbooks they deemed subversive, and sought bans on books written by, in the words of one prosegregationist Mississippi group, "leftwingers, liberal[s], integrationists, and subversive writers." In this regard, integration, communism, and anti-American activism became synonymous evils; women Birchers along with members of the Daughters of the American Revolution and Mississippi's State Sovereignty Commission all pushed to rid schools of alien ideas and led a similar fight to keep pro–civil rights and other progressive books out of schools and to "keep our schools American."[20]

Birch women were among the earliest antibusing activists, seizing on an issue that later became infamous. Responding to proposals to racially integrate Indianapolis's schools, Bircher Lori Bergman led a group of mothers in drafting a letter arguing that mandatory busing trampled the freedom of local communities to determine their own fate. Bergman and other local mothers sent the letter to every school in the city, hoping to educate the community's leadership, and she urged the society to follow the chapter's lead in mobilizing against forced busing nationwide. In Brooklyn a female member recommended that the society recruit activists from the antitax group Parents and Taxpayers Coordinating Council "to halt forced school busing."[21] In the 1970s female activists in Boston pelted school buses with eggs while handing out Birch literature. Indeed, Birch pamphlets and Birch ideas became the lingua franca of the antibusing movement. One student wrote to the Boston judge hearing a busing case, saying that the integration movement might be related to communism, an argument the Birchers helped popularize. Another woman— she didn't say whether or not she was a Bircher—became an almost full-time antibusing activist. She distributed Birch literature, adopted the

Birch technique of holding organizing meetings in her home, wrote more than two hundred letters each week, and handed out antibusing signs at nearby schools while organizing antibusing motorcades—the kind of boots-on-the-ground activism that distinguished many Birch women as they fought for the causes they cared about.[22]

From education mandates, it was only a short leap to get more involved in electoral politics. What better way to enlighten the public and challenge the policies they loathed than through political campaigns? In Austin, member Ella Hancock urged the society to teach the rank and file about recall elections to scare and "straighten" out a few liberals after their 1964 victories. Birch women in Michigan organized as a slate, running for positions as delegates in their precincts to aid the congressional primary campaign of Theodore Johnstone, a Republican ally who was running against a Romney-backed opponent and who had recently attended a twenty-five-dollar-a-plate dinner for Robert Welch. The *Detroit Free Press* ticked off the names of women powering Johnstone's run: "Mrs. Mary Degentenar, of Warren, a member of the Birch Society and Breakthrough [another ultraconservative group]; . . . Mrs. Sally Schloegel, of St. Clair Shores, a Birch Society member; and Jane Stocking, of St. Clair Shores, a Birch Society member."[23]

Some women broke the mold, taking on high-profile positions within their professions and publicly advocating Birch stances from there. Suspected member Ever Curtis, a Gloucester, Massachusetts, doctor who served as president of the Essex South District Medical Society, defended the Birch Society, saying, "I can't understand why anyone would attack any organization that is simply trying to educate the people."[24] One of Curtis's chief motivations was to fight the creation of Medicare, which she and other Birch women deemed socialistic and an affront to personal freedom. To that end she worked with the American Medical Association and appeared on Clarence Manion's radio show, attempting to defeat the Medicare bill in Congress.[25]

Others sought to inculcate in their fellow Americans opposition to public health measures backed by reputed scientists. Although studies had clearly demonstrated that adding fluoride to drinking water reduced tooth decay and prevented cavities in children, for instance, Birch women viewed the policy as a liberal-communist plot. Some allied with the Greater New York Committee Opposed to Fluoridation, an organization that tracked where the process had become mandatory. Bircher Arlene Best of Pennsylvania informed the home office that she was vehemently opposed to attempts to bring this plan to her hometown and vowed to enlighten others to fight the freedom-trampling practice.[26]

Not all male Birchers were comfortable with the activism of women who worked in the organization's headquarters. In contrast to women's empowerment at the chapter level, a cadre of male supervisors at the home office closely policed female staff, especially in the Member's Monthly Message (MMM) Department. The society asked its members to send them letters each month, and the rank and file obliged. Criticisms of the MMM staff were laced with sexist stereotypes, which bulked large in the archives.

Richard McKinney, a son of Birch PR spokesman Harold McKinney and chapter leader Anna McKinney, helmed the MMM office. McKinney's team had a big job. Staffers processed, read, and replied to thousands of members who had sent letters that flagged concerns about conditions in their communities and conveyed their hopes, fears, anxieties, and recommendations. Every missive necessitated a well-crafted, unique reply.[27] The messages served multiple purposes. They gave ordinary members a chance to voice grievances and proffer suggestions, to report on the state of their respective chapters, to forge a connection between an individual member and the national organization, and to provide intelligence to the society's top leaders. But to answer thousands of messages each month, the society had to staff up. The MMM office started with one person in 1959 and had expanded to twenty-one full-time employees by 1966.

These jobs created opportunities for women to find paid work at the society, and they constituted roughly half of the correspondents.[28] The work felt important, and staffers logged long days, as reflected in their weekly time sheets. One week in June 1965, for example, volunteer staffer Margaret Edwards clocked in around 7:55 a.m. daily, took forty-five to sixty minutes for lunch, and left work at 5:00 p.m. During four days in August, she processed 550 messages.[29] The work of McKinney's office was instrumental to the movement, ratcheting up pressure on the staff. His team had to write letters to temper the feelings of disgruntled members, to ensure that dues were paid on time, to promote the society's literature, to burnish Welch's reputation, and to field questions on race, religion, boycotts, policies, and numerous other topics.

McKinney reminded his staff that each of them "speaks for the Society," and their correspondence needed to evince a uniform level of excellence. He added elsewhere that most members' "only impression of the Home Office and Mr. Welch will be through the MMMs." The department was a repository where members "can complain, let off steam, praise and pray and know that we will understand, encourage, soothe, and help. We are all part of a family and we must be willing and able to help everyone who writes in."[30]

The culture of the message department could be punishing and acidic for both sexes but especially for women. All workers had two fifteen-minute coffee breaks (one in the morning, one in the afternoon) and an hour for lunch, "but," McKinney admonished, "all other time belongs to Mr. Welch." McKinney spot-checked each employee's letters and at various times assessed their quality based on multiple criteria: "typing," "neatness," "grammar and spelling," "quality," "content," "quantity." Another set of criteria monitored the employees' conduct. Women and men were to be judged on "Quantity" ("Is he occasionally slow or late with his work?"); "Quality" ("Does he make too many mistakes?"); "Industry" ("Is he often late or absent? . . . Is he a time-waster?"); "Initiative" ("Is he practicing self-development?"); "Relationship with Supervisor" ("How does he react to constructive criticism?"); and "Ability to get along with Others" ("Is he generally cheerful, sociable, and easy to get along with?").[31]

In truth the metrics reflected a workplace plagued by obsessive perfectionism and servility. One office supervisor chastised the staff for their shoddy work: "Quite frankly, I have been ashamed to send some of the memos to Mr. Welch that have been handed to me—with words crossed out and writing scrawled on the top or the paper wrinkled. Just out of respect for the man alone, we should be careful. . . . If Mr. Welch were able to personally supervise each of the employees everything would be right for he is a perfectionist. It would be a big weight off his shoulders if he could count on us to do the job right."

Such berating was commonplace, as were reminders that keeping up the highest of standards was an ethical obligation that served the society's larger mission. "We are a tightly-knit group, which acts as a body and thinks as one concerning the conspiracy and the items on the agenda," one memo reminded. Department employees were expected to be role models. "They will learn from what they see us 'the Home Office experts' do. Our members consider us the ideal and they have a right to think this way—so—we must live up to it."[32]

If chapters gave women the autonomy to turn ideas into action, headquarters offered them a stultifying, paternalistic milieu. Male supervisors often castigated women in barbed terms, demeaning them with sexist stereotypes. Men faced sporadic criticisms, too ("*Problem*—spending too much time on own work," read a memo about a staffer named George Edwards), but McKinney reserved his harshest broadsides for women. He commanded team members to cease their endless talking "across the desks or aisles," which he called "a tremendous distraction to others who might be just in the middle of an important thought or thinking how best to phrase a reply out and time is wasted." (He added, for good measure, "With regard to coffee breaks, Mr. [Tom] Davis has asked that I make clear that these are not a necessity but more or less of a fringe benefit.")[33]

Supervisors kept minute track of the women's habits and performance, repeatedly complaining that they were derelict, deficient, or both—a stream of commentary that made the climate dysfunctional and hierarchal. Employee Sally Riley received a barrage of gendered reproach. In a handwritten note, a supervisor wrote on January 6, 1966, that she "refused to take orders, dislikes criticism, haughty to annoyance of others. Work sloppy." McKinney wrote her another note, though he included "a touch of humor so as to soften the blow." She sent it back to him and threatened to complain about him to Welch or Davis. When she uttered an acerbic remark about a coffee break time sheet, McKinney catalogued it as another instance of insubordination. He also upbraided Riley for tardiness: "Work starts at eight o'clock and it is certainly not good for the spirit of the office to be continually arriving late, even though the time may be made up by short lunch hours which I do not approve of nor does Mr. Davis. This also goes for leaving before five in the evening. We are all here for a much bigger reason than our 'job' and dedication can most certainly be encouraged by example."[34]

A supervisor of Helen Tobin, who was employed at headquarters off and on between 1965 and 1969, misidentified her as "Ellen" and wrote, "Does fair work—has problems." Cynthia Newman, 1966: "Spends time reading on job—talking with others . . . is belligerent will not take supervision, kindly or otherwise." Jeri Yabbacio, 1967: "sloppy—very poor work—waists [sic] too much time." McKinney apparently asked her to resign, and she departed.[35]

The relentless assessments were matched by a punishing workload. From February 5 to July 9, 1965, a supervisor tracked the letter production of employee Peggy Smith and found the results wanting. Averaging between thirty-five and forty-two letters per day, Smith came under pressure to show better work habits and increase her output. On August 25 a supervisor checked her correspondence again and judged it mostly "neat," adding that she was "a little mushy on answers, but has a little imagination and creative ability." Still, she was "easily distracted." By fall the supervisor put a note in her file saying that Smith was "constantly reading personal mail—newspapers etcetera and is the first to share this news w/ others—constant distraction." The supervisor rated her as "poor" and ordered her to "stop talking and writing personal letters and to increase her average in the next two weeks from thirty-five to fifty." Smith acknowledged "talking too much" and promised to reform her ways, but her file covered only one year, 1965, so she may have resigned or been fired.

Not all the feedback was negative. A supervisor described staffer Francis Flanagan as "a great team worker." McKinney praised the performance and temperament of Marcia Humphress, a summer intern, writing to her parents in Florida that "her ability to get along with us Yankees alone was truly remarkable!" And some women clearly found their Member's Monthly Message work rewarding. Marilyn Lord left her job reluctantly because she had to move with her husband. "I would like nothing more," she wrote McKinney, "than to stay with this department and answer the increasing numbers of MMM's."[36]

For the most part, though, Birch women accomplished much more when free of the condescending, cramped patriarchy of the home office. With greater independence at local chapters, they forged a politics of social conservatism that was thoroughly modern and gained adherents among upwardly mobile middle-class suburbanites. They bound Birchism to other causes such as barring sex education from the classroom, policing the books that students could access in schools and libraries, and forging laws and polices based on their ideas of Christian morality. They artfully described the New Deal as inimical to self-reliance and, above all, rose up and mounted a crusade against liberal trends in society. Female Birchers fought to educate the public, control the realm of information and ideas, force citizens to respond to them, and steer the conversation back to their version of a moral code. Largely unsung, they helped launch a culture war that reverberates to this day.

Chapter 8

FRINGE

BY THE MID- TO LATE 1960S, HAVING SURVIVED GOLDWATER'S EPIC
electoral loss, Birchers defied easy categorization. In a 1965 survey of
650 members (including dozens of chapter leaders), political scientist Fred
Grupp asked about their motivations for belonging and reported that the
organization was ideologically heterogeneous and that the composition of
its membership was changing.[1] Approximately 60 percent of respondents
said they had joined for ideological reasons such as to save the United
States from communism and to promote individual liberty. Some 33 percent reported that their membership gave them social or political "satisfaction." Around 20 percent enjoyed mixing with "people who see things
the way I do" and viewed the group as enhancing their social status rather
than as a reflection of what historian Richard Hofstadter, in his 1955
Pulitzer prize–winning book, *The Age of Reform*, termed status anxiety.[2]
A small number of Birchers said their membership helped them to be
"better informed" and to "learn the truth" about events, while a handful
of others said they wished to "work for God" and "fight the anti-Christ,"
and a few cited more prosaic reasons: they wanted "to meet girls."

Some members went out of their way to assert their rational side, rejecting the sneers and ridicule they encountered from mainstream culture. Bircher William Lingeman called members "community leaders" who belonged to upstanding groups like Kiwanis, the Junior Achievement Program, and Industrial Management Clubs. Some Birchers proposed actions like placing anti-Medicare pamphlets in doctors' offices and advocating the abolition of the sales tax.[3]

As the society's notoriety grew, its membership patterns shifted. Before the summer of 1964 most members joined at the behest of friends and relatives. By 1965 they joined after hearing about the group through the mass media, and more new members came from the East Coast. Grupp concluded that the rapid growth of the society and the surge of applications from individuals unknown to the membership "had a divisive effect upon the organization."[4]

Never particularly harmonious, by 1966 the society splintered further. The home office investigated reports of infighting and created a "derogatory file" that catalogued members' transgressions. Mrs. V. O. Schwegel complained that some of her fellow chapter members lacked "Good Citizenship." In 1966, after the manager of a Birch library in Philadelphia feuded with other Birchers (the issue was unclear), he resigned. His replacement discovered a stack of pornographic films and books hidden in the library, prompting the ex-member to concoct a story and inform friends that his true dissatisfaction was that the society, in the words of field director Thomas Hill, was "not anti-Semitic enough."[5] Some Birchers, Hill lamented, had not understood what it meant to be "informed patriots," and others lacked "enthusiasm," a signature Birch asset.

Once flush, the organization was also now bedeviled by financial problems. The society had to refund money to lifetime members who had been expelled, recoup borrowed projectors and film reels from chapters, and figure out how to handle members who had lost their own money on Birch-affiliated bookstores.

Welch accused members of putting their personal agendas above the society's and issued an ultimatum: follow him or resign. In August 1966, the *New York Times* reported, "acrimonious disputes" had forced Welch to travel the United States to try to resolve problems one chapter at a time. During this period Hill informed his field staff that recruitment was flagging and a change was needed. A star major coordinator, Ernest Brosang, who covered the East, had pioneered a new sales pitch that every coordinator was now required to adopt. Over two full days recruits had to listen to a program called *One Dozen Trumpets*, in which Welch detailed his conspiracy theories and his plans for the counterrevolution on twelve four-sided albums, twenty-two minutes per side. The nine major coordinators, all men, had to hold these grueling recruitment meetings in cities from Nashville to Oklahoma City, Spokane to Detroit. Although attendees were free to smoke, pace, and grab coffee, they often needed to skip Sunday church services so that each coordinator could "indoctrinate and convert ten individuals to our program."[6]

Adding to the dissension and recruitment woes, Birchers who joined in the mid- to late 1960s increasingly thrived on discord and menace. While many new members were still driven mainly by a desire to rout communism, years of public attacks had made the society appear brash, somewhat unhinged, even prone to violence—and many extremists liked what they saw. They wanted in on the action.

In light of the rhetoric coming from the top, this trend was hardly shocking. The leaders' message—that the tentacles of the conspiracy continued to lengthen—appealed to fanatics searching for a community of the like-minded. At a July 4, 1967, rally in Boston, Welch thundered that the communist conspiracy was going "to destroy the family" and create "one homogeneous worldwide mass of undifferentiated robots." Fighting back required courage "greater than that called for in meeting an armed enemy . . . on a physical battlefield." The darkest impulses of the far right found a home in the society's ranks late in the decade, and those impulses went beyond the formal membership. The Birchers were breeding a sprawling movement, opening a Pandora's box to a more militant, disruptive far right. For all the attention paid to left-wing mayhem in the 1960s (Yippies, Weather Underground, Black Panthers), the Birchers and their allies were forging their own tradition of violent extremism on the right, privileging fisticuffs over the ballot. Back in 1962, at the peak of the national debate about Birchism, *The Nation* warned that by arguing that the enemy was already inside the gates, Birchers were extending "an invitation to engage in civil war, guerilla-style."[7] Several years later, the Birchers were demonstrating that such fears were valid.

In addition to fueling violence in its most problematic members, the society served as a gateway group for all kinds of volatile and bigoted extremists. Some considered it a potential springboard to armed revolt. Some made common cause with nonmembers, rallying behind a belligerent creed. Many focused on Jews as a source of America's troubles, complained that the society was insufficiently antisemitic, and urged it to be more aggressive. David Mends of Connecticut resigned due to "basic differences of opinion"; the society appended a note to his file calling him a "troublemaker" and "very anti-semitic." In September 1968 Robert Jones resigned because he found the society soft on the Jewish question. "Whoever holds the propaganda power holds the real power," he explained, "and the tragic thing about the Jews is that although they are very important in the field of propaganda here, most of them do not relate to being Americans first." Bob Weedn informed the home office that fellow members Mr. and Mrs. James Lowry were "violently anti-semitic" and recommended that "we let them phase themselves out." Weedn lamented, "I got my hands full of anti-semites since [neo-Nazi leader George Lincoln] Rockwell organized his group. . . . Looks like we'll have another 'purge' shortly."[8]

Danger seemed to cling to the society, and the threats both rained down from the top and bubbled up from below. Some leaders seemed to go out of their way to justify combat. At a chapter meeting at the San Francisco home of a retired army colonel, a key coordinator announced, "World War III has begun." James Kearney of Freeport, New York, arrested in 1966 for using a broken bottle to cut a man's face in a bar fight, was kicked out. New Yorker Bill Miller stepped down to find a more overtly violent organization that would attack the federal government, which had done "nothing to fight the Communists."[9] Although the society officially condemned lawbreaking as counterproductive and sometimes expelled unruly members, there were enough fractious Birchers to make it hard for headquarters to track them all. The fact was, the society attracted explosive personalities.

Inspired by the society, army veteran Donald Lobsinger befriended many Birchers and attended meetings but ultimately decided that he wanted a more aggressive, street-fighting approach. To that end he formed Breakthrough, a group whose goal was to "break through" the communist propaganda coursing through left-wing protest movements in his home city of Detroit. The group had roughly fifty to one hundred and fifty members and hundreds more supporters, and the Birch Society lent it ideological ballast, tactical aid, and personnel. With Birchers at his side, Birch films playing at his meetings, and a Birch front group called Truth About Civil Turmoil (TACT) distributing literature blaming inner-city riots on communist agents (a "communist-inspired insurrection"), Lobsinger and his men prepped for combat. He once told an investigator for the National Advisory Commission on Civil Disorders that Breakthrough wished to "arm the whites and keep them in the city, because 'once the city becomes black, then the blacks could wage guerilla warfare on the suburbs.'" The group formed a Douglas MacArthur shooting club sanctioned by the National Rifle Association, and in the fall of 1967 it organized gun-carrying whites in Detroit into block patrols and urged residents to store "provisions as suggested on the survival sheet and to purchase sufficient arms and ammunition for your own home defense."[10] Its slogan was "Study, Arm, Store Provisions, and Organize."[11]

Lobsinger echoed the Birchers' most potent messages. He lacerated the UN and the mass media (accusing it of "deliberate deceit of the American people"), and Breakthrough distributed a wanted poster offering a $1,000 reward for a citizen's arrest of moderate GOP governor George Romney, the perennial Birch nemesis.[12] He told seven hundred sympathetic listeners at a Detroit-area high school, "If it is going to take violence to save this country then violence it shall be." When an African American speaker gave a talk in a largely white suburb of Detroit in 1970, Birchers and members of Lobsinger's organization protested and, according to the *Baltimore Afro-American* newspaper, threatened, "N*****, we're going to lynch you."[13]

As the society both spread fringe ideas and served as a portal for them, association with it became something of a rite of passage on a journey to ever more radical activism. In the late 1960s Bircher Louis Byers left to establish the National Youth Alliance (NYA) to stop the perceived communist surge on the nation's campuses. Members learned karate, and NYA published bomb-making instructions and pledged to fight civil rights, hippies, and leftists. Byers's newspaper, *Attack!* (which echoed those dreaded leftists when it called on readers to "Smash the System" and urged "Death to the Establishment!"), was funded by Willis Carto's white supremacist Liberty Lobby. Carto, a leading Holocaust denier branded by the ADL as "the mastermind" of a massive hate network on the far right, was yet another ex-Bircher disaffected by the society's comparatively permissive posture toward Jews.[14] Still, an attorney for the Liberty Lobby acknowledged Carto's debt to the Birchers when he said, "It takes a lot of little old ladies in tennis shoes to support this operation."[15]

Some Birch members were too unstable to be confronted. Roger Mellinger, a Klansman, was a member of the society before resigning in late 1971. "He is a fanatic that I consider to be dangerous," one Bircher wrote. This member feared that any conversation with either Mellinger or his wife, who remained a Bircher, could end in violence.[16]

The Birch Society also inspired violence from its opponents. At the end of 1972, two shaggy-haired "beatnik-type" men allegedly hurled Molotov cocktails into the windows of an American Opinion Bookstore in Memphis, torching it.[17]

It was hardly surprising that so many fringe figures passed through the society. Birch language, ideas, and style sent members down a rabbit hole of conspiracies and resonated with those who viewed the growing tide of antiwar protesters, hippies, Black Power activists, and urban uprisings as signs that the communist-led apocalypse was finally at hand. The society continued to endorse films, books, and audio records that trafficked in conspiratorial thinking, such as *Brainwashing in the High Schools, Bi-Partisan Treason, The Case Against Fluoridation*, and a publication depicting Martin Luther King Jr. as a communist collaborator. (Birchers also sponsored hundreds of billboards showing King at "communist training school," which was actually a school for labor organizers and civil rights activists.) Other Birch books warned that rising crime rates required citizens to bone up on "every kind of weapon legally available to the civilian in the United States" and to self-deputize so they could act as vigilantes.

The war on poverty, a Birch-approved book asserted, had fostered "prole-
tarian violence and revolution."[18]

In the ever-present tension between mainstream and fringe, the fringe
was winning. It was becoming harder to argue that the current membership measured up to Welch's original concept of "the best known,
most highly regarded, and most influential conservatives in our country," a group "unpierced by the 'lunatic fringe.'" The society was attracting conspiracy-minded members whose views were hardly at the fore of
sixties-era conservatism and who were, at best, a minor faction in the
GOP's coalition. Mr. and Mrs. G. H. Peterson of Nebraska urged the
society to investigate an arm of the government that could "control all
of the employment in the United States without anyone knowing it until
too late." Lars J. Been Jr. of New Jersey said that the Boy Scouts "seem
to push NASA and ZIP Code and regimentation of young people with
uniforms and Advertising Council plug, and other suspicious ways."[19]
The society had to play whack-a-mole with Klansmen, Nazis, and a bevy
of other antisemites and racists, seeking to keep them out of its ranks,
even as the society's philosophy seduced them into thinking theirs was
a natural alliance. Four white supremacists in Dedham, Massachusetts,
who had studied the Birch movement urged headquarters to join with
them and the Nazi party to overthrow the US government and "give
America back to the White race. Let us begin now to send all the n*****s
back to Africa and make our country like Australia, a truly white man's
country. That is what we want and we know that is what you want."
By the mid-1960s, the home office in Belmont was expending considerable time and resources on stopping the "kooks + nuts" from becoming
card-carrying Birchers.[20]

In the days after Goldwater's defeat, it appeared plausible that the society could avoid the path of militants like Lobsinger and become a power
broker within the GOP. The Goldwater campaign had given the society
a boost, making it more widely known and organizationally robust. In
1964, the society spent an estimated $300,000 on advertising, and in
May 1965 it reached more than seven million homes by inserting a paid
sixteen-page pro-Birch color booklet in Sunday newspapers—a provoca-
tion to the hated mainstream media. One estimate put its membership

in mid-1965 at around eighty thousand, while Welch claimed a hundred thousand members, five thousand chapters, and a $5 million annual budget.[21]

Birchers felt the momentum, and their passion was unmissable. From roughly July 1964 to July 1965, the society experienced explosive growth, with twenty-seven thousand Americans joining its ranks, totaling one-third of its membership. So many messages flooded headquarters that one lifetime member waited four months for a response from the home office. Apologetically, Welch's assistant wrote, "You could not possibly understand how hectic things in this office have been for the last three or four months." Even as late as January 1967, the Member's Monthly Message Department received eighty-five hundred messages and more than $26,000 in donations and orders for Birch publications, and the pace held steady.[22]

Some Birchers eyed the GOP as still the best vehicle for bringing their ideas to a broad cross section of the country. Birchers active in local politics conferred advantages on the GOP too. New Jersey's Alfred Mierzejewski allowed his sixteen-year-old son to join the society, which deepened the son's devotion to partisan politics. To Alfred's delight, after becoming a member the teen still worked hard in school, continued his accordion lessons, and organized a Republican club for his peers. He recruited more than fifty members who were "working with more zeal toward the election of conservative Republicans than most of the adults." In Grupp's survey, about 60 percent of Birchers identified as Republican. (A far smaller percentage were Democrats who appended "conservative," "Goldwater," or "Southern" to their stated partisan preferences, and a strong minority of respondents professed independence from both parties.)[23]

In the wake of Goldwater's stinging defeat, some Birchers redoubled their commitment to two-party politics. Perhaps, then, the society was going to become a real wing of the GOP, a permanent fixture that might continue to pull conservatives and moderates within the party further toward the edge. Despite an official policy barring candidate endorsements, Birchers sometimes used meetings to discuss upcoming elections, debating whom to support. Members encouraged one another to participate in the arena and held candidate meet-and-greets. They understood that electoral politics brought sterling opportunities, including through the use of free media, to educate people on "the methods, progress, and personalities of the steadily encroaching tyranny." But sometimes they fractured over candidates—Howard Jarvis versus Loyd Wright in California, segregationists Lester Maddox versus Bo Callaway in Georgia. In 1965, reacting to Birch political activism in North Dakota, Welch reiterated his stance that individual members could decide for themselves whether they wished to support a candidate or to abstain from electoral politics altogether.[24]

Ultimately, however, the prospect of a Birch-GOP alliance fizzled, and any bonds that had formed in 1964 quickly frayed. Birchers remained a firm minority within the Republican Party, and their efforts to radicalize the GOP yielded few tangible dividends. Some Birchers ran for local or statewide office as Republicans, but they often got trounced. Others supported third parties. Birchers held few leadership positions in Republican politics and had no members in Congress between 1963 and 1970. In the late 1960s Birch ideas—whether anti-interventionism, conspiracy theories, white supremacy, or pro-Christian culture wars—and Birch tactics hardly seemed destined for the Republican center.

For their part, few Birchers saw the GOP as a vehicle for their cause after Goldwater's campaign. Birchers' distrust of GOP leaders—a motif since the society's inception—deepened. Boston lawyer and National Council member Robert Montgomery considered his own trajectory "typical." In January 1960 Montgomery had joined about thirty others (including Bircher Clarence Manion) at Chicago's Union League Club to establish Citizens for Goldwater to draft him into the presidential race. Montgomery had qualms about Goldwater even then. The senator had refrained from criticizing the GOP's "left-wing" 1960 platform, and later Montgomery "lost a lot of confidence" when Goldwater declared himself a Republican loyalist and when he seemed to affirm *National Review*'s attacks on the Birch Society.

In the fall of 1964 Montgomery's disappointment stiffened. He recalled that a local Goldwater committee official "asked me to attend a meeting to organize for precinct work," but when Montgomery questioned whether the state chairman really wanted Birchers involved, "I never heard from the committee again." Goldwater's campaign "excluded the members of the John Birch Society from an active part" in the general election and "made it clear that they did not want them even to attend rallies." Despite these slights, Montgomery and other Birchers worked hard for a Goldwater victory.

In defeat, Goldwater disappointed yet again when he stepped up his criticisms of Welch and the society's secrecy. Montgomery called it "the crowning blow." Birchers "had succeeded in doing more than had ever been done" to move the GOP to the right, yet "Goldwater turned all that had been gained over to the old gang and made it next to impossible for a conservative ever to run again as a Republican. He has added insult to injury by attacking Bob Welch and the Society and trying to destroy it."[25]

Bill Grede, one of Welch's closest allies, also soured on Goldwater. In 1966 Goldwater accused the society's "Welch wing" of "ulterior motives," embracing "conformity, the hallmark of communism," as it sought to gain control of the Republican apparatus. He then broke from his usual practice of confining his rebukes to Welch, bemoaning how "the worst job of politics is done in districts run by the Birch people. If you gave them control of the state organization, you wouldn't have a Republican candidate elected in [Arizona]."[26] After reading those criticisms in the *Milwaukee Journal*, an infuriated Grede, who had seen Goldwater's nomination as "a great victory," wrote the senator and countered that Birchers were "intelligent, effective, dedicated Americanists" and that Welch had "foresight and genius." Goldwater, he continued, had shown his true colors, becoming one of "those conservatives who join the battle cry of the Communists for the destruction of the Birch Society. . . . We are deeply concerned about the advice you are getting." Grede pointed out that his own state assemblyman was a Birch Republican, while another Birch Republican was running for a second seat in a nearby district, and added, "To have a prominent Republican like yourself condemn them with this release at this time greatly strengthens the position of their Democrat opponents." While Goldwater observed that Grede's note wasn't as "personal and abusive" as the other pro-Birch missives landing on his desk,

Grede had essentially called the senator a "com-symp"—just about the harshest denunciation imaginable.[27]

By the 1966 midterm elections Republican leaders were divided over the best strategy for dealing with the extremists within their ranks. When conservative leaders such as Buckley and Goldwater publicly criticized the society, they were careful to train their fire primarily on Welch, denouncing his conspiracy theories while refusing to alienate all Birchers. They wanted Birch energy and money but not the taint.

But Buckley's allies took offense when Nixon implied that they were worse than the Birchers. Nixon's aide Pat Buchanan had to assure Buckley and *National Review* publisher William Rusher that Nixon considered Buckley a respectable conservative; it was the Birchers who posed the true threat. "A conservative who repudiates the Birch Society becomes a much stronger candidate than one who refuses to do so," Buchanan wrote them. "Mr. Nixon is firmly convinced that the best interests of conservatives are served by their joining and working within the framework of the Republican Party. It would be a tragedy for this nation if conservatives should abandon the GOP to form splinter parties. The result of such divisions would mean permanent minority status for both conservative ideas and the Republican Party."[28] In a letter to Nixon, Rusher agreed that conservatives ought to resist "all forms of 'kookery.'"

National Review's readers evinced a similar ambivalence about the society's proper place in the conservative firmament. Clearly some subscribers admired the Birchers. An internal 1965 poll of 836 subscribers revealed that 5.6 percent ranked *American Opinion* as their favorite or second-favorite magazine. Still, 66 percent said they agreed with Buckley's anti-Welch editorials (14 percent were opposed). "Your growing intensification on the replacement of Bob Welch as the leader of the John Birch Society" was wise and persuasive, one reader wrote in a supportive note. Buckley never fully excommunicated the society, and tensions between mainstream conservatives and the Birchers continued to fester.[29]

Reagan showed similar caution during his 1966 campaign for governor of California, approaching the Birchers with a calculated mix of acceptance and rejection. Some of his positions, like his assertive law-and-order stance, comported with their views. Reagan and the Birchers also shared an enemy: Senator Thomas Kuchel of California, a moderate Republican, who had issued some of the harshest denunciations of Birchers of any politician. Moreover, a committee backing Reagan included not just moderate and conservative GOP leaders but also Birch supporters like optometrist Nolan Frizelle (who once said, "I don't consider the John Birch Society extremists—except maybe extremely American") and Bruce Reagan (no relation to Ronald), a founder of United Republicans of California, a Birch-friendly group whose endorsement Nancy Reagan cheerfully reported to Buckley.[30]

At other times Reagan kept his distance. He issued a statement criticizing Welch's conspiracy theories, and his campaign worked behind the scenes to keep Birchers at arm's length. A member of Reagan's kitchen cabinet sneered that Birchers were "a bunch of kooks," while press secretary Lyn Nofziger had a rule that Reagan was required to follow: no pictures with Birchers.[31] Reagan didn't want to end up like Goldwater, who loudly defended extremism as a higher calling, then paid dearly on Election Day; nor did he want to be Nixon, abandoned by the Birchers and subject to their attacks. Like most right-wing politicians of the era, Reagan tried to stop Welch from tarnishing his candidacy while making it easy for rank-and-file Birchers to join his cause. His victory in November validated this strategy.

Other Republican leaders took a harder line. They denounced the far right as a threat to their party's electoral prospects and a danger to democracy that was out of step with the values of the party's establishment. They attempted to freeze out the society completely, expelling radicals from their ranks while painting Democrats as the ones who refused to extirpate extremists from theirs. As pragmatic legislative and party leaders, they felt they had a responsibility to expunge Birchers from their rosters. As the far left began to outstrip the far right as the most visible emblem of the perils of American radicalism, some in the GOP saw a prime chance to paint Democrats as the true fringe.

In September 1965 the party's two most powerful elected leaders, House minority leader Gerald Ford and Senate minority leader Everett Dirksen, held a joint press conference devoted to repudiating the John Birch Society. Birchers, Dirksen emphasized, were "NOT a part of the

Republican Party" and resembled the "Know-Nothings" of the nine-teenth century. "We do not believe in extremism," he added, arguing that the GOP stood for policies such as supporting the UN, not the society's "get out" campaign. The society's views of Eisenhower and John Foster Dulles were "at complete variance with a whole tradition of the Republi-can Party," Ford, future vice president and president, said, and the GOP's legislative record was "in substantial conflict with the views of the John Birch Society."[32]

Three months later, Dirksen and Ford introduced a resolution, adopted by a Republican Coordinating Committee, urging every Republican to "reject membership in any radical or extremist organization includ-ing any which attempts to use the Republican Party for its own ends or which seeks to undermine the basic principles of American freedom and constitutional government." Republican Party chairman Ray Bliss chal-lenged Democrats to repudiate the far left and urged every Republican to reject extremism, especially its Bircher variant.[33]

Taking on Birchers gave Dirksen, Ford, and Bliss a way to reassert control. The GOP was no longer Ike's, but it also wasn't Welch's. Some Republicans and Democrats continued to regard Birchers as a useful foil, campaigning on a platform of anti-Birch sanity. In 1964 Ohio Demo-cratic senator Stephen Young ran for reelection with a campaign flier that pictured him in boxing gloves, shorts, and a T-shirt, the words "Pull-no-punches" across it. "In Senator Young's corner are the people," the ad stated, the "plain, ordinary folks whose best interests Senator Young has the courage to defend" against the Birch fringe.[34]

Establishment politicians in both parties agreed that Birchers were in retreat. Throughout the decade liberals saw themselves as spearheading the fight, but they urged the so-called responsible right to deliver the knockout blow. Back in 1962 Joseph Rauh, the vice-chairman for civil rights and civil liberties at Americans for Democratic Action, had warned that Birchers were "bent on destroying the very structure of democratic society. If their philosophy prevailed, what we now see as an ugly swell on the horizon would turn into a tidal wave that would engulf all free thought and free enquiry." But Rauh also believed that the liberal coali-tion had weakened the Birchers and expected conscientious conservatives to banish them for good, denying them a path to power. "Fortunately," he explained, "the Birch Society and its traveling companions now only look like a poor man's Secret Army Organization," referring to the San Diego–based paramilitary group. "And they will stay that way if conservatives will have nothing to do with them."[35]

Five years later the ADL's Arnold Forster and Benjamin Epstein echoed Rauh's analysis, predicting that "America will reject the John Birch Society and its allies." They had grounds for optimism. Goldwater's crushing defeat had seemingly showed the power of the liberal coalition to repulse the Birch Society, and the ADL's own efforts to expose the movement had extremists scrambling to defend themselves. Still, Forster and Epstein worried that the "hazy borderlines" they saw separating Republicans from the Birchers were inadequate to keep the far right in check.[36] Conservatives' failure to destroy their right-most flank might someday prove disastrous, allowing it to regroup, mutate, and eventually unleash an even greater menace inside the United States.

GEORGE WALLACE'S 1968 AMERICAN INDEPENDENT PARTY PRESIDENtial run made clear just how much the Birchers had soured on the Nixon-Reagan-Goldwater Republican Party. Birchers hadn't abandoned all hope for electoral politics, and Wallace's fiery third-party bid resonated with Birchers who saw his candidacy as a prime chance to take their country back. Talk of forming a third party, present since the society's earliest days, had picked up after Goldwater's defeat. John Weisman of Monkton, Maryland, wondered whether third-party discussions between Edwin Walker, Bob Welch, and Georgia governor Lester Maddox had gone anywhere, while Birchers Kent and Phoebe Courtney continued to entertain the option.[37] When a credible third-party presidential campaign finally materialized that year, many Birchers flocked to join it.

Despite their agreement with Richard Nixon's calls for law and order, most Birchers refused to back the GOP presidential nominee, whom they had long ago demonized as conniving and fuzzyheaded. They sowed doubts about rising conservative Republicans too. Although the society included Reagan's famous 1964 speech, "A Time for Choosing," among its promotional materials, its bookstore business manager also hyped

"She's Not Really My Type At All—I Just Love Her For Her Money"

When Ronald Reagan ran for governor of California in 1966, Herblock shifted his depiction of Birchers to reflect the derogatory portrayal of "little old ladies in tennis shoes." In this cartoon, a dour woman—perhaps Reagan's political wife?—struts through the house while Reagan confides that he's not attracted to her "at all"; "I just love her for her money." The tension pitting mainstream conservatives against the far right—their alliances and their mutual antagonisms—became a fault line in the modern GOP.
A 1966 Herblock Cartoon, © The Herb Block Foundation

The society said that its membership was open to anybody, but in practice the vast majority of members were white Christians. This Birch exhibit lets slip that fundamental to their agenda was the need to "Preach Christ." Birchers infused public life with their conception of Christian morality, prefiguring the rise of the most hard-line elements of the religious right.
Photo by Spencer Grant/Getty Images

The Birch Society served as a gateway extremist group with ties to numerous violent and white supremacist organizations. Donald Lobsinger, the founder of Breakthrough, found inspiration in the society's ideas and rhetoric, and some Birchers joined his Detroit street-fighting movement. Here, Lobsinger is photographed scuffling with abortion rights marchers in 1979. He was arrested multiple times for assault and disorderly conduct. *Susan Morse—USA TODAY NETWORK*

"America's tomorrow begins . . . at a John Birch Society Summer Camp," said a brochure advertising the society's summer getaways for teenagers. There was the standard camp fare—volleyball, tug-of-war, and campfires. But the society also promised unsummerlike seminars covering such classic Birch subjects as the "controlled media," "establishment education," and "political assassinations." The camp pictured here, in California's San Bernardino National Forest, shows cabins decorated as part of a contest to see which bunk could be the most patriotic. *Photo by Gina Ferazzi/Los Angeles Times via Getty Images*

On September 17, 1983, Georgia's segregationist former governor Lester Maddox led a parade of approximately four hundred Birchers through the streets of Marietta in honor of slain Birch congressman Larry McDonald. A passenger aboard Korean Air Lines Flight 007 (which the Soviets accidentally shot down), McDonald became a martyr to many Birchers. A doctor before he entered politics, he befriended Ron Paul. In death, McDonald took a place in Birch lore as the ultimate victim of the communist conspiracy.
AP Photo/Rudolph Faircloth

In 2014, in Fort Worth, Texas, the Birch Society operated a table at a forum for GOP candidates. By then, far-right ideas—explicit racism, anti-interventionism, conspiracy theories, and a more apocalyptic, violent, and antiestablishment mode of politics—had begun to gain primacy within the Republican Party. The Birchers provided a political tradition that inspired the Tea Party and other extreme-right activists and organizations.
J. G. Domke/Alamy Stock Photo

Kent Steffgen's *Here's the Rest of Him*, a book criticizing Reagan as a so-cialist wolf in conservative garb.[38] In 1967 Phoebe Courtney expressed support for a Reagan White House run, but most Birchers looked outside the GOP for a candidate.[39]

Wallace, Alabama's segregationist governor, had stood in a schoolhouse door and vowed, "Segregation now, segregation tomorrow, segregation for-ever," defying the Supreme Court and the 1964 civil rights law. His cam-paign answered the Birchite call to arms. He claimed to speak for white working-class voters disturbed by street crime, supposedly communist ri-ots, and communist-liberal domination of the airwaves, government, and universities. He spoke their language, and many Birchers felt inspired.

Starting around 1965 Welch funneled the names of Birch Society members to Sheriff Jim Clark of Selma, Alabama, whose forces had clubbed nonviolent civil rights demonstrators on Bloody Sunday. Welch hoped to lay the groundwork for a Wallace campaign, which he thought could "save our country from being taken over by the Communists." One report put the number of Birch chapters in Birmingham and its suburbs at more than one hundred. After Wallace announced his candi-dacy, Birchers, versed in organizing and messaging, recruited and trained nearly four thousand volunteers in California alone. "In state after state outside the South," Wallace biographer Dan Carter wrote, "dedicated Birchers stepped into the organizational void in the 1968 campaign; they dominated the Wallace movement in nearly a dozen states from Maine to California."[40]

Yet even some Wallace supporters were wary of the Birch stigma. While the candidate's team understood members' unmatched exuber-ance and their invaluable role as a field army, they feared that the as-sociation tethered the candidate to far-right extremists and spooked mainstream voters. One of Wallace's top aides viewed Birch supporters as fanatics. "We have all the nuts in the country," a senior aide told his boss, pleading with him to balance the ticket by choosing a relatively moderate vice-presidential nominee. "We have all the Ku Klux Klan, we have the Birch Society. We have the White Citizens' Council." If Wallace selected a middle-of-the-road running mate, "we could get some decent people—you working one side of the street and he working the other side."

When word leaked that Wallace had heeded this advice, some Birchers rebelled, forcing him to scotch his first choice. Instead, he tapped retired Air Force general Curtis LeMay, the real-life inspiration for the cigar-smoking General Jack D. Ripper, who bellowed about a "conspiracy to sap and impurify all of our precious bodily fluids" in *Dr. Strangelove*, Stanley Kubrick's satiric 1964 film. An architect of firebombing in World War II, LeMay had a fascination with nuclear weapons and drew howls of outrage when he endorsed their use while on the campaign trail.[41] Although LeMay had a record of innovative military leadership, Wallace's choosing him as a running mate was perceived as empowering Birchers and the far-right fringe.

Birch leaders such as Tom Anderson, Dan Smoot, and Colonel Laurence Bunker endorsed Wallace's third-party bid.[42] Bunker, a former aide to Douglas MacArthur and a member of the society's National Council, led the Massachusetts fundraising efforts. Addressing a hundred Wallace enthusiasts at a Birch supporter's estate in 1968, Bunker advocated fringe positions on Vietnam (he proposed outlawing antiwar dissent), immigration (some immigrants, he said, never learned American principles), and schools (he noted that equality in education "destroys initiative"). Bunker called Martin Luther King Jr. an "apostle of violence" and darkly hinted that both Democratic nominee Hubert Humphrey and Nixon wished to establish a national police force, unlike Wallace, who had vowed to "untie the hands of local police." Wallace, he declared, was "anti-narrow-minded, Ivory tower, professorial socialists."[43]

Other Birchers saw Wallace as a redeemer of the lost promise of America. When she wasn't writing police potboilers, California-based novelist Elizabeth Linington composed Birch pamphlets, delivered pro-Birch speeches, and donated office supplies. A chain-smoker who, like her mother, was a lifetime member, she wore a gold birch leaf of an "extremist size," stockpiled food in anticipation of economic collapse, likened the United States to post–World War I Germany, and strongly supported Wallace's White House run.[44]

The candidate had spent years speaking in the Birch idiom, leading the massive resistance to civil rights and characterizing the movement as a communist-led conspiracy. As Dan Carter wrote, "In the context of a decade and a half of anticommunist hysteria led by the FBI's J. Edgar Hoover," such red-baiting "nestled comfortably in a public rhetoric that accepted careless public slander and guilt by association."[45]

Wallace's authoritarianism—his refusal to follow federal civil rights law—appealed to Birchers' antimajoritarian convictions, namely that states' rights superseded federal law. The society's members were generally more upscale, educated, and business-oriented than Wallace's white working-class constituency, but the two factions united in their disdain and resentment of liberal elites. Birchers supplied Wallace with troops and the power of their ideas, while Wallace provided a skilled folksy touch that brought Birch issues more forcefully to the public consciousness. Wallace said, "We don't have a sick society, we have a sick Supreme Court," whose decisions had barred prayer in schools while permitting the distribution of pornography. The message owed a debt to Birchers' "Impeach Earl Warren" campaign.[46]

On Election Day, Wallace won five states and took 13 percent (almost ten million voters) of the total electorate—a strong showing for a third-party candidate. Perhaps more significantly, the far-right alliance of well-off Birchers with a campaign aimed at truckers, police officers, and steelworkers presaged a gradual realignment and a new coalition—a fusion of white economic and cultural factions, contemptuous of liberal elites, that promised to be powerful and durable. Politicians from Pat Buchanan to Ronald Reagan watched and learned.

DISDAINFUL OF HIS LONGTIME FOES, PRESIDENT RICHARD NIXON mostly tried to avoid antagonizing the Birchers. He didn't tangle with them as he had in 1962. He did, however, remain vigilant, and his Department of Justice's Interdependent Information Unit monitored the society, while the IRS's Special Service Staff swept the society into its investigations of ideologically driven groups. Occasionally the Nixon White House aided Republicans supportive of the Birch movement, such as Indiana representative Richard Roudebush, whom Nixon had asked to challenge incumbent Democratic senator Vance Hartke in the 1970 midterm elections. On the stump, Vice President Spiro Agnew labeled Hartke a "radical-liberal," while Hartke charged that Roudebush had

Birch ties and had endorsed To Restore American Independence Now (TRAIN), a Birch front group aimed at diminishing the power of international institutions. Roudebush ran an ad showing a Vietcong soldier pointing his rifle at the camera and accused Hartke of supplying the enemy with "weapons used to kill American servicemen" by supporting trade with communist countries. "Isn't that like putting a loaded gun in the hands of our enemies?"[47] It was almost a winning message, but the Birch-friendly challenger lost by a small margin.

Still, Nixon's GOP had put Birchers in something of a box. In order to succeed in Nixon's Republican Party, Birchers had to minimize their ties to the fringe and profess loyalty to Nixon. Although Nixon and some Birchers found common ground in their appeal to "forgotten" white Americans and paeans to the flag and love-it-or-leave-it remonstrations, Birchers were hardly a major strain of Nixon's politics or policies.

In the 1970 midterms, Republicans John Schmitz and John Rousselot were exceptions who proved the rule, candidates with Birch ties who won seats. But in order to succeed as Republicans, both had to play down their Birch connections and pledge to back Nixon's agenda and mute their criticisms once they entered Congress. Schmitz, thirty-nine, was the lone Bircher in the California State Senate in the mid- and late 1960s. "Unlike most John Birch Society members I've known, he has a sense of humor," a Democratic colleague said. He first gained a following for sponsoring a bill, which became law, barring the teaching of sex education in schools without parents' consent and enabling parents to vet any sex-related materials before they were introduced in the classroom. (Critics claimed that the new law had a chilling effect, stopping schools from teaching about human anatomy and venereal diseases.) Schmitz championed an end to federal income taxes and full privatization of the University of California system, which, he said, would end campus turmoil. He earned the ire of Governor Reagan when he became the only Republican in the legislature to vote against his tax plans.[48]

In his bid for US Congress, Schmitz represented Nixon's hometown, San Clemente, including part of Nixon's district from the late 1940s. Schmitz's campaign manager was also a Bircher, and a primary opponent bashed the candidate as a "Bircher masquerading as a Republican."

When asked why he had joined the society, he quipped, "I had to do something to get the middle-of-the-road vote in Orange County." Although Nixon reportedly dispatched a top lieutenant to intervene and stop Schmitz's nomination, he reluctantly voted for Schmitz—quietly, by absentee ballot. White House press secretary Ron Ziegler told reporters that the president's vote was a private matter. Still, Schmitz had to pledge that he would be loyal to the White House.[49]

Rousselot had lost a reelection race in 1962 and left his post as the Birch public relations director in 1967 but remained a member. In his comeback bid, he campaigned for Congress on an antinarcotics, anticommunist, antiwelfare platform. He distanced himself from the society, claiming that voters had tired of the Birch issue. He had a point. By 1970 the society was no longer a sexy story, and the media was more interested in left-wing than right-wing radicals. The narrative—that the far left was a greater menace than the far right—had shifted since the early sixties. This change, in mindset above all, enabled the far right throughout the 1970s to gain ground without facing the kind of opposition it had in the early and mid-1960s. Assumptions about progress—that America was ultimately better than the right-wing fringe; that the "kooks" and "nuts" had been successfully marginalized; that the nation would rise above its darkest impulses—became embedded in the political culture.

This optimistic view regarding the future of Birchism was understandable in the context of Nixon's first term. Both Rousselot and Schmitz had to tone down their Birch ties to be viable GOP congressional candidates. They reassured the White House that their criticism of Nixon would be muted even if, on occasion, they voted against his positions once they entered Congress. They defeated their Democratic opponents by roughly two-to-one margins in heavily Republican districts, the first Birchers to win seats since 1962.[50]

Once in office, however, Schmitz took on his party and the Republican president, refusing to abide by his pledge of support. In resorting to his Birch ways, he inadvertently revealed just how far outside the Republican mainstream he stood. Schmitz excoriated price and wage controls aimed at fighting inflation as a policy best suited to the Soviet Union. He denounced the Communist Party in the United States as a terrorist movement, linked the nation's social disintegration to Supreme Court decisions dismantling laws that had targeted communist instigators at home, and railed that the FCC's fairness doctrine was a way to give the enemy free airtime. Court-ordered busing to achieve school integration was "social engineering" at war with the Constitution, while a family-planning bill would induce "a contraceptive mentality" and represented "a first step toward national suicide." When Nixon announced his visit to China, Schmitz phoned a White House aide, withdrew from a planned cruise aboard the presidential yacht, and fumed, "I have disestablished relations with the White House as long as they pursue their suicidal policy of surrendering to international communism."[51]

His primary opponent's description of Schmitz as a Bircher masking as a Republican now seemed on the mark. But with an anti-Birch Republican as president, fears of a Birch takeover of the GOP, so intense in 1964, had abated. The Birch wars faded as an issue for members of Congress too. The organization seemed like less of a menace to democracy, wilting into near irrelevance. To liberals and the New Left, Nixon was a far greater threat and wilier foe. To them, the society seemed to have hit rock bottom.[52]

AFTER WALLACE'S CAMPAIGN, THE SOCIETY CONTINUED TO SHUN THE GOP, hitching its star to another diehard segregationist. While in the past the society had felt it was under a microscope and treaded carefully on issues of race and bigotry, by around 1970 the movement seemed more open to joining the ranks of white supremacists and participating in massive resistance to civil rights. It feted the likes of Lester Maddox, the Georgia governor, and became transparent about its links to his ilk. Before entering electoral politics, Maddox had made his views clear: he shuttered the Pickrick, his Atlanta-area restaurant, rather than allowing Black customers to eat there, as required by law. He believed the civil rights movement was un-American, communist inspired, and freedom destroying. He brandished an axe handle as his own symbol of massive resistance and gave out handles to fans. In February 1970 white residents of Sandersville, Georgia, mounted a campaign to defy federal law and refused to promote African American store workers beyond the job of clerk. They fired their pistols at Black churchgoers, shot bullets into cars driven by civil rights activists, and attempted to bomb African American targets. When local whites, including a member of the Birch Society, complained that the head of the state law enforcement team investigating the violence was "too soft" on civil rights protesters, Maddox removed the investigator from the case.[53]

Shortly thereafter, Maddox said at a Birch National Council dinner in Los Angeles that "deadly communist enemies" who promoted civil rights were committing "this monstrous crime" against free Americans. The Nixon administration, he said, "has proceeded to order police state forces to stomp the South, slap our children and kick public education in the teeth." When Maddox was invited to speak at that summer's God, Family and Country rally, race again emerged front and center. A mezzanine in the Statler-Hilton Hotel in Boston was bedecked with American flags, and an African American Birch member from Watts, Los Angeles, gave a lecture claiming that communists were using the Black Power movement to control the United States. One of the sixty-one exhibits was from the Reverend McBirnie's radio show *Voice of Americanism*, which, the *New York Times* reported, sold mace, police flashlights, and "heavy metal black judo sticks advertised as having 'two business ends.'" At a booth run by the Conservative Society of America, Bircher Kent Courtney warned that "busing and forced integration of the schools is destroying education," while the man at the Federation of American Citizens of German Descent booth was blunter: "There's something about the white race, the Aryan race, that is superior."[54]

Birchers were unfazed. Introducing Maddox, Welch called him "an honest man." After thundering against "Communist plans to force racial integration . . . upon public education and bring our country to its knees," Maddox received a raucous ovation. But he was so toxic that even the Buckley-backed Young Americans for Freedom (YAF), which in the past had set up exhibits at the Birch convention, boycotted the entire rally that year, and its Massachusetts leader said that he was "repulsed" by the Maddox invitation. "How do you go back to campus and sell Lester Maddox?" he said. "We sharply disagree when he advocates hitting people with pickaxes. Our conservatism stresses maximum individual freedom. Racism is antithetical to individualism."[55]

Courtney blamed Buckley for YAF's decision to withdraw from the event, charging that he "dictated this boycott," and huffing to the *New York Times*, "When one conservative calls another a racist, there's a n***** in the woodpile and he was it." Although three African Americans delivered remarks following Maddox's appearance, the presence of white supremacy was inescapable, and the civil rights issue animated much of the literature and set the tone for the proceedings. An article by Welch on display alleged that "black power militants" were actual communists who had completely taken control of Newark. Willis Carto's Liberty Lobby had a booth at the rally, featuring pamphlets decrying the "leftists" on the Supreme Court who had voted "to increase race mixing."

The flirtation with open white supremacy isolated the Birchers, and they drifted even further from the mainstream. "Bircher" remained a political slur, and few Americans thought that the far right had a serious shot at winning power. By the end of the sixties, many Americans believed that the magnitude of the Birch threat had receded. To a self-described expert on right-wing extremism like Gordon Hall, the Birch Society appeared to be frailer than ever, and he took a victory lap in the summer of 1969 when he asserted that Wallace's American Independent Party had supplanted the society as the leader of the far right. The society's annual July 4 God, Family and Country rally was somnolent, with fewer attendees than in years past, and Hall wrote that Welch, whom he called so uncharismatic that it was hard to see how he had ever attracted such loyal followers, walked through the convention with Birchers trailing him, the shyer ones reaching out to touch him, as if he were the Messiah.[56]

When Hall attended the rally in 1970, his judgment was even harsher: Birchers were "in very deep trouble." "What was once a gathering of far right luminaries from across America has become an annual hustlers' contest among obscure religious fanatics and racist crackpots," he proclaimed. Although Maddox spoke at the event, such Birch stalwarts as Billy Hargis, Edwin Walker, John Rousselot, Tom Anderson, and Democratic representative John Rarick were no-shows. "The far right," Hall declared, "remains the same politically futile and curious amalgam of crank economist theorists, a declining number of retired military figures, bizarre and rigid religious fundamentalists, racial bigots and otherwise well-intentioned but utterly naïve little old ladies in tennis shoes who seem to believe anything as long as it is cloaked in anticommunism."[57]

Occasionally, some observers mapped scenarios in which the future of the far right looked bright. In the summer of 1970, for example, *Los Angeles Times* reporter Nick Thimmesch speculated that another Wallace White House bid could reassemble the bloc of Birchers, White Citizens' Councils, and other far-right extremists under a more popular banner. If the United States lost in Vietnam, Thimmesch speculated, this fringe could "attract huge segments of the American population." If events broke the way of the Birchers, the far right could mount a comeback. This threat also concerned some of Nixon's top advisers, but Thimmesch concluded that a "right-wing surge and constricting isolationism are only distant possibilities."[58]

Most Americans agreed. In a Gallup survey of college students in early 1971, only 2 percent had a highly favorable view of the Birch Society, while a mere 4 percent of the general public viewed it favorably; if anything, the society's popular support had been frozen in place for the past decade, having hit a hard, low ceiling. Meanwhile, 48 percent of students and 38 percent of the public held strongly negative views. Around this time, the North Carolina GOP adopted a moderate platform recognizing integration as settled law, while one of its leaders bragged that "some of our John Birch Society members and some of our kookiest elements joined the American Party," bidding those fringe individuals good riddance.[59]

Unlike in the early 1960s, when Birchers reaped tangible benefits even in defeat, by 1970 the society appeared to have become an embarrassment in public life, and associations with it became harder to stomach. When syndicated columnist Jack Anderson revealed that the US Army had made an "outrageous goof" by publishing a 433-page tome "which sees the world through John Birch Society glasses," alleging a vast communist plot between the Nixon administration, the UN, the Supreme Court, and Martin Luther King Jr., the army promptly recalled and destroyed virtually all 137 copies of the book. Chastened, the military claimed it had been issued without the brass's knowledge. In 1970 estranged Birch member Gerald Schomp published *Birchism Was My Business*, an exposé billed as "the first public critique" by a former paid state coordinator, and the society began looking over its shoulder for traitors within. The same year, Chicago attorney Elmer Gertz sued over an article in *American Opinion* painting him as a Marxist member of the "Communist National Lawyers Guild." Gertz, who had represented a family in a wrongful-death suit, alleged that the society had falsely claimed that he had tricked the family into suing the Chicago Police Department. He ultimately won $50,000 in damages, dealing a blow to the society's public image, and the Supreme Court upheld the ruling.[60]

Other signs of the society's extreme bent abounded. In 1970 Bircher Nord Davis Jr., a JFK conspiracy theorist and onetime IBM executive who threatened to sue an ADL operative for her letters to the editor attacking the society, made a quixotic bid as an American Party candidate for the US Senate against Ted Kennedy of Massachusetts. Davis proposed ending the Vietnam War "by stopping the aid and trade we give to our enemy countries." He won barely any votes. He later moved to North Carolina, where he became a "prepper" (preparing for the destruction of the United States). By the 1990s he kept a .45-caliber semiautomatic pistol beneath his Bible, vowed to murder FBI agents responsible for the Waco and Ruby Ridge standoffs, and declared that white Americans "are God's special people."[61]

As the society lost the national spotlight and electoral ground, its rhetoric grew even more outlandish. While it had always trafficked in surreal assertions, now it was distributing *Rules for Revolution*, a pamphlet pushing yet another communist plot. The rules—disseminated at Birch rallies, reprinted in far-right and small-town publications, and pasted across bulletin boards in Boston police stations—were purportedly devised by communists to foment disorder in American society by promoting sex education, gun control, and other supposed evils. University libraries, the Library of Congress, and the National Archives concluded that the "Rules" were fake and not, as the pamphlet alleged, captured by Allies from communists after World War I.[62]

Around the same time, *American Opinion* published a sixteen-page article claiming that the ubiquitous peace sign—which at the time appeared as medallions around countless necks, on stickers and posters affixed to every surface, and in the notebook doodles of American youth far and wide—was a communist symbol that traced its origin to medieval anti-Christian crusades. According to the theory, the "eyes of the demon" appeared in an ancient woodcut of the devil and were "exactly like the peace symbol being promoted by the Reds."

"Yes," the *American Opinion* article went on, "I admit that this business is weird. But it does explain the comments in the Establishment press about a resurgence of satanism, and the proliferation of black magic shops in areas where leftist students and radicals gather." The peace signs, the author concluded, were "symbols of the anti-Christ." Questioned by a *New York Times* reporter, *American Opinion* editor Scott Stanley replied that "almost everything we do is controversial" and that the article had generated some two hundred thousand reprint requests.[63]

As an organization, the Birch Society had shriveled. Although its membership rebounded for a time in the early 1970s, its publications, associations, and style repelled even most conservatives. Birchers tended to view Richard Nixon as an apostate and were contemptuous of his policies of détente, Vietnamization, and the open door to China. At the same time, the society had suffered politically from the decade-long assault waged by politicians, pundits, the ADL, Group Research, and other political leaders and institutions. The ADL in particular had weaponized the information it had gleaned from its spying, publishing damning reports while exposing Birchers' most unsavory ideas and connections, branding it as beyond the bounds of legitimate democratic discourse. Although the Birch leadership was at pains to renounce its bigoted and violent members, the ADL and other liberal groups exposed the society as a way station for extremists.[64]

Paradoxically, however, just as the movement withered organizationally, Birch ideas, tactics, and strategies found a new life in the political culture. Although around 1970 critics rejoiced in the society's demise, and as the nation emerged from the crises of the 1960s scathed but intact, the society begat a host of canny successors that kept its spirit alive, burrowing into the political culture. It offered the far right a language, style, and ideology—confrontational, nationalistic, moralistic—that proliferated in subsequent decades until they finally became the norm within the American right. Its approach featured conspiratorial thinking and an antiestablishment, burn-it-down sensibility. More than any other far-right group, and more than the most hard-line Goldwater, Nixon, or Reagan Republicans, the Birch Society staked out a vigorous challenge to conservative orthodoxy and bequeathed to subsequent generations an extreme antigovernment zeal and rhetorically violent appeal.

Birchers' continuing influence derived from spotlighting issues, provoking opponents into a response, and garnering media coverage that nudged their ideas into the mainstream. They flashed the ability to command the stage and helped polarize politics at a time when the two major parties were sorting out ideologically and the liberal Cold War center was cratering. Most fatefully, they demonstrated over and over that the intense activism of thousands of Birchers could have a bigger impact than the votes of millions of citizens—a superpower wielded from the group's earliest years that ultimately become irresistible to establishment Republicans.

Haltingly, over decades, this fringe usurped the party's center. The trajectory was alterable, not inevitable, contingent rather than certain. Many Republican leaders worked to stop it, until they didn't. The society fostered apocalyptic thinking about the country's direction, mistrusted elites as traitors, and raised the specter that only drastic remedies, including violence, could save the country. Its brand of mass politics fed money, energy, and ideas to conservative Republicans. And by offering a home for conspiracy theorists, racists, and antisemites, some Republican leaders emboldened the right's most noxious and violent bigots. The GOP establishment's effort to court this fringe and keep it in the coalition allowed it to gain a foothold and eventually cannibalize the entire party. Over time, this uneasy alliance came to seem commonplace, part of the zeitgeist—more and more alarming yet no longer shocking.

Chapter 9

SUCCESSION

IN 1978, TWO DECADES AFTER ROBERT WELCH INVITED SEVENTEEN "A-1 men" to a hush-hush but not "even remotely conspiratorial" meeting to discuss saving the country from an internal communist plot, a new batch of invitations went out to a much larger group. Marking "the Twentieth Anniversary of the exact date of the founding of The John Birch Society," the twenty-four-dollar-a-plate gathering would include "some reminiscences about the early days" and speeches by society luminaries like Welch, cofounder William Grede, and the featured speaker, Governor Meldrim Thomson Jr. of New Hampshire, a rare Bircher in high elective office and someone who claimed that Martin Luther King Jr. was a communist sympathizer.

On December 9, about eight hundred Birchers met at the Fairmont Hotel in Dallas to celebrate the society's prescience, its successes, and its bright future and to announce, to themselves and the world, that they were not dead. "Actually," said Welch, "our influence today is about four times what it was in 1966." If some Americans were under the impression that the Birch Society had faded out, its leaders told the *New York Times*, that was because the organization had made "a conscious

decision" to keep a "low profile" and regroup. Since 1966, Welch explained, "we've been smeared so much that we couldn't get . . . new
members. They thought we were going to die." But now membership
was slowly picking up, and, the *Times* reported, leaders were "apparently
convinced" that the country "was catching up to what they'd been saying since the Eisenhower administration."

Several other attendees noted that the society had simply been too prophetic too early. "If the society has had a fault, it's that maybe what we
said, we said before it was popular to say it," observed Representative
Larry McDonald of Georgia, a Bircher since the early sixties and the only
one in Congress. "The vast majority of Americans are in essence highly
sympathetic with the views, attitudes and programs of the John Birch
Society." Grede recalled that in the early days, "it was almost a disgrace
to be a member," but now "we're quite respectable."[1]

Outside the Fairmont ballroom, however, reports of the John Birch Society's life were greatly exaggerated. Throughout the 1970s, despite an uptick
in members, the society continued to lure many diehard segregationists and
vigilantes, and Gordon Hall, a Boston-based expert who tracked extremist
movements, called Birchers "yesterday's men." Members like Allen King, of
Rochester, New York, found that the association had hurt their businesses
and that friends had distanced themselves—all because, King said, he had
tried "to reveal the conspiracy." In 1975, he finally quit.[2]

Organizational and money woes mounted. The society grew dependent
on Texas billionaire Nelson Bunker Hunt for financial support. The Vietnam War wound down, depriving the far right of some kindling, while
détente with China and the Soviet Union undercut the society's core conspiracy theory about the internal Red threat. So did the Republican Party's growing hostility to the welfare state. By the twentieth-anniversary
party, even Welch had to admit that his group had failed to persuade
Americans that "pro-Communist big shots of the self-perpetuating liberal cabal" were conspiring to take control of the country.[3]

In the 1970s, as the Birch Society devolved into a spent force, liberals
wielded its name as the ultimate put-down, using it as code for far-right
fanatics living in a fact-free universe and longing for a mythic past.[4] Even
in a nation moving rightward, the society had come to serve as shorthand

for the lunatic fringe. When Nixon nominated Assistant Attorney General William Rehnquist to the Supreme Court in 1971, reporters and liberals charged that Rehnquist had once been a Bircher. His name, other critics alleged, had appeared on a list of Arizonans for America alongside other prominent Birchers.[5] The charges were explosive, and they weren't altogether implausible. Rehnquist, a staunch foe of civil rights and school busing, had once allegedly showed up at a polling place and intimidated Black voters waiting in line to cast their ballots. As a clerk for a justice in 1952, he had written a prosegregation memo arguing that *Plessy v. Ferguson* should be upheld and *Brown v. Board of Education* rejected.[6]

Yet there was no evidence for the claim that Rehnquist was a Bircher. After he issued a vigorous denial ("I'm not now and never have been a member"), Ted Kennedy, the FBI, and Goldwater defended him. He had seemingly become the victim of a smear and won Senate approval—sixty-eight to twenty-six. But the point had been made: "Bircher" was one of the ugliest names in American politics; it was worse than being branded a segregationist.[7]

The occasional Bircher victory only underscored that the society was running on fumes. In Marietta, Georgia, after losing a congressional race in 1972, Birch spokesman and Democrat Larry McDonald won in 1974. But his tenure became a decade-long showcase for Birch fanaticism rather than an exercise in the deft use of power. A onetime urologist with unorthodox medical views (he claimed the apricot extract laetrile cured cancer), McDonald acquired a reputation as the most extremist member of Congress. His license plate said "JBS1," and a GOP opponent called him a "fascist," which hardly seemed hyperbolic for a politician who hung a portrait of Generalissimo Francisco Franco in his office. While in Congress, McDonald built his own private intelligence agency to discredit subversives, allegedly stockpiled guns at his campaign headquarters, and once suggested that Nazi war criminal Rudolf Hess should be nominated for a Nobel Peace Prize.[8] (McDonald died in what looked to some like the ultimate communist conspiracy but turned out to be a horrifying coincidence: in 1983 he was a last-minute passenger on Korean Air flight 007, a civilian flight, when Soviet fighter pilots, mistaking it for a spy plane, shot it down, killing all 269 people on board.)

As the remnants of the Birch Society indulged its most outlandish impulses, its trusty old attacks no longer landed. Birchers faulted Nixon's Vietnamization strategy as a sop to the communists, while a Birch film accused "pinko" senators of conspiring to secure America's defeat. Birchers' role in the 1972 presidential campaign likewise suggested weakness and confirmed that the society had become more afterthought than vanguard. Bircher congressman John Schmitz lost his Republican primary, and after George Wallace was shot and paralyzed, Schmitz stepped up and won the American Party's presidential nomination. This third-party challenge to Nixon was far weaker than the one in 1968. Numerous Birchers backed Schmitz, who excoriated Nixon as a patsy, cracking that he wasn't opposed to Nixon's China visit; "I'm only opposed to his coming back."[9]

Whatever the appeal of Schmitz's wit, it could not compensate for his or his fellow Birchers' extremist beliefs. He wrote the introduction to *None Dare Call It Conspiracy*, a 1971 tract filled with baseless, twisted theories, and called the book his bible. When a reporter asked its author, Bircher Gary Allen, about Schmitz's praise, Allen explained, "Richard Nixon has knowingly been an agent of the Rockefeller family, which is the ruling force in the Council of Foreign Relations, which favors a one-world superstate, which they would control." (Allen's son, Mike, later became one of DC's best-known journalist-pundits—and far from a Bircher.)[10]

Meanwhile, on Election Day, Nixon romped to reelection, delivering a clear verdict not just on George McGovern but also on the Birch Society's public appeal: Schmitz got a meager 1.1 million votes—1.4 percent of the total, a steep fall from Wallace's 13 percent in 1968. Schmitz insisted that his supporters "took a stand for what made the American Republic great," but he received zero electoral votes in Nixon's forty-nine-state landslide.

When Schmitz lost, a telling message surfaced among his allies, a note of defiance rooted in their contempt for democracy: if voters refused to return the nation to its rightful owners, then Birchers and their allies would take it back by force. One American Party official, an insurance salesman from Arizona, described the party under Schmitz as "a distillation of the John Birch Society, the Christian Crusade and the Minutemen. We're revolutionaries. We're getting together to try to work through the system. But I'll say this. We'll have constitutional government in this country and if we don't get it through the ballot box, we'll get it in the streets." Constitutionalists were entitled to rule, and either they were going to work within the system to achieve their vision of "constitutional government," or, if the ballot failed them, they were going to take up arms. By 1974, some members identified violence as the only solution to the ills plaguing the United States. The group's most prominent African American orator at the time, Charles Smith, told the society's annual Rocky Mountain Rally in Colorado that political elites had imposed "planned shortages" of consumer goods on the country, thereby committing an act of treason. Eventually, he predicted, enough Birch allies would win enough elections, and the traitors would face consequences. "We're going to take Nixon and Kissinger, McGovern, Fulbright—politicians of that sort—and we're going to try them for treason, and they'll be hanged," Smith promised. "Newsmen, take that message and publicize it. . . . The message they'll get is, 'The Americans are coming.'" Some four hundred Birchers in the crowd gave him a standing ovation.[11]

The society occasionally resurfaced in the late 1970s and 1980s—three players for the San Diego Padres were outed as members in 1984, becoming a news story for a few days—but the organization never came close to matching the intensity and impact that it had achieved in the 1960s. Most observers seemingly agreed with a *Los Angeles Times* reporter, who predicted that the society's "ideology may be so narrowly based and require so much precise faith" that "gaining mass popular support" would be near-impossible. In 1985 Welch died, two years after suffering a stroke, leaving an organization wracked by internecine feuds. His widow, Marian, repudiated his replacements, part of a series of factional disputes. Headquarters moved from Belmont, Massachusetts, to Appleton, Wisconsin (Joe McCarthy's hometown), and reams of files were stuffed in a dumpster, then eventually donated to Brown University. Enfeebled, the society held on, barely.[12]

It would have been tempting in the mid-1980s, the peak of Reaganism, to pronounce the John Birch Society a thing of the past. But it would have been a mistake.

WHAT FEW PEOPLE AT THE TIME REALIZED WAS THAT EVEN AS THE SOCI-ety faded from public view, its tactics, ideas, and rhetoric were being taken up by a mix of right-wing groups that thought Ronald Reagan was not going far enough in pursuing their goals. These included a variety of evangelicals, antifeminists, anti-immigrant outfits such as the Federation for American Immigration Reform (FAIR), and white-power militias that formed in response to a perception of betrayal in the Vietnam War.

From 1958 to 1972 big victories eluded the Birch Society, but it led the far right. After the decline of the society as an organization, Birchers handed off a set of ideas to those who came after them. These successors—inspired by the Birchers' example but more sophisticated in their politics—picked up the pieces, developed the project, and boosted the far right's power.

From 1972 until the end of Ronald Reagan's presidency in 1988, Birch successors held a fairly diverse range of ideas, and their representatives, typically white and Christian, built on the coalition of the working, middle, and upper classes that George Wallace had started to forge in 1968. Some took up the Birch housewives' focus on public morality, while others pushed for drastic government cutbacks, saw conspiracies proliferating, or sought to defend US sovereignty from internationalists and to defend the US "republic" from an increasingly multiracial populace. Many successors agreed that the greatest threat to the country lurked within. They blamed elites who, they claimed, had trashed the Constitution, family values, and economic freedom. But even as they inched closer to the center of the GOP, they remained on the fringe of American politics and policy, dissidents and rebels trying to claw their way to power.

Throughout the 1970s the country seemed to them to be moving in the wrong direction, plagued by presidential scandal, sexual liberation, economic stagnation, an ineffectual American foreign policy, and deepening cynicism about government. Birch successors skillfully exploited all this turbulence. The society's most consequential offspring in the 1970s and 1980s were culture warriors, the most ardent of them on the Christian right. From its earliest days, the society had a Christian bent. It took its name from a fundamentalist Baptist minister and barred the secular from membership—professed atheism was a surefire way to have an application rejected. It drew support from many preachers, priests, and ministers, including the Reverend Billy James Hargis, Boston archbishop Cardinal Cushing, and D. A. Waite, a fundamentalist Baptist pastor and Welch's full-time assistant, who warned that a "communist slave state" threatened freedom of religion. "Religious fundamentalists," Waite wrote a member in Oregon, "are some of our best possible allies, and [I] am doing everything I can to win more to our cause."[13]

Conservative Christians evolved into the Republican Party's largest, most dependable voting bloc. The Birch Society's religious proclivities, its apocalyptic rhetoric and faith in the end times, spoke to Christian activists who were growing concerned that the nation's moral fiber was rotting from within, and that communists had corrupted America's children with satanic ideas. The society's successors included both the individuals who influenced grassroots politics and the organizations that sustained those movements. Phyllis Schlafly's Eagle Forum, Jerry Falwell's Moral Majority, and Pat Robertson's Christian Coalition drew people and ideas from the Birch movement, and these larger, politically savvier groups helped radicalize the right in general.

Sometimes the links between Birchers and the religious right were direct and straightforward. Schlafly was a Bircher before apparently resigning in 1964. She had befriended Welch, written a best-selling pro-Goldwater book (*A Choice Not an Echo*), and, like so many Birch women, used her identity as wife and mother as a springboard to her moral agitation. (In 1962 she canceled her *National Review* subscription to protest Buckley's criticism of Welch and asked Buckley to send the refund to Welch or Pope John Paul.) A mother of six with degrees from Washington University and Radcliffe College, she challenged Betty Friedan's argument, in *The Feminine Mystique*, that women yearned for professional careers outside the home, though she herself had a thriving one.[14] At least a few of Schlafly's acolytes, like Dorothy Slade, who led the movement against the Equal Rights Amendment (ERA) in North Carolina, were also Birchers. The society's spokesman John McManus recalled that Birchers were extremely active in Schlafly's campaign; they "distributed literature, presented speakers, and informed legislators at the state level about the need" to block the amendment's ratification. Birch leader John Schmitz authored "Look Out! They're Trying to Draft Your Daughter" in *American Opinion*, a tract that received wide distribution among anti-ERA activists. And two Birchers—Oklahoma state senator Mary Helm and retired army general Andrew Gatsis—delivered anti-ERA lectures nationwide. Two years before the issue burst into the national conscience, the Birch Society derided the ERA as a threat to "women's freedom."[15]

The society also helped pioneer some antiabortion rhetoric and tactics, and religious activists and leaders later helped push the issue toward the center of the conservative movement. In 1970 Bircher and Wisconsin state representative Kenneth Merkel said a federal court decision that liberalized abortion in early pregnancy was "typical of the sickness that is contagious in our federal courts." Joining with Catholic leaders, Merkel helped lead a "right to life" effort in Wisconsin. In the early 1970s Larry McDonald and Schmitz picketed clinics where abortions were performed. Birchers excelled in dramatizing issues in lurid ways. Abortion was equated with murder. At a Birch Society summer camp for youths, which the society started hosting in the late seventies, a Birch leader brought a vial that she said held a dead fetus and had campers pass it around. By the late 1970s Schlafly was also organizing around the issue, and when a handful of antiabortion GOP candidates won surprise Senate victories in the 1978 midterms, evangelical leaders realized that abortion could galvanize voters as a moral catchall.[16] Other facets of the society's moral agitation—policing the schools and warring with the mass media—presaged the Moral Majority and the Christian Coalition, two of the most influential grassroots religious-right groups of the 1980s. Both Birch successors drew on the society's language and ideas, and several former Birchers helped lead these organizations.

Falwell, a Baptist minister from Virginia, launched his organization in 1979, which owed much to the Birch Society. Falwell evinced the society's apocalyptic fervor, arguing that if fundamentalists failed to stop abortion and porn, "America will face the judgment of God." His Moral Majority updated the society's idea that America was decaying from within, railing against the encroachments of teachers' unions, feminists, secular humanists, and other "degenerates."[17] Like the Birch Society, the Moral Majority, though mostly Baptist, set aside theological differences and even included Catholics. Like Birchers, Moral Majority members belonged to chapters, received membership cards, tuned in to their own media programs, and tapped clergy to infuse religious purpose into social life. Bircher enemies—the ADL, NAACP, and AFL-CIO—were almost identical to the Moral Majority's. Falwell's rhetoric echoed Welch's, with its fear-mongering about "militant homosexuals, atheists . . . , arsonists and saboteurs," as well as pornographers, communists, and schemers in Washington.[18]

Other people and groups in the religious right absorbed the society's ideas, energy, and tactics while also moving the culture war in new directions. While serving as a pastor at the Scott Memorial Baptist Church in San Diego in the 1960s and 1970s, Tim LaHaye regularly lectured and ran training seminars for the Birch Society. LaHaye helped lead on several causes popular with the religious right. In 1978 he worked to pass California's Proposition 6, which banned gays and lesbians from teaching in public schools. As gay rights became a flashpoint in the 1970s, former Birchers such as LaHaye seized on it as a code for the far-left's alleged antifamily agenda, adapting the Birch Society's worldview to a hot-button social issue. LaHaye lobbied for bans on pornography, served on the Moral Majority's board, and cofounded the Council for National Policy (CNP), a coalition whose goal was to bring "focus and force" to the conservative cause. LaHaye wished to "remove all humanists from public office and replace them with pro-moral political leaders." The council's members included onetime Birchers, and the military veterans, wealthy businessmen, and evangelical leaders who belonged to it bore some resemblance to the makeup of the early Birch membership. CNP operated in secrecy, with one critic describing it as "a slick, updated re-packaging of Birch Society philosophy" and "creating a rightist counterpoint to established power." One CNP goal was to counter the Council on Foreign Relations, which Birchers and their allies considered a Rockefeller-driven plot to control US foreign policy. Allen's *None Dare Call It Conspiracy* inspired the CNP, and Bircher Nelson Bunker Hunt, the pro-Birch Coors family, Amway executive Richard DeVos, and Birch founder Fred Koch's children Charles and David Koch helped fund the CNP. Bircher James Quayle (father of the senator and future vice president) also provided support.[19]

Consisting of small prayer circles that mobilized women to fight feminism, abolish abortion, and ban "obscene" books, Concerned Women for America, founded by LaHaye's wife, Beverly, also took up Birchite themes and methods. Her group established chapters in virtually every state and sought to defend Christianity, US sovereignty, a patriotic education, and traditional gender roles. Like Birchers, Beverly LaHaye helped lead a movement of Christian parents battling a school board in Hawkins County, Tennessee, to ban textbooks that allegedly promoted "secular humanism" and were anti-Christian. Echoing the language of Birchers and drawing on the sustaining power of Birch women, Beverly LaHaye once told members of her organization that "you will be strong, noncompromising and speaking boldly for truth" and urged them to "wake up Americans and wake up women to stand strong in this evil day."[20]

Bircher themes and individuals also inspired Christian reconstructionist theologian R. J. Rushdoony's movement in the 1960s and 1970s. Rushdoony served as a pastor in Santa Cruz, California, befriended Robert Welch, and praised the society as an effective moral instrument with "a plan of operation which has strong resemblance to the early church" because both were "criticized, hated, and attacked." After Goldwater's defeat he delivered a series of lectures outlining his philosophy, and "many of his early supporters were in the John Birch Society," his son, Mark, told an interviewer. Rushdoony contributed the idea of Christian Reconstructionism—the use of biblical law as the basis for rebuilding society—decried state-run schools as a blight, spurred on the homeschooling movement, railed at a one-world "super-state," and offered what one historian described as "a massive cultural indictment of twentieth-century America on biblical grounds"—echoing at least some of the Birch Society's rhetoric and stands.[21]

As the power of the religious right's grass roots became apparent to Republican conservatives, they drew on another Birch tradition: fusing disparate philosophies of the right and far right. Birchers had used front groups such as the Committee Against Summit Entanglements to mobilize activists who didn't always see eye to eye. By rallying behind a single, common cause, they could sublimate their differences and join hands to achieve a shared goal. In 1978 that goal was to block the proposed treaty to return the Panama Canal to Panama, and conservative leaders summoned mainstream conservatives who tended to support a strong US role in the world to unite with more zealous anti-interventionists in opposition.

Four US presidents—from Lyndon Johnson to Jimmy Carter—had negotiated for the canal's return, and the treaty enjoyed bipartisan support in the Senate. Both these attributes were flashing red lights for Birchers. Amid détente with the USSR and defeat in Vietnam (not to mention treachery stretching back decades to Yalta, Korea, and Hungary), conservative nationalists argued that a canal paid for in American blood and treasure should stay in American hands. Still game for the occasional inflammatory sound bite, Robert Welch charged that with the proposed treaty, "the most powerful nation on earth" was "helping and encouraging Torrijos, Castro, and Brezhnev"—all left-wing dictators—on behalf of "a poor little pipsqueak domain." (*New York Times* columnist Tom Wicker called Welch's argument a "fierce polemic" grounded in "hysterics.") Others in the mainstream and far-right wings of the conservative movement picked up the Birch charge that elites had sold out national sovereignty. Barry Goldwater corresponded with Bircher Spruille Braden, the former ambassador, who also conferred about the issue with Welch. Even as mainstream conservatives such as Goldwater and Reagan led the effort to oppose the return of the canal, they made peace with Birchers and drew on Birch ideas about sovereignty to stop the treaty in the Senate.[22]

Although the Senate ultimately ratified the treaty, the alliance that formed in support of the opposition showed the possibilities: the religious right's grassroots energy had joined with populist defenders of US sovereignty to create a mass movement replete with rallies, campaign appeals, and fired-up activists. Birch successors also had some actual victories in the late 1970s: Schlafly's movement halted passage of the ERA. Jerry Falwell founded the Moral Majority, thrusting "prolife" advocacy into the pantheon of right-wing wedge issues. And several wins that suppressed the push for gay rights forced Republican leaders to heed the concerns of this mostly white bloc of religious voters. Though some evangelicals had supported the born-again Jimmy Carter in 1976, they ultimately broke with him, disappointed that he governed as a progressive on social issues.

Economic libertarianism—another Bircher cause—was on the ascent as well. At times it was able to mix radical antigovernment ideas on issues of business regulation, taxes, and spending with Christian morality in an uneasy combination. But in other instances libertarians emphasized their dramatic antistatist positions. In the 1980 Libertarian Party presidential campaign, for instance, strategists for presidential and vice-presidential nominees Ed Clark and David Koch (whose brother Charles, like his father, had once been a Bircher) described one of the campaign's cornerstones as "non-interventionist foreign policy," as distinct from Reagan's internationalist approach.[23]

REAGAN UNDERSTOOD THAT BUILDING A COALITION REQUIRED KEEPING elements of the Birch movement—anti–civil rights Wallaceites, white working-class voters motivated by the idea that a liberal culture sought to erode their identities and values—in his camp. He kicked off his 1980 general election campaign in Neshoba County, Mississippi, where three civil rights workers had been murdered in 1964, and declared, "I believe in states' rights," a statement that resonated with Birchers and allies who resisted the civil rights revolution. Reagan went on to extol local and private control and to decry "giving powers" to the federal government "that were never intended in the Constitution." Updating Nixon's so-called southern strategy of dividing working-class voters along racial lines, he didn't mention race, but he didn't have to; the strategy, deployed by adviser Lee Atwater, called for coded, rather than explicit, racism. In this vein, Reagan stoked the anger of his base with tales of luxurious public housing and egregious welfare fraud, railing against a Cadillac-driving, fur-wearing woman from the South Side of Chicago who scammed the government out of thousands of dollars. With each telling, he varied the sums and other details about the "welfare queen" scammer, but as president he successfully leveraged the supposed epidemic of welfare fraud to enact cuts to food stamps and aid to families with children and to mount a broad assault on the welfare state. (The changes tightened eligibility requirements and slashed benefits but did not address fraud.) Conservatives who bristled at the idea of government support for "those people" were gleeful.[24]

Using speeches, rallies, party platforms, and high-profile appointments, Reagan signaled that he was broadly sympathetic with at least some aspects of the far right's agenda; they had a spot in his orbit. For the first time, in 1980 the Republican platform condemned the ERA and abortion while endorsing prayer in schools. Reagan gave a talk to students at Bob Jones University, which banned interracial dating and had ties to segregationists and Birchers. (In 1965, the society even recommended Bob Jones University—the nation's "most Conservative and patriotic" college—to a nineteen-year-old Oberlin dropout, and Birch National Council member Tom Anderson held an honorary law degree from BJU.) Bob Jones III, the university's president, implored the students to "take the word to family and friends," a tacit endorsement of Reagan's candidacy. Reagan attended a meeting of the National Religious Broadcasters at Falwell's Liberty University, a sign of his support for Birchite social causes. The Supreme Court, he declared on that occasion, had "expelled God from the classroom," echoing the Birch prayer-in-school argument. Renouncing his decision as governor to sign a law liberalizing abortion, Reagan endorsed a constitutional amendment to ban the procedure. Beverly LaHaye joined Reagan's Family Policy Advisor Board during his presidential campaign, establishing a formal link between socially conservative Christian women activists and his campaign.[25] He needed their votes, their fundraising, their energy, and their activism, so he took steps to win their support.

Once in office, his policy record notched a handful of wins for the far right, including his appointment of antiabortion judges to the federal judiciary, pleasing abortion's opponents, and breaking the air traffic controllers' strike in 1981, hobbling the already declining US labor movement.[26] Occasionally he tried to assure the far right that the Republican Party was a viable long-term home for it. Early in his administration he repeated a Birch-friendly conspiracy theory that Russian communists were puppeteering America's nuclear freeze movement. On racial issues his most significant sop to the Birch successors was his statement at a press conference that Martin Luther King Jr. may have been a communist sympathizer, a favorite Birch falsehood. Former New Hampshire Governor Meldrim Thomson Jr., the featured speaker at the Birchers' twentieth-anniversary dinner, had helped shape Reagan's views, writing to him that King had "well established" subversive ties and urging the president to veto legislation memorializing King's birthday as a national holiday. In a private letter, Reagan, who had opposed both the Civil Rights Act of 1964 and the Voting Rights Act of 1965, cast doubt on King's virtuous reputation, replying that "the perception of too many people is based on an image, not reality." When the communist smear provoked a firestorm, however, he backtracked, apologizing to King's widow and ultimately signing a bill to create a national holiday commemorating King.[27]

For the most part, however, Reagan governed as a mainstream conservative, often angering and antagonizing successors to the Birch movement. Reagan cut taxes, but he also raised them multiple times. He put the prochoice justice Sandra Day O'Connor on the Supreme Court, signed a bipartisan agreement to strengthen Social Security, extended the Voting Rights Act for twenty-five years, signed comprehensive immigration reform giving workers a path to citizenship, signed a bill that apologized and paid reparations for placing Japanese Americans in internment camps, and established a new cabinet-level bureaucracy, the Department of Veterans Affairs, a seeming slap in the face to far-right activists, who equated expanding federal power with treason.

He defied the Birch Society's America First isolationist approach, pursuing interventionism and alliance building instead. Rather than rejecting the post–World War II international order, Reagan in many respects embraced it. He boosted NATO and kept the United States as a member of the United Nations. He sent US Marines on an ill-fated peacekeeping mission to Lebanon (241 US troops lost their lives in a suicide bombing), invaded the Caribbean island of Grenada, defended the Western alliance as the cornerstone of a free world, established a free-trade agreement with Canada, and—most galling of all—after calling the Soviet Union "the evil empire" in 1983, he changed course and outdid Ike, holding three summits with Mikhail Gorbachev, embracing arms-control negotiations, and enacting an Intermediate Nuclear Forces (INF) agreement that helped ease tensions with the USSR and contributed to the end of the Cold War.

To some on the far right who were doubtful that the Cold War had actually ended, Reagan was not a hero but just the latest Republican president to practice subversion. As the INF treaty was being debated in 1988, far-right activists (and even some more moderate conservatives) mobilized to block it. At one strategy retreat for about twenty-four leaders of right-wing groups claiming to represent organizations with a combined one to two million members, an anonymous participant told the *New York Times* that Reagan was a disappointment. The participants discussed, one of them said, "what to do about Reagan's relationship with Gorbachev—the idea being that Reagan was appeasing liberals in Congress, appeasing the Communists, caving in on taxes, putting moderates like Frank Carlucci at Defense, and cutting deals with the evil empire." In 1992, after Gorbachev and Reagan had left office and both the Berlin Wall and the USSR had collapsed, Gorbachev paid a visit to the Ronald Reagan Presidential Library, which sat atop a mountain in Simi Valley, California, in a reunion of what the *New York Times* called "super-power retirees." Reagan described Gorbachev as "my friend," presented him with the first Ronald Reagan Freedom Award, and said that his "shining legacy will live forever." As they basked in smiles and mutual praise, at the bottom of the mountain at least a dozen Birchers protested with signs that read: "Socialism Is Not Dead" and "Gorbachev to the Gulag." Reflecting the distrust felt by many Birchers, one protester expressed disdain that Reagan "would be having a social event with this man, this communist criminal." A Southern California Birch leader said that real Birchers had "never bought into Ronald Reagan," who had ultimately failed in the fight against communists. "We believe the agenda for these insiders is that they intend to have it totally consolidated—a one-world government—by the end of the '90s," he complained. "Evil is never going to go away."[28]

Reagan viewed government as a problem, but he rarely went as far as the Birchers' all-encompassing antigovernment conspiracy theories. Reagan typically did not view civil rights as a communist plot, and on reparations for internees and renewal of the Voting Rights Act and relenting to make King's birthday a national holiday, Reagan demonstrated a willingness to resist the most hard-right members of his coalition. In the end Reagan also failed to repeal *Roe v. Wade*, ban pornography, add a constitutional amendment legalizing school prayer, rein in Hollywood's excesses, or dismantle the gay rights movement, which had continued to organize as the administration minimized and mostly ignored the HIV/ AIDS epidemic.

REAGAN'S TRIUMPH RESTED ON THE MOVEMENT KNOWN AS THE NEW Right as well as the network of think tanks, publications, and issue organizations that Sidney Blumenthal called the "counter-establishment." By and large, these institutions supported Reagan and his brand of conservatism. But within this panoply of right-wing organizations, Birch influence could still be seen and felt—notably in the free-market advocacy of the Koch brothers, the Second Amendment absolutism of the National Rifle Association (NRA), and, to some extent, the conferences of the influential Conservative Political Action Coalition (CPAC).

The pro-free-enterprise, well-funded side of the Birch movement was making inroads, and Birch founder Fred Koch and early supporter Harry Bradley bequeathed a heavily financed far-right infrastructure that survived long after the society's peak organizational influence. Two of Koch's sons laid the groundwork for a deregulated, union-free, antitax, antiregulation future, priorities that the Republican Party soon adopted as its own. The Koch brothers formed a foundation that seeded think tanks and funded academics and activists to lobby GOP leaders on their core concerns. Recalling the rabid antiunion rhetoric and actions of Koch père, Grede, and many other Birch leaders, the Koch brothers set out to weaken organized labor, train new generations of far-right leaders, back preferred candidates, and advocate for and against policies with ad campaigns, rallies, and protests. To press its causes the Koch fringe used a host of anodyne-sounding groups and surreptitious means—most notoriously "dark money," which their advocacy against campaign-finance restrictions helped legalize. The seeding of causes with funds from a single super-wealthy donor, or a handful of them, owed a debt to the Birchers, who often relied on big donors to finance their projects. A former Senate committee counsel told journalist Jane Mayer that Charles Koch "was so far right he was off in the ether. They thought Reagan was a sellout."[29]

CPAC's annual conferences reflected some of the ways that far-right activists clashed with a more mainstream conservative sensibility. These events subsumed large swaths of the American right, drawing libertarians, traditionalists, neocons, and more, and an internal 1986 survey of 402 CPAC members conducted by GOP pollster Arthur Finkelstein offered a window into the fringe as a growing minority within the conservative movement. Conservatives polled were split on the issues that motivated Birchers and their successors. Sixty-nine percent of CPAC attendees thought that the Reagan administration needed to reach an arms-control agreement with the Soviet Union, a position at odds with the Birchite antitreaty sentiment. But 51 percent of respondents wanted the United States to withdraw from the United Nations, a position the Birchers had helped to forge. When asked whom they supported for the GOP presidential nomination, establishment figures George Bush, Jack Kemp, and Bob Dole took the top three slots, while Jesse Helms and Pat Robertson garnered 5 percent and 3.5 percent, respectively. Although about two-thirds of respondents endorsed the restoration of voluntary prayer in public schools, about one-quarter opposed the idea. All in all it was a mixed bag: the Birchers' legacy had become part of the fabric of the broad conservative coalition, but it remained a minority view and ideology.[30]

The National Rifle Association over time became more and more Birchite in its language and ideology, seeing a communist plot to destroy the Second Amendment. Birchers were early progun activists, urging the society's home office to partner with the NRA. In 1964, one year after Oswald had used a gun purchased through the NRA to kill President Kennedy, Bircher Michael Carlucci pushed the society's leadership "to preserve the 2nd Amendment." R. G. Johnson, who belonged to Chapter 960 in Rogers, Arkansas, urged the society to oppose "the registration of fire arms within the United States," which, he asserted in 1964, would obliterate freedom, and suggested a Birch-NRA alliance. "NOW IS THE TIME FOR ALL GOOD MEN TO COME TO THE AID OF FREE GOVERNMENT!" Johnson declared. "Not tomorrow, that will be too

LATE." In 1977, at the NRA's Cincinnati convention, a faction of hard-right rebels successfully ousted a bipartisan group of NRA leaders and proceeded to transform the organization into a no-holds-barred culture warrior. For roughly a century the NRA's agenda had featured conservation, hunting, and shooting. Now it became absolutist and moved in a classic Birch vein. Its new crop of leaders drew on the Birchite notion that "communists" in the federal government were seeking to take away people's guns and quash their liberties, employed Birchite language that any firearms restrictions inevitably led to government tyranny, embraced conspiracy theories (NRA hard-liner Clifford Neal Knox alleged that antigun fanatics had carried out the political assassinations of the 1960s in order to generate public sympathy for gun control), and bashed the media as "a force that dwarfs any political power or social tyrant that ever before existed on this planet."[31]

Successors to the Birch Society gained some influence in the late 1980s. They radicalized existing organizations, and the far right became better coordinated, with more funding and activists more focused on making a future in the fickle world of electoral politics. Descendants to the Birchers had proven their resiliency and their mettle. The far right never died. Its ideas and tactics lived on.

Chapter 10

CRACK-UP

Although Reagan had kept the right-wing fringe in his camp for part of his time in the White House, far-right extremists regarded his final days in office with a mix of trepidation and discontent. Was he truly on their side? His January 1989 farewell address mostly pointed to the negative, sounding several notes that conflicted with their highest priorities. His praise of small government resonated, though it was not quite as stridently hostile to federal authority as they would have preferred. More disconcertingly, Reagan's speech extolled immigrants who came to the United States in search of freedom, and it celebrated the nation's renewed international purpose—themes that clashed with the far right's nativism and isolationism.

Reagan's departure from office hinted at an impending struggle for the future of the Republican Party. Reagan had been dominant for so long that it was hard to imagine conservatism without his presence. No other modern leader had brought about such a clear rightward shift in the country's center of gravity, and no one else possessed the broad appeal to maintain his coalition.

A battle between ultra- and mainstream conservatives filled the vacuum. From 1989 to 2000 the tell-tale signs of Birchite influence on the far right were the apocalyptic tone, the knee-jerk extremism and hatred, the preoccupation with the notion of elites manipulating everything. The conspiratorial interpretation of national events coupled with a constricting isolationism also were signatures of the fringe during those years. In contrast, Reagan, Bush, and Dole ideas featured supply-side economics (income tax cuts), curbs on some federal social-spending programs, a post–Cold War internationalism, and a pragmatic streak. By the mid-nineties, however, it was harder at times to separate the fringe from the center in the American right.

Reagan's departure, coinciding roughly with the end of the Cold War, renewed foreign policy disputes between internationalist mainstream conservatives and isolationists on the far right. While the political establishment, left and right, saw the collapse of communism starting in 1989 as a victory for democracy and a validation of US Cold War leadership, supporters of America First ideas like isolationism, nativism, and tariffs repudiated the premise of an American-led world order and saw an opportunity to retreat from global entanglements. With only one remaining superpower, isolationists saw the post-USSR reshuffling as only strengthening their long-held conviction that the United States should not be the world's policeman. The bipartisan post–World War II foreign policy consensus (supportive of foreign aid, military interventions, alliance building, and international institutions), they believed, had carried steep costs and was now more misguided than ever. They wanted a new approach emphasizing defense of the nation's sovereignty, and they intended to fight for it.

As before, conspiracy theories were among their most potent weapons of choice, and the far right proved nimble at adapting them to the new international realities. With communism in eclipse, they never completely relinquished their most tried-and-true bogeyman, but they demoted it, elevating other trusty villains to pick up the slack. Bankers, the Council on Foreign Relations, media elites, and the United Nations now assumed larger roles as puppet masters in the plot against America, seeking to wreck people's freedoms and drain the nation's hard-won treasure. Those who predicted that the fall of communism and the attendant neutering of the far right's most durable rhetorical enemy would usher in "the end of history" or would puncture the zeal of far-right extremists were once again underestimating their creativity, resilience, and determination.[1]

THROUGHOUT THE REAGAN YEARS, WHEN CONSERVATIVE AIDES AND AL-lies wanted their president to quit listening to moderates and fulfill his promise, they would say, "Let Reagan be Reagan." None of them ever said, about his vice president and successor, "Let Bush be Bush." George H. W. Bush was the establishment made flesh. A Connecticut senator's son and a fixture of Washington's elite institutions, he was a former CIA director and ambassador to China and the United Nations. If he was unpopular among mainstream conservatives like George Will, he was loathed by the Birch Society; even though he renounced a lot of his pre-1980 politics (when he was prochoice and anti–supply side), many conservatives (not just ultras) thought him a squish. Even moving to Texas in the late 1940s and raising his children there over decades couldn't erase his patrician Yankee aura. When Bush sought election as the chairman of Texas's Harris County GOP, he tried to bring Birchers into his coalition, but a friend warned, "George, you don't know these people. They mean to kill you!" In 1964, Bush sought a US Senate seat from Texas. Birchers charged that his father-in-law was publishing a communist magazine, *Redbook* (which, despite the "red" in its title, was nothing of the sort), and they scorned Bush as a "One-World tool of the Communist-Wall Street internationalist conspiracy."[2]

Bush did what he thought necessary to win that election: he declared his opposition to the Civil Rights Act, the United Nations, and JFK's 1963 Nuclear Test Ban Treaty. He got trounced just the same and later told his minister in Houston, "I took some of the far-right positions to get elected. I hope I never do it again." Twenty-four years later, hoping to succeed Reagan during his campaign for president, Bush faced a similar test: Just how far would he go for a win?

Reagan's loyal vice president did not have a lock on the nomination. Senator Bob Dole was running for president, and Reverend Pat Robert-son's presidential primary campaign posed a thorny dilemma for Bush.

Robertson's political base was proof that Birch philosophy had staying power in the struggle to define the post-Reagan GOP.

Robertson was perhaps the most influential of all the religious-right leaders. Soft spoken, well dressed, and seemingly unflappable in front of a camera, Robertson, like Falwell, was a Baptist minister from Virginia. Starting in 1966 he hosted a TV show, *The 700 Club*, on his pioneering cable channel, the Christian Broadcasting Network (CBN), which reached millions of viewers, made him wildly rich, and formed the cornerstone of a vast media, educational, and business empire. Robertson's annual Road to Victory conventions later became must-stops for GOP presidential hopefuls, who grasped the political influence of Robertson's supporters, making him a power broker as well. But his warm manner and trace of a Southern accent clashed with his persistent affection for all manner of conspiracies, such as the notion that the Council on Foreign Relations controlled all US foreign policy, or that a one-world superstate was a goal of the UN and would impose socialism on freedom-loving Americans.

The Birch Society had bequeathed to him a set of allies and causes, and Robertson's interpretation of global affairs was glossed with Birch ideas about hidden forces usurping America's sovereignty at home and abroad. During the primary he distributed an audiotape warning that children in public schools were "being subjected to psychological manipulation which moves them away from their Judeo-Christian mindset and moves them into a humanistic mold and from the humanistic mold into the socialist worldview and ultimately into the Communist International." E. J. Dionne called the formulation a "garden-variety conspiracy theory associated with groups such as the old John Birch Society—and I'm not sure I'm being entirely fair to the Birchers."[3]

The society may have been old, but Robertson showed that its ideas still had an audience. Robertson argued that the United States had endured "moral decay" at the diabolical direction of liberal elites. In one campaign speech he pledged as president to fire most of the one hundred thousand government workers in the State Department and get rid of "the influence of the Council on Foreign Relations—the trilateral commission it is called, the Eastern liberal establishment." Then, he said, he intended to put Americans in these jobs "who would stand up for the United States of America and stop trying to move us toward a one-world socialist Government."[4]

Robertson's dire warnings—that anti-American government officials dictated US foreign policy; that US sovereignty had disappeared; that liberals indoctrinated children with smut—picked up on some classic Birch thought patterns, weaving together alleged anti-American plots hatched at the highest levels of government. Robertson's presidential run revealed how a fringe candidate with the right ideas and strategic savvy could make a dent in the universe. Activists found a lot to like in his message. Competing hard in low-turnout caucus states where candidates with fired-up supporters typically did well, Robertson won four states in the 1988 primary. Most importantly his supporters showcased the fervor of the extreme right within the post-Reagan GOP.

Reagan had checked some of his far-right backers' excesses. But when Robertson ran for president he unleashed them, waging a war on what he viewed as establishment conservatives. In Michigan Robertson's supporters were so hostile to pro-Bush antagonists that one of Bush's aides called the state "the Beirut of Republican politics." Robertson's go-for-broke backers, many of them affiliated with the religious right, looked as if they came straight out of "the bar scene [in] Star Wars," the chairman of the Michigan GOP quipped.[5] But they were also well organized and devoted to a cause.

The tactics Robertson's supporters used in Georgia were rooted in Birch aggression. At the state's Republican convention, Robertson's people contested the process of delegate selection and shouted down some speakers. The Associated Press reported that the "chaos" forced the convention into an adjournment. In neighboring North Carolina Robertson's supporters boycotted the state's Republican Party due to alleged mistreatment by entrenched Republicans who had denied them key roles. Robertson only won 10 percent of the primary vote in the state, but his voters were vocal and stronger than their numbers suggested.[6]

Robertson won the Washington State caucus by turning out tens of thousands of supporters. His youngest delegate, Matt Dentino, twenty-seven, told the *Seattle Times* how he recruited volunteers and voters by going from church to church. "We would find the spark plugs, the John the Baptists in the church," he said. "There was always one Rambo kind of person and we would plug them in. It was fun and exciting." In Washington Robertson established what one reporter called "a new right wing of the Republican Party, building a loyal following from the state's growing fundamentalist ranks, anti-abortion groups, and other conservatives who felt left out of politics."[7]

Robertson's army pushed the GOP to accept its culture-war agenda more fully and made the far-right Christian Coalition an even more influential voice in the post-Reagan conservative universe. In state after state Robertson's relatively neophyte activists sought to win slots as delegates to the national convention and push the GOP to write a platform that reflected their key concerns. After Robertson lost the Republican nomination for president, they applauded Bush's strong stands on social issues—his antiabortion, profamily values—even as they kept one eye on attempting to turn the party rightward. "We're not going away," a leader of Robertson's campaign told supporters in Michigan. "We're here to stay."[8]

Indeed, Republicans recognized the power of Robertson's army, with its more than one million members, its nearly two-million-household mailing list, and its extensive television empire. In the years following his 1988 campaign, they acted accordingly. Conservative luminaries such as William Bennett, Newt Gingrich, Oliver North, Jack Kemp, Jesse Helms, and Dinesh D'Souza happily appeared at Robertson's Road to Victory conferences. As a presidential candidate in 1995, Senator Bob Dole, a pillar of the Republican establishment who was widely disliked by the far right, told Robertson's followers, "I am proud to stand up here and say that I've been awarded a 100 percent voting record in '93 and 100 percent in 1994 and 100 percent in 1995" from Robertson's group, the Christian Coalition.

Robertson received a speaking slot at the 1988 Republican National Convention, and the GOP platform reflected his priorities. His success underscored the staying power of the Birch movement. Robertson's mostly Christian evangelical supporters stayed politically active and entered "the mainstream of Republican politics," reporter Susan Gilmore wrote.[9]

Despite beating Robertson for the GOP presidential nomination in 1988, Bush had to move to the right to shore up his support during the general election. The vice president picked up on some of Robertson's themes, tarring the Democratic nominee, Massachusetts governor Michael Dukakis, as vaguely foreign, unpatriotic, and soft on crime, using his infamous "Willie Horton" ad to scare white voters about Black criminals on the loose. It also sent a clear message to the far right: Bush could speak their language. He had the cojones. The ad comported with Birchers' willingness to be ruthless, their defend-your-local-police stand, their cunning use of wedge issues, and their racism.[10]

Partly to please the Robertson far right, Bush chose as his running mate Dan Quayle, a forty-one-year-old, socially conservative senator from Indiana. Many mainstream critics dismissed Quayle as callow and dim and charged Bush with shameless pandering—not to the right wing but to young voters and women. But Quayle's real allure lay in his "family values" bona fides and his far-right bloodlines. He was a wealthy scion too, but his parents, James and Corinne, had been Birchers. "I'm not ashamed of it at all," James Quayle said about his membership in the Birch Society after Bush put his son on the ticket. (Robert Welch, he added, was like "a Nostradamus . . . whose vision has come true in some sense today.") When Dan Quayle worked for Indiana's attorney general, he befriended another Birch offspring, Clarence Manion's son Daniel. As a senator in 1986 he urged the Reagan White House to tap the younger Manion as a federal judge.[11]

Once the two were in power, however, the Bush-Quayle record—like that of Reagan—was a disappointment for the extreme right. More pragmatic than conspiratorial, carrying into the White House strong congressional relationships, Quayle, ultimately savvy, worked to fend off far-right criticisms of the president's agenda, including times when Bush compromised with Democrats on taxes and spending.

In the view of the far right, Bush had a lot to compensate for—and at times he overcompensated. After the retirement from the Supreme Court of Thurgood Marshall, the first Black justice and a civil rights legend, Bush nominated Clarence Thomas to replace him. A hard-right ideologue, Thomas bitterly opposed affirmative action and pledged to undo the Warren court's jurisprudence. His wife, Ginni, was a far-right activist. She held a leadership post on Tim LaHaye's Council for National Policy, and she, too, had some ties to the Birch Society. A childhood neighbor recalled that Ginni Thomas's parents were active in a losing 1968 referendum campaign in Omaha to ban putting fluoride in the water supply. "My Republican parents, who knew them well, certainly considered them Birchers," journalist Kurt Andersen recalled. As an activist, Ginni Thomas's apocalyptic rhetoric ("Our house is on fire!") and warnings that leftists were "arsonists" combined with her progun extremism ("May we all have guns and concealed carry to handle what's coming!") to bring a Birchite perspective to the center of the conservative movement.[12]

In the end, however, the extreme right suffered from a lack of clout during Bush's presidency. Many of Bush's policies were abominable, as bad as Eisenhower's, according to the far-right activists, and their embitterment deepened. In domestic policy, Bush endorsed immigration reform, signed the landmark Americans with Disabilities Act, enacted the Clean Air Act, decried the bigotry of ex-KKK Grand Wizard David Duke, and, in his greatest act of perfidy, decided in 1990 to raise taxes (after vowing, "Read my lips: no new taxes") as part of a bipartisan budget agreement.[13]

His foreign policy amounted to an even graver rebuke of the vision that animated his party's anti-interventionist activists, with his mobilization of a UN coalition to expel Iraq's Saddam Hussein from Kuwait and, even more so, with his proclamation of a "new world order." As research analyst Chip Berlet explained, the president had employed "the Birch secret buzz word," making "a tremendous error in judgment."[14] Such rhetoric alarmed Birch successor organizations. Rather than seeing a triumph of American values, they substituted the "new world order" for "communism" as the conspiracy's culprit, and Bush's unforced error ratified this view.

But the Cold War's end also enabled the far right to press an advantage: with communism dead, they argued, America no longer needed its foreign alliances; it could prioritize its own spiritual renewal and expose the conspiracy of one-world socialists. In 1991 Pat Robertson published *The New World Order*, which held that scheming government leaders, including Bush, were working to set up "world government, a world police force, world courts, world banking and currency, and a world elite in charge of it all." Like the Birchers (and others) before him, Robertson named the Council on Foreign Relations, the Trilateral Commission, and the Illuminati as part of the conspiracy. As far back as 1980 he had warned of a plot "to destroy nationalism in favor of an interdependent one-world government." Robertson's book, which sold about half a million copies, pinned the blame for the one-worldist putsch on a tangled historical web that at every turn featured the hand of the Rothschilds, the family of Jewish bankers. Robertson drew many of his ideas from Nesta Webster, an antisemitic conspiracy theorist.[15]

Falwell, Robertson, and their legion of followers had become more embedded in state Republican Parties and remained a part of Bush's political coalition. But a recession caused Bush's job approval ratings to dip, and when he sought reelection in 1992, he faced a stiff primary challenge from Pat Buchanan. At the same time, the Birch Society was making a bit of a comeback. The society had mostly declined between 1965 and 1985 and came close to collapsing. But thanks to Bush's "new world order" address in defense of his post–Cold War vision of international coalition building to police rogue states, by 1992 the society saw a surge in membership. Buchanan's primary run provided yet more ballast.

Buchanan had once worked as a speechwriter for Nixon, and he had always pushed the president toward right-wing, populist positions. Even as he became an influential Washington pundit, Buchanan defied mainstream conservative orthodoxy on many issues, dashing to the far right of the spectrum. His 1992 campaign slogan, "Make America First Again," echoed the America First Committee, the World War II–era isolationist group led by aviator Charles Lindbergh, a Nazi sympathizer, and seized on Birch ideas that America's international alliances and treaties had diluted American strength. Many of Pat Robertson's supporters flocked to Buchanan's campaign.[16] On the stump in New Hampshire, Buchanan pounded views that often comported with Birch ideology. Opposing free trade, immigration, Bush's tax hike, and internationalist foreign policy, Buchanan decried globalism and open borders, lashed Bush's pragmatic streak, and represented an increasingly influential fringe in the GOP coalition. Following in the tradition of George Wallace, John Schmitz, and Robertson, Buchanan lost. But in winning more than a third of the New Hampshire GOP primary vote against an incumbent president, Buchanan channeled far-right antiestablishment discontent with Bush and the mainstream Republican Party.

To strengthen his position during his 1992 presidential run, Bush brought culture warriors more fully into the party and made it clear that even moderate established Republicans needed to court the base on social issues and politely ignore or downplay their conspiracy theories. Rather than excommunicate Buchanan after he dropped out of the race, Bush accommodated him. His campaign dedicated the convention's third night to the theme "family values," featuring fiery speeches by Marilyn Quayle (the vice president's wife), Missouri senator John Ashcroft, and Robertson, who told the delegates that the GOP platform had a foundation rooted in Christian scripture. Bush's opponent Bill Clinton, Robertson averred, had "a radical plan to destroy the traditional family and transfer many of its functions to the federal government." Bush's GOP handed Buchanan a prime-time slot on the convention stage, where he infamously proclaimed a culture war for America's soul. The delegates on the floor of the Houston Astrodome, Buchanan recalled, loved the speech. Bush's high command praised it when he exited the stage. "That speech was then, and is now, consistent with the heart and soul of the Republican Party," Buchanan later said. "The country-club and the establishment Republicans recoil from the social, cultural and moral issues which many conservatives and evangelicals have embraced." One elder statesman who admired its fiery message was the eighty-three-year-old Barry Goldwater, who called it "superb" and added in a note to Buchanan, "You brought a lot of fire back to a very dull affair."[17]

Ultimately, a recession, a series of political blunders, and the public's sheer pent-up frustration with twelve years of Republicans in the White House converged to make Bush a one-term president. But his efforts to merge the fringe and the center right into an uneasy union inched the GOP closer to the Birchers' alternative political tradition. His embrace of Robertson and Buchanan illustrated how their rhetoric and appearances, even in defeat, shaped the party's ideological and strategic direction. Despite lacking ideological kinship with the fringe, Bush provided the apocalyptic, conspiratorial, and anti-interventionist far right with a firmer spot in the GOP's ever-shifting constellation.

Bush's loss to Bill Clinton in 1992 imparted another lesson, this time for future Republican candidates for high office: by antagonizing some of his party's most vocal activists, Bush had contributed to the demise of his presidency. Republican leaders made mental notes. To them Bush stood as a cautionary tale, and they resolved to avoid a repeat of his mistake.

As the first Democrat to win the White House since 1976, Bill Clinton, one Birch leader quipped in 1993, was "the best recruiter for the John Birch Society we've had since Jimmy Carter."[18] Clinton's presidency fueled the right wing's worst impulses and gave it a bigger place in the Republican Party. Paradoxically, Clinton also was fairly effective at containing the far right, using it as a foil to show what could happen when one party courted extremists, condoned their ideas, and let them sway a party's agenda.

Although the far right surged during the Bush and Clinton presidencies, Clinton combatted it through a strategy of "triangulation"—forging a position above the left position and the right position, pulling away from both in a new way. One political scientist credited this policy and a recent surge of extremism with showing "the public how bad it could be if you were to elect someone of the extreme left or the extreme right."[19] For a time the strategy checked the radicals' growing influence in the GOP.

Clinton used his bully pulpit to tie the GOP to far-right militants like Timothy McVeigh, the Oklahoma City mass murderer, and Randy Weaver, the white separatist who triggered a bloody confrontation with the FBI at Ruby Ridge. After McVeigh's powerful homemade bomb tore through the Murrah Federal Building in Oklahoma City in 1995, Clinton attended a memorial service in Oklahoma City and urged Americans "to purge ourselves of the dark forces which gave rise to this evil. They are forces that threaten our common peace, our freedom, our way of life," and, he vowed, "we will stand against the forces of fear." Some right-wing talk show hosts and politicians, he added, had to realize that their "incendiary talk" moved fanatics to action. Their "constant bashing of government, and relentless assumption that forces beyond our control run our government" had spread dark views of federal employees and could trigger yet more bloodshed.[20]

By linking Republican leaders to violent white militias, Clinton conjured up the danger of antigovernment zealots holding the reins of power. That argument aided his reelection and helped keep pragmatists such as him in office. GOP leaders struggled to respond to his criticisms.

Still, Clinton couldn't stop the march of the fringe altogether. His first term also served to widen the network of the far right and gave conspiracy theories and apocalyptic notions—many of them targeting the Clintons—a fresh life. Although the Birch Society never came anywhere near its heyday (in terms of membership, impact, or notoriety), it slowly spilled into the broader political culture. It was simultaneously an oddity and a force. Its leadership continued to obsess over the internal conspiracy; communism hadn't faded, Birch leader John McManus explained in 1993. The plot against America had remained virtually unchanged. "The growth of government power leading to total government power is what Americans should be concerned about," he warned. Birchers called global warming a hoax cooked up to justify the government's seizure of Americans' property. Despite such braggadocio Birchers and their successors still embodied a far-right fringe defined variously by conspiracy theories, white supremacy, isolationism, and culture-war belligerence. According to one Bircher, McManus described neoconservative television host Ben Wattenberg as "a slimy New York Jew."[21]

To much of the far right, Bill Clinton was an amalgam of everything they loathed in American liberalism. When he won the White House, the fringe finally faced a president they despised more than Bush. Their scorn for Clinton helped radicalize the right during his presidency and at the same time posed a fresh dilemma for Republicans: How far were they willing to go to oppose the president? Clinton embodied the kind of "moral decay" responsible for the nation's decline that Robertson invoked in 1988. A Rhodes Scholar, he had studied at Oxford, marched against the Vietnam War, visited the Soviet Union, and grown his hair long. His boyhood hero was JFK. When seeking the presidency Clinton promised "two for the price of one," referring to his wife, Hillary Clinton, which infuriated those who thought the First Lady was as bad as her husband.

To numerous Birch successors, the Clintons represented the progovernment, communistic ideology that had sapped Americans' freedoms.

In response, far-right individuals, tactics, and ideas gained clout as lines between ultra- and mainstream conservatives grew blurrier. The GOP's pattern of accommodating or benignly neglecting the extreme right persisted, and during the Clinton years the conspiratorial thinking became harder and harder to distinguish from the outlook of the Republican Party. While the relationship wasn't always harmonious, the Birch successors found an uneasy but expanding home inside the organizations of the American right and the Republican Party.

The funding that had animated the Birch Society was now being used to fund conspiracy theories about Clinton. Conservative billionaire Richard Mellon Scaife sent investigators to Arkansas to dig up dirt on the president's past, and when they failed they settled for salacious fabrications that Bill Clinton was part of a drug-smuggling ring. Jerry Falwell started selling a forty-three-dollar videotape that, among other charges, said Clinton was responsible for the deaths of "countless people." More anti-Clinton conspiracies proliferated: His serpentine ties to a Georgetown professor constituted a plot to create the new world order. The Clintons had ordered the murder of White House counsel Vince Foster to hide their financial wrongdoing. (Foster, a close friend of the Clintons' from Arkansas, had died by suicide, leaving a note indicating that his mental anguish sprang from relentless public sniping from the right.)[22]

In an article for the *Washington Post* titled "Calling All Crackpots," conservative-turned-liberal author Michael Lind warned that the GOP credo of "no enemies on the right" was playing with fire. He noted that the party's gatekeepers had refused to condemn Pat Robertson's conspiracy theories and Charles Murray's book *The Bell Curve*, which lamented that welfare "subsidizes birth among poor women, who are disproportionately at the low end of the intelligence distribution," and that Black babies and Latino immigrants were lowering America's collective IQ. Lind concluded by predicting that if tolerance of such extremism brought electoral gains, the consequences would be chilling. "The GOP strategy of welcoming the formerly excluded far right will appear to be vindicated," he warned. "The moderate conservative majority in the GOP may learn that their cause has not been harmed, and may even be helped, by welcoming antisemitic conspiracy theorists, pseudo-scientific racists and nativists back into the fold. For the short-sighted opportunism of the conservatives, all of America may eventually pay a heavy price."[23]

The most lurid and consequential conspiracy theory about Clinton nearly brought down his presidency. As with Robert Welch's sprawling communist writings, many claims were false and several dots failed to connect, but no matter. With assists from Birch successors like Falwell, Scaife, and Independent Counsel Ken Starr and his team, the so-called scandal of the century linked ginned-up charges surrounding a failed Ozarks land deal with salacious but true allegations of Clinton's relations with a White House intern, which Starr then pumped up into charges of obstruction of justice and other allegedly impeachable offenses. In effect, far-right strategists sought to wound a Democratic president not because of what he had done—have sex with an intern—but as part of what Hillary Clinton famously labeled "a vast right-wing conspiracy" that tied sex acts to "high crimes and misdemeanors." Like the Birch conspiracies of the 1950s and 1960s, this one wove together baseless conjecture, distortions, half truths, and actual truths (Vernon Jordan did try to help the intern, Monica Lewinsky, get a job; the semen stains on her blue dress were from Clinton) into a massive, misleading plot. Unlike those past conspiracies, however, these caught on with the mainstream press—not just with fresh, Birch-toned voices like Matt Drudge, Rush Limbaugh, and the hosts on Rupert Murdoch's new conservative cable network, Fox News.

Few Republicans tried to rein in the conspiratorial voices in their party. Instead, the GOP continued its incremental radicalization. Where Nixon, Buckley, Goldwater, and Reagan had criticized Welch's outlandish charge that Eisenhower was a communist, Republican leaders in the nineties mostly amplified baseless theories about Clinton's alleged crimes or kept mum and let the fringe go to work unimpeded.

Several controversial issues also helped to radicalize the GOP, especially guns. In 1992 Birchers appeared at protests to block new firearms restrictions; one Birch sign read: "God and the Constitution: Your Gun Permit," and the National Rifle Association more and more often channeled Birch themes, arguing that the federal government had undertaken a plot to steal Americans' liberties. The NRA's rhetoric was now virtually indistinguishable from the fevered warnings of a communist-led Armageddon woven through a typical issue of *American Opinion* from the 1960s. In 1995, one week prior to the Oklahoma City bombing, an NRA fundraising letter signed by Executive Vice President Wayne LaPierre charged that "in Clinton's administration, if you have a badge, you have the government's go-ahead to harass, intimidate, even murder law-abiding citizens." The letter echoed Birchers in its fear of "a new wave of brainwashing propaganda aimed at further destroying our Constitutional freedoms." "Most Americans don't realize that our freedoms are slowly slipping away. They don't understand that politicians and bureaucrats are chipping away at the American way of life. They're destroying business, destroying our economy, destroying property rights, destroying our moral foundation, destroying our schools, destroying our culture." This formulation— "politicians" were "destroying our culture"—connoted many things, but above all it rallied NRA members to defend white, Christian gun owners from the communist conspiracy. George H. W. Bush found the rhetoric so offensive—particularly the bit likening federal law enforcement agents to murderers—that he resigned his NRA membership. Then again, his political career was over, and he no longer needed the organization's support in his campaigns.[24]

Though House Speaker Newt Gingrich, with his scorched-earth tactics, is often blamed for the deterioration of functional governance, his 1994 Republican Revolution drew on elements of the Birch movement: a stance that accused the establishment of selling out American principles, a defense of Christian family values from decades of moral turpitude, a conviction that enemies required a warlike response to head off Armageddon. Gingrich rose in Republican politics in Georgia shortly after Birch leader Larry McDonald won office in that state. As a Republican candidate for Congress from Georgia's Sixth Congressional District in 1978, Gingrich adopted a slash-and-burn style that bore similarities to McDonald's. Both accused the Republican establishment of weakness. Gingrich thundered that every Republican leader of his lifetime—Eisenhower, Nixon, Ford—had committed acts of cowardice, and that they had "done a terrible job, a pathetic job!"

Gingrich had absorbed the insurgent, us-against-them mindset of the Birch movement. "One of the great problems we have in the Republican Party is that we don't . . . encourage you to be nasty," he told a group of college Republicans during his 1978 bid for office. His apocalyptic interpretation of the stakes drew on the Birch notion that politics meant battling a mortal enemy to the death. "You're fighting a war," he warned the young Republicans. "It is a war for power."[25]

In 1994, for the first time in forty years, Republicans won control of the US House of Representatives, and although many of their legislative positions (tax and spending cuts, term limits) fell into the mainstream conservative camp, they brought a Birchite burn-it-down sensibility into power. Many of them governed in the spirit of a comment from Bircher Anthony Ferlanto, who in 1965 assured Welch that after watching a society recruitment presentation, "I will fight these atheistic diabolical corrupt mass inslavers [sic] with my every heartbeat and every fibre of my bein [sic] and spread the knowledge to everyone I meet." His letter included a stamp with words from Goldwater's convention address: "Extremism in the defense of liberty is no vice."[26]

Republicans at times also took a turn toward an isolationist, America First ideology. Not only did they decry the United Nations; they rallied opposition to foreign aid and voiced skepticism of nation building. In 1995, scores of House Republicans voted to cut off funding for the US military mission to defend Bosnian Muslims from Serbia's aggression.[27]

By the mid-nineties some of the lines separating the Birchite fringe from the conservative mainstream had blurred. Simmering conspiracy theories increasingly boiled over into the core of conservative thought, the detestation of establishment Republicans intensified, and suspicion of elites, international institutions, and interventionist policies deepened.

Emboldened by the 1994 Republican Revolution, Buchanan made a second bid for president in 1996, this time exhibiting more bile. Appearing at a nearly all-white rally in Iowa, he warned that immigration on the southern border represented a major national security threat: "I'll build that security fence, and we'll close it, and we'll say, 'Listen Jose, you're not coming in this time!'" Mexicans, he thundered elsewhere, have "no right to break our laws and break into our country and go on welfare, and some of them commit crimes." Speaking the language of right-wing conspiracists and isolationists, he said, "When I raise my hand to take that oath of office, your New World Order comes crashing down"—a surefire crowd-pleaser. Buchanan wove conspiracy theories holding that international organizations were dragging America's sovereignty through the mud, citing deals such as the North American Free Trade Agreement (NAFTA), international bodies such as the General Agreement on Tariffs and Trade (GATT) and the World Health Organization (WHO), and Latin Americans as injurious to self-determination. Foreign aid, he argued, should be abolished; America's "rich allies" had to "pay the full cost of their own defense." He demanded "a foreign policy that puts America First—not the United Nations." The Cold War's end, Bush's internationalism, and growing fury at immigration, free trade, and military interventions gave far-right ideas a new life, and Buchanan went further than the Gingrich Republicans, vowing to restore states' rights, abolish affirmative action, outlaw abortion, eliminate cultural "pollution," and defend Americans' Second Amendment gun rights. Laced with invective against dark-skinned "aliens," Buchanan's oratory, more than that of any other presidential candidate since Wallace, updated the Birch tradition within the American right.[28]

Occasionally a Republican would stand up to the far right. Arlen Specter, a GOP presidential candidate and moderate US senator from Pennsylvania, assailed Robertson and Buchanan as leaders of the "intolerant right." But such dissenting voices—profact, proscience, and proreason—lost the internal debate over how to treat the fringe, and moments of truth-telling by Republicans at all levels were fleeting and increasingly rare.[29]

On his third try for president, in 2000, Pat Buchanan's alliance with the Birch phenomenon came even more clearly to light. Buchanan selected Ezola Foster, a public school teacher for thirty-three years and a Birch national spokesperson, as his running mate on Ross Perot's Reform Party ticket. Buchanan defended the Birch Society ("not a racist group"), but Foster's views belied this benign spin: a Black woman, she had labeled public schools "socialist training camps," called civil rights leaders "Leninist race-baiters," defended the Confederate flag and Jim Crow, said Africans came to America to fulfill God's freedom agenda, and described the ticket as "Americanists who believe in the Constitution and America first." One *Washington Post* reader captured the dilemma facing the GOP, asking Foster if at bottom she was a Republican rather than a member of a true third party. The reader surmised that Republicans were seeking "to leave the scary, extremist, elitist, hate-mongering elements of the Republican party at the door," even as those elements remained a part of the GOP's coalition.[30]

COULD REPUBLICAN LEADERS HAVE BANISHED THE BIRCH SOCIETY's progeny through a more forceful campaign of excommunication in the 1990s? It's instructive to examine what happened in some of the few instances when they did. Reagan defied hard-liners in his administration and among his allies to summit with Gorbachev and reach an important treaty agreement, drawing flak from the extreme right. Still, Reagan was sui generis, able to fend off far-right criticism, and his reputation as a conservative stalwart soared after he left office. As the most capacious and successful conservative leader of the second half of the twentieth century, Reagan had more latitude than most.

After 1988 most Republicans who tried to combat the extreme right came away bruised. When George H. W. Bush directly challenged far-right orthodoxy on taxes and foreign policy, he paid a steep price, losing reelection. His invocation of a "new world order" energized anti-internationalists in his coalition, including Robertson and Buchanan. Bush's willingness to cut deals and his acceptance of some federal initiatives (voting rights, clean air, disability rights)—his belief that one could be conservative and govern pragmatically and responsibly—outweighed any goodwill he had generated among the right wing through his nomination of Clarence Thomas and his antiabortion and anti-flag-burning stands.

To defy the fringe was to court peril in almost any campaign. Bob Dole learned this lesson the hard way. When he sought the GOP's presidential nomination in 1996, the pro-gay-rights Log Cabin Republicans sent him a campaign check for $1,000. After he finished tied in an Iowa straw poll with his primary rival, the Texas senator Phil Gramm, who journalist Mark Shields joked was "running considerably to the right of Pepin the Short," however, Dole decided to return the Log Cabin group's money.[31] Running to the right, Dole won the party's nomination, but he was ultimately an institutionalist, not a culture warrior. Like Bush, he hadn't come from the right-wing fringe, and he was far more at ease in the corridors of the Capitol than in the fevered swamps of a Birch-sponsored rally. The far right continued to view him with skepticism; for a variety of reasons, Dole lost the general election. With Clinton winning a second term, by the late 1990s most Republicans had watched, studied, and learned: to go against the right-wing fringe carried political risks that were mostly intolerable to them. Doing so sacrificed more than votes and funding; it potentially invited a primary challenge that might end their careers.

Treating the fringe as allies rather than banishing it was a choice. Through much of the late twentieth century, the Birch successors mostly stood outside the gates, shouting in protest. The leaders of the GOP did not have to placate them, did not have to let them knock the metal down, inch by inch, until the gates fell and the renegades stormed the grounds.

Chapter 11

TAKEOVER

GEORGE W. BUSH'S RELATIONSHIP WITH THE FAR RIGHT WAS A fraught blend of alliance building punctuated by mutual animus. Those who subscribed to conspiracy theories, isolationism, nativism, and white supremacy eyed him suspiciously. His last name summoned bad memories of his dad's vision of a "new world order," and his time as a member of Yale's Skull and Bones, a secretive club that some fringe activists likened to the Illuminati, raised doubts about his character. As one conspiracy theorist predicted in a 1999 blog post, if Bush won the White House, he was going to copy the "Antichristian policies and attitudes of President Clinton."[1]

When Bush, a Republican, ran for president in 2000, he knew that to have any hope of winning, he would need to avoid alienating his party's far-right fringe. As Texas governor and in his White House run, he played up the idea that he was not his father's son. "The biggest difference between me and my father," he once said, "is that he went to Greenwich Country Day and I went to San Jacinto Junior High." While both George Bushes descended from New England WASP aristocracy, the younger one wore cowboy boots and spoke with a twang. Adviser Karl Rove noted that there was "more bubba in him." A born-again Christian, he had stronger ties to the socially conservative wing of his party, and many conservative evangelicals accepted him as, if not one of their own, at least an ally.[2]

Bush became the most conservative president since the 1920s. He had none of his father's ambivalence about abortion or supply-side economics and on the whole governed solidly from the right. That said, he was still not in line with the ultraright fringe. In his politics and policy positions he was closer to Reagan than to his dad, even arguably to the right of Reagan. This in fact underscores that the rift was not between the old-line eastern establishment Bush Sr. types and the "movement conservatives"; it was between *both* those groups and the Birchy far-right types.

Although George W. Bush was more religious and socially conservative than his father, he shared with him, Reagan, and other GOP leaders the recognition that the far right was a cohort that needed to be managed. Courting the votes, funding, and passion of extreme conservatives was essential, and he fully accepted that sometimes dirty hands were the cost of victory. So in early 2000, after losing by a stunning eighteen-point margin to Senator John McCain in the New Hampshire GOP presidential primary, Bush headed to the conservative state of South Carolina under no illusions about his next move. One of his first campaign stops was at Bob Jones University, which had long promoted segregation and still banned interracial dating. (Its president once called Bush Sr. "a devil.") After initially defending his appearance at the school, Bush apologized (as his father had belatedly done for the Willie Horton ad)—not for speaking at Bob Jones but for his silence on the interracial ban. His disavowals were similarly wan when McCain, who had adopted a baby girl from Bangladesh, blamed Bush's team for a smear campaign that included anonymous phone calls in which fake pollsters asked South Carolinians, "Would you be more or less likely to vote for John McCain . . . if you knew he had fathered an illegitimate black child?" Bush turned his real fury not on the racist phone calls but on a retaliatory McCain ad stating that Bush "twists the truth like Clinton."[3]

At the same time, Bush knew that such racist appeals risked turning off suburban Republicans, especially women. He sought to unite these more mainstream conservative voters with those further right by highlighting their shared hostility toward the New Deal and the Great Society. He spoke about tax cuts ("It's not the government's money, it's the people's money") and about deregulation measures to encourage churches and private charities to support the needy. His campaign spun these policies into a philosophy called "compassionate conservatism." He said, "The truest kind of compassion doesn't only come from more government spending, but from helping citizens build lives of their own."[4]

Again, though, when the entire presidential election hung on the votes of a shockingly small number of Floridians, Bush took extreme measures. He understood the calculus, and when the results became ensnared in a highest-of-stakes recount, he brought in the ultimate pragmatist from his dad's administration, James Baker, to get the job done. Within days of the inconclusive election, a few dozen almost all-white and male Republican operatives and congressional staffers descended on a ballot-counting room in Miami-Dade County. Clad in blazers and button-downs (hence the moniker "Brooks Brothers riot"), they shouted, "Voter fraud" and "Let us in" and banged on doors and windows. One Democratic official caught in the melee said he felt that he was in physical danger. He later reflected that the rioters used "violence, fear and physical intimidation" to influence "the outcome of a lawful elections process." The aggressive tactics worked. Miami-Dade officials scrapped their recount. In a five-to-four vote, the Supreme Court stopped a statewide recount, and Bush entered the White House. If Birchian bullying was what it took to win, so be it.[5]

Still, Bush managed to enter office with his mainstream conservative credentials intact. His orientation—proimmigrant, muscular interventionism, education reform, a conservatism leavened with "compassion"— clashed with the norms and ideas that his fringe supporters held on all those key questions. It was in this conflict that the ground was laid for a shift in power from mainstream conservative to fringe. As Bush prepared to take the oath of office, his presidency hardly seemed bound to be the most consequential chapter yet in the Birchification of the American right and the GOP. But that is what it became.

LESS THAN EIGHT MONTHS AFTER HIS INAUGURATION, PRESIDENT BUSH, who had campaigned against nation building and spoke of projecting "a humble nation, but strong," faced a steep challenge to the "humble" part. When Islamist terrorists flew planes into the World Trade Center and the Pentagon, the president united most of the country behind his response—a "war on terrorism"—and his approval ratings soared.[6]

But some of his subsequent policies empowered the country's most extreme voices, Birchian and otherwise. After gaining support from much of the world for the invasion of Afghanistan, his administration twisted intelligence to accuse Iraqi president Saddam Hussein of possessing weapons of mass destruction and collaborating with the 9/11 terrorists, and then, based on those false allegations, he invaded Iraq. After toppling Saddam, Bush reneged on his (and the Birch successors') stated antipathy toward nation building and sought to build democracy in the heart of the Middle East. His administration's countenance of torture, which flouted international norms and the Geneva Conventions, drew on the Birch tradition of denouncing international institutions as injurious to US sovereignty.

On the domestic front Bush elevated the ideas of the Birchite fringe on a handful of occasions. Wooing prolife Christians, his administration supported federal intervention to keep Terri Schiavo on life support against the wishes of her husband, who had made the heartrending decision to end her fifteen years in a vegetative state. Bush also delighted white evangelical supporters and others on the far right when he appointed John Ashcroft as attorney general. A self-made graduate of Yale and the University of Chicago Law School, Ashcroft had attained one of the most conservative records in the US Senate, earning the highest possible ratings from the American Conservative Union. He advocated imposing a ban on almost all abortions. Like Bush, he spoke at Bob Jones University. After accepting an honorary degree, he delivered a speech where he elevated God above civic rule in America: "There's a difference between a culture that has no king but Caesar, no standard but the civil authority, and a culture that has no king but Jesus, no standard but the eternal authority. . . . We have no King but Jesus."[7]

Like Birchers, Ashcroft sometimes saw segregationists as allies, and he took a dim view of the civil rights and voting rights revolution of the 1960s. In 1998 then-Senator Ashcroft gave an interview to *Southern*

Progress, a pro-Confederate publication, in which he endorsed Lost Cause mythology: "Your magazine also helps set the record straight. You've got a heritage of doing that, of defending Southern patriots" like the Confederate leaders Stonewall Jackson, Robert E. Lee, and Jefferson Davis. (The interview's introduction hit a Birchian note when it lauded Ashcroft as a "jealous defender of national sovereignty against the New World Order.") With Ashcroft's appointment as attorney general, an editorial writer stated, "the neo-Confederate cause is no longer the fringe"; it's "part of the mainstream debate over how we read America's past and how we design America's future."[8]

As governor of Missouri from 1985 to 1993, Ashcroft had twice vetoed bills that would have established the same rules for voter registration in Democratic St. Louis as those that applied in the Republican suburbs. He justified the veto by raising concerns about voter fraud, without giving evidence that such fraud existed. As US attorney general he took up this issue in the Justice Department's Civil Rights Division, announcing a Voting Rights and Integrity Initiative that grew into a long-term, far-reaching campaign that used unsupported claims of fraud to erode voting rights.[9]

Bush's second attorney general, Alberto Gonzales, continued this crusade. He oversaw the firing of nine US attorneys who were deemed insufficiently loyal to Bush because they declined to prosecute weak accusations of voter fraud in their locales (mainly heavily Black and Democratic strongholds).[10]

Bush also made common cause with the far right when he ran for reelection against Senator John Kerry in 2004. A Bush-aligned super PAC, the Swift Boat Veterans for Truth, promoted a conspiracy theory that hinged on a book titled *Unfit for Command*, coauthored by Jerome Corsi, which claimed that Kerry's heroic actions in the Vietnam War were fabrications. The campaign used classic Birch techniques: take evidentiary shards, spin them into a false story, and depict the person as an enemy of the republic.[11]

But Bush couldn't control what the campaign had unleashed. Corsi was an extremist in the Birch tradition. In 2007 he made clear his unhappiness with the Bush administration in his book *The Late Great U.S.A.: The Coming Merger with Mexico and Canada*, an attack on free trade and immigration. "I kept asking myself why, six years into the war on terror, was Bush not securing the border?" Corsi said. His answer: Bush intended to replace US sovereignty with a superstate called the North American Union. Among those who helped Corsi spread this conspiracy theory were far-rightists and sometime Birch allies such as Representative Ron Paul of Texas and Phyllis Schlafly. The Birch Society itself, itching to recapture its long-ago relevance, referred to the fictional North American Union as a "satanic" plot to kneecap US autonomy and spent an entire issue dissecting the topic in its *New American* magazine. When asked about the conspiracy theory, Bush made clear he had no truck with it. "If you've been in politics as long as I have, you get used to that kind of technique, where you lay out a conspiracy and then force people to try to prove it doesn't exist. That's just the way some people operate."[12]

The attacks from Corsi, Schlafly, and the rump Birch Society reflected the fact that for all Bush's efforts to appease the far right, once in office he rejected much of their agenda. Bush championed free trade, forged close ties to Mexico and Canada, strengthened some of America's alliances overseas, and ultimately increased the size and scope of the federal government during his two White House terms. He added a Medicare prescription drug benefit, established national education standards for all public schools, spent heavily to stem Africa's HIV/AIDS crisis, and created the Millennium Challenge Corporation to provide infrastructure funding to the developing world. Although hardly an environmentalist, Bush did, late in his presidency, sign a centrist, bipartisan bill that raised fuel emission standards.[13]

On race, Bush was more opportunist than civil rights proponent. But he found it convenient to punish expressions of extremism and forced Senator Trent Lott to step down as Senate minority leader for his remarks praising Strom Thurmond's segregationist 1948 presidential run on the Dixiecrat ticket. Bush also signed a renewal of the Voting Rights Act (which had been passed unanimously by the Senate). Six days after the 9/11 terrorist attacks, he stood with a group of Muslim Americans at a Washington mosque and said, "The faith of terror is not the true faith of Islam. . . . Islam is peace." He added that Muslim Americans "make an incredibly valuable contribution to our country" and that "in our anger and emotion, our fellow Americans must treat each other with respect." Most detestable of all to the far right, in 2006 Bush delivered an Oval Office address urging Congress to pass comprehensive reform that included a path to citizenship for undocumented immigrants. "We must remember that the vast majority of illegal immigrants are decent people who work hard, support their families, practice their faith, and lead responsible lives," Bush said.[14] After howls of disgust (pundits like Ann Coulter cried "amnesty"), the anti-immigrant wing of his party helped tank the bill, and much of the fringe disowned him. Republicans inclined to support immigration reform took notice and pulled back for the foreseeable future.[15]

The affronts to the far right piled higher and higher. Despite his previous calls for small government, Bush had built a domestic security state, similar to Truman's national security architecture early in the Cold War, employing vast powers to monitor suspected terrorists at home (via the Patriot Act) and establishing the Department of Homeland Security (the third-largest cabinet agency).[16]

By 2007, as the wars in Afghanistan and Iraq were becoming unpopular, isolationist sentiment ticked upward. Discontent over both wars, which came to be seen as never-ending quagmires to many Americans late in Bush's tenure, gave ammunition to the anti-interventionists in the GOP fringe and helped discredit Bush's militarily aggressive internationalism. Pew Research found that two-thirds of Americans thought the Iraq War was "not going well," and a majority of respondents said they wanted "troops home as soon as possible." The preemptive Iraq War and President Bush's call to aid "the growth of democratic movements and institutions in every nation and culture" had worn thin.[17] Isolationist, far-right activists, whose stock had plummeted after the Cold War's end seemed to have vindicated internationalism, now won a new hearing and pushed for more power within the GOP. Tucker Carlson, then with CNN, decried Bush's faltering attempts to democratize the Middle East, while Fox News's Glenn Beck slammed his "Wilsonian" approach to spreading democracy overseas. Corsi called for his impeachment.[18]

In September 2008 Bush's response to the collapse of the nation's credit markets and the ensuing financial crisis infuriated the far right.

To restore liquidity, the US government would buy Wall Street banks' distressed debt—pouring billions of taxpayer dollars into the same private firms whose greed and recklessness had brought on the predicament in the first place. Distasteful as it was, most Democrats held their noses and supported the Troubled Asset Relief Program (TARP) as necessary to stave off a depression, but a surprising number of Republicans balked, some of them blasting the plan as creeping socialism (though socialist governments do not tend to funnel large sums of public money to private banks).[19]

During nail-biting negotiations at the White House, Bush seemed hapless, unable to referee what one participant called an "internal GOP ideological civil war." When TARP ultimately passed, many Republicans in Congress decried it as an apostasy. They charged that Bush had bailed out Wall Street bankers at taxpayer expense. Bush had pledged to curb federal economic influence, but the TARP law seemingly undercut that promise. Shortly thereafter, the president agreed to use TARP funds to bail out the auto industry as well. Bush's erstwhile allies on the far right stewed.[20] Although TARP helped avert financial meltdown, it couldn't prevent the onset of the deepest and longest economic slump since the Great Depression. As Bush left office unemployment was soaring, and Main Street was reeling.

The perception that mainstream conservative governance had failed gave opportunities not only to the Democrats but also to the far right. Bush's failures overseas and with the economy (as well as his policies on immigration, education, health care, and other issues) scrambled Republican politics and ultimately helped the fringe do what it had long desired: topple conservative GOP institutionalists. It was in the fissures that had grown by pitting the fringe against Bush's governance and in the subsequent repudiation of Bush by a variety of activists that the far right at last gained an edge in the war for the GOP. In explaining the far right's takeover of conservatism, the Bush presidency was perhaps the most significant chapter of all.

BUSH FATIGUE WAS RAMPANT DURING THE 2008 PRESIDENTIAL CAMpaign. The president's approval ratings hovered around 30 percent, and he skipped the GOP convention, addressing the delegates only by video—a far cry from the triumphant victory laps taken by Reagan in 1988 or Clinton in 2000. Several ideas and individuals with roots in the Birch movement filled the vacuum, but perhaps none better embodied the Birch tradition than Texas congressman Ron Paul. A onetime libertarian and a lifelong exponent of key Birch ideas, Paul gave those ideas a second wind when he ran for president in 2008 and again in 2012. "I have a lot of friends in the John Birch Society," he said. "They're generally well educated, and they understand the Constitution. I don't know how many positions they would have that I don't agree with."[21]

His 2008 campaign promised a break from party orthodoxies with rhetoric that often sounded Birchian. He urged the government to eliminate foreign aid, withdraw from the UN, and "end the Fed." A longtime isolationist, Paul had been one of only six Republicans in 2002 to vote against the Bush administration's resolution authorizing the use of force that led to the war in Iraq. He argued that Saddam Hussein's regime posed "no threat to our national security," that the resolution gave the president too much power, and that it compelled the United States to follow the "dictates of the United Nations." Six years later, his messages resonated with a striking number of Republicans and unaffiliated young men who were new to politics. His campaign broke fundraising records, reeling in some $4.2 million in a single day in late 2007, a so-called money bomb.[22]

Athletic, energetic, and slight, his doctor's office filled with economics textbooks, Paul's charm was that he came off as a bit of a kook. He kept most of his savings in gold and silver because he distrusted the US money supply. He repeatedly claimed that Social Security was unconstitutional.[23]

Paul grew up opposing the New Deal. In 1964 he supported Goldwater and opposed the Civil Rights Act. In 2004, he was the only US representative to vote against the fortieth-anniversary commemoration of that landmark act, which banned discrimination based on race, color, religion, sex, or national origin, because, he said, it "did not improve race relations or enhance freedom. Instead, the forced integration dictated by the Civil Rights Act of 1964 increased racial tensions while diminishing individual liberty." He was also part of a small House minority to vote against the 2006 reauthorization of the 1965 Voting Rights Act.[24]

Although Paul said that he didn't share Birchers' belief in conspiracy theories—"that 12 or 15 people for hundreds of years get together and plan the world"—in fact he embraced many far-fetched plots, including Corsi's warnings of a North American superstate. Paul's presence on-stage during the presidential race legitimized some of the fringiest ideas within the Republican Party. During a primary debate on November 28, 2007, a voter asked Paul if he believed "a conspiracy theory regarding the Council on Foreign Relations and some plan to make a North American Union by merging the United States with Canada and Mexico," as some of his online fans claimed. Paul denied that this was a conspiracy theory—"These are real things"—and said sardonically, "CFR exists, the Trilateral Commission exists, and it's a, quote, 'conspiracy of ideas.'" His answer drew a loud round of applause. John McCain, standing at the next lectern, raised his eyebrows and grimaced. "Some people believe in globalism, others of us believe in national sovereignty," Paul continued. "And there is a move on toward a North American Union. . . . They're planning on millions of acres taken by eminent domain for an international highway from Mexico to Canada, which is going to make the immigration problem that much worse."[25]

When an especially loyal constituent died, Paul inherited a four-acre property in a joint ownership arrangement with the Birch Society. Although never a member of the society, he subscribed to *American Opinion*, appeared in Birch videos, and spoke at Birch events, including its fiftieth-anniversary celebration, where he fondly reminisced about Larry McDonald, a close friend and onetime Birch spokesman. In the mid-1970s, Paul recalled, he and McDonald were the only doctors in Congress *and* the only members of Congress to vote against funding for a flu vaccine.[26]

Paul's office was once led by chief of staff and former Birch lifetime member Lew Rockwell, who had worked in the society's Member's Monthly Message Department before resigning after a fallout with Birch leaders (a supervisor called his work "sloppy . . . lacks imagination").[27] Like many other Birchers-turned-activists in the religious-right and libertarian movements of the 1970s, Rockwell thirsted for political combat and embraced incendiary behind-the-scenes social and culture-war commentary. Paul's aides also said that Rockwell had authored the lion's share of the anti-Black, antigay articles that appeared in the *Ron Paul Survival Report*, a newsletter, while serving as vice president of Ron Paul and Associates from 1985 to 2001. Some of the more racist passages in the newsletter reportedly included, "Order was only restored in L.A. when it came time for the blacks to pick up their welfare checks," and black protesters should "gather at a food stamp bureau or a crack house." Rockwell founded the Ludwig von Mises Institute, where he and libertarian economist Murray Rothbard promoted neo-Confederacy views and the Austrian school of economics that called for the dismantling of state intervention in market economies. The men argued that attracting working-class whites to the movement would help mainstream libertarianism, and they praised ex-KKK grand wizard David Duke's 1990 Louisiana GOP Senate run. They also backed Ron Paul's 1988 Libertarian Party presidential campaign and Pat Buchanan's 1992 White House run.

The newsletters, long ignored by the news media, suddenly became an issue as Paul caught fire in the 2008 primary race. Although Paul told CNN in early 2008 that he had "no idea" who had written the newsletters, the *Washington Post* found that Paul likely not only knew that it was Rockwell but had signed off on the newsletters himself. Two reporters from *Reason* wrote, "To this day, Rockwell remains a friend and advisor to Paul—accompanying him to major media appearances; promoting his candidacy on the LewRockwell.com blog; publishing his books; and peddling an array of the avuncular Texas congressman's recent writings and audio recordings."[28]

Hard-core racists flocked to Paul's cause. It was hard for any member of the fringe to build a wall and keep out those even further on the right—including neo-Nazis and white supremacists. Paul was a favorite among readers of the neo-Nazi website Stormfront, and Don Black, a former Klan boss who ran Stormfront, said the newsletters were one reason they endorsed Paul's candidacy. "We understand that Paul is not a white nationalist," Black told the *New York Times*. "We think our race is being threatened through a form of genocide by assimilation, meaning the allowing in of third-world immigrants into the United States." But although Paul didn't ascribe to such beliefs, the Stormfront members still liked his "aggressive position on securing our borders" and his plan to abolish the Federal Reserve. "Our board," Black said, "recognizes that most of the leaders involved in the Fed and the international banking system are Jews."[29]

Paul was willing to accept the support of racists to infuse his cause with money and zeal, declining to repudiate them outright. More than most GOP leaders, Paul channeled their fury, tapping anger at civil rights, income inequality, and fear of government.[30]

For a losing candidate, Paul's influence was substantial, opening the Republican Party to previously unthinkable views. The North American Union surfaced as a topic whenever the 2008 GOP presidential candidate Mitt Romney held town halls. Thirteen states passed resolutions denouncing the fictitious union, and Virginia Republican representative Virgil Goode introduced a House resolution condemning it. Paul's criticisms of Bush's inclusive immigration policies helped inflame an already charged issue, raising it to the status of GOP litmus test. His even more frequent denunciations of NAFTA and Bush's trade agenda fed an outcry that jeopardized all future trade deals. When Paul ran for president again in 2012, Jesse Benton, his campaign chair, exulted in Paul's influence on the GOP platform. He pointed out that just eight years earlier, it was only "fringy people in the John Birch Society" who advocated policies like auditing the Federal Reserve. "Now it's the Republican Party."[31] Score another one for the fringe.

IN 2000, SOON AFTER BUSH BACKERS' SMEAR AGAINST JOHN MCCAIN help sink McCain in South Carolina, the Arizona senator had taken a brave stand against the evangelical far right. In a school gym in Virginia Beach, Virginia, not far from the headquarters of Pat Robertson's Christian Coalition, he said that those who engage in "the politics of division and slander" are "corrupting influences on religion and politics, and those who practice them in the name of religion or in the name of the Republican Party or in the name of America shame our faith, our party and our country." He singled out Robertson and Falwell by name and called them "agents of intolerance." McCain, whose campaign bus was dubbed the Straight Talk Express and who was leading what he called a "reformist crusade" to redirect the GOP away from the fringe, told the Virginia audience, "We are the party of Ronald Reagan, not Pat Robertson. We are the party of Theodore Roosevelt, not the party of special interests. We are the party of Abraham Lincoln, not Bob Jones."[32]

Emphasizing his own support of conservative positions on such issues as abortion and taxes, McCain made clear that his comments went deeper than politics, to morality. Not since Nelson Rockefeller at the 1964 convention had any Republican stood up to the party's far-right wing with as much conviction and fervor. But in 2008, when McCain ran for president again, he faced the indisputable reality that no Republican could win without substantial support from white evangelical voters, who represented almost 25 percent of the American electorate. "One of 2000's big lessons," the *Arizona Republic* asserted, "was that a Republican candidate cannot ride the support of independents, Democrats and media to victory in the GOP primary process."[33]

So McCain backtracked, reconciled with Falwell, and addressed graduates at his Liberty University. For more than a year he sought the endorsement of Texas televangelist John Hagee, who had called the Catholic Church "the great whore" and said that the Holocaust was part of God's plan to send the Jews "back to the land of Israel." Upon receiving Hagee's endorsement, McCain said he was "very honored." (Later, in the face of media criticism, he backpedaled on his backpedaling, and Hagee ultimately withdrew his endorsement.)

McCain saw that it was no longer possible to navigate the tension between the far right and the mainstream because by 2008, in the Republican Party, the fringe had begun to gain the upper hand. If he wanted to win, McCain had little choice but to violate his own principles. Critics chided McCain for flip-flopping on torture, lobbying reform, public funding of elections, and the so-called Swiftboating of John Kerry in 2004. Journalists and voters who had once admired his straight talk now wondered, if McCain wasn't going to stand strong against the encroaching successors to the Birch movement, who was?[34]

McCain struggled in the general election to deal with the far right—needing their votes but reluctant to be pulled into the extremist swamp. At one campaign event, when a supporter attacked Democratic presidential candidate Barack Obama, calling him "an Arab," Mc-Cain took the microphone from her and said, "He is a decent person and a person you don't have to be scared of as president of the United States."[35]

He faced another momentous ideological test when choosing his running mate. Forty-four years old and the first woman to appear on a Republican presidential ticket, Sarah Palin was a dynamic, socially conservative governor of Alaska with a strong antiestablishment bent. A self-professed "hockey mom," she liked to say that she and McCain were a "team of mavericks." She presented herself as a whistleblower who, as governor, had taken on Big Oil and the political establishment.[36] She was also given to Birch-style rhetoric about "elites" and "cabals" subverting the government. In a 1995 photo she provided to the *New York Times* for a profile, the Birch magazine *New American* is clearly visible in front of her. She denied any connection to the society (constituents sometimes sent her reading material), but whether she was a subscriber or just a victim of happenstance, the image was apt, emblematic of her affiliations and her political allegiances.

At first, McCain's choice of Palin electrified the Republican faithful. In her speech at the Republican convention in St. Paul, she invoked the Birch motif, accusing elites of weakening American values and taking aim at a ring of insiders who had no connection to real Americans.[37]

Her rise in politics, too, owed a debt to Birchers and their allies. When Palin ran for mayor of Wasilla in 1996, she drew support from the Alaskan Independence Party (AIP), whose members advocated secession from the United States and allied themselves with the Birch Society. Her husband, Todd Palin, had been a member of the AIP for seven years, and both Palins sympathized with its radical antistatist agenda, which carried Birch echoes. "I've got no use for America or her damned institutions," founder Joe Vogler, a gold miner, once declared. AIP supporter Steve Stoll (nicknamed "Black Helicopter Steve" for his love of conspiracy theories) had allegedly "wrapped his guns in plastic and buried them in his yard so he could get them after the New World Order took over." Active in Wasilla's Birch movement, he campaigned for and donated to Palin, and she and Stoll later pushed a law that empowered militias in the state. As mayor, Palin tried to appoint him to an open seat on Wasilla's city council but was blocked by a council member.[38]

Palin's 2008 convention speech quoted Westbrook Pegler, a right-wing syndicated columnist whose column ran in *American Opinion* and who, referring to Robert F. Kennedy, wrote in 1965 that he wished "some white patriot of the Southern tier will spatter his spoonful of brains in public premises before the snow flies." While Palin chose an inoffensive Pegler quote—"We grow good people in our small towns, with honesty and sincerity and dignity"—the decision to quote a pro-Birch columnist with a record of inflammatory commentary gave hints as to her ideological affinities.[39]

Palin also talked a lot about the "real America," by which she probably did not mean her Democratic opponent's home city of Chicago, or his birthplace, Honolulu. When she charged that Obama had been "palling around with terrorists," the gist was equally clear: Obama would betray the United States. "This is not a man who sees America the way you and I see America," she warned an almost entirely white audience on another occasion. During one rally speech, Palin denounced Katie Couric's gotcha interview tactics (the reporter had tripped up Palin when she asked what newspapers Palin liked to read). Livid supporters turned toward the journalists' section and hurled obscenities. One told an African American soundman, "Sit down, boy." The mention of Obama's name was enough to rouse crowds to shout, "Traitor," "Treason," and "Kill him."[40]

Palin's vice-presidential campaign was a harbinger. Her rallies started to draw more supporters than McCain's. By the time McCain lost the general election, Palin had become a source of internal acrimony within the campaign, and most voters had concluded that she wasn't ready for the White House. But her popularity on the right suggested that she, rather than McCain, might represent the party's future.[41]

Reacting to Obama's victory, people in big cities in blue states literally danced in the streets. An exhausting, confounding era had ended, and even many independents and some Republicans shared in a spirit of hope and renewal.

But one election could not wipe away developments that were decades in the making, and any hopes for a country where Americans moved past their divisions proved fleeting. The United States remained a fractured polity, cleaved along racial, gender, regional, and class axes. The fractures within American conservatism worsened as well. The far right was now entering the mainstream of the Republican Party, bringing with it the legacy of the John Birch Society.

THE RISE OF THE FAR RIGHT IN POLITICS WAS MIRRORED BY ITS ASCENT within the right-wing media sphere. During the 1990s conservative media outlets had often partaken of Birch-inflected conspiracy theories and apocalyptic imagery. The Drudge Report debuted in 1995, Fox News launched in 1996, and both helped lead the impeachment effort against Bill Clinton by having primed their viewers to think he was evil incarnate. But from around 2006 to 2010 the conservative media universe became even friendlier to Birchite causes, acting as a kind of de facto enforcer of ultraconservative ideas and individuals. Longtime talk radio kingpin Rush Limbaugh championed Sarah Palin as "the head of the party" following the Bush years and picked up on some Birch themes when he faulted Bush's soft-on-the-border policies as a threat to "our sovereignty." "We've had two people in our party literally, John McCain and George W. Bush, grant amnesty to how many millions of illegal Hispanics in the country," he said.[42]

The breakout media star of the far right was Alex Jones, whose namesake show on his website InfoWars gained power and notoriety coinciding with the debut of YouTube in 2005. Jones combined a Birch affection for all manner of conspiracies with a government-as-evil philosophy. He got his start in broadcasting on an Austin local-access television channel, where he railed at the FBI raids in Waco and Ruby Ridge that had occurred early in Clinton's presidency and falsely pinned the 1995 Oklahoma City bombing on the federal government.[43] His roots also lay in the Birch movement. As a young teen, he spied a book on his father's bookshelf: Birch Society PR director Gary Allen's *None Dare Call It Conspiracy*. Allen's polemic chronicled a conspiracy of international bankers to establish a one-world superstate, and Jones loved what he read there. Allen had provided Jones with a template, part stylistic, part ideological, and Jones was adept at adapting it to his own ends. Jones essentially concluded that conspiracies held the key to delineating American life. He invoked Birchite boilerplate tales of "a new world order" that would control the nation's institutions, and he claimed that the terrorist attack of 9/11 was an inside job. More inventively, he said that Barack Obama and Hillary Clinton smelled like sulfur—the scent of the devil—proving they were demons from hell, bent on planetary destruction.[44] But more than his fellow conspiratorial shock jocks, Jones added what became a trademark: cruelty. After a deranged, heavily armed twenty-year-old killed twenty six- and seven-year-old children and six adults at Sandy Hook Elementary School in Newtown, Connecticut, in December 2012, Jones tirelessly spread the obscene story that the massacre had been a "staged" operation organized by gun-control lunatics to make the gun-rights side look bad. (Jones was later sued for libel and ordered to pay millions of dollars in damages to some of the shooting victims' families.) Just as Birchers had sometimes spun theories far removed from the Cold War and alleged that liberals generally were forever engaged in sinister plots to kill innocents, Jones wove webs of fantasy and deception that enraged and empowered his audiences.

During Obama's presidency, Jones had an estimated 7.5 million unique viewers on his website each month. Though treated as a fringe figure, he promulgated far-fetched notions that reached a massive audience. And some Republican leaders amplified Jones's most incendiary allegations. New Hampshire state representative Stella Tremblay falsely charged that the 2013 Boston Marathon bombing was orchestrated by the federal government, echoing Jones. Some Fox News hosts such as Lou Dobbs repeated and basically condoned Jones's baseless theories, while Republicans in Congress such as Jim Jordan and Jason Chaffetz held hearings that investigated Jones's allegation that the Obama administration was buying special bullets that could be used by unnamed federal agents to assassinate law-abiding citizens. Ron Paul and his son Rand, who was elected to the Senate in 2010, were interviewed on Jones's show, and the younger Paul stole a page from the Birchers when he accused Obama of leading an "anti-American globalist plot against our Constitution."[45]

Conservatives who rejected Jones's ideas rarely confronted or condemned him. When social media platforms banned Jones for his foul rants in 2018, the Birch Society even came to Jones's defense, tweeting that the "deep state" was conspiring to quiet him.[46] The Birch successors who ruled this nebulous right-wing media world—a swashbuckling mix of outrage, entertainment, hype, and nefarious tales of big government plots—fueled the fringe's ascent atop the GOP, making it hard to distinguish Republican leaders from activists, donors, and talking heads. Politicians who lost their races signed fat contracts to appear as Fox News pundits. Those still in office who dared take an independent stand were slapped down.

Another rising star, Fox's Glenn Beck, tapped the society's anti-interventionism, conspiratorial, and white supremacist traditions, fusing them into a blend of lurid anti-Obama entertainment. Beck's show debuted on Fox the day before Obama's 2009 inauguration, and soon three million viewers were tuning in nightly. Beck grafted conspiracy theories onto his Birchian view that virtually every American institution had been corrupted by foreign ideology, bloodthirsty bankers, and other globalist evils. Beck's histrionics—he cried, screamed, rambled, pleaded—hid the appeal that his ideas carried when he packaged them for Fox's audiences. Obama was a perfect foil for Beck's brand of politics. America's first Black president, Beck claimed, harbored "deep-seated hatred for white people," desired a "New World Order" dictatorship, and planned to detain citizens in government-run internment camps.[47]

Two books written by the late Birch author and spokesman W. Cleon Skousen helped inspire Beck's understanding of the world. *The Naked Communist* (1958) traced the communist conspiracy to the progressive movement, and *The 5,000 Year Leap* (1981) described the US Constitution as a God-ordained document. (Skousen had also published a 1963 pamphlet titled *The Communist Attack on the John Birch Society*.)[48] Beck never hid his sympathies for the Birch movement. He interviewed society spokesman and Welch biographer G. Edward Griffin, who once said that *The Protocols of the Learned Elders of Zion* explained "much of what is happening in our world today."[49]

As Beck's and Jones's popularity surged in early 2009, CNBC correspondent Rick Santelli stood on a Chicago trading floor and ranted about the bailouts stemming from the previous fall's financial crisis. At the end of his tirade, he turned to the traders behind him and shouted, "This is America. How many of you people want to pay for your neighbor's mortgage that has an extra bathroom and can't pay their bills?" To a chorus of boos, he then asked, "President Obama, are you listening?" Obama had been in office for one month.

The social movements that formed in response to Santelli's rant—widely called the Tea Party—bore conspicuous continuities with the Birch Society of the 1960s. Conspiracy theories of a Birchite hue surrounding the president bulked large. A Tea Party convention speaker named Steve Malloy called Obama "an international socialist" aiming for "a one-world government." Judge Roy Moore, who later ran for US Senate from Alabama and was accused of sexually violating young teenagers, warned Tea Party activists that Obama sought "a U.N. guard stationed in every house."[50] Like Birchers, Tea Partiers viewed media, banking, academic, and political elites as sworn enemies.

There was also a great deal of overlap in the Birch-Tea Party policy agendas. Some Tea Party activists urged abolition of the income tax, the Federal Reserve, and cabinet agencies, and viewed federal laws as unconstitutional.[51] Like the Birch Society, the Tea Party fused Christian nationalism with government-as-the-enemy ideas, twinning morality with notions of elite betrayal. Like the Birch Society, the Tea Party contained multitudes, drawing libertarians and Christian moral agitators alike, and it sometimes attracted violent individuals and groups. The Oath Keepers—a militia mostly composed of former police and military veterans who thought Obama planned to impose martial law and detain "patriots" in camps—appeared at Tea Party rallies. When Obama gave speeches, armed men sometimes showed up carrying signs that called for watering the "tree of liberty" with "the blood of tyrants." Similar language had surfaced among the Birch Society's offshoots a generation earlier and was eerily reminiscent of Don Lobsinger's Breakthrough movement.[52]

Like the Birch Society, the Tea Party relied on men and women who fought in the trenches, working for candidates, spreading the message, appearing at forums, and running for elective office themselves. In

Florida and New Jersey, Tea Party activists protested the fluoridation of the drinking water. Typical was one activist, a high school teacher who alleged that the government was "medicating us without our consent."[53] Yet just as the Birchers had been funded by moguls like Fred Koch and Harry Bradley, so the Kochs, the Bradleys, the Adelsons (conservative megadonors), the DeVoses, and other families with deep roots in the far right backed the Tea Party, building a cross-class alliance.

But there was at least one significant tactical difference between the Birchers and Tea Party activists. In 2010, rather than flirt with a third party or abandon electoral politics as Birchers had sometimes done, the Tea Party allied with politically savvy groups such as FreedomWorks and the Koch-funded Americans for Prosperity and took advantage of the GOP's primary process to begin to unseat conservative Republican incumbents and effectuate a far-right takeover of key congressional seats and governors' offices. The Tea Party's focus and achievements far exceeded anything Birchers had done in electoral politics, with the possible exception of the Birch support for Barry Goldwater in the 1964 GOP presidential primary. Targeting Republicans who had failed a test of purity as defined by Tea Party activists, donors, and groups, this movement succeeded in ending the careers of many established and rock-ribbed conservative officeholders. Between 2010 and 2014, numerous incumbent Republican members of Congress lost primary challenges to right-wing insurgents.[54] The Tea Party also had a more popular set of ideas with which to appeal to voters than the Birch Society had: they agitated against abortion rights, gay rights, voting rights, gender equality, and progressive education in public schools. Reagan and two generations of Bushes had failed to reverse these trends—and such failures, time after agonizing time, imbued the Tea Party movement with a firm sense of mission.

Unlike in the mid-1960s, the Republican Party of the early 2010s failed to check the extreme right. There was no counterpart to the relentless local and national press exposure—the negative associations with racism and antisemitism at the height of the civil rights movement—that had weakened the Birchers. On the contrary, social media and the ubiquitous, sophisticated right-wing media amplified the far right's most inflammatory claims. Above all, conditions in the country had grown more favorable to the far right. The United States was increasingly non-white, the middle class seemed to have stagnated, an economic crisis had been triggered by Wall Street, and a war in Iraq had failed, giving the old Birch claims and aspirations—isolationism, more explicit racism, nativism, and culture battles—even more salience.

The Tea Party was also adroit at exploiting popular anger toward Obama's agenda: government regulations, bailouts, economic stimulus, and landmark health care reform (that allegedly authorized "death panels"). Diligently, it worked to gain the upper hand within the Republican Party. Targeting conservatives who had transgressed, the Tea Party ousted Senators Robert Bennett and Richard Lugar and Representatives Cliff Stearns and Jean Schmidt. In 2014 economics professor and Tea Party favorite Dave Brat defeated Eric Cantor, the House majority leader, because Cantor had allegedly proposed "giving citizenship papers to illegal immigrants." Fox's Laura Ingraham called Brat's victory "an absolute repudiation of establishment politics."[55]

In other elections from around this time, the Tea Party continued to rack up wins. Inspired to enter politics after stewing over what he considered the Bush administration's big-spending record, South Carolina's Mick Mulvaney won a House seat. He once claimed that Social Security was "a Ponzi scheme," suggested on Facebook that the Zika virus did not cause birth defects, and openly campaigned at a meeting of the Birch Society, telling Birchers that the Federal Reserve intentionally had "devalued the dollar." "You all put out some really good stuff and it's always interesting," Mulvaney praised the members.[56] Other far-right victors during the Tea Party surge of 2010 to 2014 became leaders of the Republican Party, including Rand Paul, Ted Cruz, Ron Johnson, and Mike Lee. Sometimes the connections to the Birchers were overt. In 2014 Kentucky businessman Matt Bevin challenged Senate Majority Leader Mitch McConnell during the GOP primary and captioned a photo on his Facebook page showing him "enjoying time with the John Birch Society in Union, Ky." Rand Paul's and Representative Thomas Massie's aides also attended that event, and Massie later keynoted the society's sixtieth anniversary celebration.[57] What once had been considered fuzzy lines that kept the fringe and the center apart, however imperfectly, now had come to seem essentially illegible.

In contrast to Birchers in the 1960s and 1970s, the far right of the 2010s established a firm base in Congress. In 2011 the Tea Party Caucus (later renamed the Freedom Caucus) counted fifty-two members. Caucus founder Michele Bachmann of Minnesota was also influenced by the Birch Society. Like Birchers, she approached public health via conspiracy theories, claiming, for example, that the vaccine against the human papillomavirus caused mental retardation. Bachmann also joined the ministry of former Bircher and church leader David Noebel.[58]

The Birch Society made other cameos during the Tea Party's surge. It cosponsored the 2010 Conservative Political Action Conference, prompting *New York Times* columnist Frank Rich to quip that Birchers had "re-emerged after years of hibernation." By the early 2010s CPAC had become a far more radical organization than it was at its founding in 1974. Reagan had keynoted the first CPAC meeting, invoking his favorite image of the United States as "a city on a hill," supporting immigration and an active American presence overseas. His un-Birchlike address continued when he sang the praises of aviator and war hero John McCain, who had recently been released from a Vietnam prison after enduring years of torture. But by 2010 CPAC had become a hotbed of Birch ideas. Speakers promised to punish GOP leaders who were insufficiently militant. South Carolina Republican senator Jim DeMint told delegates, "We're causing a little trouble for the establishment" and warned that "when Republican senators don't do the things they say they believe in, voters should have a choice of a new Republican, a real Republican."[59]

The Tea Party's signature conspiracy theory—that Obama had been born outside the United States and thus was ineligible for the presidency—also had Bircher resonances. Birchers had insisted that communists controlled the civil rights movement. They painted it as a foreign-directed plot rather than an organic homegrown struggle. "Birthers" unwittingly tapped this inheritance. They spun a related theory that America's first Black president had been born overseas. They implied that Obama promoted ideas foreign to the United States. He had perpetrated on the people a hoax so immense that it had to be stopped at all costs. One implication was that Black Americans reaching for power were frauds and charlatans, an echo of the Bircher view of the civil rights movement. And Birtherism was more popular than the Birch Society had been. In the 1960s polls typically showed that roughly 5 percent of the public supported Birchers; in 2011 a Gallup poll reported that 38 percent of the public said Obama "definitely" was born in the United States. Only 47 percent of Republicans said Obama was eligible for the presidency, according to Fox News.[60] The far right had assailed Eisenhower as a communist agent, painted Clinton as a drug-smuggling kingpin, fingered George W. Bush as a sovereignty-sapping North American Unionist. But for the first Black president, the far right fixated on his birthplace: he wasn't really American. He was probably Muslim, likely from Kenya. Birchers' conspiracy theory about civil rights was having its own consequential afterlife.

BIRTHERISM HAD A LOT GOING FOR IT AS A CULTURAL PHENOMENON. Conspiracy theories could be incredibly profitable (one of Corsi's books was a best seller, and one of John Stormer's sold seven million copies). The mainstream media also gave the conspiracy theory a great deal of oxygen, even though it was patently absurd (Obama, as both his short- and long-form birth certificates proved, was born in Hawaii).

In 2011 ABC's *The View* hosted Donald Trump, where he spread the Birther conspiracy theory before a network news audience. "Why doesn't he show his birth certificate?" Trump said to viewers. "I wish he would because I think it's a terrible pall that's hanging over him. . . . There's something on that birth certificate that he doesn't like."[61] A master of innuendo and misdirection, Trump elsewhere said, "I'm starting to think that he was not born here." Far-right activists and pundits aided Trump's cause. Joseph Farah, publisher of WorldNetDaily.com, told the 2010 Tea Party convention in Nashville, "My dream is that if Barack Obama seeks reelection in 2012 that he won't be able to go to any city, any town in America without seeing signs that ask, 'Where's the birth certificate?'" Trump consulted Farah. Corsi published the book *Where's the Birth Certificate?: The Case That Barack Obama Is Not Eligible to Be President*, and

Trump consulted Corsi. Dirty trickster Roger Stone Jr., an old Nixon hand, also provided advice. Sarah Palin, by then a contributor to Fox News, endorsed Trump's vision, telling the *Washington Post*, "More power to him. He's not just throwing stones from the sidelines. He's digging in, he's paying for researchers to find out why President Obama would have spent $2 million to not show his birth certificate." (Trump never hired any investigators.)[62]

Conservative media either affirmed or failed to refute the falsehood about President Obama's birthplace. Most Republican elected officials stayed silent. Former Massachusetts governor Mitt Romney, who would later stand up to Trump on several issues, at the time was still courting Trump's endorsement for the 2012 presidential nomination, in large part because Trump had become, as ABC News said, "the birther movement's most prominent spokesman." Romney visited the mogul's Las Vegas hotel, held a news conference, and accepted Trump's endorsement.[63] In other ways, too, Romney in 2012 muted his former moderation, much as McCain had in 2008.

Bircher thinking had penetrated the culture more than it had in the sixties, and observers were beginning to notice the uncanny resurgence of Birch ideas. Around this time, historian Sean Wilentz argued that the Tea Party's rise "marks a revival of ideas that circulated on the extremist right half a century ago, especially in the John Birch Society and among its admirers."[64] Once ensconced, the Tea Party's beliefs and attitudes would prove difficult to dislodge. Although Obama won a second term, the structure of national politics—the major concerns of the voting public, trends in the nation's economy and culture, shifts in conservative politics and media—favored the far right. Faith in institutions had plummeted; income inequality remained stubbornly large; fears of Black, Latino, and Asian American political power increased; and with Syria's civil war and the Islamic State's grisly beheadings beamed worldwide, anger at immigrants and at Islamic terrorism shaped the internal conservative debate. The balance of power within the American right shifted in the Birch direction. The Republican Party's leaders and conservative activists grew radicalized in Obama's second term.

After Obama defeated Romney in 2012, the GOP famously conducted an "autopsy" on itself, trying to assess where it had erred and rec-
ommending strategies that could lead it to victory in future presidential
elections. The report encouraged Republicans to embrace immigration
reform, do more to woo Latinos, Asian Americans, and women, and
adjust to the increasingly diverse American electorate by enlarging the
party's tent. Institutionalists were seeking to take back power from the
growing influence of radicals in their ranks.[65]

But the changes were never adopted. Another path beckoned.

Chapter 12

RADICALIZATION

THE RADICALIZATION OF THE AMERICAN RIGHT CANNOT BE AT-tributed to one man alone. Tapping into the Birchers' alternative political tradition, Donald Trump became a savvy exponent of a set of ideas that had been simmering on the extreme right for decades. His background enabled him to piece together a far-right coalition, bringing it to power in the Republican Party and in the country.

Donald Trump's family history was rooted in some elements of modern right wing extremism. In the 1920s his father, Fred, had been arrested after reportedly attending a Ku Klux Klan rally. In the 1970s the Justice Department successfully sued father and son for housing discrimination, underscoring the Trumps' contempt for minorities and rejection of federal civil rights law. Donald, born in 1946, came from New York City, where there was a substantial Birch presence in the 1960s; despite its liberal reputation the city was a logical home for a bombastic leader of the fringe. Roy Cohn, a former senior counsel to Joe McCarthy, mentored Donald Trump, teaching him how to weaponize conspiracy theories, and Cohn had served on the board of Larry McDonald's Western

Goals Foundation, which had numerous Birch members. (Cohn claimed to dislike Birchers for reasons that remain unclear.)[1]

During Obama's presidency, a belief among the political class held that the far right would not take over. A commitment to progress, reason, and social tolerance would prevail; the fringe, it was thought, would ultimately be repudiated. When Trump appeared at the 2011 White House Correspondents' Dinner as a guest of the *Washington Post*, this belief underpinned Obama's mockery of Trump, who at the time starred on NBC's hit reality television show *The Apprentice*. The president joked that now that he had released his birth certificate, Trump could "finally get back to focusing on the issues that matter, like: Did we fake the moon landing? What really happened in Roswell? And where are Biggie and Tupac?"[2] Birchers, too, had been mocked—and the attacks empowered their resentment and humiliation and inspired them to exact their revenge.

When Trump announced his presidential campaign as a Republican in 2015, pundits and politicians dismissed him as a freak rather than treating him as a serious contender. In a speech that year to Georgetown University students, the 2012 Republican nominee, Mitt Romney, argued that Americans typically elected "good people" to the presidency and promised that Trump would not be the party's nominee. Americans, *Washington Post* columnist Dana Milbank wrote, would never let Trump "murder" democracy.[3]

But Trump adapted the Birch notion of Americanism to appeal to the electorate. He said that he might intern Muslim Americans (who, he said, threatened citizens' lives), questioned whether a Mexican American judge was truly American, and refused to repudiate KKK grand wizard and former Republican fringe candidate David Duke. Invoking a Christian moral order that was being "stolen" from white Americans, Trump implied that unless he took power the America his supporters knew and loved would be destroyed.

Trump benefited from the rhetorical and ideological legacy that Birchers had bequeathed to subsequent generations. He stood on the shoulders of far-right giants and presidential candidates such as George Wallace, John Schmitz, and Pat Robertson, and he campaigned on a set of Birch-toned themes, ideas rooted in the history of the extreme right.

Conspiracies, white supremacy, the sense that the United States had been hijacked by alien ideas, and the mantle of oppression and victimhood that Birchers had donned were all present in Trump's 2016 White House run and in the policies his administration later pursued.

Breaking with decades of accepted conservative foreign policy doctrine, Trump argued that he would put America first, meaning that Birchers' anti-interventionist principles and disgust with the internationalist arrangements following World War II would govern the country. Trump's isolationist, anti-free-trade rhetoric rejected, in so many words, decades of mainstream conservative foreign policy, stretching from Eisenhower more or less through George W. Bush's administration. He called NATO "obsolete," the UN full of "utter weakness and incompetence," and NAFTA, which had enjoyed bipartisan support, "the worst trade deal ever made." Insisting that decades of elite misrule had diluted the nation's sovereignty and imperiled its heritage, Trump promised to build "a big, beautiful wall" along the southern border and keep out nonwhites.[4]

Trump's apocalyptic oratory and conspiracy theories helped mobilize his supporters and framed his message. Trump argued that he needed to save Americans from a "deep state" that was destroying the Constitution and stealing people's rights, updating the Birch canard about "insiders" orchestrating America's decline.[5] Trump's final televised ad of the 2016 presidential campaign conveyed many of the conspiratorial ideas that had been building in the far right for decades, drawing on antiestablishment, antisemitic themes. As dollar signs and pictures of villains—the Clintons, Jewish bankers (George Soros, Janet Yellen, Lloyd Blankfein)—flashed on-screen, Trump warned, in Birchite tones, that a political establishment "trying to stop us is the same group responsible for our disastrous trade deals, massive illegal immigration, and economic and foreign policies that have bled our country dry. . . . It is a global power structure that is responsible for the economic decisions that have robbed our working class, stripped our country of its wealth, and put that money into the pockets of a handful of large corporations and political entities."[6] Laying the blame at the feet of the political establishment, Trump described the fight as a battle between patriots and un-American elites.

Early in the 2016 presidential race, as Trump's inflammatory comments multiplied and he topped polls of GOP primary voters, at least a handful of conservatives feared that the far right was gaining momentum and that more needed to be done to stop the reality TV star. In late 2015 *Weekly Standard* editor and onetime Quayle chief of staff Bill Kristol tweeted, "Trump has entered John Birch Society/Pat Buchanan territory," and that it was "important to save conservatism from him."[7] Trump had entered such territory years earlier, however, with his Birther comments, and it was unclear who could stop him. By then, the far right had several advantages over the conservative mainstream in the struggle for the GOP: a dynamic, attention-grabbing candidate; a Republican Party that for decades had accommodated extremists; and above all a series of external shocks that had made Trump's presidential bid more viable than his critics had imagined was possible.

TRUMP HAD A KEY IF UNWITTING ALLY DURING THE PRIMARY CAMpaign: he was running against Jeb Bush, the brother of George W. and the son of George H. W., whose last name invoked establishment evil for many on the far right. By 2016 a Bush had been either vice president or president for twenty of the previous thirty-six years, making the Bushes by far the most powerful family in modern Republican politics. Trump used Jeb Bush as an exquisite foil. Jeb had a strong record as a mainstream conservative Florida governor, and Trump used the Bush family history—with all its old-boy patrician and dynastic connotations—to discredit mainstream conservative governance. He told Jeb on a debate stage that Jeb's brother's decision to go to war in Iraq was "a big, fat mistake," accused George W. Bush of lying about the presence of weapons of mass destruction, faulted George W. Bush for failing to protect Americans from the 9/11 terrorist attacks, and argued that George W. Bush's policies had enabled "Islamic terrorism" to "[eat] up large portions of the Middle East."[8]

Other mainstream conservative policies had seemingly failed, and many Republicans were willing to give the far right's approach a new look. The free-trade deals championed by a generation of Republicans had not halted the loss of manufacturing jobs or led to higher living standards for non-college-educated white workers. China had grown into the nation's leading economic rival, in spite of bipartisan pledges to curb China's influence. TARP was unpopular, deficits were rising, and most of the Christian fundamentalist social agenda had never become law, despite vows by Reagan and both Bushes to make it so. Now was the time for a change, Trump argued. Growing economic inequality framed Trump's appeal: between 1971 and 2019, the percentage of middle-class households in the United States had dropped from 61 percent to 51 percent; between 1989 and 2016 the wealthiest 1 percent had increased its share of national wealth from 30 percent to 39 percent, while 90 percent of Americans saw their proportion of the nation's wealth fall from 33 percent to 23 percent. These developments aided Trump's cause, giving his protectionist, anti-interventionist, and nativist themes a wider audience.[9]

The nation's growing diversity had also empowered some of the Birch successors' attacks on civil rights as diabolically antifreedom. Trump made this agenda his own. He exploited a 2016 terrorist attack that occurred at Pulse nightclub in Orlando, the fears of the Islamic State fueled by the group's beheadings in the Middle East, and the refugee crisis overwhelming parts of Europe and triggered by the ongoing civil war in Syria. Trump's more explicit racism—calling Mexicans "rapists," for example—updated the Birch argument that civil rights was an alien creed, federal enforcement of those laws trampled individual liberties, and the nation's true heritage was under threat. With the share of the country's white population dropping from 88.6 percent in 1960 to 72 percent in 2010 (and the Hispanic population increasing by 43 percent between 2000 and 2010), Republican voters appeared increasingly receptive to Trump's more explicitly racist campaign appeals.[10]

The Birch inheritance not only colored Trump's campaign but also informed his White House agenda. Trump's victory in 2016 gave the far right a chance to enact some of its ideas and air its most aching grievances via the bully pulpit. Had another Republican defeated Trump during the primaries, that nominee and his colleagues almost certainly would have pursued some of the same policies that Trump did. They would have tried to repeal Obamacare, enacted corporate tax cuts, loosened business regulations, expanded fossil fuel production, and minimized the threat of climate change. And under almost any Republican who had won in 2016, the judicial appointments would have been virtually identical, drawing from names on the same list of candidates vetted and endorsed by the Federalist Society. A President Ted Cruz or a President Jeb Bush could plausibly have named the same justices—Neil Gorsuch, Brett Kavanaugh, and Amy Coney Barrett—to the Supreme Court.

But on many of the biggest issues facing the United States, Trump broke with long-standing conservative orthodoxy, built on the work of the Sarah Palin–led Tea Party, and molded the GOP further in his far-right image, in terms of both ideology and style. Rejecting the Reagan-Dole-Bush ideas of yore, Trump adopted Birchite positions on issues and topics ranging from immigration and foreign affairs to civil rights, trade agreements, and conspiracy theories. Trump's repudiation of US global leadership and US-led military and economic interventions was consonant with Birch calls to defend America's sovereignty from foreign ideology and get the United States out of corrupt international alliances and institutions. While Trump called out what he saw as foreign adversaries, he identified the greatest enemies as internal to the United States, a classic Birch stance. Upending the foreign policy touchstones that had guided conservative and moderate Republicans for decades, he denigrated NATO as ripping off US taxpayers, withdrew the United States from NAFTA and the Trans-Pacific Partnership, and pulled the United States out of the World Health Organization while denouncing traditional Western allies such as Germany.

Trump's anti-immigrant oratory and policies overthrew the Reagan-Bush-McCain view of immigration as an "act of love" (in Jeb Bush's words) and their decades-long support for comprehensive immigration reform that included a path to citizenship for the undocumented. Stephen Miller, the president's chief domestic policy advisor, drew anti-immigration rhetoric from white nationalist publications like the 1973 French novel *The Camp of the Saints*, which envisions hordes of immigrants obliterating Western civilization.[11] Under Miller's prodding the Trump administration started to build a border wall (after declaring a national emergency) and enacted an immigration agenda based on child separation at the southern border and a wholesale rejection of virtually all asylum claims.

Trump drew energy, as Birchers had, from white supremacists, militias, and nativists and brought them into his coalition. His alliances with the white nationalists who rioted in Charlottesville ("fine people"), with the far-right, all-male Proud Boys ("stand back and stand by"), and with the deep-state-obsessed, conspiratorial QAnon ("people that love our country") blended racism and conspiracy theories in ways that harked back to the mix of racism, antisemitism, and conspiracy theories that drew many Birchers to their movement.[12]

The more explicit racism was hardly confined to the president. Jeff Sessions, Trump's first attorney general, echoed a Bircher trope by calling the NAACP and ACLU "communist-inspired" groups that were "trying to force civil rights down the throats of people who were trying to put problems behind them." As publisher of *Breitbart News*, Steve Bannon, Trump's first White House political advisor, had featured anti-immigrant, antigay, and anti-Black theories that could have been found in an earlier generation of far-right publications, including *American Opinion* and *American Mercury*. During the 2016 GOP convention, Bannon described his magazine as the publication of the "alt-right."[13]

Another Birch hobbyhorse—imposing Christian prayer and "Americanist" teachings on public schools—became a plank of the administration's policy agenda. Education Secretary Betsy DeVos, an heir to the Amway family fortune, championed public funding of Christian schools, backed the home-school movement (supported by many evangelical Christians), and helped lead the effort to advance patriotic teachings. Although mainstream conservatives had also embraced such causes, the Trump administration focused far less on education reform (such as the No Child Left Behind agenda of George W. Bush) and far more on molding public schools in the pro-Americanist ideas enunciated by the Birchers.[14]

The Birch Society's view of public health policies as a statist plot to quash individual liberties entered the conservative mainstream during the Trump administration's response to the COVID-19 pandemic. Trump and his allies adjusted the Birchite conspiracy theories about fluoridated drinking water to fit the COVID challenge. Trump called the coronavirus "a hoax," predicted that "one day—it's like a miracle—it will disappear," and insisted that the antimalaria drug hydroxychloroquine was an effective treatment for it. Some of his allies said that the government-made vaccines were killing citizens and that the nation's leading infectious-disease doctor, Anthony Fauci, had engineered the coronavirus in order to harm Trump's reelection chances in 2020. (Michael Flynn also said that George Soros and Bill Gates had manufactured the pandemic to "rule the world" and get rid of Trump.)[15]

Trump's governance helped turn conservative antigovernment ideology into a government-as-the-enemy, root-of-all-evil philosophy. His insistence that federal judges, FBI and CIA agents, and government civil servants (the so-called deep state) were plotting a coup against him drew on Birch notions that traitors within the federal bureaucracy posed the most serious threat to Americans' freedoms and lives. Trump once said, "We're saving the world from a radical left philosophy that will destroy this country," a statement that comported with the Birch Society's view of their opponents as "commie-symps."[16]

AFTER TRUMP'S LOSS TO DEMOCRAT JOE BIDEN IN THE 2020 PRESIDEN-tial election, he claimed that the left had committed massive voter fraud and stolen the presidency. The accusation forged conspiratorial Birchite hostility to democracy into a potent catch-all: elites had deprived citizens of their rightful leader; the destruction of the country had commenced. Trump was hardly the first on the right to cast doubt on election results. During the 2008 presidential campaign, Republican nominee John McCain and former Missouri senator John Danforth were among the GOP leaders who alleged that the progressive voter-mobilization group ACORN was engaged in election fraud.

Nonetheless, in Trump's hands, allegations of a left-wing plot to steal power from the people on Election Day represented a more acute break from his GOP predecessors' occasional issuance of disinformation. Singling out predominantly African American cities such as Atlanta, Philadelphia, and Detroit as hotbeds of systemic fraud, Trump weaponized conspiracy theories and cast democracy as unconstitutional to keep himself in power.[17]

There is, however, an important distinction between the way Birchers approached elections and how Trump reacted to his defeat in 2020. When

Birchers participated in electoral politics, they occasionally questioned the results. The Birch Society's infatuation with conspiracy theories gave some of its members a sort of ideological permission slip to peddle baseless allegations, including those involving election cheating. During the 1964 presidential race, for example, one Bircher urged the home office in Belmont to "organize poll-watchers in areas of potential deceit," though the nature of the supposed deceit was unclear. In Brockton, Massachusetts, Warren Appleton, a Bircher, actually persuaded local police to investigate his allegations that a public health official and other proponents had lied about fluoride's benefits during a referendum contest to determine whether to fluoridate the town's drinking water. (It's unclear if the police ever found evidence of coercion.) Nevertheless, most members of the society didn't argue that LBJ had stolen the election from Goldwater.[18]

Still, the continuities and parallels are striking. Just as Birchers took a dim view of democracy, Trump questioned the integrity of elections in which millions of people of color voted. The White Citizens' Councils, Breakthrough, the Minutemen, the violent Jewish Defense League's Meir Kahane (an ex-Bircher formerly known as Michael King), the Liberty Lobby, and other far-right individuals and groups had ties (direct and indirect) to the Birchers, and those alliances reflected the bitter Birchite opposition to multiracial democracy.[19] Trump implied that easy and universal access to the ballot meant Armageddon for white Christian patriots; elites, people of color, globalists, and the media all conspired to silence the one man who was protecting his overwhelmingly white voters' God-given constitutional rights.

Birch activists and leaders also bequeathed to Trump a penchant for inciting political violence. The society's conspiracy theories spurred men like Donald Lobsinger to use physical violence against their putative communist foes. Such theories were potent tools of mobilization, but they were also inextricably bound with antisemitism, racism, and violence. Trump's conspiracy theories inspired white militias such as the Proud Boys and the Oath Keepers along with QAnon adherents and various others to travel to Washington and "stop the steal" of the presidential election on January 6, 2021, the day Congress was convening to certify the results of the election.

At a rally prior to the insurrection at the US Capitol, far-right leaders told thousands of Americans to "fight like hell" (Trump), to "go to the streets and be . . . violent" (Louis Gohmert), to "not go quietly into the night" (Ted Cruz), to "have trial by combat" (Rudy Giuliani), and to remind their enemies that "we're coming for you" (Donald Trump Jr.). Trump promised his supporters, "We will not take it anymore. You'll never take back our country with weakness. You have to show strength." Robert Welch once described Birchers as "a phalanx of tens of thousands of spears, which can be hurled simultaneously as one mighty weapon against any vulnerable spot in the Communist line." The insurrectionists who marched on the Capitol operated as if they were that "one mighty weapon" and launched themselves against the police lines defending one of the world's symbols of democracy. Trump's admonitions were Birchian. He told supporters to rise and defend their republic in order to save it. He said the socialists and their sympathizers had been ruining the United States for decades. Action in the streets was the only remedy for the greatest heist in American history.[20]

Signs and images displayed at the insurrection affirmed conspiracy theories and encouraged the faithful to defend their way of life through force. "Stop the Steal" became as iconic in its defiance as "Impeach Earl Warren" or "Support Your Local Police." One rioter wore a "Camp Auschwitz" sweatshirt. Another carried a Confederate flag. Capitol police later testified that rioters called Black officers "n*****" as they beat the officers with fists and flags. A noose and gallows erected on the Capitol grounds, accompanied by chants of "Hang Mike Pence," the vice president, invoked the Birch argument that leaders had committed treason and deserved to be punished. Threats aimed at reporters were reminiscent of the Birch trope that journalists were procommunist. The insurrectionists' beliefs—that people of color were replacing white Christians, pedophiles were in charge of the government, and the enemy of the republic lurked within the federal government—harked back to Birchite sensibilities and ideology.

One study estimated that among the roughly twenty-one million Americans (about 8 percent) who supported the insurrectionists and thought that violence was necessary to reinstall Trump in office, the most commonly held belief was in the Great Replacement theory, which held that "elites" were plotting to wipe out the white race by replacing them with immigrants and racial and ethnic minorities. The militias on hand that day, including the Oath Keepers and the Proud Boys, shared a lineage with the Minutemen and Breakthrough and other violent offshoots inspired by the Birchers.[21]

The seven-hundred-plus insurrectionists who were arrested also echoed some aspects of Birch membership. The majority of them were white, middle-class professionals with stable employment. They were doctors, architects, small-business owners, veterans, and police officers, and many had college degrees. But they also enjoyed more popular support than the Birchers had. More tellingly, the Big Lie—that the election had been stolen—had gone mainstream in a way that Birch ideas had never quite done. According to a CBS News/YouGov poll taken in the summer of 2021, two-thirds of Republicans believed that "the election was rigged and stolen from Trump."[22]

By THE TIME THE FAR RIGHT TOOK CONTROL OF MUCH OF THE PARTY, long-time Republican politicians believed they had almost no choice but to be subservient. Cross the bosses and you're harassed and primaried into oblivion. Even in safe districts, crossing Trump almost guaranteed a primary challenge and meant the likely end of one's career. As long as Trump enjoyed overwhelming support from Republican voters, there was going to be only token opposition to him within the ranks of the GOP.

Trump's Make America Great Again movement also reflected a Birchite pattern of far-right radicalization. The society had always had some racists and conspiracy theorists in its membership, but many Birchers also staked a claim to outward respectability. Welch once said that some members evinced the "utmost integrity," and that the John Birch Society gave their lives meaning, allowing them to *act* on their deepest principles. In the late sixties, however, as the society turned to those who preferred action and disruption, it became even more aggressive and drew even more bigots to its fold. It was a vicious cycle: radicals drew still more radicals, and conspiracies attracted more extremists.

A similar dynamic defined the MAGA movement. The tie-clad wealthy businessmen such as cabinet secretaries Steve Mnuchin and Wilbur Ross were in a coalition that included white nationalists like Richard Spencer. Movements of the far right that may have aspired to respectability in one form or another quickly devolved, and its most violent and racist members became some of its most energetic and influential leaders.

MAGA paralleled the Birch movement in another key respect: the conspiracism, white supremacism, and take-your-country-back rhetoric attracted individuals who believed at least some of what their leaders were telling them. Donald Trump had drawn supporters to Washington on that fateful day who believed in his lies; his incendiarism primed them for war—and launched them into battle. Birch leaders sometimes tried to police their own fringe (the fringe of the fringe). This task proved impossible. Rank-and-file Birchers often treated the leadership's messages as reality, and words became weapons beyond the realm of traditional political clashes and policy debates. Like the Birch leaders, MAGA leaders lost some control of the movement they had forged. By the time hundreds of Americans stormed the US Capitol in a bloody insurrection, the extreme right had achieved what in many ways was the logical end point of the Birch-slash-MAGA movement: an actual war on the government, waged in the name of taking their country back.

CONCLUSION

OST OBSERVERS AGREE THAT WHEN TRUMP WON THE GOP PRESI-
dential nomination in 2016, it was a clear sign that the American
right had been radicalized. But how the process unfolded is a matter of
dispute. Some recent histories imply that the far right had led conservatism for much of the twentieth century, driving politics and policy, and
that it was only a matter of time until the fringe took power. Other studies have focused on developments fueling the radicalization over the past
three decades, citing the corrosive influence of internet and cable news—
Fox News propaganda, social media, and extremist forums such as 4chan
where individuals get exposed to conspiracy theories and find positive
reinforcement, reveling in the idea of violence against their liberal and
left-wing enemies.

Other explanations of how conservatism became radicalized have also
surfaced with some frequency. Observers have argued that the Supreme
Court's *Citizens United* ruling, which permitted corporations and individuals to spend unlimited sums to influence political campaigns, enabled the wealthiest individuals and businesses to dictate politics and
policy and implement their far-right agenda, thwarting the will of the
American majority. Other critics pointed out that the GOP primary

process enabled Tea Party and MAGA activists to unseat conservative incumbents seen as unfaithful to the far right's highest priorities, giving the fringe a path to power.[1]

Social media, dark money, and Republican primaries are tools for spreading ideas and enforcing a set of pro–Tea Party and pro-Trump norms among party officials. But they are merely tools, and they don't really explain how millions of Americans became open to believing in the extreme right's core ideas, such as the desire to withdraw the United States from its role as a world power, the overturning of free and fair elections, and heaping blame on the GOP, media, and other elites as the root of the nation's decline.

To answer the question, we ought to turn our sights to the longer history of the GOP, American conservatism, and the John Birch Society from 1958 to 2022. Birchers were hardly the only movement that helped to radicalize conservatism and the Republican Party. But more than most mass mobilizations on the far right, the Birch Society begat a host of canny successors that put extremist themes, ideas, and techniques into general circulation. They picketed. They protested. They mailed letters to politicians' offices and corporate headquarters, signed petitions, recruited friends and neighbors, delivered and attended lectures, spread ideas on the radio, ran for school board seats, and organized politically through third parties and the GOP to create the impetus for public action on their priorities. Their tactics also included harassing their foes, shouting down speakers, disrupting civic meetings, and threatening unspecified harm against their critics. Their apocalyptic faith that the country was on the eve of destruction led them to brand liberals, the media, the left, civil servants, and moderates from both parties as communist traitors.

To understand how a large swath of the public became radicalized, we need to look to mass movements, to seemingly extremist individuals who seeded fringe ideas that became more popular as the country evolved. A history of Birchers also suggests that the very notion of what constitutes political extremism is more fluid than fixed. Some Birchers' views—allegations of plots to poison the water supply, a belief that the news media was under communist control—were considered extremist in the 1960s.

But many members of the Birch Society, and their successors, also had one foot planted in the mainstream. Far-right activists worked as doctors, dentists, lawyers, and industrialists who were respected in their communities. They sometimes participated in venerable civic groups and charitable organizations such as Rotary Clubs, the YMCA, their churches, Little League baseball, and the American Medical Association. Most were hard-line but not antediluvian. But even at their most outlandish—the fringe of the Birchian fringe—Birch extremism was not separate from the nation's culture, traditions, and politics. The view that Black people's aspirations for equality imperiled white power and efforts to mold a culture on the basis of Christian morality was a longtime feature of the American landscape with deep roots. Endemic and homegrown, that notion sprang from the soil of a country that often dismissed Birchers as unnatural or backward looking.

Further, the Birchers' history highlights how external shocks—terrorist attacks, financial collapse—can rearrange the landscape and make ideas once dismissed as "extremist" seem popular and reasonable. Conspiracy theories found millions of adherents. Efforts to subvert democracy came to be seen as steps to defend an "American" way of life. The fact that Birchers failed to enact most of their agenda (stopping the Khrushchev summit, impeaching Earl Warren, discrediting civil rights as a Red plot) didn't mean that they lost the larger war. In defeat, they planted seeds that later bore fruit. Their successors picked up on their ideas and campaigned for their causes and over decades gained more and more traction. In the long run, Birchers won by losing.[2]

Americans often conceive of political history as broken into discrete themes and decades. We label these periods "eras" (e.g., the Progressive Era). Sometimes we call them "ages" (the Age of Jackson, the Gilded Age). There are also "revolutions" (the Reagan Revolution, the 1994 Republican Revolution). Viewing the past as a series of thematic periods contains a certain logic as it sheds light on electoral coalitions that cohere and dominate American politics, suggesting that one set of ideas, represented by a particular coalition, replaced another. These demarcations are thus a useful shorthand.

But such frameworks fail to give the Birch Society and the far right their due. These entities don't really have their own epoch—and perhaps Birchers and their allies on the far right deserve one. From roughly 1958 to the present, the Birch style of politics provided an alternative political tradition that challenged the left, liberals, and mainstream conservatives on multiple fronts. The Republican Party and American conservatism tried to keep the fringe inside their coalition, speaking at racist institutions, flirting with conspiracy theories and their exponents, using coded language to push the Birchers' culture war issues. But the fringe grew embittered as its agenda got stymied, and the Republican establishment ultimately lost control of the far right even as it continued to cater to its concerns. We need to find space in our periodization of American politics for fringe traditions in general and the rise of the Birchers in particular. Call that period, from 1958 to 2022, the Bircher Years.

The Birchers' long-term achievements hinged partly on external developments that gave the extreme right an opening. High unemployment and inflation in the late 1970s undermined liberal Keynesian economics as a dominant governing ideology. The ongoing loss of manufacturing jobs, plummeting union membership, and the increased allegiance of working-class white voters to Republicans gave the far right opportunities to assemble a more durable cross-class coalition, while cultural developments like support for abortion rights, gender equality, civil rights, and the environmental movement also enlarged the audience for those who viewed these trends as threats to their lives and livelihoods. Varied expressions of right-wing nationalism, racism, and antisemitism surged, placing the far right on sturdier political terrain. The United States' role as a world leader defending liberal democratic capitalism turned out to be ephemeral rather than permanent. The end of the Cold War in 1989, followed by growing popular discontent with the US-led war on terror starting around 2006, created conditions that favored hard-right isolationists, who argued with greater popular support for closed borders, against military interventions, and for more attention paid to Americans' economic problems.[3]

During the height of the Cold War in the 1950s and 1960s, a robust liberal coalition proved effective at containing the far right, ensuring that it would remain, in the realm of electoral party politics, relatively marginal. But as this coalition fractured in the 1970s and 1980s, and mainstream conservatives led by Reagan took power, the far right gained a seat in the Republican coalition and a voice in its power. Its adherents clashed with conservatives much of the time, but the GOP also legitimized extremist voices and concerns, setting the stage for further gains down the road. The broad assault on the federal government as a problem opened more space in the culture for harsher attacks on it as the center of conspiratorial evil.

When Trump announced his presidential candidacy with a meandering speech in the lobby of Trump Tower, condemning virtually all Mexican immigrants as "rapists" and criminals, commentators derided him as clownish and a sideshow. His ideas were so beyond the bounds of acceptable discourse that few American voters were going to tolerate them, pundits and politicians agreed. Such observers lost sight of what some liberal leaders in the 1960s had come to see as a painful facet of modern America. Liberals back then knew that capitalism and democracy had almost collapsed during the Great Depression and the crisis of fascism. They grasped a truism that many Americans missed amid the glow of Barack Obama's landmark presidency.

They had forgotten a liberalism of fear. Political scientist Ira Katznelson described the liberalism of fear as "a kind of persistent anxiety that sometimes things can get worse." It was "a liberalism that aims . . . at preventing cruelty." Among the things that liberals feared and worked to oppose, scholar Judith Shklar pointed out in her essay on the topic, were "the dangers of tyranny," generally thought of by liberals as mass movements that oppose multiracial democracy and that wish to impose Christian theology on a secular nation. Birchers and their allies also fear tyranny, of course, but by contrast they see it as an elite-driven plot to destroy free enterprise, Christianity, and national sovereignty.

The Birchers ultimately took a dim view of democracy, preferring to see the United States as a "republic." That meant different things to different people. To some Birchers, a republic meant that checks and balances curbed the will of the popular majority, ensuring that as the country became more ethnically and racially heterogeneous, it could retain its white, Christian character, and the rights of white Christians would be defended. To others, a republic meant that an original set of values and people—white Christians who favored strict moral codes, detested the New Deal, and clamored for unfettered free enterprise—had a constitutional and God-ordained right to live their lives however they pleased without dictatorial edicts destroying their liberties from foreign ideologies controlling Washington. It was not a big leap from this idea—democracy is pernicious—to the notion that elections were being manipulated by voters of color and by other unseen and un-American forces and depriving certain citizens of their inherent right to rule the country.

This belief prompted Birchers to engage in extreme tactics. Although there were not high-profile instances of far-right mob violence outside the South in the 1960s, Birch opponents feared that if Birchers and their allies had their way, they would launch a campaign of harassment, intimidation, and belligerence. Such tactics seemed beyond the bounds of typical discourse, substituting a form of brute force and even violent rhetoric and actions for free and fair elections, replacing nonviolent tactics and reasoned debates about politics and policy with accusations of treason and the use of force as an acceptable way to gain power. Birchers, then, bestowed to subsequent generations a fraught legacy—a politics of the street, where armed militias, QAnon adherents, white supremacists, and their leaders lived in the spirit of what Abraham Lincoln once warned against. In 1838, concerned that mob violence imperiled the nation's fledgling democratic institutions, Lincoln predicted that the gravest "danger" to democracy was never going to originate overseas but "must spring up amongst us. . . . If destruction be our lot, we must ourselves be its author and finisher."[4]

ACKNOWLEDGMENTS

ARCHIVISTS, WHO OVERSEE THE COLLECTIONS SO CRUCIAL TO STUDYING history, made a major contribution to the completion of this book. At the Library of Congress, Sara Duke, Jeff Flannery, and Ryan Reft tracked down documents and photographs, offered tips, and went out of their way to aid my search in the library's vast holdings. The Lyndon Baines Johnson Presidential Library's Allen Fisher provided me with details about its collections that were extremely helpful. In New York, the American Jewish Historical Society's Melanie Meyers, deputy director and chair of collections and engagement, offered timely feedback and sure-footed guidance. From Yale University to Brown University's John Hay Library, the Wisconsin Historical Society, the University of Oregon Libraries, Stanford University's Hoover Institution Library and Archives, and the University of California, Berkeley's Bancroft Library, archivists and other staff were consistently gracious, patient, and thoughtful.

Other individuals and organizations lent their aid to this project. Christopher Buckley permitted me to conduct research in William F. Buckley, Jr.'s papers at Yale. The Anti-Defamation League kindly allowed me to review some of the historical records in its archives. Ernie Lazar used Freedom of Information Act requests to uncover a trove of important documents about the history of the John Birch Society and other far-right organizations. He put all the documents online, available for free. A fount of knowledge about the Birchers, Ernie gave this manuscript a careful read, offering thoughts and primary source material. His efforts not only aided this book; they will advance the cause of research into right-wing extremism for years to come.

At Stanford University, I was fortunate to be the recipient of a summer visiting scholar position from the Bill Lane Center for the American West that seeded the research for this book. Thanks go to the center's founding director, historian David Kennedy, and to its current director, political scientist Bruce Cain, who has served as a mentor to me and as a model of teaching and scholarship.

My employer, George Washington University, supplied the kind of institutional backing that made it possible to write this book. A GW University Facilitating Fund award provided the funds that allowed me to consult a wide array of archival collections. George Washington University also granted my request to take a sabbatical, which allowed me to draft the manuscript, and the Gelman Library staff and archivists provided advice. I couldn't have asked for better, more supportive colleagues in GW's College of Professional Studies and Graduate School of Political Management: Todd Belt, Lara Brown, Casey Burgat, Christopher Deering, Natalia Dinello, Sarah Gunel, Suzanne Farrand, Melissa Feuer, Jack Prostko, Liesl Riddle, and others assisted in my research, posed queries, and believed that the study of history could shed light on contemporary politics and American society.

Two excellent research assistants, Emma Young and Elijah Weiss, helped find newspaper articles that aided my analysis of how Birchers influenced the evolution of the modern far right. A host of friends and scholars gave feedback and enriched the book-making process through all sorts of informal conversations. My thanks go to Elisabeth Anker, Eric Arnesen, Mark Brilliant, Vincent Cannato, Steven Cook, Thomas Guglielmo, David Karol, Jeff Kelman, Dane Kennedy, Ethan Porter, Jonathan Schoenwald, Michael Signer, Jeremi Suri, Murray Waas, and Sarah Wagner. A pair of top-flight historians, Joseph Crespino and Jeff Shesol, suggested themes, floated ideas, and provided insights, inspiration, and friendship.

My reading group—named the Red Line because everyone at one time lived near Washington, DC's, Red Line metro—was phenomenal. Marie-Therese Connolly, Mary Ellen Curtin, Robyn Muncy, and Philippa Strum read the entire manuscript, crystallized my thoughts, helped focus my arguments, and contributed edits, title suggestions, laughter, and comradeship. Each "Red Liner" is an amazing author, scholar, and teacher in her own right, and their fifteen years of friendship fueled the book writing.

Susan Chumsky read almost the entire book in manuscript form and provided incredible edits that sharpened each chapter and gave the book a narrative arc. Susan was generous with her time, was patient, and served as an all-around excellent sounding board. I'm also indebted to David Greenberg, a great historian and friend. David proposed ideas for the book, helped me think about the historiography on the far right, and graciously edited the book's introduction and three of its later chapters. I'm grateful for his fantastic edits and, above all, for his almost three decades of friendship.

My agent, the late John Wright, helped the book find a publisher and gave sage advice on all book-related matters. His guidance, humor, and insights will be missed. At Basic Books, I had a roster of all-star editors who were committed to making this book as good as possible. Publisher Lara Heimert and then–senior editor Dan Gerstle acquired the book and encouraged me to broaden it chronologically and conceptually. When Dan changed jobs to help lead another imprint, vice president and editor in chief Brian Distelberg became my editor. Brian shaped the book's themes and ideas and helped me tell a better story. His encouragement, comments, and counsel made this a much better book. Associate editor Michael Kaler offered a detailed, penetrating critique of a first draft of the manuscript, and his input enormously improved the book's structure and arguments. Brandon Proia provided a first-rate line edit that sharpened the prose; Alex Cullina aided with the interior artwork and captions; production editor Katie Carruthers-Busser skillfully led the book across the finish line; copyeditor Kelley Blewster refined sentences, flagged inconsistences, posed shrewd questions, and her final polish on the manuscript was copyediting at its best. The art department at Basic Books created the book jacket.

My family erected the scaffolding that enabled me to write the book. My sister Rebecca Dallek and her family—Mike, Hannah, and Ethan Bender—and my mother-in-law Judy Sarathy provided love and moral support. My parents Robert and Geri Dallek read parts of the manuscript, tracked down photographs for the interior artwork, helped care for their grandchildren, and provided inspiration. They have both had extremely successful careers, but, most importantly, they are great parents and grandparents.

This book wouldn't be in the world without the heroic efforts of my lovely wife, Tara Sarathy. Her passion, intelligence, verve, willpower, and cooking helped see us through the pandemic. As I tried to write the book, Tara went back to school to get a master's degree and left the law behind for a new career as a special-education advocate, consultant, and reading interventionist. Tara provided the kind of moral example and loving partnership that enriched and made possible the research and writing.

She also provided a loving home for our children. Sammy, eleven, and Eli, nine, contributed in ways that they can't fully appreciate. They are two of the most creative people I know and make every day joyful. Sammy's observations of the world, his concern for others, and his shrewd efforts to help me track down the Trump reference in the ADL memo were inspirational. (Sammy also kindly took the author's photo for this book.) Eli brought to this project his skill as a joke-teller, his love of facts, his kindness toward all living creatures, and his sweet disposition to make the process of book writing more pleasurable. Their curiosity, decency, and intelligence were daily sustenance. Finally, Sammy and Eli took loving care of our family pets, Bogart, Peanut Butter and Jelly, Greenie, and Lightning, for which I am also grateful.

ARCHIVAL COLLECTIONS

Below is the list of archival collections on which this book is based.

ADLC   Anti-Defamation League, John Birch Society Collection, Identifier: I-510, American Jewish Historical Society, New York City.

AFP   Arthur J. Finkelstein Papers, 1945–2017, Manuscript Division, Library of Congress, Washington, DC.

BGP   Personal and Political Papers of Barry M. Goldwater, 1880s–2008, FM MSS 1, Arizona State University Library, Greater Arizona Collection, Tempe, Arizona.

CRGBR   Committee to Re-elect Governor Brown Records, 1961–1962, BANC MSS 67/34 c, Bancroft Library, University of California, Berkeley.

DBP   David S. Broder Papers, 1910–2012, MSS86014, Manuscript Division, Library of Congress, Washington, DC.

ELFF   Ernie Lazar Freedom of Information Act Files, https://archive.org/details/@ernie1241.

HGP   Herbert Gold Papers, 1942–2001, BANC MSS 2011/186, Bancroft Library, University of California, Berkeley.

HPP   Herbert A. Philbrick Papers, 1849–1977, MSS84356, Manuscript Division, Library of Congress, Washington, DC.

JBSR   John Birch Society Records, 1928–1990, Ms. 2013.003, John Hay Library, Brown University, Providence, Rhode Island.

JFKPL   John F. Kennedy Presidential Library, Boston, Massachusetts (accessed digitally at jfklibrary.org).

JRP   Joseph L. Rauh Jr., Papers, 1913–2008, MSS62041, Manuscript Division, Library of Congress, Washington, DC.

LBJPL   Lyndon Baines Johnson Presidential Library, Austin, Texas.

LSP Lawrence E. Spivak Papers, 1917–1994, MSS40964, Manuscript Division, Library of Congress, Washington, DC.

RKP Roger Kent Papers, 1947–1974, BANC MSS 74/160 c, Bancroft Library, University of California, Berkeley.

RNAACP Records of the National Association for the Advancement of Colored People, 1842–1999, Manuscript Division, Library of Congress, Washington, DC.

RNPL Richard Nixon Presidential Library, Yorba Linda, California (accessed digitally at nixonlibrary.gov).

SBP Spruille Braden Papers, Rare Book and Manuscript Library, Columbia University, New York City.

SDC Sara Diamond Collection of the US Right, BANC MSS 98/70 cz, Politics and Protest: Collections from the Bancroft Library, University of California, Berkeley.

WFBP William F. Buckley, Jr. Papers, MS 576, Manuscripts and Archives, Yale University Library, New Haven, Connecticut.

WFKP William F. Knowland Papers, 1900–1974, BANC MSS 75/97, Bancroft Library, University of California, Berkeley.

WJGP William J. Grede Papers, 1909–1979, MSS 341, Division of Library, Archives, and Museum Collections, Wisconsin Historical Society, Madison.

NOTES

Introduction

1. Patricia R. Hitt, "From Precinct Worker to Assistant Secretary of the Department of Health, Education, and Welfare: Oral History Transcript / and Related Material," interview by Miriam Stein, 1977, 52–55, Oral History Center, Bancroft Library, University of California, Berkeley; and *Departments of Labor and Health, Education, and Welfare Appropriations for 1970: Hearings Before a Subcommittee of the House Committee on Appropriations*, 91st Cong. (1969), 1081.

2. Several studies focus on divisions between conservative and moderate Republicans, and on the rise of mainstream movement conservatism. See, for example, Geoffrey Kabaservice, *Rule and Ruin: The Downfall of Moderation and the Destruction of the Republican Party, from Eisenhower to the Tea Party* (New York: Oxford University Press, 2012); Rick Perlstein, *Before the Storm: Barry Goldwater and the Unmaking of the American Consensus* (New York: Hill and Wang, 2001); and Lisa McGirr, *Suburban Warriors: The Origins of the New American Right* (Princeton, NJ: Princeton University Press, 2001).

3. BoogieFinger, *Anarchy USA—1966 John Birch Society Film*, video, YouTube, February 10, 2017, www.youtube.com/watch?v=T6UAgm3cgIs; Commission on Professional Rights and Responsibilities, *Suggestions for Defense Against Extremist Attack: Sex Education in the Public Schools* (Washington, DC: National Education Association, March 1970), 4, https://files.eric.ed.gov/fulltext/ED042255.pdf; Rebecca Onion, "The 'Wanted for Treason' Flyer Distributed in Dallas Before JFK's Visit," *Slate*, November 15, 2013, https://slate.com/human-interest/2013/11/jfk -assassination-flyer-distributed-in-dallas-by-edwin-walker-s-group-before-his-visit .html; Jane Wilson to Mr. Spivak, May 21, 1961, B: 45, F 4: "Meet the Press Viewer Mail, Program Response, Robert Welch, 5/21/61," LSP; C. Jacobsen to Lawrence Spivak, May 23, 1961, B: 45, F: 2, "Program Response, Robert Welch, 5/21/61," LSP; and Hitt, "From Precinct Worker," 52–55.

4. Barry Goldwater, *The Conscience of a Conservative* (Washington, DC: Regnery Gateway, 1960), 18.

5. "Goldwater Takes Turn to the Left," *New York Times*, February 15, 1964, www.nytimes.com/1964/02/15/archives/goldwater-takes-turn-to-the-left-finds -arizona-audience-too.html; interview with Goldwater, *Human Events*, April 7, 1961, p. 212, B: 14, F: John Birch Society, WFBP. When asked if he agreed with calls to impeach Warren, Goldwater replied, "No, I don't." Patrick Buchanan, introduction, in Goldwater, *The Conscience of a Conservative* (1990 ed.), xi. The Birch members who served in Congress were Edgar Hiestand, John Rousselot, John Schmitz, and Larry McDonald.

6. For an example of Birch antipathy to international trade, see Carl Dick to Welch, November 30, 1964, B: 1, F: 6, JBSR. George B. Wallace, a Bircher, wrote headquarters to complain that foreign imports and international trade agreements such as GATT harmed US lumber, steel, and textile industries. These "national policies definitely [fit] the Communist program of world domination by sapping our strength and independence."

7. For a biography of John Birch, see Terry Lautz, *John Birch: A Life* (New York: Oxford University Press, 2016). Membership numbers: D. J. Mulloy, *The World of the John Birch Society: Conspiracy, Conservatism, and the Cold War* (Nashville: Vanderbilt University Press, 2014), 2. Mulloy estimates that the society peaked at around one hundred thousand members in 1965–1966, stood at around sixty thousand members in 1968, and had between fifteen thousand and twenty thousand by the mid-1990s.

8. Jonathan Schoenwald, *A Time for Choosing: The Rise of Modern American Conservatism* (New York: Oxford University Press, 2001), 186; and Richard Hofstadter, "The Paranoid Style in American Politics," *Harper's Magazine*, November 1964. Hofstadter's definition of who qualified as a member of the far right focused on conspiracy theories, and it was overly narrow, emphasizing irrationality as the key trait when it was merely one element in a vaster universe of ideas and attitudes.

9. Research Department to R. L. Powell Jr., March 21, 1962, B: 2, F: 4, JBSR.

10. For discussions of who joined the Birch movement and their motivations, see McGirr, *Suburban Warriors*; Michelle Nickerson, *Mothers of Conservatism: Women and the Postwar Right* (Princeton, NJ: Princeton University Press, 2012); and Perlstein, *Before the Storm*.

11. "We're a republic, not a democracy" became a popular slogan among Birchers in the 1960s, but, arguably, it meant different things to different people. The concept has roots in the nation's early years, when founders warned against adopting a form of pure democracy (in which all male citizens debated and voted on laws) as practiced in ancient Athens. The modern provenance of the idea, as historians Nicole Hemmer and Lawrence Glickman argue, emerged in opposition to the New Deal. Franklin D. Roosevelt had argued that the New Deal was vital to defend and preserve democracy, but critics complained that the United States wasn't a democracy and that FDR was destroying "the checks and balances of our republic." FDR's opponents believed that he was using totalitarian methods to quash individual liberties, and many of their arguments had economic connotations. Birchers picked up on this theme that the New Deal state imperiled the republic, which prioritized property rights, free enterprise, and individual freedom. For other Birchers,

however, the phrase also implied that some citizens—white, Christian—inherited the country and had a right to rule. A republic was superior to democracy, they suggested, because republics protected the rights of minority factions and individuals to do as they pleased rather than mandating equality for all. During the heyday of the civil rights movement, the "we're a republic" argument became a way for Birchers to assert the moral primacy of white Christian elites and to contend that in a republic the federal government had no constitutional power to mandate civil rights. In 2020, Senator Mike Lee tweeted the slogan, suggesting that the far-right found something sinister about democracy as a threat to the rights of shrinking numbers of white people. One scholar wrote for the Heritage Foundation in 2020 that efforts "to weaken our republican customs and institutions" and unleash "the potential excesses of democratic majorities" undermined "the social, familial, religious, and economic distinctions and inequalities that undergird our political liberty." See Bernard Dobski, "America Is a Republic, Not a Democracy," Heritage Foundation, June 19, 2020, www.heritage.org/american-founders/report/america-republic-not-democracy; Jamelle Bouie, "Alexandria Ocasio-Cortez Understands Democracy Better than Republicans Do," *New York Times*, August 27, 2019, www.nytimes.com/2019/08/27/opinion/aoc-crenshaw-republicans-democracy.html; and Zach Beauchamp, "Sen. Mike Lee's Tweets Against 'Democracy,' Explained," *Vox*, October 8, 2020, www.vox.com/policy-and-politics/21507713/mike-lee-democracy-republic-trump-2020.

12. Edward Miller and Rick Perlstein, "The John Birch Society Never Left," *New Republic*, March 8, 2021, https://newrepublic.com/article/161603/john-birch-society-qanon-trump; and John S. Huntington, *Far-Right Vanguard: The Radical Roots of Modern Conservatism* (Philadelphia: University of Pennsylvania Press, 2022), 4. A trio of insightful books trace the radicalization of the American right to the 1990s: Nicole Hemmer, *Partisans: The Conservative Revolutionaries Who Remade American Politics in the 1990s* (New York: Basic Books, 2022); Jeremy Peters, *Insurgency: How Republicans Lost Their Party and Got Everything They Wanted* (New York: Random House, 2022); and Julian E. Zelizer, *Burning Down the House: Newt Gingrich, the Fall of a Speaker, and the Rise of the New Republican Party* (New York: Penguin Press, 2020).

13. Sam Rosenfeld and Daniel Schlozman, "The Long New Right and the World It Made" (working paper, American Political Science Association, January 2019 version), 16–17, https://static1.squarespace.com/static/540f1546e4b0ca60699c8f73/t/5c3e694321c67c3d28e992ba/1547594053027/Long+New+Right+Jan+2019.pdf. For valuable recent studies of the far right that tend to stress its centrality to modern conservatism's evolution, see David Austin Walsh, "The Right-Wing Popular Front: The Far Right and American Conservatism in the 1950s," *Journal of American History* 107, no. 2 (September 2020): 411–432, https://doi.org/10.1093/jahist/jaaa182 (Walsh reports, "Most *National Review* contributors had bylines in the Maguire-run *American Mercury*"); Huntington, *Far-Right Vanguard*; Edward H. Miller, *A Conspiratorial Life: Robert Welch, the John Birch Society, and the Revolution of American Conservatism* (Chicago: University of Chicago Press, 2022); Mulloy, *The World of the John Birch Society*; and Rick Perlstein, "I Thought I Understood the American Right. Trump Proved Me Wrong," *New York Times Magazine*, April 11, 2017, www.nytimes.com/2017/04/11

/magazine/i-thought-i-understood-the-american-right-trump-proved-me-wrong. html. For more on Buckley's relationship to electoral politics, see Alvin S. Felzenberg, *A Man and His Presidents: The Political Odyssey of William F. Buckley, Jr.* (New Haven, CT: Yale University Press, 2017), 79, 81.

14. Buckley's quote appears in the editorial, "Why the South Must Prevail," *National Review*, August 24, 1957. Alvin Felzenberg, "The Inside Story of William F. Buckley, Jr.'s Crusade Against the John Birch Society," *National Review*, June 20, 2017, https://nationalreview.com/2017/06/william-f-buckley-john-birch -society-history-conflict-robert-welch/; Geoffrey Kabaservice, *Rule and Ruin*, 25– 26; William F. Buckley and L. Brent Bozell, *McCarthy and His Enemies: The Record and Its Meaning* (Chicago: Regnery Publishers, 1954), 326; Samuel Bennett, "'A Critic Friendly to McCarthy': How William F. Buckley, Jr. Brought Senator Joseph R. McCarthy into the American Conservative Movement Between 1951 and 1959," EliScholar, 2019, https://elischolar.library.yale.edu/mssa_collections/20; Walsh, "The Right-Wing Popular Front"; and Kim Phillips-Fein, "Ultras: The Rise of America's Far Right," *The Nation*, January 11, 2022, www.thenation.com/article /society/john-huntington-far-right-vanguard/. For more examples of Buckley's ties to the Birchers, see Douglas Caddy to Buckley, "Young Americans for Freedom (Still in Formation)," October 19, 1960, B: 14, F: Young Americans for Freedom (1960), WFBP. Scott Stanley Jr., a future editor of *American Opinion*, was also an early YAF director. YAF's National Advisory Board had more than half a dozen men who were Birchers or had ties to the society, including Adolphe Menjou, J. Bracken Lee, Clarence Manion, Charles Edison, George Schuyler, and Maj. Gen. Charles Willoughby. Buckley to Revilo Oliver, February 10, 1960, B: 11, F: Oliver, Revilo (1960); and Buckley to T. Coleman Andrews, June 7, 1961, B: 13, F: Anderson-Andrews, WFBP. Buckley's approach to the far right was a stew of contradictory impulses. He befriended and held lively debates with fringe leaders while also denouncing publications that, as he put it in a note to Revilo Oliver in 1960, were "issued out of the fever swamps of right wing crackpottery." Buckley called Oliver, an antisemite, one of "my closest friends." And although Buckley criticized Welch, he also described him to Birch leader T. Coleman Andrews as "one of the finest men we'll ever meet."

15. For the late nineteenth- and early twentieth-century roots of ultraconservatism, see Huntington, *Far-Right Vanguard*, 14–21. Some studies of the Old Right, or paleoconservatism, include Leo Ribuffo, *The Old Christian Right: The Protestant Far Right from the Great Depression to the Cold War* (Philadelphia: Temple University Press, 1983); and Linda Gordon, *The Second Coming of the KKK: The Ku Klux Klan of the 1920s and the American Political Tradition* (New York: Liveright Publishing, 2017). Also see David Greenberg, "An Intellectual History of Trumpism," *Politico*, December 11, 2016, www.politico.com/magazine/story/2016/12 /trumpism-intellectual-history-populism-paleoconservatives-214518.

16. Remarks by Louis Ruthenburg, "The John Birch Society," August 5, 1965; Ruthenburg to Buckley, November 27, 1965, B: 37, F: Ruffin, Martha, WFBP.

17. James T. Patterson, *Grand Expectations: The United States, 1945–1974* (New York: Oxford University Press 1996), 7–8.

18. Patterson, *Grand Expectations*, 145, 166; Schoenwald, *A Time for Choosing*, 66.

19. William Hitchcock, *The Age of Eisenhower: America and the World in the 1950s* (New York: Simon and Schuster, 2018), 405–406, underscores the depth of the electoral rout for the Republicans. The GOP lost thirteen Senate seats and forty-eight in the House. Robert R. Nathan, Americans for Democratic Action, press release, November 6, 1958, B: 12, F: 6, Americans for Democratic Action, June–December 1958, JRP.

Chapter 1. "God's Angry Men"

1. Robert Welch to T. Coleman Andrews, October 27, 1958, November 12, 1958, ELFF, https://archive.org/details/DocumentaryHistoryOfJBS/page/n1/mode/2up?q=t+coleman+andrews; Welch to William Grede, November 14, 1958, B: 14, F: 8, WJGP; and "Capacity Crowd Hears Welch, Founder of the Birch Society, Tell of Its Origins, Methods, and Purposes," *Executives' Club News*, May 11, 1962, B: 27, F: 54, JBSR.

2. Welch to Andrews, November 12, 1958, ELFF; Thomas Rosteck, *See It Now Confronts McCarthyism: Television Documentary and the Politics of Representation* (Tuscaloosa: University of Alabama Press, 1994), 92; Welch to William Grede, November 14 and 17, 1958; and Welch to Grede, November 4, 1958, B: 14, F: 8, WJGP. For a nuanced view of Dice's anticommunist activism and her involvement in progressive women's clubs, see Annabelle Long, "A Biography of Marguerite Dice: Daughter of Republicanism and Mother of Conservatism" (unpublished manuscript, UC Berkeley Library, 2022), https://escholarship.org/uc/item/1j63q9n2.

3. Max P. Peterson, "The Ideology of the John Birch Society" (master's thesis, Utah State University, 1966), 4, https://digitalcommons.usu.edu/etd/7982.

4. I. R. Witthuhn to Grede, August 27, 1952, B: 25, F: 1, WJGP; Welch to Grede, January 27, 1953, B: 14: F: 8, WJGP; and Isadore Zack to Daniel Prelack, April 1, 1966, B: 5, F: 6, ADLC. T. Coleman Andrews was a member of Ike's administration. William Grede, an army second lieutenant during World War I, served as president of the YMCA's national council, president of NAM, and a director of the Federal Reserve's seventh district. He also spoke to a Kiwanis convention. Glenn Fowler, "William J. Grede Is Dead at 92; Joined in Founding Birch Society," *New York Times*, June 7, 1989.

5. "Man from Revenue," *Time*, October 24, 1955; James Best, "A Few Words from an IRS Commissioner Under Eisenhower," What Would the Founders Think?, accessed July 30, 2022, www.whatwouldthefoundersthink.com/a-few-words-from-an-irs-commissioner-under-eisenhower-2; and "Andrews' Drive Opens Tomorrow," *New York Times*, October 14, 1956, https://timesmachine.nytimes.com/timesmachine/1956/10/14/107159370.pdf?pdf_redirect=true&ip=0.

6. Fred Koch to William Kent, January 2, 1959, B: 14, F: 8, WJGP.

7. Dick Hauserman, "'Fitz' Scott: Architect of Vail Village," *Vail Daily*, August 3, 2002, www.vaildaily.com/news/fitz-scott-architect-of-vail-village/; Daniel Schulman, *Sons of Wichita: How the Koch Brothers Became America's Most Powerful and Private Dynasty* (New York: Grand Central Publishing, 2014), chapter 3. For examples of Grede's involvement in antiunion organizing and in the 1952 campaign, see Philip Cortney to Grede, November 5, 1952, and Ray Jandall to Grede, November 14, 1952, B: 25, F: 1, WJGP.

8. Remarks by Louis Ruthenburg, "The John Birch Society," April 5, 1965; Ruthenburg to William Buckley, November 27, 1965, B: 37, F: Ruffin, Martha, WFBP; and Rosemary Feurer, *Radical Unionism in the Midwest, 1900–1950* (Champaign-Urbana: University of Illinois Press, 2006), 104. During the New Deal years, Ruthenburg was active in antiunion organizing in Indiana.

9. G. Edward Griffin, *The Life and Words of Robert Welch, Founder of the John Birch Society* (Thousand Oaks, CA: American Media, 1975), 67–68; "Mr. Robert Welch," Biographical sketch, n.d., B: 27, F: 20, JBSR; Jonathan Schoenwald, *A Time for Choosing* (New York: Oxford University Press, 2001), 65; Jonathan Houghton, "Welch, Robert Henry Winborne, Jr.," in *Dictionary of North Carolina Biography*, ed. William Powell (Chapel Hill: University of North Carolina Press, 1996); James Phelan, "Mutiny in the Birch Society," *Saturday Evening Post*, April 8, 1967; and Edward Miller, *A Conspiratorial Life* (Chicago: University of Chicago Press, 2022), 37, 46–47, 60.

10. Mr. Robert Welch, biographical sketch, n.d., B: 27, F: 20, JBSR.

11. Robert Welch, *The Road to Salesmanship* (New York: Ronald Press Company, 1942), 6–7.

12. Miller, *A Conspiratorial Life*, 66–68, 89. "Welch had deep isolationist tendencies when it came to Europe, largely because of what he saw as the absurdity and waste of America's involvement in World War I," Miller reports. Bart Verhoeven, "The Rear Guard of Freedom: The John Birch Society and the Development of Modern Conservatism in the United States, 1958–1968" (PhD diss., University of Nottingham, 2015), 16.

13. Miller, *A Conspiratorial Life*, 83, 93–97, 100; Schoenwald, *A Time for Choosing*, 66; and D. J. Mulloy, *The World of the John Birch Society* (Nashville: Vanderbilt University Press, 2014), 6–7.

14. Albert C. Wedemeyer, "Appeasement in China: Where It Leads," *Human Events*, November 17, 1958, B: 28, F: 10, JBSR. For a discussion of how debates about Asia shaped the Birch Society, see Joyce Mao, *Asia and the Making of Modern American Conservatism* (Chicago: University of Chicago Press, 2015). Kohlberg sent Knowland a copy of a letter in which he had stated that "the Pacific Ocean is as important to [Americans] as the Atlantic." Kohlberg to Major General J. F. C. Fuller, April 11, 1956, C: 273, F: Kohlberg, Alfred, 1956, WFKP.

15. Herbert Hoover to William Knowland, December 31, 1949, C: 273, F: special correspondence, Hoover, Herbert, WFKP. Truman's sacking of General MacArthur triggered outrage. See William Knowland to Tony De Lap, April 20, 1951, C: 273, F: Knowland, Sen. William; Statement of William F. Knowland, n.d., C: 273, F: Knowland, Sen. William, WFKP.

16. Robert Aura Smith, "One Man's Opinions," *New York Times*, November 16, 1952; Welch to Grede, April 18, 1955; Welch to Grede, May 26, 1955; and President, American Mailing Committee, Inc. to "the Reader," n.d., B: 14, F: 8, WJGP. Also see Schoenwald, *A Time for Choosing*, 75.

17. Smith, "One Man's Opinions."

18. Griffin, *Life and Words of Robert Welch*, 179.

19. Welch to Knowland, October 25, 1953, C: 241, F: Personal Captain John Birch, WFKP; "Capacity Crowd Hears Welch"; and "Captain John Birch," biographical sketch, n.d., B: 27, F: 20, JBSR.

20. Jonathan Soffer, "The National Association of Manufacturers and the Militarization of American Conservatism," *Business History Review* 75, no. 4 (2001): 776, https://doi.org/10.2307/3116511.

21. "Capacity Crowd Hears Welch"; Kim Philips-Fein, *Invisible Hands: The Making of the Conservative Movement from the New Deal to Reagan* (New York: Norton, 2009); Verhoeven, "Rear Guard of Freedom," 16–17; and Miller, *A Conspiratorial Life*, 171. For an overview of Grede's life, see Craig Miner, *Grede of Milwaukee* (Wichita, KS: Watermark Press, 1989). NAM's ideological conflicts can be found in Jennifer A. Delton, *The Industrialists: How the National Association of Manufacturers Shaped American Capitalism* (Princeton, NJ: Princeton University Press, 2020), 187–198, 205.

22. Michelle Nickerson, *Mothers of Conservatism* (Princeton, NJ: Princeton University Press, 2012), xvii, xix; Welch to members of the NAM Board, January 10, 1955, B: 14, F: 8, WJGP; and Welch to Dr. Edwin Lee, April 1, 1953 B: 14, F: 8, WJGP.

23. Delton, *The Industrialists*, 187–209; Schoenwald, *A Time for Choosing*, 62–63.

24. Welch to "Dear Reader," a letter to subscribers, November 29, 1957, B: 14, F: 8, WJGP.

25. Welch, "A Brief Report to Friends on My Trip to the Far East," September 2, 1955, B: 14, F: 8, WJGP. Welch started writing this report on the plane home. He was in the habit of typing lengthy letters and reports to friends who shared his contempt for communism.

26. Rus Walton, "Turning Political Ideas into Government Program," interview by Gabrielle Morris, in "Internal and External Operations of the California Governor's Office, 1966–1974: Oral History Transcript and Related Material," 1983, iii, 3, Oral History Center, Bancroft Library, University of California, Berkeley.

27. F. E. Masland Jr. to Grede, September 23, 1955; Grede to Masland Jr., October 5, 1955, B: 14, F: 8, WJGP.

28. David Brion Davis, ed., *The Fear of Conspiracy: Images of Un-American Subversion from the Revolution to the Present* (Ithaca, NY: Cornell University Press, 1971), xiii.

29. Kathryn Olmsted, *Real Enemies: Conspiracy Theories and American Democracy, World War I to 9/11* (New York: Oxford University Press, 2009), 1–5.

30. For more on conspiracy "entrepreneurs" and this "long and central tradition in our nation's history," see Robert Goldberg, *Real Enemies: The Culture of Conspiracy in Modern America* (New Haven, CT: Yale University Press, 2001), x. For a chronicle of the evolution of right-wing media in the Cold War, see Nicole Hemmer, *Messengers of the Right: Conservative Media and the Transformation of American Politics* (Philadelphia: University of Pennsylvania Press, 2016).

31. Edward H. Miller, *Nut Country: Right-Wing Dallas and the Birth of the Southern Strategy* (Chicago: University of Chicago Press, 2015), 57–58. Miller sums up how far-right purveyors of conspiratorial plots against America bore religious undertones: "The greatest conspiracy of all was Satan's ongoing battle against Christianity."

32. Welch to Philip Cortney, March 20, 1954, B: 23, F: 7, WJGP.

33. Miller, *A Conspiratorial Life*, 171–174.

34. Welch to Grede, May 17, 1957, and Editorial Advisory Committee disclaimer, n.d.; Welch to Grede, June 3, 1957, B: 14, F: 8, WJGP.

35. Welch to All Members of the Editorial Advisory Committee of *One Man's Opinion*, Confidential, June 25, 1957, B: 14, F: 8, WJGP.

36. Welch to Andrews, September 29, 1958; Welch to J. W. Clise, February 25, 1959, ELFF, https://archive.org/details/clise-james-w.-papers/page/n109/mode/2up.

37. Robert Welch, *The Blue Book of the John Birch Society*, 5th ed. (Belmont, MA: Western Islands Publishing, 1961), introduction.

38. "Capacity Crowd Hears Welch."

Chapter 2. "Some Rather Frightening Aspects"

1. Spruille Braden to William Buckley, April 3, 1959, B: 7, F: Braden, Spruille (1959), WFBP. Braden shared Buckley's concern about the alleged prevalence of communists on Yale's faculty and endorsed the use of campus loyalty oaths. For more on Braden's career and anticommunist views, see *Diplomats and Demagogues: The Memoirs of Spruille Braden* (New Rochelle, NY: Arlington House, 1971).

2. A brief biographical description of Merwin K. Hart's career can be found here: Merwin K. Hart Papers, University of Oregon Libraries, Special Collections and University Archives Collections Database, accessed August 31, 2022, https://scua .uoregon.edu/repositories/2/resources/2043. For Smoot's impact on far-right media, see Heather Hendershot, *What's Fair on the Air? Cold War Right-Wing Broadcasting and the Public Interest* (Chicago: University of Chicago Press, 2011), chapter 2.

3. Donald T. Critchlow, *Phyllis Schlafly and Grassroots Conservatism: A Woman's Crusade* (Princeton, NJ: Princeton University Press, 2008) 338–339.

4. Herb Philbrick to Frank Willette, May 28, 1959; Philbrick to Welch, August 4, 1959, B: 121, F: 6, HPP.

5. "A Confidential Report to Members of the Council of the John Birch Society," January 21, 1960, B: 15, F: 1; Welch to Grede, December 26, 1959, B: 14, F: 8; and Grede to Welch, May 13, 1959, B: 15, F: 1, WJGP.

6. Don Rothberg and Doris Klein, "Debate on Extremism Boosts Its Membership, Birch Society Says," *Chicago Sun-Times*, September 6, 1964; "Confidential Report No. 1," December 19, 1958, B: 14, F: 8, WJGP; Welch to Grede, December 11, 1958; and Grede to Welch, December 18, 1959, B: 14, F: 8, WJGP.

7. Welch to Grede, December 11, 1958, December 13, 1958, December 22, 1958; Grede to Welch, December 18, 1959, B: 14, F: 8, WJGP.

8. Wire News Service, "Birch Society's Aims, Functions Examined," *Wichita Eagle*, October 27, 1960, B: 14, F: Welch, 1960; Welch to Grede, January 27, 1959, February 26, 1959, B: 14, F: 8, WJGP. Welch explained, "I found out at Boca that not only are the 'wives' extremely interested, but also most helpful to have present."

9. Welch to Grede, December 11, 1958, December 13, 1958; Grede to Welch, December 18, 1959; Welch to Grede, February 26, 1959, B: 14, F: 8, WJGP. "They are waiting for some prodding from you," Welch wrote Grede. Grede to Welch, May 13, 1959, B: 14, F: 8, WJGP. "I have neglected the group that [was] at your meeting," Grede apologized in a note to Welch.

10. Welch to Grede, February 26, 1959, May 18, 1959, B: 14, F: 8, WJGP. Bradley, Loock, and a man named Harvey Peters agreed to fund the entire cost of putting Welch's pitch on film, which Welch figured would run to $35,000. It was

unclear if the Bradley-Loock $25,000 pledge was separate from or part of the funding to film the founder's lecture.

11. "A Confidential Report to Members of the Council of the John Birch Society," January 21, 1960, B: 91, F: 1, WJGP; Grede to Welch, May 13, 1959, February 3, 1960, B: 15, F: 1, WJGP. Cardinal Cushing endorsed the society, citing shared "dedication to the fight against the atheistic Communist conspiracy." Cornelius Hurley, AP, "Cushing Recants Talk Against Birch Society," *Worcester Daily Telegram*, April 24, 1964.

12. T. Walker Lewis to Grede, May 23, 1960; Grede to Lewis, May 31, 1960, B: 15, F: 1, WJGP.

13. "Comments Extracted from Very Recent Correspondence," quote from "A Housewife in Calfiornia," n.d., attached to letter, Welch to "All Members of the Council," May 17, 1960, B: 15, F: 1, WJGP.

14. *Bulletin*, November 30, 1959, B: 121, F: 6, HPP.

15. "Confidential Report to Members of the Council of the John Birch Society," January 21, 1960, B: 15, F: 1, WJGP.

16. Michelle Nickerson, *Mothers of Conservatism* (Princeton, NJ: Princeton University Press, 2012), 138.

17. Welch to Grede, February 26, 1959, B: 14, F: 8, WJGP.

18. Jane Mayer, *Dark Money: The Hidden History of the Billionaires Behind the Rise of the Radical Right* (New York: Doubleday, 2016), 38–39.

19. Fred Koch to Wm. Kent, January 2, 1959, B: 14, F: 8, WJGP.

20. Fred Koch to "Dear Friends," January 17, 1959, B: 14, F: 8, WJGP; Koch to Welch, January 15, 1960, B: 15, F: 1, WJGP.

21. Gene Grove, *Inside the John Birch Society* (Greenwich, CT: Fawcett Gold Medal, 1961), 95–97; Group Research Inc., *The National Right to Work Committee* (Washington, DC: December 13, 1962), www.prwatch.org/files/rtw_group _research.pdf.

22. Fred Koch to "Dear Friends," January 17, 1959, B: 14, F: 8, WJGP.

23. Tom Anderson, "Straight Talk," *Farm and Ranch*, October 1959, B: 121, F: 6, HPP; "A Confidential Report to Members of the Council of the John Birch Society," January 21, 1960, B: 15, F: 1; Welch to "Present Members and Prospective Members," August 7, 1959, B: 15, F: 1; Welch to Grede, May 7, 1959, B: 15, F: 1; Welch to "Fellow American," May 28, 1959, B: 15, F: 1; Welch to "All Members of the Council," May 17, 1960, B: 15, F: 1, WJGP; and ADL Press Release, n.d., B: 10, F: 34, ADLC.

24. "A Confidential Report to Members of the Council of the John Birch Society," April 11, 1960, B: 15, F: 1, WJGP; Welch to "All Members of the Council," May 17, 1960, B: 15, F: 1, WJGP; and "Committee Against Summit Entanglements," August 3, 1962 (Group Research Inc.), B: 122, F: 31a, BGP.

25. Welch, *Bulletin*, March 1, 1961, B: 3, F: Robert Welch, SBP.

26. Harry Barr to *Racine Journal-Times*, August 31, 1959; "Voice of the Old Gang," *Racine Journal-Times*, August 26, 1959; Barr to Grede, September 1 and 2, 1959, B: 14, F: 8, WJGP; and Anna Mathiesen to Welch, August 31, 1959, B: 28, F: 10, JBSR.

27. "Comments Extracted from Very Recent Correspondence," attached to Welch to "All Members of the Council," May 17, 1960, B: 15, F: 1, WJGP.

28. D. J. Mulloy, *The World of the John Birch Society* (Nashville: Vanderbilt University Press, 2014), 10; Isadore Zack to Milt Ellerin, October 22, 1959, B: 5, F: 8, David Breen, ADLC.

29. *Bulletin*, December 31, 1959, 12, B: 121, F: 2; Herb Philbrick to Frank Willette, May 28, 1959, B: 121, F: 6, HPP; and Grove, *Inside the John Birch Society*, 80.

30. *Bulletin*, August 31, 1959; *Bulletin*, November 30, 1959, B: 121, F: 6, HPP.

31. Zack to Jerry Bakst, April 27, 1966; Bob Creamer, "He Was a Bircher While in NAACP," *Boston Traveler*, April 28, 1966, B: 7, F: 9, Galary, Richard, ADLC.

32. Welch to Grede, December 11, 1958; Welch to Home Chapter Members, February 28, 1959, B: 14, F: 8, WJGP; and Zack to Ellerin, October 22, 1959, B: 5, F: 8, David Breen, ADLC.

33. *Bulletin*, August 31, 1959, B: 121, F: 6, HPP.

34. Don Rueber to Welch, February 14, 1960, B: 15, F: 1, WJGP. The tapes were especially motivational. On the night after the school ended, the Ruebers played recordings for a St. Petersburg, Florida, resident, William O'Grady, who had stayed late just to hear them. D. Carotta to Grede, March 7, 1960, B: 15, F: 1, WJGP. Welch praised the Ruebers in a note to Grede as "doing an extremely good job." Welch to Grede, February 18, 1960, B: 15, F: 1, WJGP. And on March 7, Don Rueber stopped by Grede's office for advice on finding industrialists willing to fund newspaper ads in Wisconsin.

35. Grove, *Inside the John Birch Society*, 95–97.

36. Welch to "All Members of the Council," May 17, 1960, B: 15, F: 1, WJGP. For a discussion of *Operation Abolition*, see Seth Rosenfeld, *The FBI's War on Student Radicals, and Reagan's Rise to Power* (New York: Farrar, Straus and Giroux, 2012), 94–95, 97.

37. Grove, *Inside the John Birch Society*, 97–103.

38. "A Confidential Report to Members of the Council of the John Birch Society," April 11, 1960, B: 15, F: 1, WJGP; "A Confidential Report to Members of the Council of the John Birch Society," January 21, 1960, B: 15, F: 1, WJGP; and *Bulletin*, November 30, 1959, B: 121, F: 6, HPP.

39. "A Confidential Report to Members of the Council of the John Birch Society," April 11, 1960, B: 15, F: 1, WJGP.

40. Welch, "To All Members," December 7, 1959, B: 121, F: 6, HPP. "Our members have been complying with our letter-writing requests," Welch informed his readers. C. P. Trussell, "Senators Query U.N. Aide's Death," *New York Times*, October 10, 1961; *Bulletin*, August 31, 1959; and *Bulletin*, November 30, 1959, B: 121, F: 6, HPP.

41. A. G. Heinsohn to D. Hayes Murphy, February 5, 1960, B: 15, F: 1, WJGP.

42. "The John Birch Society," Testimonial Dinner for Mr. Robert Welch, Part I, B: 14, F: John Birch Society, WFBP; *Bulletin*, November 30, 1959, B: 121, F: 6, HPP; and Welch to Grede, January 16, 1960, B: 15, F: 1, WJGP.

43. For more on the aggressive protests against the Johnsons by a group dubbed Dallas's "mink coat mob," see Edward Miller, *Nut Country* (Chicago: University of Chicago Press, 2015), 86–87. For the attacks on Young, see Mulloy, *The World of the John Birch Society*, 21.

44. Kristin Gates, "Montana and the Backwater of Birchism: The Origins of the John Birch Society in the Treasure State, 1961–1964" (unpublished paper, University of Montana, December 11, 2019, in author's possession), cited with Gates's permission.

Chapter 3. Witch Hunt

1. "A Confidential Report to Members of the Council of the John Birch Society," April 11, 1960, B: 15, F: 1; Welch to "A Good American," October 5, 1959, B: 14, F: 8, WJGP. "We avoid publicity as well as we can," Welch informed prospective members.

2. Drew Pearson, "The Washington Merry-Go-Round," *Times Pawtucket-Central Falls R.I.*, April 23, 1962.

3. Richard Hofstadter, "The Pseudo-Conservative Revolt," *The American Scholar*, Winter, 1954-1955; Richard Hofstadter, *Anti-Intellectualism in American Life* (New York: Random House, 1963), 42; Jonathan Schoenwald, *A Time for Choosing* (New York: Oxford University Press, 2001), chapter 3; and Richard Hofstadter, "The Paranoid Style in American Politics," *Harper's Magazine*, November 1964.

4. Edward Miller, *A Conspiratorial Life* (Chicago: University of Chicago Press, 2022), 207; D. J. Mulloy, *The World of the John Birch Society* (Nashville: Vanderbilt University Press, 2014), 16–17.

5. Law Offices of Clark, Rankin, Nash, Emmerling and Spindler to *The Milwaukee Journal*, August 10, 1960, B: 15, F: 1; Wire News Service, "Birch Society's Aims, Functions Examined," *Wichita Eagle*, October 27, 1960, B: 14, F: Buckley, 1960; and Welch to "All Members of the Council," August 11, 1960, B: 15, F:1, WJGP. Just to be safe, however, Welch asked some of his friends to whom he had sent *The Politician* to return their copies to him.

6. Fred Waterous to Grede, August 9, 1960; H. E. Humphreys Jr. to Waterous, August 25, 1960; anonymous to Grede, August 3, 1960; anonymous handwritten letter to Grede, July 31, 1960, B: 15, F: 1, WJGP.

7. Grede to Welch, August 19, 1960, B: 15, F: 1, WJGP.

8. Grede to Eisenhower, August 22, 1960; Grede to "Our Officers and Staff," August 4, 1960, B: 15, F: 1, WJGP.

9. Grede to Eisenhower, August 22, 1960; Frederick Mueller to Grede, August 24, 1960, and attached "Mueller draft," n.d., B: 15, F: 1, WJGP.

10. The correspondence relating to the contretemps can be found here: Welch to Grede, August 24, 1960; Grede to Welch, August 19, 1960; Grede to Eisenhower, August 22, 1960; Grede to Mueller, August 26, 1960; Grede to Eisenhower, August 29, 1960; Grede to William Heller Sr., August 8, 1960; Eisenhower to Grede, August 30, 1960; Grede to Waterous, August 12, 1960, B: 15, F: 1, WJGP.

11. Welch to Fred Schwarz, September 6, 1960, B: 121, F: 7, HPP; Welch to "All Members of the Council," August 11, 1960, B: 15, F: 1, WJGP.

12. Welch to Doctor S. M. Draskovich, August 1, 1960; Welch to "All Members of the Council," August 11, 1960; "Members and friends of John Birch Chapter #74" to Welch, August 8, 1960; Grede to "Our Salaried Employees," August. 5, 1960; Grede to "our officers and staff," August. 4, 1960; Ernest Swigert to Frederick Mueller, August 24, 1960; Grede to William Heller Sr., August 8, 1960; Grede to Fred Waterous, August 12, 1960; Henry W. Marx to Grede, August 10, 1960; Ida

Breit to Grede, August 13, 1960 (Breit, a teacher, believed that the *Journal* wanted to help John Kennedy win the presidency); DC to Grede, September 6, 1960; John Alexander to Grede, August 6, 1960; Law Offices of Clark, Rankin, Nash, Emmerling and Spindler to the *Milwaukee Journal*, August 10, 1960; Welch to "All Members of the Council," August 11, 1960, B: 15, F: 1, WJGP.

13. Miller, *A Conspiratorial Life*, 232; Mulloy, *The World of the John Birch Society*, 19–22; AP, "Senator Scores Group Calling Eisenhower a Red," *New York Times*, March 9, 1961; and Russell Baker, "Senator Who Brought Birch Unit to Public Notice Fears Reprisal," *New York Times*, April 18, 1961.

14. Welch to "Members of our Council and a Few Other Friends," April 1, 1961, B: 14, F: John Birch Society, WFBP.

15. Robert Welch, *Bulletin*, March 1, 1961, B: 3, F: Robert Welch, SBP; "The Movement to Impeach Earl Warren," Birch Society pocket petition, n.d., B: 14, F: John Birch Society, WFBP.

16. James Eastland, "The Supreme Court's 'Modern Scientific Authorities in the Segregation Cases' in the Senate of the United States," May 26, 1955, archive.org /details/1955Eastland/mode/2up; "Confidential Report to Members of the Council of the John Birch Society," January 21, 1960, B: 15, F: 1, WJGP; and Robert Welch, *Bulletin*, March 1, 1961, B: 3, F: Robert Welch, SBP.

17. Welch to "All Coordinators, Section Leaders, and Chapter Leaders," June 18, 1963, B: 27, F: 4, JBSR.

18. Welch to "Patriotic Groups, Publications, and Individuals," January 1961; "The Movement to Impeach Earl Warren," n.d.; and "An Essay Contest for the American Undergraduate," n.d., Part I, B: 14, F: John Birch Society, WFBP. The five judges of the contest were Tom Anderson; Salt Lake City mayor J. Bracken Lee; prep school president Doane Lowery; Arizona Supreme Court justice M. T. Phelps; and professor of history Charles Callan Tansill.

19. Author interview with Philippa Strum; and Strum, email message to author, March 30, 2022.

20. Laurence Swanson to Robert Welch, week of November 2, 1964, B: 1, F: 6, JBSR; Rabbi M. J. Merritt to Welch, February 11, 1961, reprinted in the *Bulletin*, March 1, 1961, B: 3, F: Robert Welch, SBP.

21. James J. Kilpatrick to Buckley, March 27, 1961, B: 15, F: Kilpatrick, James J. (1961); Kilpatrick to Buckley, June 1, 1960, B: 15, F: Kilpatrick, James J. (1961); and Buckley to John Leonard, October 10, 1961, B: 15, F: Leonard, John (1961), WFBP.

22. Swanson to Welch, week of November 9, 1964, B: 1, F: 6, JBSR; George Todt, "A View of the News: George Todt's Opinion," *Los Angeles Herald Examiner*, February 10, 1961; "The South: Hello, Earl," *Time*, February 22, 1963, http:// content.time.com/time/subscriber/article/0,33009,827999,00.html; and Jim Newton, "The Nation Earl Warren Made," interview with Terry Gross, *Fresh Air*, NPR, December 7, 2006, www.npr.org/templates/story/story.php?storyId=6592640.

23. Welch, *Bulletin*, March 1, 1961, B: 3, F: Robert Welch, SBP.

24. Claire Conner, *Wrapped in the Flag: A Personal History of America's Radical Right* (Boston: Beacon Press, 2013), 57; Schoenwald, *A Time for Choosing*, 279; Stanley Mosk to Pat Brown, July 7, 1961, B: A204, F: 3, John Birch Society, 1961– 65, RNAACP.

25. UPI, "The Story of Thomas Storke: Man of Achievement," *Desert Sun*, May 1, 1963, https://cdnc.ucr.edu/?a=d&d=DS19630501.2.111&e=-------en--20--1--txt -txIN--------1; "Thomas More Storke Is Dead; Editor Attacked Birch Society," *New York Times*, October 13, 1971, www.nytimes.com/1971/10/13/archives/thomas -more-storke-is-dead-editor-attacked-birch-society-publisher.html.

26. Alan F. Westin, "The John Birch Society," *Commentary*, August 1961; Hans Engh, "The John Birch Society," *The Nation*, March 11, 1961.

27. Stanley Mosk to Pat Brown, July 7, 1961, B: A204, F: 3, John Birch Society, 1961–65, RNAACP.

28. Article, *Manchester Union Leader*, August 12, 1964, B: 9, F: 5, McCrossen, Vincent A., ADLC; "Past on Parade: John Birch Society a Local Issue in 1961," *Pasadena Star-News*, May 22, 2011, www.pasadenastarnews.com/2011/05/22/past -on-parade-john-birch-society-a-local-issue-in-1961/; Mulloy, *The World of the John Birch Society*, 20–21.

29. Hy Rosen, *Pecking Away*, photograph, 1961, www.loc.gov/item/201668 4063/.

30. President John F. Kennedy, News Conference 10, April 21, 1961, JFKPL.

31. "He Was a Man of Principle," *New Republic*, December 25, 1961, https:// newrepublic.com/article/93204/he-was-man-principle. Liberals feared that veterans and enlisted men would become radicalized under the sway of the John Birch Society, and the JBS indeed appeared to have its share of ex-military in its ranks. In the fall of 1962 the society's New England coordinator, for example, was about to return from active duty and resume his job with the Birch Society. "He will be in touch with our Chapter Leaders throughout New England in the very near future," field director Thomas Hill informed colleagues.

32. Mulloy, *The World of the John Birch Society*, 43-44; Buckley to Edwin Walker, July 5, 1961, B: 17, F: Walker, Gen. E. A. (1961), WFBP; "Thunder on the Right," *Newsweek* (Cover), December 4, 1961.

33. Joseph Crespino, *Strom Thurmond's America* (New York: Hill and Wang, 2012), 157–158. In 1963, Walker denounced John F. Kennedy's brother, Attorney General Robert Kennedy, as "little stupid brother Bobby." Walker also conspiratorially implied that the government had tried to assassinate him, stating, "They had to [arrest and] get rid of me because I knew too much about Mississippi." Seven months before John F. Kennedy was assassinated in Dallas, according to the Warren Commission, Lee Harvey Oswald tried to assassinate Walker, firing a single shot into his Dallas home that came within about an inch of Walker's head. Bill Minutaglio and Steven L. Davis, "The Man Oswald First Tried to Kill before JFK," *Daily Beast*, October 3, 2013, www.thedailybeast.com/the-man-oswald-first-tried -to-kill-before-jfk; John Judis, *William F. Buckley, Jr.: Patron Saint of the Conservatives* (New York: Simon and Schuster, 1988), 206.

34. Pearson, "The Washington Merry-Go-Round."

35. Otis Chandler to Roger Kent, April 17, 1961, B: 6, F: Chandler, Otis, 1927, RKP.

36. Mulloy, *The World of the John Birch Society*, 24, 49.

37. Kent to Chandler, April 12, 1961, B: 6, F: Chandler, Otis, 1927; Fred M. Standley to Kent, March 13, 1964, B: 27, F: Standley, Fred Mack, RKP. "The very thought of their gaining control of one of the major political parties is frightening

beyond comprehension," the New Mexico Democratic activist opined. A Birch takeover of any segment of the GOP, he predicted, "in the long run . . . would be very detrimental to . . . the nation."

38. "Storm over Birchers," *Time*, April 7, 1961.

39. Westin, "The John Birch Society."

40. "Storm over Birchers," *Time*; Jim Stack, "Judge Tangles with Senator in Birch Probe," *Manchester Union Leader*, April 27, 1961.

41. AP, "Truman Asserts Superpatriots Ill," n.d., newspaper article in Part I, B: 14, F: John Birch Society, WFBP; Stanley Mosk to Pat Brown, July 7, 1961, B: A204, F: 3, John Birch Society, 1961–65, RNAACP.

42. Address by John F. Kennedy at California Democratic Party dinner, Los Angeles, California, November 18, 1961, JFK Library, www.jfklibrary.org /asset-viewer/archives/JFKPOF/036/JFKPOF-036-020; David Wise, "Kennedy Assails Rightists," *Boston Sunday Globe*, November 19, 1961.

43. Harold Collins, "Liberalism Is Out," *Boston Sunday Herald*, September 24, 1961, B: 5, F: 38, Collins, Harold, ADLC.

44. Press Release, NBC News, "Television News Pioneer Lawrence Spivak Dies at 93," May 5, 1994, Dole Archives, University of Kansas, dolearchivecollections .ku.edu/collections/speeches/089/c019_089_013_all.pdf, accessed September 6, 2022; NBC, Transcript, *Meet the Press*, May 21, 1961, B: 215, F: Welch, Robert, LSP.

45. Jane Wilson to Mr. Spivak, May 21, 1961, B: 45, F: 4, "Meet the Press Viewer Mail, Program Response, Robert Welch, 5/21/61"; Mr. and Mrs. W. Cardon to Lawrence Spivak, May 21, 1961, B: 45, F: 4, "Meet the Press Viewer Mail, Program Response, Robert Welch, 5/21/61"; and Blanche Bell to NBC TV News, May 23, 1961, B: 45, F: 2, "Program Response: Robert Welch, 5/21/61," LSP.

46. Lois Hefferman to Spivak, May 21, 1961, B: 45, F: 3, "'Meet the Press Viewer Mail,' Program Response, Robert Welch, 5/21/61, #3"; C. Jacobsen to Spivak, May 23, 1961, B: 45, F, 2: "Program Response, Robert Welch, 5/21/61"; Clair Starrett Linton to Spivak, May 25, 1961, B: 45, F: 2, "Program Response, Robert Welch, 5/21/61"; Pearl Stein to "Gentlemen," May 25, 1961, B: 45, F: 2, "Program Response, Robert Welch, 5/21/61"; and Mr. and Mrs. Charles McClung to "Gentlemen," May 21, 1961, B: 45, F 4: "Meet the Press Viewer Mail, Program Response, Robert Welch, 5/21/61," LSP.

47. Genevieve Hatch Stetson to Spivak and Staff, May 21, 1961; Mrs. Carl H. Leger to Spivak, May 21, 1961, B: 45, F: 4, "Meet the Press Viewer Mail, Program Response, Robert Welch, 5/21/61," LSP.

Chapter 4. Shock Troops

1. William Buckley to Kent Courtney, December 16, 1959; "New Party Rally in Chicago Draws 1,000 from 34 States," "'No Difference Between Old Parties' says Tom Anderson," and other news coverage, B: 7, F: Courtney, Kent (1959), WFBP. Buckley had a habit of holding contradictory positions and developed complex relationships with numerous members of the right-wing fringe. He praised Kent Courtney for keeping the crackpots and antisemitic groups away from the convention, but asked to be seated at the banquet next to the antisemitic scholar Revilo Oliver. In May 1960, however, Buckley informed Oliver that he was removing him

from *National Review*'s masthead. Buckley to Oliver, May 16, 1960, B: 11, F: Oliver, Revilo (1960), WFBP. Courtney and Medford Evans, staunch segregationists, earned rapt encomiums from Buckley; see Buckley to Courtney, October 21, 1959; Buckley to Courtney, November 3, 1959, B: 7, F: Courtney, Kent, WFBP. See also Buckley to Medford Evans, October 2, 1959; and Evans to Buckley, September 27, 1959, B: 7, F: Evans, Medford, WFBP. "We are running Kent for Governor of Louisiana on the States Rights Party ticket," Evans apprised Buckley.

2. Research Department to Henry Forster, November 5, 1962, B: 2, F: 4, Member's Monthly Message (MMM) 1962, JBSR; Clayton Knowles, "Race Is Dropped by Conservative," *New York Times*, July 20, 1962; and Thomas Anderson to Patrick Carr, January 7, 1960, B: 10, F: Anderson to Anti-Defamation League (1960), WFBP. Anderson figured that a third party, even one with no shot at victory, was worthwhile if it pushed "the Socialist Republican Party and the Socialist Democrat Party . . . toward Constitutional government, states rights, freedom, and capitalism."

3. Birch leader Ernest Swigert urged Robert Welch to back Nixon in the 1960 election. Swigert to Welch, July 20, 1959, B 14, F: 8, WJGP. Welch feared that Nixon "will probably try to outdo [Nelson] Rockefeller . . . in his internationalism." Welch to Grede, July 8, 1959, B: 14, F: 8, WJGP.

4. Statement of Senator Strom Thurmond (D-SC) on Senate Floor, February 2, 1961, B: 17, F: Thurmond, Sen. Strom (1961), WFBP.

5. "Hussey & Cupples Clash at St. Francis John Birch Debate," *Wells-Ognquit Star*, April 26, 1962; Isadore Zack to Milt Ellerin, May 1, 1962, B: 6, F: 1, Cupples, Walter W., ADLC; Herb Philbrick to Robert Welch, October 30, 1959, B: 121, F: 6, HPP; and Helen Schmeling to "Gentlemen," MMM, February 5, 1962, B: 2, F: 4, JBSR.

6. Wire News Service, "Birch Society's Aims, Functions Examined," *Wichita Eagle*, October 27, 1960, B: 14, F: Welch, 1960, WFBP; RBM to Mr. J. Goldberg, February 6, 1962, B: 1, F: 4, JBSR; Robert Bragner to "Gentlemen," MMM, October 6, 1962; and Research Department to Robert Bragner, November 5, 1962, B: 2, F: 4, JBSR. JBS's Research Department replied that "one of the Saners" was heading for defeat in his US Senate race in Massachusetts and praised the member for his achievement.

7. Robert Montgomery, letter to the editor, *Boston Herald*, September 17, 1962.

8. Zack to Ellerin, September 17, 1963, B: 7, F: 60 Kahian, Leo, ADLC.

9. "Own Pastor Bircher's Rival," article, n.d., B: 5, F: 15, Bunker, Col. Laurence D., ADLC.

10. Josh Indar, "Nothing New Under the Sun," *Chico News and Review*, September 30, 2004; Tom Leonardi, "Joan Baez, Trouble in Paradise, 1957," KZFR, April 26, 2013, http://kzfr.org/broadcasts/195; "Teacher's Rights an Issue on Coast; Panel of California Assembly Told of Legion's Pressure," *New York Times*, February 23, 1964; Jonathan Zimmerman, "Teachers in Paradise: Extinguish the Fires of Political Polarization," *Pittsburgh Post-Gazette*, November 18, 2018; and "Hell Breaks Loose in Paradise," *Life*, April 26, 1963.

11. Sen. Gale McGee to Mike Feldman, August 14, 1963, B:106, F: Right-wing movement, JFKPL; Dale Johnson, "Birch Member Defends the Society," *The Retort*, Eastern Montana College, March 3, 1967.

12. Thomas Hill to Major Coordinators and Coordinators, May 7, 1964, B: 27, F: 5, JBSR; Sen. Gale McGee to Mike Feldman, August 14, 1963, B: 106, F: Rightwing movement, JFKPL.

13. Research Department to Mr. and Mrs. F. C. Quill, February 27, 1962, B: 2, F: 4, JBSR; Richard C. Fuller, "George Romney and the Michigan Gubernatorial Campaign—1962" (master's thesis, Brigham Young University, 1964), https://scholarsarchive.byu.edu/cgi/viewcontent.cgi?article=5701&context=etd; and Bentley Historical Library, University of Michigan, "'George Romney Announcing His Candidacy for Governor' Footage," video, February 10, 1962, https://bentley.mivideo.it.umich.edu/media/1_mwtj295a.

14. Zack to Ellerin, December 13, 1961, B: 10, F: 16, Rousselot, John H., ADLC.

15. Mike Feldman to President John F. Kennedy, August 15, 1963, B: 63, F: Feldman, Myer, 1963, JFKP; Kent Courtney to Members of the Conservative Society of America in California, May 17, 1962, B: 61, F: 17, RNPL.

16. Rus Walton, "Turning Political Ideas into Government Program," interview by Gabrielle Morris, 1983, 3–4, in "Internal and External Operations of the California Governor's Office, 1966–1974," oral history transcript and related material, Oral History Center, Bancroft Library, University of California, Berkeley. Walton reports that he had to quit his post at NAM due to his role in Shell's campaign. NAM supported Nixon, and perhaps burned by the negative publicity from NAM's ties to Welch, NAM wanted no part of a Birch-backed Shell campaign. Margaret Meier to H. R. Haldeman, May 28, 1962, and one-page typewritten attachment, n.d., B: 61, F: 17; Richard Nixon, White House files, B: 61, F: 17; and Background Memo, Nixon and California—1962, May 14, 1962, B: 54, F: 9, RNPL.

17. "Per Pat Hitt from Margaret Sangster," uncorroborated report that Barbara Shell had spread rumors of Pat Nixon's "breakdown," May 26, 1962; Edwin Halvorson to "Sir," May 21, 1962, B: 61, F: 17, RNPL.

18. Patricia R. Hitt, "From Precinct Worker to Assistant Secretary of the Department of Health, Education, and Welfare: Oral History Transcript/and Related Material," interview by Miriam Stein, 1977, 107, Oral History Center, Bancroft Library, University of California, Berkeley. Stephen Hess, *Bit Player: My Life with Presidents and Ideas* (Washington, DC: Brookings Institution Press, 2018), 62.

19. Richard Bergholz, "Hiestand and Rousselot Promised GOP Backing," *Los Angeles Times*, March 8, 1962; Walter Knott to "Dear Fellow American," letter endorsing Joe Shell, April 16, 1962, and pro-Shell newsletter, "The Feeling Is Growing in California Republican Circles," April 4, 1962. Knott praised Shell for being an original supporter of the state's anticommunist loyalty oath and for backing "tougher penalties for narcotics peddlers." Citizens for Freedom press release, "A Pre-Primary Election Message," May 21, 1962, B: 61, F: 17, RNPL.

20. Kent Courtney to Members of the Conservative Society of America, n.d.; Courtney to Members of the Conservative Society of America in California, May 17, 1962, B: 61, F: 17, RNPL.

21. Rick Perlstein, *Before the Storm: Barry Goldwater and the Unmaking of the American Consensus* (New York: Hill and Wang, 2001), 172; Mike Feldman to President John F. Kennedy, August 15, 1963, B: 63, F: Feldman, Myer, 1963, JFKPL; Stuart A. Morrison to Clarence Edmonds, March 8, 1962; Oouise to Tom Saunders, n.d., attached to Morrison correspondence, B: 3, F: John Birch Society, Letter,

March 8, 1962, CRGBR. Morrison referred to himself as "president" of the Sutter County JBS, but heads of chapters were typically called "chapter leaders."

22. "The Passing of the Patriot: Excerpts from the Speech That Launched Max Rafferty into Politics in 1961," reprinted in *New York Times*, September 1, 1968, https://timesmachine.nytimes.com/timesmachine/1968/09/01/88959865.pdf?pdf _redirect=true&ip=0; Franklin Parker, "Roots of the New Right: School Critic Max Rafferty (1917–82)" (paper, West Virginia University, 1985), https://files.eric .ed.gov/fulltext/ED257728.pdf.

23. Les Ledbetter, "Max Rafferty, 65, Conservative Who Ran California Schools, Dies," *New York Times*, June 14, 1982, www.nytimes.com/1982/06/14/obituaries /max-l-rafferty-65-conservative-who-ran-california-schools-dies.html; Drew Pearson, "Merry Go-Round," *La Habra Star*, October 31, 1962.

24. Perlstein, *Before the Storm*, 171–172; Parker, "Roots of the New Right."

25. Hitt warned Kuchel that denouncing the Birchers "was committing potential political suicide" based on what she had seen befall Nixon in 1962. Hitt, "From Precinct Worker," 116–117; Bryan W. Stevens, *The John Birch Society in California Politics, 1966* (West Covina, CA: Publius Society, 1966); Gladwin Hill, "Libel Apologies End Kuchel Case," *New York Times*, June 29, 1965, https://times machine.nytimes.com/timesmachine/1965/06/29/97215226.html?pageNumber =17; and Lawrence E. Davies, "Kuchel, Target of Rumors, Fights Back and Takes His Accusers to Court," *New York Times*, February 28, 1965, https://timesmachine .nytimes.com/timesmachine/1965/02/28/98453687.html?pageNumber=69.

26. *American Opinion Bookstore Manual*, n.d., B: 5, F: 1; Sally Riley to American Opinion Libraries, November 13, 1963, B: 5, F: 2; Wholesale Bookstore Division to All American Opinion Libraries and Associate Bookstore Units, August 22, 1966, B: 5, F: 2; and American Opinion Wholesale Book Division Purchase Order, n.d., B: 5, F: 2, JBSR.

27. Riley to American Opinion Libraries, April 25, 1963; Riley to American Opinion Libraries, February 19, 1963, B: 5, F: 2, JBSR. The society urged proprietors to stock their shelves with children's books for elementary-school-age kids. "You'd be amazed how many enthusiastic comments have been heard about them," one official marveled.

28. Thomas Hill to Home Office Coordinator and MMM Departments, June 17, 1968, B: 27, F: 2, JBSR.

29. Mike Feldman to President John F. Kennedy, August 15, 1963; and "Financial Scope of the American Right-Wing," August 1963, President's Office Files, B: 106, F: Feldman, Myer, 1963, JFKPL.

30. Hill to All Major Coordinators and Coordinators, December 16, 1964, B: 5, F:2, JBSR.

31. Feldman to JFK, August 15, 1963; and "Financial Scope of the American Right-Wing," August 1963, President's Office Files, B: 106, F: Feldman, Myer, 1963, JFKPL. Zack to Samuel Bloomberg, January 4, 1962, B: 10, F: 16, Rousselot, John H., ADLC; Research Department to Mrs. Grace Bennett, September 18, 1962, B: 2, F: 4, JBSR; and Research Department to John Parrish, September 18, 1962, B: 2, F: 4, MMM 1962, JBSR.

32. Knott to "Friend (and fellow conservative)," August 20, 1962, and attached bulletin from Willis Stone, B: 126, F: 14, Knott, Walter, 1962–1971, HPP.

33. W. A. Barnett to D. A. Waite, October 3, 1963, B: 2, F: 5, JBSR.

34. UPI, "Bircher Predicts Integration Part of Commie Plot," *Las Vegas Sun*, September 22, 1963, B: 121, F: 10, HPP. For details about some aspects of the society's membership, see "John Birch Society Membership," posted by Ernie Lazar, rev. January 27, 2021, ELFF, https://sites.google.com/site/aboutxr/jbs-members.

35. Ellerin to Arnold Forster, April 16, 1963, B: 7, F: 27, Hargis, Billy James, ADLC; Sasha Issenberg, "The Wild Road Trip That Launched the Populist Conservative Movement," *Smithsonian Magazine*, September 2018, www.smithsonianmag .com/history/wild-road-trip-rallied-conservatives-180970033/.

36. Zack to Ellerin, November 19, 1963, B: 7, F: 60, Kahian, Leo, ADLC.

37. Sen. Gale McGee to Feldman, August 14, 1963, B: 106, F: "Right-Wing Movement," JFKPL.

38. Douglas Martin, "Myer Feldman, 92, Advisor to President Kennedy, Dies," *New York Times*, March 3, 2007, www.nytimes.com/2007/03/03/obituaries /03feldman.html.

39. Feldman to JFK, August 15, 1963, and "Financial Scope of the American Right-Wing," August 1963, President's Office Files, B: 106, B: 63, F: Feldman, Myer, 1963, JFKPL.

40. Feldman to JFK, August 15, 1963, and "Financial Scope of the American Right-Wing," August 1963, President's Office Files, B: 106, B: 63, F: Feldman, Myer, 1963, JFKPL.

Chapter 5. "A Dirty War"

1. Carl Linde, Adlai Stevenson at Dallas Memorial Auditorium Theatre, photo, October 24, 1963, *Dallas Morning News*, Tumblr, "Looking Back at Dallas," https://dallashistory.tumblr.com/post/50926630115/oct-24-1963 -ambassador-adlai-stevenson-was; "Long Before Colin Kaepernick, 3 San Diego Padres Joined John Birch Society," *Dallas Morning News*, November 3, 2017, www.dallasnews.com/news/politics/2017/11/03/long-before-colin-kaepernick -3-san-diego-padres-joined-john-birch-society/.

2. D. A. Waite to Robert Welch, November 29, 1963, B: 2, F: 5, JBSR. Some Birchers questioned whether Jack Ruby might have used aliases (such as Rubinstein or Rubenstein) and wanted to check his birth certificate to verify his real name. D. A. Waite to Mrs. Welch, n.d., B: 2, F: 5, JBSR; "The Radical Right," memo on the "impact of Dallas," March 1964, B: 8, F: 11, Kennedy, John F. (assassination), ADLC.

3. Arnold Forster to National Civil Rights Committee, December 24, 1963, B: 8, F: 11, Kennedy, John F. (assassination); "The Radical Right," memo on the "impact of Dallas," March 1964, B: 8, F: 11, Kennedy, John F. (assassination), ADLC.

4. Drew Pearson, "Baker Filed Modest Income Taxes—Birch Soc. in Campaign for Members," *Foster's Daily Democrat*, December 23, 1963; Arnold Forster to National Civil Rights Committee, December 24, 1963, B: 8, F: 11, Kennedy, John F. (assassination), ADLC.

5. "The Radical Right," memo on the "impact of Dallas," March 1964, B: 8, F: 11, Kennedy, John F. (assassination), ADLC.

6. Isadore Zack to Finger, March 25, 1967, B: 5, F: 6, Blumenfeld, Samuel, ADLC.

7. ADL memo on Samuel Blumenfeld, February 1966, B: 5, F: 6, Blumenfeld, Samuel; Arnold Forster to National Civil Rights Committee, December 24, 1963, B: 8, F: 11, Kennedy, John F. (assassination), ADLC.

8. Editorial, "Dispelling the Fog of Extremism in Attleboro," *Providence Journal*, February 17, 1965; Ezra Taft Benson, "An Internal Threat Today," *American Opinion*, n.d. The quotes come from a speech he was scheduled to deliver in Boise, Idaho, in December 1963, which was canceled due to the weather. B: 21, F: 31, JBSR. AP, "Welch Lays Assassination on U.S. Reds," *New Bedford Standard Times*, December 26, 1963. Benson's role in the John Birch Society is chronicled in Matthew L. Harris, ed., *Thunder from the Right: Ezra Taft Benson in Mormonism and Politics* (Champaign: University of Illinois Press, 2019); and Matthew L. Harris, *Watchman on the Tower: Ezra Taft Benson and the Making of the Mormon Right* (Salt Lake City: University of Utah Press, 2020).

9. Harvey Schechter to Milton Ellerin, December 11, 1963, B: 8, F: 11, Kennedy, John F. (assassination), ADLC.

10. ADL Memo, n.d., B: 8, F: 11, Kennedy, John F. (assassination), ADLC.

11. Laurence Swanson to Welch, "Member's Monthly Message Department: Suggestions," week of November 23, 1964, B: 1, F: 6, JBSR.

12. MEV to Welch, November 23–27, 1964, B: 1, F: 6, JBSR; Mary Lou Gray to Welch, November 30, 1964, Member's Monthly Message: Comments and Suggestions, B: 1, F: 6; and Swanson to Welch, week of October 19, 1964, B: 1, F: 6, JBSR. Swanson's memo discusses a section leader named Maddox, who complained that Oliver's speech in Glendale was so unhinged that the society lost "some good prospects."

13. Waite to Robert Barbaras, July 29, 1963, B: 2, F: 5, JBSR.

14. "Nixon, Goldwater? No, Say Rightists," *Chicago Daily News*, April 14, 1961, B: 5, F: 42, ADLC; Thomas Hill to All Major Coordinators and Coordinators, May 7, 1964, B: 27, F: 5, JBSR.

15. "Goldwater Takes Turn to the Left," *New York Times*, February 15, 1964, www.nytimes.com/1964/02/15/archives/goldwater-takes-turn-to-the-left-finds -arizona-audience-too.html; Richard Norton Smith, "Nelson Rockefeller's Last Stand," *Politico*, October 21, 2014, www.politico.com/magazine/story/2014/10 /nelson-rockefellers-last-stand-112072/; Barry Goldwater, *The Conscience of a Conservative*, 30th anniv. ed. (Washington, DC: Regnery Gateway, 1990), 18, 30; and "Text of Goldwater Speech on Rights," *New York Times*, June 19, 1964, www .nytimes.com/1964/06/19/archives/text-of-goldwater-speech-on-rights.html.

16. "Goldwater Denies Knowing He Joined Birch Front Group," *New York Times*, October 10, 1964, www.nytimes.com/1964/10/10/archives/goldwater -denies-knowing-he-joined-birch-front-group.html; "Goldwater, Senator Barry M.," June 11, 1962, Group Research Inc., B: 122, F: 31a, BGP.

17. Goldwater to Spruille Braden, July 25, 1961; Braden to Goldwater, July 28, 1961; Goldwater to Braden, September 8, 1964; Braden to Goldwater, August 17, 1964, B: 1, F: Barry Goldwater, SBP.

18. "Goldwater Gets H. L. Hunt Backing; but Texas Rightist Won't Criticize the President," *New York Times*, November 1, 1964, www.nytimes.com/1964/11/01 /archives/goldwater-gets-hl-huntbacking-but-texas-rightist-wont-criticize-the.html.

19. Zack to Finger, March 25, 1967, B: 5, F: 6, Blumenfeld, Samuel, ADLC; "Right Wing Gains in Coast GOP Organizations," *New York Times*, May 3,

1964, www.nytimes.com/1964/05/03/archives/right-wing-gains-in-coast-gop
-organizations.html. Goldwater had challenged critics to "name some names" of his
allegedly fringe backers, and the *Times* uncovered some. "Birchers Told to Campaign as Individuals," *Boston Herald*, July 23, 1964.

20. A few takes on Buckley's varied efforts to deal with the Birch Society can
be found here: Carl Bogus, *Buckley: William F. Buckley and the Rise of American Conservatism* (New York: Bloomsbury Press, 2011), chapter 4; William F.
Buckley Jr., "Goldwater, the John Birch Society, and Me," *Commentary*, March
2008, www.commentary.org/articles/william-buckley-jr/goldwater-the-john
-birch-society-and-me/; and Alvin Felzenberg, *A Man and His Presidents: The
Political Odyssey of William F. Buckley, Jr.* (New Haven, CT: Yale University
Press, 2017).

21. Frank Meyer to William Buckley, March 26, 2961; M. R. B. to Buckley,
March 29, 1961, B: 14, F: John Birch Society, WFBP.

22. William Rusher to Buckley, April 6, 1961, B: 14, F: John Birch Society,
WFBP.

23. See Lewis Kirby to Buckley, March 21, 1961, B: 14, F: John Birch Society,
WFBP.

24. Buckley to Clarence Manion, December 27, 1961, B: 15, F: Manion, Clarence (1961), WFBP.

25. "Goldwater Denies Knowing He Joined Birch Front Group"; Rick Perlstein,
Before the Storm (New York: Hill and Wang, 2001), 154–156; Cormac Kelly, "William F. Buckley and the Birchers: A Myth, a History Lesson, and a Moral," *Salon*, April 3, 2021, www.salon.com/2021/04/03/william-f-buckley-and-the-birchers
-a-myth-a-history-lesson-and-a-moral/; and Buckley, "Goldwater, the John Birch
Society, and Me." A sympathetic and detailed account of Buckley's efforts to expunge the Birch Society from conservatism's ranks can be found in Alvin Felzenberg, "The Inside Story of William F. Buckley, Jr.'s Crusade Against the John
Birch Society," *National Review*, June 20, 2017, https://nationalreview.com/2017/06
/william-f-buckley-john-birch-society-history-conflict-robert-welch/.

26. Rusher to Cable Ball, March 11, 1963, B: 26, F: John Birch Society; Buckley
to T. Coleman Andrews, October 8, 1963, B: 24, F: T. Coleman Andrews; and
Daniel Bell to Buckley, April 4, 1963, B: 24, F: Bell, Prof. Daniel (1963), WFBP.

27. Louis Ruthenburg to Buckley, November 27, 1965, B: 37, F: Ruffin, Martha,
WFBP. One of Buckley's informants noted that a Manhattan Birch chapter leader
had attended one of Buckley's campaign rallies. At the New York City seventh anniversary dinner for the JBS, Buckley's confidante observed "many Buckley buttons
in evidence, and everyone I talked to said they are voting for him, 'regardless of
what he says against the JBS.'" Agatha Schmidt to Buckley, October 11, 1965, B:
35, F: John Birch Society (1965), WFBP. Buckley attacked his foes on terms that
likely would have been familiar to the JBS home office in Belmont. He wrote Goldwater in the summer of 1964 that Buckley's sparring partner Gore Vidal was "your
favorite pink queer. . . . Vidal, by the way, asked on television what were my relations with Senator Goldwater. I was terribly tempted to reply, 'normal.'" Buckley to
Goldwater, August 11, 1964, B: 30, F: Goldwater, Barry, WFBP.

28. Ruthenburg to Buckley, November 27, 1965, B: 37, F: Ruffin, Martha,
WFBP; "Goldwater Takes Turn to the Left."

29. Research Department to Mrs. Garrett Leonard, November 7, 1962, B: 2, F: 4, JBSR.

30. Julius Duscha, "Fevered Pitch Brings on Chill at Right-Wing Rally," *Chicago Sun-Times*, August 30, 1964.

31. Research Department to Mrs. John Napier, November 5, 1962, B: 2, F: 4, JBSR; Perlstein, *Before the Storm*, 149.

32. 1964 Goldwater Campaign Ad 1, "In Your Heart You Know He's Right," video, Dan Rather: American Journalist, accessed July 16, 2022, https://danratherjournalist .org/political-analyst/election-coverage/1964-election/compilation-1964-general -election-materials/video; Richard Hutchinson to "Gentlemen," MMM, July 1963, B: 1, F: 6, JBSR; Waite to Hutchinson, September 6, 1963, B: 1, F: 6, JBSR.

33. Perlstein, *Before the Storm*, 486.

34. *Support Your Local Police* (Birch Society pamphlet), n.d., B: 21, F: 27, JBSR; essay, *American Opinion*, June 1965, 12–15. See Michael W. Flamm, *Law and Order: Street Crime, Civil Unrest, and the Crisis of Liberalism in the 1960s* (New York: Columbia University Press, 2005), 218–219. The Anti-Defamation League issued a bulletin, "John Birch in Uniform," warning of the danger posed by Birchers who did double duty as police officers, and Flamm reports that at one town hall sponsored by the Birch Society, nearly five hundred people attended, "most of them off-duty officers," wearing badges signaling their affiliation with the police. "A Communist Plot Against the Free World Police," Senate Subcommittee Transcript of Hearing to Investigate the Administration of the Internal Security Act and Other Internal Security Laws, June 13, 1961, B: 27, F: 52, JBSR.

35. Perlstein, *Before the Storm*, 483; W. E. Dunham to Welch, August 17, 1964, B: 27, F: 52, JBSR; and *Support Your Local Police*.

36. Thomas Davis to Welch, February 18, 1965, B: 27, F: 52, JBSR.

37. Perlstein, *Before the Storm*, 487; Philadelphia Committee to Support Your Local Police, *What to Do* (brochure), December 1964, B: 27, F: 52, JBSR.

38. Paul Corbett to Welch, February 16, 1965, B: 27, F: 52; AP, "Tate Says Birchist Police Limit Own Use," *Baltimore Sun*, November 14, 1964, B: 1, F: 6, JBSR.

39. Hill to Major Coordinators and Coordinators, May 7, 1964, B: 27, F: 5, JBSR.

40. Michelle Nickerson, *Mothers of Conservatism* (Princeton, NJ: Princeton University Press, 2012), 158–167. As Nickerson argues, the moral crusade was an effort by the Goldwater campaign to sow fear of liberals, leftists, and other anti-American forces that allegedly had led to rising crime rates, student protests, drugs, and loose sexual mores. And, she adds, "the 'religious right' or 'pro-family movement' gradually replaced anticommunism, with Christianity as the core organizing principle of the American right." Just as the Birchers would do, "Goldwater generated enthusiasm among conservatives for federal and state enforcement of 'morality.'" The society prefigured efforts by the religious right to lobby against the ERA, sex education, prayer in schools, and *Roe v. Wade*.

41. Thomas Hill to All Major Coordinators and Coordinators, May 7, 1964, B: 2, F: 5; Birch Society to John Weisman, July 19, 1965, B: 1, F: 6, JBSR. Although Birchers had a handful of college chapters, the society recommended that college students join preexisting chapters off campus. Campus life was so distracting that it made setting up chapters a challenge, in the view of Birch leaders.

42. Kelly, "William F. Buckley and the Birchers." Also see Perlstein, *Before the Storm*, 476–477.

43. Hill to Major Coordinators and Coordinators, May 7, 1964, B: 27, F: 5, JBSR.

44. MEV to Robert Welch, October 15, 1964, B: 1, F: 6, JBSR.

45. "5 Birch Members Win on the Coast; Gain G.O.P. Nominations for U.S. and State Offices," *New York Times*, June 4, 1964. The five men were Robert Muncaster, William C. J. VanMastright, John G. Schmitz, Jack B. Azevedo, and Donald R. St. John.

46. Perlstein, *Before the Storm*, 381–382.

47. Rus Walton, "Turning Political Ideas into Government Program," interview by Gabrielle Morris, 1983, 19–21, in "Internal and External Operations of the California Governor's Office, 1966–1974," oral history transcript and related material, Oral History Center, Bancroft Library, University of California, Berkeley.

48. Niels Bjerre-Poulsen, *Right Face: Organizing the American Conservative Movement, 1945–1965* (Copenhagen: Museum Tusculanum Press, University of Copenhagen, 2002), 254.

49. Darcy Eveleigh and Damon Darlin, "A Short History of Convention Speech-Booing," *New York Times*, July 23, 2016, www.nytimes.com/2016/07/23/upshot/a-short-history-of-convention-speech-booing.html; Smith, "Nelson Rockefeller's Last Stand."

50. Rothberg and Klein, "Debate on Extremism Boosts Its Membership, Birch Society Says," *Chicago Sun-Times*, September 6, 1964.

51. Louis Shanks oral history transcript, interview by Gina Gianzero, August 20, 1987, 2–3, LBJ Library Oral Histories, LBJ Presidential Library, www.discoverlbj.org/item/oh-shanksl-19870820-1-07-01.

52. Ana Steele to Buckley, September 23, 1964, B: 32, F: Steele, Ana M. (1964), WFBP.

53. Carmen Steele to Editor, *New York Times*, September 24, 1964; Ana Steele to Buckley, September 23, 1964, B: 32, F: Steele, Ana M. (1964), WFBP.

54. Bob Dunim to "Gentlemen," MMM, November 15, 1964; Oliver Kelso Jr. to Gentlemen, November 12, 1964; Eugene Rodgers to Gentlemen, November 9, 1964; Mrs. Walsh (no first name appears in the document) to Gentlemen, November 1964; MFW to Mrs. Walsh, December 30, 1964; and MFW to Mrs. Bateman, December 30, 1964, B: 2, F: 7, JBSR.

55. Don Rubin, "Society's Ranks in State Doubled Within 8 Months," *New Haven Register*, August 19, 1965; Hill to All Major Coordinators and Coordinators, December 16, 1964, B: 5, F: 2, JBSR; Member's Monthly Message Department to Mrs. Bateman, January 5, 1965, B: 2, F: 7, JBSR; Wolfson to Lerner, November 30, 1964, B: 10, F: 36, Skousen, W. Cleon, ADLC; and Mrs. Martin Carlson to "Gentlemen," MMM, November 11, 1964, B: 2, F: 7, JBSR.

56. Zack to Jerome Bakst, January 21, 1964, B: 6, F: 13, DePalo, Thomas P., ADLC.

57. Herb Brin, "The Birchers," *Southwest Jewish Press*, March 12, 1964, B: 6, F: 13, DePalo, Thomas P., ADLC.

58. Marie Howard to Gentlemen, November 1964, B: 2, F: 7; Mr. and Mrs. C. Gandy to Gentlemen, September 11, 1964, B: 1, F: 9, JBSR.

59. The society's headquarters understood members who wished to keep their membership secret. "We have notified our Home Office coordinator for your area to send your bulletins in a plain envelope in the future." MFW to Mrs. Reiswig, January 4, 1965, B: 2, F: 7; Vivian E. Reiswig to Gentlemen, November 9, 1964, B: 2, F; 7; John C. Peterson to Gentlemen, November 19, 1964, B: 2, F: 7; and Sally Riley to Welch, Month of November, B: 1, F: 6, JBSR.

60. Waite to Peter Brown, August 14, 1963, B: 1, F: 9, JBSR.

61. Waite to Shirley Hoover, August 14, 1963, B: 1, F: 9; Waite to Guy Banister, August 14, 1963, B: 1, F: 9; James Burks to Gentlemen, November 12, 1964, B: 2, F: 7, JBSR.

Chapter 6. Birch Watchers

1. Isadore Zack to Arnold Forster, March 30, 1964, B: 9, F: 45, ADLC. The agent's identity, Zack assured Forster, was also "known to [Jerry] Bakst," ADL's research director.

2. Forster to Zack, February 3, 1964, B: 9, F: 45, ADLC. "Any chance of our getting our hands on the typescript copy of that article?" Forster had asked Zack. "I would love to see its anti-Semitism. We may need such evidence in the near future."

3. Report #26, Bos #4, "Conversations with Robert Welch and Tom Hill (Major Coordinator)," April 4, 1964; B: 9, F: 45, Pegler, Westbrook, ADLC. An official with the ADL scribbled on a letter to the editor from a Bircher named Harold Collins, "File under name." Harold Collins, "Liberalism Is Out," *Boston Sunday Herald*, September 24, 1961, B: 5, F: 38, Collins, Harold R., ADLC.

4. Alan F. Westin, "The John Birch Society," *Commentary*, August 1961.

5. "GRI: A Reuther Idea?," n.d., B: 42, F: 2, WJGP. For background information on Group Research, see "Biographical Note," "Group Research Inc. Records, 1955–1996," Columbia University Libraries Archival Collections, accessed July 17, 2022, www.columbia.edu/cu/lweb/archival/collections/ldpd_5010936/. Editorial, "Dispelling the Fog of Extremism in Attleboro," *Providence Journal*, February 17, 1965; "Hall, Expert on Extremism, Claims Birchers Love, Misunderstand U.S.," *Harvard Crimson*, February 17, 1965, www.thecrimson.com/article/1965/2/17/hall-expert-on-extremism-claims-birchers/.

6. Arnold Forster and Benjamin Epstein, *The Trouble-Makers: An Anti-Defamation League Report* (Garden City, NY: Doubleday, 1952), 19–20; and foreword (by Meier Steinbrink), 13; Arnold Forster and Benjamin Epstein, *The Radical Right: Report on the John Birch Society and Its Allies* (New York: Random House Trade Paperbacks, 1967), 4–5.

7. Steven J. Ross, *Hitler in Los Angeles: How Jews Foiled Nazi Plots against Hollywood and America* (New York: Bloomsbury, 2017), 2–4; Walter H. Waggoner, "Benjamin Epstein, Director of League Fighting Prejudice," *New York Times*, May 4, 1983; Margalit Fox, "Arnold Forster, Who Fought Anti-Semitism with B'nai B'rith, Is Dead at 97," *New York Times*, March 26, 2010.

8. For more on Zack, see "Guide to the Isadore Zack–U.S. Army Counter Intelligence Corps (CIC) Papers, 1942–1997," University of New Hampshire, www.library.unh.edu/find/archives/collections/isadore-zack-us-army-counter

-intelligence-corps-cic-papers-1942-1997. Bryan Marquard, "Isadore Zack; Intelligence Work Led to Fight for Justice," *Boston Globe*, May 11, 2011.

9. John F. Kennedy, "Remarks of the President at 50th Annual Meeting, Anti-Defamation League of B'nai B'rith," January 31, 1963, President's Office Files, Speech Files, F: Remarks to B'nai B'rith Anti-Defamation League, 31 January 1963, JFKL; Lyndon B. Johnson, Address Before a Joint Session of the Congress, November 27, 1963, LBJPL.

10. "Johnson Seeking Extremism Plank," *New York Times*, August 5, 1964.

11. See, for example, Zack to Florence Seldin, March 26, 1959, B: 10, F: 3, ADLC. Also see Zack to Justin Finger, October 15, 1964, B: 6, F: 9, ADLC: "I have had a second report from officer James Foreman of the Stamford, Conn., Police Department re Tom Davis," Zack informed Finger. Also see Zack to Finger, June 8, 1964, B: 6, F: 27, ADLC: "There are quite a few Jewish families around the 12 Hoitt Road address of Edwards, Sr.," wrote Zack, describing the freelancers aiding the ADL's Birch Watcher program. "Many of them know of the association of the Edwards family with the John Birch Society." (The ADL apparently received information about Birchers from "a reliable source in Belmont.") For an example of an accountant doubling as a confidential informant, see Zack to Robert Segal, January 14, 1963, B: 7, F: 38, ADLC: "Mr. S. K. Solomon . . . , an accountant . . . , has identified another Dedham resident as a sponsor of the New England Rally for God and Country and as a member of the John Birch Society. Mr. Solomon said that he was the accountant for James F. Higgins . . . and that Mr. Higgins has informed him of his membership in the John Birch Society. . . . asked Solomon to question Higgins further and establish, if possible, whether or not there is a John Birch chapter in Dedham, and, if so, who is the leader, etc. Mr. Solomon promised to give us every assistance." For an example of ADL feeding dirt on the JBS to reporters, months before the first articles on the society appeared, see Zack to Ben Bagdikian, August 28, 1959, B: 7, F: 35, ADLC. For an example of running credit checks on Birchers, see Zack to Robert Schaye, March 31, 1964, B: 10, F: 34; the confidential "Associated Credit of America, Inc.," for Angelo A. Cambio, at the request of "United Furniture"; and Zack to Finger, November 29, 1965, B: 5, F: 20, ADLC. "We would greatly appreciate it if you could arrange for a credit check in depth on both of these women," Zack wrote Schaye. "This is an extremely confidential matter. That is why this request is being hand delivered to you." Also see Zack to Finger, April 7, 1967, B: 4, F: 34, ADLC. "The Haags [hosts of a Birch meeting] are not pro-Birch," Zack reported. "They cooperated with our contact in setting up this meeting so that [Birch leader] Harold Beck could be 'interviewed.'"

12. Debra Schulz, *Going South: Jewish Women in the Civil Rights Movement* (New York: New York University Press, 2001), 180–182.

13. Zack to Forster, March 30, 1964, B: 9, F: 45, ADLC. For an example of the society's attacks on the ADL, see Arthur Spiegel to Gus Fingee, October 25, 1966, B: 6, F: 9, ADLC. "A Hartford couple . . . have been telling people to go to the Birch meeting on Thursday night to hear the truth about ADL." For ADL efforts to use the media to undercut the society, see, for instance, Arthur Spiegel to Justin Finger, September 10, 1965, B: 6, F: 34, Fenton, Francis, ADLC: "Can you . . . get a nationally known Roman Catholic leader to write a similar kind of column which

would be an attack on the John Birch Society?" Spiegel asked Finger in response to comments by Father Francis Fenton favorable to the Birchers. Also see Zack to Irving Fain, March 18, 1963, B: 6, F: 21, ADLC. Zack wrote, "I know that the [Providence] Journal is doing some digging on [Robert] Dresser's involvement with the radical right. The reporter handling the story is Robert Taylor. I have been giving him some assistance in this matter." Zack to Finger, February 18, 1966, B: 5, F: 11, Julia Brown, ADLC. White supremacist funder Olive Simes added a codicil to her will bequeathing to the society "all stock or other securities" upon her death. See codicil, signed July 16, 1965, B: 10, F: 34, ADLC.

14. Zack to Harrison Siegle, September 10, 1959, B: 9, F: 11, McKinney, Harold; Zack to Robert Segal, November 3, 1959, B: 9, F: 11, McKinney, Harold; Zack to Jerry Bakst and Milt Ellerin, February 28, 1962, B: 7, F: 57, Jenkins, Philip I.; Jerry Bakst to Zack, September 4, 1959, B: 5, F: 28, Carto, Willis; Zack to Arthur Levin, November 10, 1959, B: 7, F: 35, Heinsohn, A. G., Jr., ADLC. See, for example, Spiegel to Zack, January 8, 1965, B: 10, F: 36, Skousen, W. Cleon, ADLC. Spiegel requested that a colleague dig up a document that quoted Skousen's antisemitic remark from a right-wing event in Iowa in 1964. Zack to Seldin, March 26, 1959, B: 10, F: 3, Prince, Burton A., ADLC.

15. ADL report describing a Birch Society event in Detroit, B: 10, F: 16, ADLC. Donald Lobsinger, the founder of the far-right group Breakthrough, was spotted at the meeting by a Birch Watcher.

16. Zack to Samuel Bloomberg, January 4, 1962, B: 10, F: 16, Rousselot, John H.; Zack to Finger, March 15, 1967, B: 5, F: 6, Blumenfeld, Samuel, ADLC.

17. Zack to Ellerin, March 5, 1962, B: 7, F: 57, Jenkins, Philip I., ADLC.

18. Zack to Irwin Suall, re: Colonel Laurence Bunker, September 18, 1969, B: 5, F: 15, Bunker, Colonel Laurence E.; Arthur Spiegel to Justin Finger, September 10, 1965, B: 4, F: 37, ADLC.

19. ADL Memo, p. 2, B: 8, F: 11; Spiegel to Zack, January 7, 1966, B: 2, F: 15; and Spiegel to Zack, April 8, 1966, B: 10, F: 14, Root, E. Merrill, ADLC.

20. Confidential report on Walker-Hargis rally, April 3, 1963, B: 7, F: 27, ADLC.

21. Zack to Finger, December 2, 1964, B: 10, F: 17, Rousselot, John H., ADLC.

22. Zack to Finger, March 25, 1965, B: 9, F: 11, ADLC. "So far Robert Welch, Mrs. Welch, and Harold McKinney have worked on BS #2," Zack informed Finger.

23. Memo, "not to be shown," no author, no recipient, "Subject: Eric Butler," March 24, 1967, B: 7, F: 16, Butler, Eric D., ADLC.

24. Tracy Gordon, "In Mormon President's FBI Files, Signs of an Early Tea Partier Take Root," *Religion News Service*, November 19, 2010, https://religionnews .com/2010/11/19/in-mormon-leaders-fbi-files-signs-of-an-early-tea-partier1/; Claire Conner, *Wrapped in the Flag: A Personal History of the Radical Right* (Boston: Beacon Press, 2013), 57. For background on the FBI's Birch Society files, see Ernie Lazar, "FBI on John Birch Society," July 2021 ELFF, https://sites.google.com/site /ernie124102/jbs-1.

25. Finger to Nissen Gross et al., August 26, 1965, B: 9, F: 25, Noble, John; Zack to John Noonan, September 14, 1965, B: 4, F: 29, Ayler, Natalie, ADLC.

26. Spiegel to Finger, September 10, 1965, B: 6, F: 34, Fenton, Francis E.; Zack to Finger, October 26, 1965; and Bob Creamer, "'Freedom Ring' Voice Known," *Boston Traveler*, October 25, 1965, B: 9, F: 12, McKinney, John M., ADLC.

27. Harvey Schechter to Finger, June 15, 1966, B: 7, F: 46, Holmes, Lola Belle, ADLC.

28. Zack to Finger, January 26, 1965, B: 5, F: 11, Brown, Julia; Zack to Finger, January 7, 1965, B: 6, F: 9, Davis, Tom; and Zack to Earl and Irma Reingold, March 31, 1967, B: 9, F: 13, McManus, John, ADLC.

29. Spiegel to Zack, April 14, 1967, B: 5, F: 11, Brown, Julia; Fred Andelman to Zack, August 1, 1966, B: 6, F: 27, Edwards, George; and Finger to Zack, March 14, 1967, B: 5, F: 6, Blumenfeld, Samuel, ADLC.

30. Zack to Finger, June 25, 1965, B: 6, F: 34, Fenton, Francis, ADLC.

31. Zack to Finger, December 2, 1964, B: 10, F: 17, Rousselot, John; Zack to Finger, October 8, 1965, B: 5, F: 38, Collins, Harold R., ADLC.

32. *Bulletin*, October 2, 1961, p. 9, B: 14, F: John Birch Society, WFBP; Robert Welch, radio script, *The John Birch Society Report*, January 1966, B: 21, F: 23, JBSR; and Zack to Finger, April 27, 1966, B: 10, F: 8, Rousselot, John H., ADLC. Zack was quoting Rousselot, who said the Klan wasn't welcome in the society; Rousselot claimed, "We have helped mightily to offset the emotional and extravagant tendencies of the prejudiced and the poorly informed to blame communism on any one group or race or organization." "Philip Blair Jones," p. 2, B: 9, F: 45, ADLC.

33. ADL report, p. 3, B: 5, F: 15, ADLC; MEV to Welch, week of October 26–30, 1964, B: 1, F: 6, JBSR; and Laurence Swanson to Welch, October 26, 1964, B: 1, F: 6, JBSR.

34. Welch, radio script, *The John Birch Society Report*, January 1966, B: 21, F: 23, JBSR; Don Rubin, "Society's Ranks in State Doubled Within 8 Months," *New Haven Register*, August 19, 1965; and Welch, radio script, *The John Birch Society Report*, April 1966, B: 21, F: 23, JBSR.

35. MLG to Tom Hill, November 24, 1964, B: 1, F: 6; Mr. and Mrs. James Wornock, Comments for Dr. Waite, November 18, 1964, B: 1, F: 6, JBSR.

36. ADL Report on Lola Belle Holmes' lecture on Cape Cod, B: 7, F: 46, Holmes, Lola Belle, ADLC; Ingrid Cowan to Welch, December 3, 1963, B: 27, F: 5, JBSR. Cowan, who was proficient in firearms, announced herself "ready to do almost anything when it comes to defeating these One World Socialists." While her Birch meetings featured ten women and one man, she said the men were more "bloodthirsty" and eager to use guns and knives and join the KKK while the women were more open to waging a war of words before they resorted to violence.

37. Albin Kerbs, "Gerald L. K. Smith Dead; Anti-Communist Crusader," *New York Times*, April 16, 1976; Thomas Hill to Ronald Carnes; Hill to "Harry Browne," March 5, 1962; Carnes to "Gentlemen," MMM, February 19, 1962, B: 2, F: 3, JBSR.

38. John Baker Jr. to Welch, April 8, 1964; D. A. Waite to Baker, April 20, 1964, B: 1, F: 6, JBSR.

39. Waite to Marilyn Allen, January 9, 1964, B: 1, F: 6, JBSR. See memo on Reed Benson, p. 3, B: 4, F: 37, Benson, Reed A., ADLC. Henry Norsen to "Gentlemen," MMM, November 1961, B: 2, F: 3, JBSR; MMM Ginger to Dr. Gannon, December 13, 1961, B: 2, F: 3, JBSR; and ADL Report, Detroit meeting, p. 2, B: 10, F: Rousselot, ADLC.

40. Roberta Galler to Ellerin, May 4, 1961, B: 5, F: 2, Courtney, Kent, ADLC.

41. Zack to Art Levin, November 4, 1959, B: 7, F: 35, Heinsohn, A. G., Jr., ADLC; Forster and Epstein, *Trouble-Makers*, 202.

42. ADL Press Release, n.d., B: 10, F: 34, Simes, Olive; Harvey Schechter to Finger, June 3, 1964, B: 9, F: 32, Oliver, Revilo; and letter to the editor, draft, *Bangor Maine Daily News*, July 25, 1966, B: 5, F: 4, Bradley Bickford, ADLC.

43. Thomas Anderson, radio script, *The John Birch Society Report*, April 1966, B: 21, F: 23, JBSR; Spiegel to Finger, November 10, 1965, B: 4, F: 22, ADLC. Anderson, Spiegel wrote, "attacked just about everybody in his clever humorous way including Bill Buckley and Barry Goldwater. The former he called a butcher of the English language and the latter he called a phony."

44. ADL Pacific Southwest Regional Office to James Oviatt, January 17, 1964; ADL Press Release, n.d.; Bill Becker, "Rightist Mailings Stir Coast Clash," *New York Times*, February 9, 1964; Harvey Schechter, "Fact-Finding Report," February 18 and October 20, 1964, B: 9, F: 34, Oviatt, James, ADLC.

45. ADL, press release, n.d., B: 9, F: 34, Oviatt, James, ADLC. When ADL agents learned that Oviatt and his wife were sponsoring a Welch tribute dinner, one ADL official considered "sending another letter to Rousselot, asking him, 'nu, nu?,'" Yiddish loosely translated as "Don't do that." Schechter to Finger, April 10, 1964, B: 9, F: 34, Oviatt, James, ADLC.

46. Schechter, "Fact-Finding Report," October 20, 1964; *Oviatt vs. Senn, et al.*, n.d., B: 9, F: 34, Oviatt, James, ADLC.

47. Forster and Epstein, *Trouble-Makers*, 202. For background on George, see W. C. George Papers, 1904–1971, Wilson Special Collections Library, University of North Carolina, accessed September 3, 2022, https://finding-aids .lib.unc.edu/03822/. Carl Dick to Welch, July 25, 1963, summarizing E. Ludlow Keeney's concerns about the distribution of Birch literature alongside the racist book; Waite to E. Ludlow Keeney Jr., August, 15, 1963, B: 1, F: 9, JBSR.

48. Waite to Delores Davis, August 15, 1963, B: 1, F: 9, JBSR; John Fenton, "Birch Society Is Shaken by 'Acrimonious Disputes,'" *New York Times*, August 2, 1966. The day after Oliver's resignation, another council member, Slobodan Draskovich, resigned. In a 1982 letter explaining his resignation, Oliver cited his conclusion that Birchers had been captured by "the Defamation League" and informed an ally that "I have the full names of the four Kikes on the [JBS] supervisory committee" who allegedly had orchestrated the plot to take control of the society. Revilo Oliver to Joseph Kamp, June 12, 1982, ELFF, https://archive.org/details/06 -12-82-letter-by-revilo-oliver-to-joseph-kamp-about-oliver-resignation-from-jbs /mode/2up; Revilo Oliver to Members of the Council of the John Birch Society, August 14, 1966, ELFF, archive.org/details/ReviloOliverResignationFrom JohnBirchSociety/mode/2up.

49. Dan T. Carter, *The Politics of Rage: George Wallace, the Origins of the New Conservatism, and the Transformation of American Politics* (New York: Simon and Schuster, 1995), 274–275.

50. Rousselot to William Randolph Hearst Jr., July 31, 1964, B: 10, F: 7, Rousselot, John H.; Hyman Haves to Forster, February 24, 1964, B: 10, F: 17, ADLC.

51. "Anti-Defamation Leader Accused by Birch Official," October 6, 1966; AP, "Bircher Hits ADL Official," *Bridgeport Post*, October 6, 1966; and Thomas Davis, telegram, October 5, 1966, B: 6, F: 9, Davis, Tom, ADLC.

52. Thomas Davis, "The Jewish Community and the John Birch Society," October 4, 1966, B: 6, F: 9, ADLC; Epstein and Forster, *Report on the John Birch Society, 1966* (New York: Random House, 1966).

Chapter 7. "Little Old Ladies in Tennis Shoes"

1. Roy Fultz to Welch, July 14, 1965, B: 1, F: 21, JBSR; Anthony Ferlanto to Welch, January 4, 1965, B: 1, F: 21, JBSR; James Traub, "Potent Brew: His Name Said Beer, but His Money Helped Finance a Right-Wing Revolution," *New York Times*, December 28, 2003.

2. Welch to William Grede, January 27, 1959, B: 14, F: 8, WJGP; "Birch Society Public Relations Man Comes Here to Seek Members," *Charlotte Observer*, August 19, 1965, in FBI-Charlotte 100-9548, serial 142, https://sites.google.com/site/aboutxr/jbs-members. Thomas Davis, then the eastern regional director of the Birch Society, told a newspaper in North Carolina that approximately half the Birch membership comprised women. Lisa McGirr, *Suburban Warriors* (Princeton, NJ: Princeton University Press, 2001), 87. The California demographic estimate comes from Barbara Stone, "The John Birch Society of California" (PhD diss., University of Southern California, 1968), 87, www.proquest.com/openview/8c41593c94234082a3ce4f258b7beac3/1?pq-origsite=gscholar&cbl=18750&diss=y.

3. Herbert Gold, "John Rousselot of the John Birch Society," August 1967, C: 3, F: 49, "Rousselot of the JBS," HGP.

4. Richard Hofstadter, *The Paranoid Style in American Politics* (New York: Knopf, 2008), 67.

5. Welch to Grede, January 27, 1959, B: 14, F: 8, WJGP.

6. "American Opinion Library, Inc.: Board of Directors," n.d. circa 1964, B: 42, F: 2, WJGP; Carolyn Bertram to Anne Dennison, September 26, 1966, B: 9, F: 3, JBSR; and Isadore Zack to Milt Ellerin, July 20, 1962, B: 9, F: 9, McKinney, Anna, ADLC.

7. Center for American Women and Politics, "History of Women in the U.S. Congress," accessed September 3, 2022, https://cawp.rutgers.edu/history-women-us-congress; Ellen Fitzpatrick, *The Highest Glass Ceiling: Women's Quest for the American Presidency* (Cambridge, MA: Harvard University Press, 2016), 79–80.

8. Michelle Nickerson, *Mothers of Conservatism* (Princeton, NJ: Princeton University Press, 2012); Kathleen Blee, *Women of the Klan: Racism and Gender in the 1920s* (Berkeley: University of California Press, 1991); Elizabeth Gillespie McRae, *Mothers of Massive Resistance: White Women and the Politics of White Supremacy* (New York: Oxford University Press, 2018).

9. Nickerson, *Mothers of Conservatism*, 2–7, 8–13.

10. Grace Terkhorn to JBS, Comments from MMMs, November 11, 1964, B: 17, F: 6; Laurence Swanson to Welch, Member's Monthly Message Department: Suggestions, Week of November 23, 1964, B: 1, F: 6; MEV to Welch, November 23–27, 1964, B: 1, F: 6; Mrs. Fulmer to Welch, January 29, 1965, B: 1, F: 21; and D. A. Waite to David Diamond, July 12, 1963, B: 2, F: 5, JBSR.

11. McGirr, *Suburban Warriors*, 87; Thomas Hill to Bertram, December 16, 1965, B: 9, F: 3, JBSR; MEV to Welch, week of November 2–6, 1964, B: 1, F: 6, JBSR; Welch to Mrs. William Buckley Sr., May 5, 1961, Part I, B: 14, F: John Birch Society, WFBP; Mary Lou Gray to Welch, November 30, 1964, Member's Monthly Message: Comments and Suggestions, B: 1, F: 6, JBSR.

12. For a good discussion of women's leadership of Birch-sponsored bookstores in Los Angeles, see Michelle Nickerson, "Sarah Palin's Surprising Social Roots," *Zocalo Public Square*, September 6, 2012, www.zocalopublicsquare.org/2012/09/06/sarah-palins-surprising-socal-roots/chronicles/who-we-were/.

13. Nickerson, *Mothers of Conservatism*, 160, 169. Nickerson refers to conservative women's activism as "housewife populism." Mary Kathryn Daniels to Donald Gray, October 1, 1966, B: 9, F: 2, JBSR. McGirr argues in *Suburban Warriors* that women partly reacted to suburban anomie by finding camaraderie during daytime Birch meetings.

14. Nickerson, "Sarah Palin's Surprising Social Roots"; Swanson to Welch, week of November 9, 1964, B: 1, F: 6, JBSR; and Patricia Huster to Gentlemen, May 6, 1965, B: 1, F: 6, JBSR.

15. Nickerson, *Mothers of Conservatism*, 54–55; Mary Lou Gray to Welch, November 30, 1964, Member's Monthly Message: Comments and Suggestions, B: 1, F: 6, JBSR; and C. L. Hanson to Welch, week of October 19, 1964, B: 1, F: 6, JBSR.

16. Jane Wilson to Mr. Spivak, May 21, 1961, B: 45, F 4: Meet the Press Viewer Mail, Program Response, Robert Welch, 5/21/61, LSP; Swanson to Welch, week of October 19, 1964, B: 1, F: 6, JBSR; MEV to Welch, November 9–13, 1964, B: 1, F: 6, JBSR; Rochelle Joseph to JBS, November 9–13, 1964, B: 1, F: 6, JBSR; and Hanson to Welch, week of October 19, 1964, B: 1, F: 6, JBSR.

17. Mabel Moffat to Welch, October 6, 1963; MEV to Welch, week of October 13–16, 1964, B: 1, F: 6, JBSR.

18. Swanson to Welch, Member's Monthly Message Department: Suggestions, November 16, 1964; Catherine Kloppenburg to JBS, October 26, 1964; Swanson to Welch, week of November 4, 1964, B: 1, F: 6, JBSR.

19. McRae, *Mothers of Massive Resistance*, 197–198.

20. Marilyn Miller to Welch, September 14, 1964, B: 1, F: 6, JBSR; McRae, *Mothers of Massive Resistance*, 200.

21. Lori Bergman to JBS, December 4, 1964; Swanson to Welch, Member's Monthly Message Department, week of November 16, 1964, B: 1, F: 6; Swanson to Welch, "Suggestions," Week of November 15, 1964, B: 1, F: 6, JBSR.

22. McRae, *Mothers of Massive Resistance*, 227, 231.

23. MEV to Welch, week of November 2–6, 1964, B: 1, F: 6, JBSR; Saul Friedman, "U.S. Politics Fail to Slow with Summer Heat," *Detroit Free Press*, June 26, 1966. The seat Johnstone was contesting was solidly Democratic, but Johnstone, the *Free Press* reported, had better organization than the Romney-backed candidate.

24. "No Comment on Election Says Dr. Ever Curtis," *Gloucester Times*, April 7, 1965. Right-wing medical groups also sought to pass resolutions opposing pledges of nondiscrimination by medical doctors as the 1964 Civil Rights law required. Zack to Justin Finger, October 28, 1965, B: 6, F: 2, Curtis, Ever, ADLC.

25. Herbert Black, "Doctors Row over Birch Program," *Boston Globe*, April 6, 1965.

26. Research Department to Arlene Best, April 9, 1962, B: 2, F: 4, JBSR; Best to "Gentlemen," MMM, March 28, 1962, B: 2, F: 4, JBSR; and Zack to Finger, April 5, 1965, B: 6, F: 2, Curtis, Ever, ADLC.

27. "Review and Setting Tone for the New Year," n.d., B: 5, F: 19, JBSR.

28. Attendance/Time Sheet, "September '65," B: 5, F: 55, JBSR. One timesheet listed nineteen employees in the MMM Department during September 1965, at least half of them women.

29. Margaret Edwards to Richard McKinney, August 16–19, 1965; Weekly Time Sheet, Margaret Edwards, June 14–18, 1965, B: 5, F: 23, JBSR.

30. Richard McKinney to Mike McGagin, March 24, 1966; "Review and Setting Tone for the New Year," n.d., B: 5, F: 19, JBSR.

31. Member's Monthly Message Department, n.d., B: 5, F: 19; Guide sheet: "Quantity of Work," n.d., B: 5, F: 41, JBSR.

32. Member's Monthly Message Department, n.d.; "Review and Setting Tone for the New Year," n.d., B: 5, F: 19, JBSR.

33. "Robert Clarke," employee assessment, August 26, 1965 (and other handwritten entries), B: 5, F: 19; "George Edwards," employee assessment, October 27, 1966, and July 28, 1967, B: 5, F: 22; "Review and Setting Tone for the New Year," n.d., B: 5, F: 19, JBSR.

34. RBM to Sally Riley, June 10, 1966; Sally Riley, January 6, 1966; "I wrote this note . . . ," n.d., B: 5, F: 42, JBSR.

35. "Ellen Tobin," n.d., B: 5, F: 51; "Cynthia Newman," February 9, 1966, B: 5, F: 40; "Jeri Yabbacio," July 28, 1967, B: 5, F: 54, JBSR.

36. Richard McKinney to Mr. and Mrs. Tom Humphress, August 29, 1966, B: 5, F: 29; "Within-Office Memorandum," no names, n.d., "Talked with Peggy Smith July 13 . . . ," B: 5, F: 47; Peggy Smith to Carole, August 6, 1965, B: 5, F: 47; "Peggy Smith," handwritten tally of her letter output, B: 5, F: 47; "Peggy Smith," handwritten notes, August 25 and October 27, 1965, B: 5, F: 47; "Francis Flanagan," July 28, 1967, B: 5, F: 25; and Marilyn Lord to Richard McKinney, May 7, 1966, B: 5, F: 35, JBSR.

Chapter 8. Fringe

1. Fred Grupp Jr., "Political Activists: The John Birch Society and the ADA" (paper presented at the Annual Meeting of the American Political Science Association, September 6–10, 1966), B: 57, F: 2, WJGP. Grupp developed a contact who was on the JBS's National Council. The contact received all the respondents' completed questionnaires, removed the completed surveys from their envelopes to keep members anonymous, and gave the forms to Grupp. Grupp asked about six issues: "Impeach Earl Warren"; "Favors Liberty Amendment"; "Save Panama Canal"; "Get U.S. out of U.N. and U.N. out of U.S."; "Expose the Civil Rights Fraud"; and "Support Police." Also see Fred Grupp Jr., "Personal Satisfaction Derived from Membership in the John Birch Society," *Political Research Quarterly*, March 1, 1971, https://journals.sagepub.com/doi/abs/10.1177/106591297102400112. Grupp speculated that by 1966 recruitment to the society had become more of a slog because the Johnson Administration had stepped up its military efforts in Vietnam,

depriving the society of a chief criticism, although other factors were likely more important.

2. For a discussion of the "status thesis" in Hofstadter's and other midcentury liberal scholars' work, see David Brown, *Richard Hofstadter: An Intellectual Biography* (Chicago: University of Chicago Press, 2008), 115–119. Hofstadter discusses the "status revolution" as applied to progressive leaders in chapter 4 of *The Age of Reform: From Bryan to FDR* (New York: Random House, 1955).

3. Laurence Swanson to Robert Welch, week of November 9, 1964; C. L. Hanson to Welch, week of November 2, 1964, B: 1, F: 6, JBSR.

4. Grupp, "Political Activists."

5. Swanson to Welch, week of October 30, 1964, B: 1, F: 6; Thomas Hill to Richard Daum, May 21, 1968, B: 9, F: 3, JBSR.

6. John Fenton, "Birch Society Is Shaken by 'Acrimonious Disputes,'" *New York Times*, August 28, 1966; Hill to All Major Coordinators, December 1, 1965, and "Suggested Remarks and Procedure for Leadership Seminar," B: 27, F: 66, JBSR.

7. Robert Welch, "In Praise of Patriotism," July 4, 1967, New England Rally for God, Family and Country, B: 28, F: 11, JBSR; editorial, "False Pairing," *The Nation*, February 10, 1962, B: 2, F: 12, Americans for Democratic Action, 1962, JRP.

8. David Mends to Bob Rogerson, June 21, 1967, B: 9, F: 3; Robert Jones to Welch, September 9, 1968, B: 9, F: 2; and Bob Weedn to Donald Folkers, November 16, 1964, B: 9, F: 3, JBSR.

9. Herbert Gold, "John Rousselot of the John Birch Society," August 1967, C: 3, F: 49, "Rousselot of the JBS," HGP; within-office memo, September 23, 1966, describing the actions of James Kearney, B: 9, F: 2, JBSR; Bill Miller to Dear Sirs, April 23, 1968, B: 9, F: 3, JBSR.

10. FBI Report, Re: Breakthrough, December 7, 1966, Internet Archive, accessed July 19, 2022, https://archive.org/stream/LobsingerDonaldJ.Detroit1571028 /Lobsinger%2C%20Donald%20J.-Detroit%20157-1028_djvu.txt. Federal investigators interviewed Breakthrough chairman Donald Lobsinger amid fears on the part of the federal government of violence sowed by extremists. FBI memo, re: Breakthrough, December 7, 1966, Records of the National Advisory Commission on Civil Disorders, Office of Investigation, Organizational Files, B: E14, Breakthrough—FBI Reports, LBJPL; John K. Scales to M. C. Miskovsky, December 27, 1967, Records of the National Advisory Commission on Civil Disorders, Office of Investigation, Individual Files, B: E10, Lobsinger, Donald, LBJPL.

11. B. J. Widick, *Detroit: City of Race and Class Violence* (Detroit: Wayne State University Press, 1989), 189–190; JoEllen McNergney Vinyard, *Right in Michigan's Grassroots: From the KKK to the Michigan Militia* (Ann Arbor: University of Michigan Press, 2011), 232.

12. FBI Report, Re: Breakthrough; investigator's description of "Open Occupancy Hearings," n.d.; Don Lobsinger, Breakthrough, Newsletter, October 9, 1967; *On Firearms*, Breakthrough pamphlet, n.d.; "Wanted" George Romney Poster, July 31, 1967, Records of the National Advisory Commission on Civil Disorders, Office of Investigation, Organizational Files, B: 14E, Breakthrough, Miscellaneous, LBJPL.

13. "Williams Is Target of Hecklers, Threats," *Baltimore Afro-American*, February 14, 1970; Bill McGraw, "Detroit's Infamous Right-Wing Extremist Died and

Hardly Anyone Knew—Until Now," *Detroit Free Press*, July 9, 2020, www.freep
.com/story/news/local/michigan/detroit/2020/07/09/donald-lobsinger-death/53998
12002/.

14. For the NYA's bomb-making instructions, see David Austin Walsh
(@DavidAstinWalsh), "For instance, ATTACK!—a publication of the neo-Nazi
National Youth Alliance from the early 1970s," Twitter, November 21, 2021,
https://twitter.com/DavidAstinWalsh/status/1462465116646084619.

15. Tom Hill to Louis Byers, April 15, 1969, B: 9, F: 11; Fred Bruckman to Harold McKinney, July 12, 1965, B: 1, F: 13, JBSR. Byers once worked on the society's
field staff as the western Pennsylvania coordinator, but he resigned in early 1969,
and headquarters terminated his home chapter membership in April due to what
was described at the time as fundamental differences of opinion. Douglas Martin, "Willis Carto, Far Right Figure and Holocaust Denier, Dies at 89," *New York
Times*, November 2, 2015. Buckley said Carto was part of the "fever swamps of the
crazed Right." Upon his death, in 2015, the *Times*'s obituary reported that Carto's
"associates included neo-Nazis, Christian vigilantes, John Birch Society members
and Ku Klux Klansmen." "Liberty Lobby Proves Right Makes Right," *Los Angeles
Times*, December 10, 1970.

16. Jim McLemore, handwritten notes, May 16, 1975, B: 9, F: 3, JBSR.

17. UPI, "Birch Society's Store Burned in Memphis," *Washington Post*, December 6, 1972.

18. Dan Carter, *The Politics of Rage: George Wallace, the Origins of the New Conservatism, and the Transformation of American Politics* (New York: Simon and Schuster, 1995), 158; Donald Gray to All Bookstore Managers, October 3, 1967, October
27, 1967, April 12, 1968, and May 23, 1968, B: 5, F: 11, JBSR.

19. Mr. and Mrs. G. H. Peterson, MEV to Welch, November 23–27, 1964, B: 1,
F: 6; Lars J. Been Jr. to Welch, October 26, 1968, B: 1, F: 4, JBSR.

20. William James Jr. et al. to Gentlemen, April 22, 1965; for "kooks + nuts," see
memo to Tom Hill, January 8, 1965, B: 9, F: 6, JBSR. See other letters, memos, and
notes in box 9, folder 6 for more examples of white supremacists seeking to join and
ally themselves with the John Birch Society.

21. Grupp, "Political Activists"; Fenton, "Birch Society Is Shaken."

22. Assistant to Mr. Welch to Fred Farrell, March 1, 1965, B: 1, F: 20; MMM
Department, January–August, 1967: see memos in B: 5, F: 89, JBSR.

23. Swanson to Welch, week of November 2, B: 1, F: 6, JBSR; Grupp, "Political
Activists" (see responses to question 27).

24. Arthur Spiegel to Isadore Zack, April 8, 1966, B: 10, F: 14, Root, Merrill
E., ADLC; Welch to Coordinators, November 7, 1962, B: 27, F: 2, JBSR; and Hill
to Home Office Coordinator and MMM Departments, June 17, 1968, B: 27, F: 2,
JBSR.

25. Robert H. Montgomery to Floyd McGowin, October 18, 1965, B: 8, F: 8,
WJGP.

26. Journal Wire Services, "Goldwater Wants Bircher Lists," *Milwaukee Journal*,
n.d., B: 8, F: 8, WJGP; AP, "Goldwater Blasts Birch Society," *Milwaukee Journal*,
September 26, 1966. Shortly after his 1964 election defeat, Goldwater complained to
Buckley that "the idiot fringe" was seeking to oust Dean Burch from his post as RNC
chair. Goldwater to Buckley, December 19, 1964, B: 30, F: Goldwater, Barry, WFBP.

27. William Grede to Barry Goldwater, November 4, 1966; Goldwater to Grede, November 10, 1966, 8, F: 8, WJGP.

28. Patrick Buchanan to Editor, *National Review*, March 8, 1966, B: 40, F: Nixon, Richard, WFBP.

29. "Editorial Preferences and Opinions of National Review Subscribers," April 1965, B: 35, F: Inter Office Memos, January 1965–June 1965; National Review Survey, Q 7, "In general, what do you think of National Review's position on . . . ," B: 35, F: Goldwater; William Rusher to Richard Nixon, November 2, 1965, B: 36, F: Nichols, Louis B., etc., WFBP.

30. Lee Edwards, "Why Californians Look to Ronald Reagan," *Human Events*, February 19, 1966, B: 18, F: 5a, BGP; Rick Perlstein, *Before the Storm: Barry Goldwater and the Unmaking of the American Consensus* (New York: Hill and Wang, 2001), 166; and Nancy Reagan to Buckley, n.d., B: 40, F: Reagan, Ronald and Nancy, WFBP.

31. Matthew Dallek, *The Right Moment* (New York: Free Press, 2000), 111, 126.

32. "The Joint Senate-House Leadership, Transcript of Comments on the John Birch Society," press conference, September 30, 1965, B: D6, F: "Ford Press Releases—Birch Society/Extremism, 1965," Ford Congressional Papers: Press Secretary and Speech File, Gerald R. Ford Presidential Library, Ann Arbor, MI.

33. RNC, news release, December 13, 1965; "Statement on Extremism by Republican National Chairman Ray C. Bless," news conference, November 5, 1965, B: 15, F: 1, DBP.

34. "Bring 'Em On," Stephen Young campaign flier, n.d., B: 1, F: 6, JBSR.

35. "Statement of Joseph L. Rauh, Jr.," January 25, 1962, B: 2, F: 12, Americans for Democratic Action, 1962, JRP.

36. "ADL Warned of Anti-Semitism in 'Radical Right,' John Birch Society," *Jewish Telegraphic Agency*, January 31, 1967, www.jta.org/archive/adl-warned-of-anti-semitism-in-radical-right-john-birch-society.

37. John Weisman to Gentlemen, May 19, 1965; MEV to Mr. Weisman, July 19, 1965, B: 1, F: 6, JBSR.

38. Gray to All Bookstore Managers, April 19, 1968, B: 5, F: 11, JBSR. Kent Steffgen, *Here's the Rest of Him* (Reno, NV: Foresight Books, 1968), introduction. Steffgen blasted Reagan as "a conservative salesman for a socialist cause."

39. "Reagan for President If . . . ," October 16, 1967; press release, *Independent American*, October 30, 1967, B: 6, F: 6, DBP.

40. Claire Conner, "My Parents Were Right-Wing Extremists," *Salon*, July 15, 2013, www.salon.com/2013/07/15/my_parents_were_right_wing_extremists/; Carter, *The Politics of Rage*, 343.

41. Carter, *The Politics of Rage*, 356–359.

42. "Endorsements for Wallace in the Conservative Journal," B: 11, F: 21, Wallace, George C., ADLC.

43. Peter Werwath, "100 Hear Wallace Aide Speak Here," *Beverly, Massachusetts Times*, October 28, 1968, B: 5, F: 15, Bunker, Laurence E., ADLC.

44. Ann Waldron, "Speaking Volumes: Past-Mistress of the Police Procedural," *Washington Post*, March 1, 1970.

45. Carter, *The Politics of Rage*, 158–159.

46. Carter, *The Politics of Rage*, 367.

47. *Intelligence Activities and the Rights of Americans: Final Report of the Select Committee to Study Governmental Operations with Respect to Intelligence Activities*, US Senate 94th Cong. (April 26, 1976), 55; R. W. Apple Jr., "Agnew's Visit to Indiana Gave Hartke Rival a Lift," *New York Times*, October 22, 1970; George Vecsey, "Hartke and Roudebush in Close Race," *New York Times*, November 4, 1970.

48. Sydney Kossen, "Sex Education Foe Runs for Congress," *Washington Post*, May 7, 1970; R. W. Apple Jr., "2 Birch Society Members Favored in Coast Races," *New York Times*, May 27, 1970; and Stephan Lesher, "John Schmitz Is No George Wallace," *New York Times*, November 5, 1972.

49. Lou Cannon, "A Sense of Humor Betrayed Him," *Washington Post*, August 3, 1972; John Carroll, "Faced with Unhappy Pick, Nixon Votes Unobtrusively," *The Sun*, June 30, 1970.

50. AP, "2 in Birch Society Elected on Coast," *New York Times*, July 1, 1970; Steven Roberts, "Birch Member and Black Among Victors on Coast," *New York Times*, June 4, 1970.

51. Adam Clymer, "Family Planning Bill Gains," *Baltimore Sun*, November 17, 1970; Don Oberdorfer, "Friends on Right Showing Disenchantment with President," *Washington Post*, August 1, 1971.

52. "Rep. Schmitz," *Los Angeles Times*, August 3, 1970.

53. Jon Nordreimer, "Rights Leader Undaunted by Violence," *New York Times*, February 14, 1970.

54. Donald Janson, "Right-Wing Rally Is Held in Boston," *New York Times*, July 5, 1970.

55. AP, "Maddox Decries Greatest Theft: Tells Birchers in California Agnew Just Stages a Diversion," *Atlanta Constitution*, March 7, 1970; Donald Janson, "Maddox Hailed at Right-Wing Rally in Boston," *New York Times*, July 6, 1970.

56. Gordon Hall, "The Birch Society is Losing Its Grip," *Washington Post*, July 29, 1969, http://jfk.hood.edu/Collection/Weisberg%20Subject%20Index%20 Files/J%20Disk/John%20Birch%20Society/Item%2003.pdf.

57. Gordon Hall, "The Diminishing Thunder on the Radical Right," *Washington Post*, August 1, 1970.

58. Nick Thimmesch, "Thunder on the Right," *Los Angeles Times*, July 8, 1970.

59. "College Students Shun Extremists," *New York Times*, February 7, 1971; Joe Doster, "Pleased GOP Doesn't Woo Radicals," *Winston-Salem Journal*, printed in the *Atlanta Constitution*, March 29, 1970. The American Party was the successor to the American Independent Party.

60. Jack Anderson, "Washington Merry Go-Round: Army Publishes Mad-Cap Book on Reds," *Washington Post*, August 29, 1970; Richard West, "Birch Society to Print Report Barred by Court," *Los Angeles Times*, November 20, 1970; "$50,000 in Libel Award Given in Birch Suit," *Chicago Tribune*, September 24, 1970; Gerald Schomp, *Birchism Was My Business* (New York: Macmillan, 1970), 11.

61. A. A. Michelson, "Senate Candidate Davis Speaks of Chappaquidick," *Berkshire Eagle*, May 30, 1970; Zack to Irwin Small, January 2, 1968, B: 6, F: 8, ADLC. Also see Edward Miller, *A Conspiratorial Life* (Chicago: University of Chicago Press, 2022), 319; Susan Ladd and Stan Swofford, "On the Brink of Doom," *Raleigh News and Observer*, June 25, 1995, https://greensboro.com/on-the-brink-of -doom/article_c601159b-835a-59dc-9323-24490165b2cc.html.

62. Donald Janson, "Communist 'Rules' for Revolt Viewed as Durable Fraud," *New York Times*, July 10, 1970.

63. Linda Greenhouse, "Flyer About Peace Symbol Disturbs Many," *New York Times*, August 3, 1970.

64. "Bill" to Justin Finger, February 14, 1964, B: 9, F: 32, ADLC. One ADL memo observed that the "[Chicago] Sun-Times article of February 12, [1964] used almost verbatim the Group Research, Inc., report on Oliver—much of which was obtained from us," suggesting the ADL's hub-like role, feeding derogatory reports on Birchers to allies and sympathetic members of the press corps.

Chapter 9. Succession

1. "Birch Society Celebrates Its 20th Birthday," *New York Times*, December 11, 1978, https://timesmachine.nytimes.com/timesmachine/1978/12/11/110981397.html?pageNumber=14; "Invitation: John Birch Society Dinner" (2018). Saffy Collection - All Textual Materials. 890, accessed July 19, 2022, https://digital commons.unf.edu/cgi/viewcontent.cgi?article=1889&context=saffy_text.

2. Gordon Hall, "A Review of the Extremist Scene for 1971," *Washington Post*, February 7, 1972; "Biographical Note," Gordon Hall and Grace Hoag Collection of Dissenting and Extremist Printed Propaganda, Brown University Library, accessed August 15, 2022, www.riamco.org/render?eadid=US-RPB-mshallhoag &view=biography; and Allen King to Gentlemen, November 24, 1975, B: 9, F: 2, JBSR.

3. Gordon Hall, "A Review of the Extremist Scene for 1971," *Washington Post*, February 7, 1972.

4. Edward Miller, *A Conspiratorial Life: Robert Welch, the John Birch Society, and the Revolution of American Conservatism* (Chicago: University of Chicago Press, 2022), 331-334; "Birch Society Celebrates Its 20th Birthday," *New York Times*, December 11, 1978, https://timesmachine.nytimes.com/times machine/1978/12/11/110981397.html?pageNumber=14; John MacKenzie, "ABA Says 2 Unfit for Court," *Washington Post*, October 21, 1971; Barry Goldwater, "A Man of the Highest Personal Integrity," *New York Times*, November 17, 1971; Donald Janson, "Bayh to Query Alleged Membership of Rehnquist in Right-Wing Organization," *New York Times*, November 18, 1971; and Ronald Ostrow, "2 Rights Leaders Call Rehnquist a 'Self-Propelled Segregationist,'" *Los Angeles Times*, November 10, 1971.

5. FBI Report, L. H. Martin to Mr. Cleveland, "William Hubbs Rehnquist," November 2, 1971, The Black Vault, accessed July 19, 2022, http://documents .theblackvault.com/documents/fbifiles/Rehnquist_William_H.-HQ-4_text.pdf.

6. "Rehnquist a Bircher?," *Chicago Daily Defender*, November 10, 1971; Adam Liptak, "The Memo That Rehnquist Wrote and Had to Disown," *New York Times*, September 11, 2005, www.nytimes.com/2005/09/11/weekinreview/the-memo -that-rehnquist-wrote-and-had-to-disown.html; Leroy Aarons and Ken Clawson, "Rehnquist: Admired yet Decried," *Washington Post*, November 3, 1971; and Glen Elsasser, "Rehnquist Assailed as Segregationist," *Chicago Tribune*, November 9, 1971.

7. "Rehnquist a Bircher?;" Aarons and Clawson, "Rehnquist: Admired yet Decried;" Elsasser, "Rehnquist Assailed as Segregationist."

8. Zach Dorfman, "The Congressman Who Created His Own Deep State. Really," *Politico*, December 2, 2018, www.politico.com/magazine/story/2018/12/02/larry-mcdonald-communists-deep-state-222726/.

9. Howard Seelye, "Orange County's Other Presidential Candidate," *Los Angeles Times*, September 3, 1972; Jack Anderson, "Air Guard Uses Birch Film on Vietnam," *Washington Post*, May 10, 1971; Howard Seelye, "Both Are Tough Runners," *Los Angeles Times*, March 27, 1972; and Everett Holless, "Anti-Nixon Drive Is Gaining Among Conservatives in California," *New York Times*, January 16, 1972.

10. Everett Holles, "Rightists Call Nixon Dupe of Left," *New York Times*, June 4, 1972; George Vecsey, "Schmitz Details Theory on Plots," *New York Times*, August 6, 1972; Frank Blatchford, "American Party Picks Vice Presidential Nominee," *Chicago Tribune*, August 6, 1972; Frank Blatchford, "Christmas Without Santa Claus," *Chicago Tribune*, August 12, 1972; editorial, "Birch Society Ticket," *Los Angeles Times*, August 8, 1972; and Mark Leibovich, "The Man the White House Wakes Up To," *New York Times Magazine*, April 21, 2010, www.nytimes.com/2010/04/25/magazine/25allen-t.html.

11. Stephan Lesher, "John Schmitz Is No George Wallace . . . ," *New York Times*, November 5, 1972; Jack Boettner, "Hope in Wake of Schmitz Defeat," *Los Angeles Times*, November 8, 1972; Kenneth Reich, "Birch Society: Tightly Knit, but Limited Appeal," *Los Angeles Times*, June 25, 1974.

12. Reich, "Birch Society"; AP, "John Birch Group Has Money Woes," *New York Times*, September 1, 1986; "John Birch Society Records: About the Collection, Acquisition," www.riamco.org/render?eadid=US-RPB-ms2013.003&view=administrative, accessed September 30, 2022.

13. AP, "Cardinal Cushing Retracts Birch Society Endorsement," *New York Times*, April 21, 1964, www.nytimes.com/1964/04/21/archives/cardinal-cushing-retracts-birch-society-endorsement.html. Cushing was never a member, but he issued a letter of endorsement in 1961, which he retracted with much fanfare in 1964. Waite to Rev. Glen Adams, July 10, 1963, B: 2, F: 5; D. A. Waite to J. R. Roaf, December 18, 1963, B: 1, F: 6; Waite to Reverend J. Lynn Cleveland, June 29, 1964, B: 1, F: 6; and Waite to Pierre Allston, December 9, 1964, B: 1, F: 6, JBSR. Waite elaborated on the society's relationship to religion in Waite to Mrs. Theodore Truska, April 29, 1964, B: 1, F: 6, JBSR.

14. Schlafly explained that she and her husband had "both joined promptly" after attending a Birch meeting in Chicago. See Phyllis Schlafly to Verne Kaub, December 5, 1959, ELFF, https://archive.org/details/schlaflyphyllisandjohnbirchsociety/mode/2up; Ronald Radosh, "Phyllis Schlafly, 'Mrs. America,' Was a Secret Member of the John Birch Society," *Daily Beast*, April 22, 2020, www.thedailybeast.com/phyllis-schlafly-mrs-america-was-a-secret-member-of-the-john-birch-society; Nicole Hemmer, "Paving the Way for Trump," *US News and World Report*, September 6, 2016; and Donald Critchlow, *Phyllis Schlafly and Grassroots Conservatism* (Princeton, NJ: Princeton University Press, 2005), 217–218, 222–223.

15. John F. McManus, "Phyllis Schlafly: Conservative Icon," *New American*, October 10, 2016, https://thenewamerican.com/phyllis-schlafly-conservative-icon-1924-2016/; Scott Melzer, *Gun Crusaders: The NRA's Culture War* (New York: New York University Press, 2009), 53.

16. "Opposition Growing in Wisconsin to US Court Legalization of Early Abortion," *New York Times*, March 15, 1970; Edward Miller and Rick Perlstein, "The Birch Society Never Left," *New Republic*, March 8, 2021; Howard Seelye, "Orange County's Other Presidential Candidate," *Los Angeles Times*, September 3, 1972; Adam Yeomans, "A New Twist on Summer Camp," *Independent Florida Alligator*, September 17, 1981; and Randall Balmer, "The Real Origins of the Religious Right," *Politico*, May 27, 2014, www.politico.com/magazine/story/2014/05/religious-right-real-origins-107133/; Gillian Frank and Neil Young, "What everyone gets wrong about evangelicals and abortion," *Washington Post*, May 16, 2022, www.washingtonpost.com/outlook/2022/05/16/what-everyone-gets-wrong-about-evangelicals-abortion/.

17. Frances FitzGerald, *The Evangelicals: The Struggle to Shape America* (New York: Simon and Schuster, 2017), 304–305; Dinesh D'Souza, "Jerry Falwell's Renaissance," *Policy Review*, C: 11, F: Moral Majority, 1 of 4, SDC; and Heather Hendershot, "God's Angriest Man: Carl McIntire, Cold War Fundamentalism, and Right-Wing Broadcasting," *American Quarterly* 59, no. 2 (2007): 373–396, www.jstor.org/stable/40068467.

18. Jerry Falwell to Dear Friend, "Your Official Moral Majority Membership Card," n.d., C: 11, F: Moral Majority, 4 of 4; Jerry Fallwell to Dear Friend, February 1986, C: 11, F: Moral Majority, 1 of 4, SDC.

19. Rob Boston, "Left Behind," *Church and State Magazine*, February 2002; Russ Bellant, "Secretive Right-Wing Group: The Council for National Policy," *Covert Action*, Summer 1990; and Michael J. McVicar, "The Religious Right in America," *Oxford Research Encyclopedia of Religion*, February 26, 2018, https://oxfordre.com/religion/view/10.1093/acrefore/9780199340378.001.0001/acrefore-9780199340378-e-97.

20. James C. Carper, "Concerned Women for America," *Britannica*, accessed July 19, 2022, www.britannica.com/topic/Concerned-Women-for-America; Concerned Women for America Staff, "CWA Founder and Chairman Beverly LaHaye's Charge at Our 40th Anniversary Gala," transcript of LaHaye Speech delivered September 12, 2019, https://concernedwomen.org/tag/beverly-lahaye/; and Arlisha R. Norwood, "Beverly LaHaye," National Women's History Museum, 2017, www.womenshistory.org/education-resources/biographies/beverly-lahaye.

21. Chad Bull, "Stalwarts of Freedom: An Inside Look at the John Birch Society," *Chalcedon*, September 1, 2006, https://chalcedon.edu/magazine/stalwarts-of-freedom-an-inside-look-at-the-john-birch-society; Molly Worthen, "The Chalcedon Problem: Rousas John Rushdoony and the Origins of Christian Reconstructionism," *Church History* 77, no. 2 (2008): 399–437, www.jstor.org/stable/20618492; and FitzGerald, *The Evangelicals*, 337–341.

22. For a capsule description of the Birchers' myriad front groups, see "Historical Note—John Birch Society," John Birch Society Records, Brown University Library, accessed September 4, 2022, www.riamco.org/render?eadid=US-RPB-ms2013.003&view=biography. See also Natasha Zaretsky, "Restraint or Retreat? The Debate over the Panama Canal Treaties and U.S. Nationalism After Vietnam." *Diplomatic History* 35, no. 3 (2011): 535–62, www.jstor.org/stable/24916432; Tom Wicker, "A Great Issue," *New York Times*, February 10, 1978; and Tom Wicker, "The Real Canal Giveaway," *New York Times*, August 30,

1977. For correspondence between Birch leaders and mainstream conservatives discussing the canal treaty fight, see Spruille Braden to Welch, September 29, 1977, B: 3, F: Robert Welch; Goldwater to Braden, January 17, 1975, B: 1, F: Barry Goldwater; Ronald Reagan to Braden, October 18, 1977, B: 2: F: Ronald Reagan; Braden to Reagan, November 1, 1977, B: 2: F: Ronald Reagan, SBP.

23. Edward Crane and Chris Hocker, "Clark for President: A Report on the 1980 Libertarian Presidential Campaign," December 1980, Koch Docs, accessed July 19, 2022, https://kochdocs.org/2019/08/27/1980-report-on-the-libertarian-presidential-campaign-of-ed-clark-and-david-koch/, p. 41.

24. Josh Levin, "The Welfare Queen," *Slate*, December 19, 2013, www.slate.com/articles/news_and_politics/history/2013/12/linda_taylor_welfare_queen_ronald_reagan_made_her_a_notorious_american_villain.html; Kevin M. Kruse (@KevinMKruse), "No, in that very interview . . . ," Twitter, June 30, 2019, https://twitter.com/KevinMKruse/status/1145371580085788672; Lou Cannon, *President Reagan: The Role of A Lifetime* (New York: PublicAffairs, 2008), 455–456; and Alexander P. Lamis, "Interview with Lee Atwater (1981)," *Grasping Reality by Brad DeLong* (blog), accessed July 19, 2022, www.bradford-delong.com/2017/03/lee-atwater-interview-with-alexander-p-lamis-rough-transcript-weekend-reading.html.

25. "Republican Party Platforms, Republican Party Platform of 1980 Online," by Gerhard Peters and John T. Woolley, The American Presidency Project, www.presidency.ucsb.edu/node/273420; John Graham to Laurence Swanson, February 2, 1965, B: 1, F: 22, JBSR; assistant to Mr. Welch to John Graham, February 9, 1965, B: 1, F: 22, JBSR; Judith Bainbridge, "In 1980, Ronald Reagan Received Warm Welcomes in Upstate," *Greenville News*, July 2, 2017, www.greenvilleonline.com/story/news/local/greenville-roots/2017/07/02/ronald-reagan/445919001/; press release, June 28, 1971, B: 4, F: 22, ADLC; and FitzGerald, *The Evangelicals*, 312–313. For a discussion of the rising power of evangelicals during the early Reagan administration, see FitzGerald, *The Evangelicals*, 304–305, 313–336; Carmen Celestini, "God, Country, and Christian Conservatives: The National Association of Manufacturers, the John Birch Society, and the Rise of the Christian Right" (PhD diss., University of Waterloo, 2018), 14.

26. Ronald Reagan, "Inaugural Address 1981," Ronald Reagan Presidential Library and Museum, accessed July 19, 2022, www.reaganlibrary.gov/archives/speech/inaugural-address-1981. For a history of the air traffic controllers' strike, see Joseph A. McCartin, *Collision Course: Ronald Reagan, the Air Traffic Controllers, and the Strike That Changed America* (New York: Oxford University Press, 2011); Kathleen Schalch, "1981 Strike Leaves Legacy for American Workers," National Public Radio, August 3, 2006, www.npr.org/2006/08/03/5604656/1981-strike-leaves-legacy-for-american-workers.

27. Ian Tyrrell and Jay Sexton, *Empire's Twin: US Anti-Imperialism from the Founding Era to the Age of Terrorism* (Ithaca, NY: Cornell University Press, 2015), 228; Francis X. Clines, "Reagan's Doubts on Dr. King Disclosed," *New York Times*, October 22, 1983, www.nytimes.com/1983/10/22/us/reagan-s-doubts-on-dr-king-disclosed.html; and "The Gipper Beyond 100," *National Review*, February 7, 2011, www.nationalreview.com/magazine/2011/02/07/gipper-beyond-100/. There were rumors that Reagan had attended a Birch Society chapter meeting in Beverly Hills

with John Wayne in the early 1960s. The FBI based the report on a single, unreliable source. Reagan at times flashed an angry antiestablishment streak. But he neither campaigned nor governed as a Birch ideologue. His time in Sacramento and, later, in Washington was mostly defined by pragmatic conservative ideas rather than conspiratorial, isolationist, and government-as-the-root-of-evil ones. His approach parted ways with the far right on some key elements of ideology and style. In 1984, as Reagan romped to reelection, Bircher Dan Smoot, the far-right media maven, lamented that "at the present low point in the degradation of our Constitutional Republic, strict constitutionalism is the most hated position that a person in public life can take." Heather Hendershot, *What's Fair on the Air?: Cold War Right-Wing Broadcasting and the Public Interest* (Chicago: University of Chicago Press, 2011), 99.

28. Hedrick Smith, "The Right Against Reagan," *New York Times Magazine*, January 17, 1988; Francis X. Clines, "A Neocapitalist Basks with Reagan," *New York Times*, May 5, 1992, www.nytimes.com/1992/05/05/world/a-neocapitalist-basks-with-reagan.html; Jenifer Warren, "Old Cold War Foes Rekindle a Firm Friendship," *Los Angeles Times*, May 5, 1992; and Dana Parsons, "Soviet Union Left, but Birch Society Is Still Right Here," *Los Angeles Times*, January 22, 1992, www.presidency.ucsb.edu/documents/ronald-reagan-event-timeline.

29. Alexander Hertel-Fernandez, Caroline Tervo, and Theda Skocpol, "How the Koch Brothers Built the Most Powerful Rightwing Group You've Never Heard Of," *The Guardian*, September 26, 2018, www.theguardian.com/us-news/2018/sep/26/koch-brothers-americans-for-prosperity-rightwing-political-group; Jane Mayer, *Dark Money: The Hidden History of the Billionaires Behind the Rise of the Radical Right* (New York: Doubleday, 2016), 143.

30. Arthur Finkelstein to David Keene, February 20, 1986, B: 11, F: Conservative Political Action Committee, 1984–1986, AFP.

31. Laurence Swanson to Robert Welch, week of November 9, 1964, B: 1, F: 6, JBSR; R. G. Johnson to Member's Monthly Message Department, December 2, 1964, B: 1, F: 6, JBSR; and Melzer, *Gun Crusaders*, 137; Joel Achenbach, Scott Higham, and Sari Horwitz, "How NRA's true believers turned a marxsmanship group into a mighty gun lobby," *Washington Post*, January 12, 2013. "Is it possible that some of those incidents could have been created for the purpose of disarming the people of the free world?" Knox asked.

Chapter 10. Crack-Up

1. See, for example, Francis Fukuyama, *The End of History and the Last Man* (New York: Free Press, 1992).

2. Robert Mackay, "Reagan Campaign to Let Reagan Be Reagan," UPI, October 11, 1984; Michael Beschloss, "George Bush," in *Character Above All: Ten Presidents from FDR to George Bush*, ed. Robert A. Wilson (New York: Simon and Schuster, 1995), 228–229; Maureen Dowd, *Bushworld: Enter at Your Own Risk* (New York: Berkeley Books, 2004), 40.

3. Dudley Clendinen, "Pat Robertson Looks to South and Evangelicals as Key to 1988," *New York Times*, June 24, 1986; Frances FitzGerald, *The Evangelicals: The Struggle to Shape America* (New York: Simon and Schuster, 2017), 365-369; Michael Lind, "Rev. Robertson's Grand International Conspiracy Theory," *New York*

Review of Books, February 2, 1995; and E. J. Dionne, "Pat and Politics," *Washington Post*, December 7, 2001.

4. Pat Robertson, "A Strong Warning That Moral Decay Is Basic Trouble Facing the Nation," campaign address, transcript in *New York Times*, January 14, 1988, www.nytimes.com/1988/01/14/us/the-speech-pat-robertson-a-strong-warning-that-moral-decay-is-basic.html.

5. James M. Penning, "Pat Robertson and the GOP: 1988 and Beyond." *Sociology of Religion* 55, no. 3 (1994): 327–344, https://doi.org/10.2307/3712057.

6. AP, "State Convention Is Disrupted," *New York Times*, May 23, 1988, www.nytimes.com/1988/05/23/us/state-convention-is-disrupted.html; AP, "Robertson Backers Set North Carolina Boycott," *New York Times*, May 25, 1988, www.nytimes.com/1988/05/25/us/robertson-backers-set-north-carolina-boycott.html.

7. Susan Gilmore, "Pat Robertson's 1988 'Army': From Rebels to GOP Mainstream," *Seattle Times*, April 13, 1992, https://archive.seattletimes.com/archive/?date=19920413&slug=1486177.

8. Pat Robertson, Address at "Rump" Convention, C-Span, January 30, 1988, www.c-span.org/video/?58-1/pat-robertson-rump-convention.

9. Lind, "Rev. Robertson's"; and Sen. Bob Dole's Remarks to the Christian Coalition conference Road to Victory '95, C-Span transcript, September 8, 1995, www.c-span.org/video/?67021-1/road-victory-95; Gilmore, "Pat Robertson's 1988 'Army.'"

10. Rachel Withers, "George H. W. Bush's 'Willie Horton' Ad Will Always Be the Reference Point for Dog-Whistle Racism," *Vox*, December 1, 2018, www.vox.com/2018/12/1/18121221/george-hw-bush-willie-horton-dog-whistle-politics; Peter Baker, "Bush Made Willie Horton an Issue in 1988, and the Racial Scars Are Still Fresh," *New York Times*, December 3, 2018, www.nytimes.com/2018/12/03/us/politics/bush-willie-horton.html; "George Bush and Willie Horton," *New York Times*, November 4, 1988, www.nytimes.com/1988/11/04/opinion/george-bush-and-willie-horton.html; and Erin Blakemore, "How the Willie Horton Ad Played on Racism and Fear," History.com, November 2, 2018, www.history.com/news/george-bush-willie-horton-racist-ad.

11. Jack Nelson and Richard Meyer, "Bush Selects Quayle as His Running Mate: Calls Indiana Senator, 41, Future Leader," *Los Angeles Times*, August 17, 1988, www.latimes.com/archives/la-xpm-1988-08-17-mn-446-story.html; Richard Meyer and Henry Weinstein, "Campaign Becomes Confrontation with Past: Privilege, Wealth Shaped Quayle," *Los Angeles Times*, August 21, 1988; George Lardner, Jr., and Dan Morgan, "Quayle Drew on Energy, Affability, in Political Rise," *Washington Post*, October 2, 1988; and John Hughes, "Quayle as Kennedy," *Christian Science Monitor*, October 7, 1988, www.csmonitor.com/layout/set/amphtml/1988/1007/eoma.html.

12. Email correspondence, Kurt Andersen to author, June 5, 2022; Kurt Andersen (@KBAndersen), "She grew up across the street from me in Omaha," Twitter, November 11, 2018, https://twitter.com/KBAndersen/status/1061602119076188161; and Jane Mayer, "Is Ginni Thomas a Threat to SCOTUS?," interview by Terry Gross, *Fresh Air*, NPR, January 27, 2022, www.npr.org/2022/01/27/1076124740/is-ginni-thomas-a-threat-to-scotus. Also see Jane Mayer, "Is Ginni Thomas a Threat to the Supreme Court?," *New Yorker*, January 21, 2022, www.newyorker.com/magazine/2022/01/31/is-ginni-thomas-a-threat-to-the-supreme-court.

13. Joel K. Goldstein, "A Reassessment: Dan Quayle as Vice President," *Indy-Star*, January 17, 2017, www.indystar.com/story/opinion/2017/01/17/reassess ment-dan-quayle-vice-president/96670656/; Gerhard Peters and John T. Woolley, "George Bush, George Bush Event Timeline Online," The American Presidency Project, www.presidency.ucsb.edu/node/347875; Errin Haines Whack, "George H.W. Bush's Legacy on Racial Issues is Complicated," AP, December 4, 2018.

14. Nancy Kruh, "The Re-Birching of a Nation," *Chicago Tribune*, February 26, 1992.

15. Rev. Robertson, *The New World Order* (Dallas: Word Publishing, 1991), 6; Lind, "Pat Robertson's"; and FitzGerald, *The Evangelicals*, 416–419. The Birch Society maintained that the CFR and the Trilateral Commission, an organization of media, business, and academic elites in North America, Japan, and Western Europe, were central to the international conspiracy against the United States.

16. Kruh, "The Re-Birching"; Gilmore, "Pat Robertson's 1988 'Army.'"

17. Pat Buchanan, "A Crossroads in Our Country's History," Presidential Announcement Speech, December 10, 1991, www.4president.org/speeches/1992/pat buchanan1992announcement.htm; Pat Robertson, address to the Republican National Convention, C-Span, August 19, 1992, www.c-span.org/video/?c4469335/user -clip-pat-robertson-speech; Video footage from the third night of the Republican National Convention, C-Span, August 19, 1992, www.c-span.org/video/?31353-1 /republican-national-convention; Adam Nagourney, "'Cultural War' of 1992 Moves In from the Fringe," *New York Times*, August 29, 2012, www.nytimes .com/2012/08/30/us/politics/from-the-fringe-in-1992-patrick-j-buchanans-words -now-seem-mainstream.html; Barry Goldwater to Patrick Buchanan, July 12, 1992, B: 2, F: 25a, BGP; and Goldwater to Buchanan, August 18, 1992, B: 2, F: 25a, BGP.

18. Mack Reed, "Still Seeing Red," *Los Angeles Times*, September 27, 1993.

19. Reed, "Still Seeing Red."

20. William Jefferson Clinton, "Oklahoma Bombing Memorial Prayer Service Address," April 23, 1995, AmericanRhetoric.com, www.americanrhetoric.com /speeches/wjcoklahomabombingspeech.htm; John Mintz, "Criticism Leveled at the NRA," *Washington Post*, April 28, 1995, www.washingtonpost.com /archive/politics/1995/04/28/criticism-leveled-at-the-nra/7d8c1769-4acb-4a96 -845a-0c5ef6775f22/.

21. Reed, "Still Seeing Red"; and Email, William Norman Grigg to Ernie Lazar, March 12, 2007, in author's possession. Grigg, a one-time senior editor of the Birch Society's *New American* magazine, asked McManus what he thought of Wattenberg after McManus had appeared on a television show with Wattenberg hosted by Pat Buchanan. That's when McManus made his antisemitic remark.

22. Murray Waas, "Richard Scaife Paid for Dirt on Clinton in 'Arkansas Project,'" *The Observer*, February 2, 1998, https://observer.com/1998/02/richard-scaife -paid-for-dirt-on-clinton-in-arkansas-project/; Christopher Reed, "Richard Mellon Scaife Obituary," *The Guardian*, July 7, 2014, www.theguardian.com/world/2014 /jul/07/richard-mellon-scaife; Robert L. Jackson, "Falwell Selling Tape That Attacks Clinton," *Los Angeles Times*, May 14, 1994, www.latimes.com/archives /la-xpm-1994-05-14-mn-57626-story.html; and Kenn Thomas, "Clinton-Era Conspiracies!," *Washington Post*, January 16, 1994.

23. Michael Lind, "Calling All Crackpots," *Washington Post*, October 16, 1994.

24. Charles Babington, "Boos Greet Gun Ban Testimony," *Washington Post*, March 11, 1992; Stuart A. Wright, *Patriots, Politics, and Oklahoma City Bombing* (Cambridge, UK: Cambridge University Press, 2007), 58; Wayne LaPierre to Dear Fellow Americans, fundraising letter, reprinted in Deborah Homsher, *Women and Guns: Politics and the Culture of Firearms in America* (New York: Routledge, 2015), 325; and Michael E. Diamond, "George H.W. Bush's Public Rejection of the NRA Exemplified His Duty to 'Honor, Duty, and Country,'" NBC News, December 5, 2018, www.nbcnews.com/think/opinion/george -h-w-bush-s-public-rejection-nra-exemplified-his-ncna944086.

25. Newt Gingrich, transcript of Address to College Republicans, Holiday Inn Airport, June 24, 1978, B: 7, F: 8a, BGP.

26. Anthony Ferlanto to Robert Welch, January 4, 1965, B: 1, F: 21, JBSR.

27. AP, "GOP Caucus Favors Cutoff of Funds for Bosnia Mission," *Deseret News*, December 15, 1995, www.deseret.com/1995/12/13/19209713/gop-caucus -favors-cutoff-of-funds-for-bosnia-mission.

28. Patrick Buchanan to Dear Friend and Fellow Conservative, Winter 1995, C: 45, F: Buchanan 1996, SDC. Under the heading "Culture War," Buchanan brought up the topic of monuments and history—vowing that "all federally funded institutions . . . will manifest a respect for America's history and values—and all monuments, battlefields, and symbols of America's glorious, if sometimes tragic, history will be protected." Buchanan to Dear Friend, March 1995, C: 45, F: Buchanan 1996, SDC; Buchanan to Dear Fellow Republican, March 1996, C: 45, F: Buchanan 1996, SDC; and James Bennet, "Politics: Patrick J. Buchanan: Candidate's Speech Is Called Code for Controversy," *New York Times*, February 25, 1996.

29. Richard L. Berke, "Joining Race, Specter Attacks the Right," *New York Times*, March 31, 1995, www.nytimes.com/1995/03/31/us/joining-race-specter -attacks-the-right.html.

30. Peter Carlson, "Pat Buchanan's Far Right Hand," *Washington Post*, September 13, 2000; "Reform Party Vice Presidential Candidate Ezola Foster," *Washington Post*, August 29, 2000, www.washingtonpost.com/wp-srv/liveonline/00/politics /freemedia082900_foster.htm; Reuters, "Buchanan Learns Running Mate Is Birch Member," *Washington Post*, August 14, 2000. The *New York Times* called Foster "the first black candidate to seek the vice presidency for what is, arguably, a major party." Michael Janofsky and B. Drummond Ayres Jr., "The 2000 Campaign: The Reform Parties; Buchanan Chooses Black Woman as Running Mate," *New York Times*, August 12, 2000.

31. Mark Shields, "Where Dole Is No Reagan," *Washington Post*, September 2, 1995, www.washingtonpost.com/archive/opinions/1995/09/02/where-dole -is-no-reagan/728c29ad-cdbd-45b7-b08f-0677929f612e/.

Chapter 11. Takeover

1. Curtis Dickinson, "Texas Governor George W. Bush Is Also a Member of the Illuminist Satanic Secret Society, Skull & Bones!," The Cutting Edge, July 1999, www.cuttingedge.org/news/n1314.cfm.

2. Nicholas D. Kristof, "A Philosophy with Roots in Conservative Texas Soil," *New York Times*, May 21, 2000, www.nytimes.com/2000/05/21/us/a-philosophy -with-roots-in-conservative-texas-soil.html.

3. David S. Broder and Mike Allen, "Bush Cites Regret on Bob Jones," *Washington Post*, Feburary 28, 2000, www.washingtonpost.com/archive/politics/2000/02/28/bush-cites-regret-on-bob-jones/ae6ee98e-cef3-4acf-b576-3e7e69a9f57c/; Richard Gooding, "The Trashing of John McCain," *Vanity Fair*, September 24, 2008, www.vanityfair.com/news/2004/11/mccain200411; Frank Bruni, "The 2000 Campaign: Campaign Memo; Bush and McCain, Sittin' in a Tree, D-I-S-S-I-N-G," *New York Times*, February 9, 2000, www.nytimes.com/2000/02/09/us/the-2000-campaign-campaign-memo-bush-and-mccain-sittin-in-a-tree-d-i-s-s-i-n-g.html; Elaine Kamarck, "A Short History of Campaign Dirty Tricks before Twitter and Facebook," Brookings, July 11, 2019, www.brookings.edu/blog/fixgov/2019/07/11/a-short-history-of-campaign-dirty-tricks-before-twitter-and-facebook/; Juliet Eilperin and Hanna Rosin, "Bob Jones: A Magnet School for Controversy," *Washington Post*, February 25, 2000.

4. Richard L. Berke, "Bush Tests Presidential Run with a Flourish," *New York Times*, March 8, 1999, www.nytimes.com/1999/03/08/us/bush-tests-presidential-run-with-a-flourish.html?searchResultPosition=19; Forrest Sawyer, "Ten Trillion and Counting," transcript, *Frontline*, PBS, accessed July 25, 2022, www.pbs.org/wgbh/pages/frontline/tentrillion/etc/script.html; Adam Nagourney, "Bush Iowa Trip Signals Real Start of 2000 Race for the Presidency," *New York Times*, June 13, 1999, www.nytimes.com/1999/06/13/us/bush-iowa-trip-signals-real-start-of-2000-race-for-the-presidency.html; and White House, President George W. Bush, "Fact Sheet: Compassionate Conservatism," press release, April 30, 2002, https://georgewbush-whitehouse.archives.gov/news/releases/2002/04/20020430.html.

5. Michael E. Miller, "'It's Insanity': How the 'Brooks Brothers Riot' Killed the 2000 Recount in Miami," *Washington Post*, November 15, 2018, www.washingtonpost.com/history/2018/11/15/its-insanity-how-brooks-brothers-riot-killed-recount-miami/. For more on the "riot," see Jeffrey Toobin, *Too Close to Call: The Thirty-Six-Day Battle to Decide the 2000 Election* (New York: Random House, 2001).

6. David W. Moore, "Bush Job Approval Highest in Gallup History," Gallup News Service, September 24, 2001, https://news.gallup.com/poll/4924/bush-job-approval-highest-gallup-history.aspx; News desk, "George W. Bush, Nation-Builder," *Chicago Tribune*, June 25, 2006, www.chicagotribune.com/chinews-mtblog-2006-06-george_w_bush_nationbuilder-story.html.

7. For an overview of the controversies about Bush's foreign policy, see James Mann, *George W. Bush* (New York: Times Books, 2015), especially 70–80. AP, "Bush Signs Schiavo Legislation," NBC News, March 16, 2005; Jeffrey Toobin, "Ashcroft's Ascent," *New Yorker*, April 7, 2002, www.newyorker.com/magazine/2002/04/15/ashcrofts-ascent; "John Ashcroft's Speech at Bob Jones University," transcript, *New York Times*, January 13, 2001, www.nytimes.com/2001/01/13/politics/john-ashcroftacutes-speech-at-bob-jones-university.html.

8. Joshua Micah Marshall, "John Ashcroft's Rebel Yell," *Slate*, December 26, 2000, https://slate.com/news-and-politics/2000/12/john-ashcroft-s-rebel-yell.html; Diane Roberts, "Ashcroft Is Bush's Gift to White Evangelical Christians," *Tampa Bay Times*, February 11, 2001, www.tampabay.com/archive/2001/02/11/ashcroft-is-bush-s-gift-to-white-evangelical-christians/.

9. "John Ashcroft: The Controversial Issues," ABC News, January 6, 2006, https://abcnews.go.com/Politics/story?id=122054&page=1; "Prepared Remarks of Attorney General John Ashcroft," Voting Integrity Symposium, October 8, 2002, www.justice.gov/archive/ag/speeches/2002/100802ballotintegrity.htm.

10. Eric Lipton and Ian Urbina, "In 5-Year Effort, Scant Evidence of Voter Fraud," *New York Times*, April 12, 2007, www.nytimes.com/2007/04/12/washington/12fraud.html; Cameron Scott, "The Real D.O.J. Scandal: Infringement of Voting Rights," *Mother Jones*, May 2, 2007, www.motherjones.com/politics/2007/05/real-doj-scandal-infringement-voting-rights/; Transcript, "Gonzales Acknowledges 'Mistakes' in Ousting U.S. Attorneys," *PBS News Hour*, March 13, 2007, www.pbs.org/newshour/show/gonzales-acknowledges-mistakes-in-ousting-u-s-attorneys.

11. Jane Coaston and Andrew Prokop, "Jerome Corsi, the Conspiracy Theorist Now Entangled in the Mueller Investigation, Explained," *Vox*, November 28, 2018, www.vox.com/policy-and-politics/2018/11/28/18112717/jerome-corsi-mueller-roger-stone-donald-trump-wikileaks.

12. Chip Berlet, "The North American Union Right-Wing Populist Conspiracism Rebounds," *Public Eye*, March 10, 2008, www.politicalresearch.org/2008/03/10/the-north-american-union-right-wing-populist-conspiracism-rebounds-2; Patrick J. Buchanan, *Where the Right Went Wrong: How Neoconservatives Subverted the Reagan Revolution and Hijacked the Bush Presidency* (New York: St. Martin's Press, 2004), introduction; Drake Bennett, "The Amero Conspiracy," *New York Times*, November 25, 2007, www.nytimes.com/2007/11/25/world/americas/25iht-25Amero.8473833.html ("If you haven't heard about the NAU, that may be because its plotters have succeeded in keeping it secret," the *Times* deadpanned); Dan Barry, "Holding Firm Against Plots By Evildoers," *New York Times*, June 25, 2009; and White House, "President Bush Participates in Joint Press Availability with Prime Minister Harper of Canada and President Calderon of Mexico," transcript of press conference, August 21, 2007, https://georgewbush-whitehouse.archives.gov/news/releases/2007/08/20070821-3.html.

13. Alyson Klein, "No Child Left Behind: An Overview," *Education Week*, April 10, 2015, www.edweek.org/policy-politics/no-child-left-behind-an-overview/2015/04; Chuck Squatriglia, "Bush Signs Energy Bill Raising Fuel Economy Standards," *Wired*, December 19, 2007, www.wired.com/2007/12/auto-industry-w/.

14. White House, President George W. Bush, "Remarks by the President at Islamic Center of Washington, D.C.: 'Islam Is Peace' Says President," press release, September 17, 2001, https://georgewbush-whitehouse.archives.gov/news/releases/2001/09/20010917-11.html; White House, President George W. Bush, "President Bush Addresses the Nation on Immigration Reform," press release, May 15, 2006, https://georgewbush-whitehouse.archives.gov/news/releases/2006/05/20060515-8.html.

15. Ann Coulter, "Read My Lips: No New Amnesty," AnnCoulter.com, May 17, 2006; White House, President George W. Bush, "President Bush Signs Voting Rights Act Reauthorization and Amendments Act of 2006," press release, July 27, 2006, https://georgewbush-whitehouse.archives.gov/news/releases/2006/07/20060727.html; Legal Defense Fund, "Case: Voting Rights Act Reauthorization, 2006," February 16, 2018, www.naacpldf.org/case-issue/voting-rights-act-reauthorization-2006/;

Hamil R. Harris and Michael Abramowitz, "Bush Signs Voting Rights Act Extension; and "President Vows to Build on 'Legal Equality' Won in Civil Rights Era," *Washington Post*, July 28, 2006, www.washingtonpost.com/archive/politics/2006/07/28/bush-signs-voting-rights-act-extension-span-classbankhead president-vows-to-build-on-legal-equality-won-in-civil-rights-eraspan/0d60601a-241f-4f92-99c3-9a71114d3069/.

16. White House, "President Bush: Information Sharing, Patriot Act Vital to Homeland Security," presidential remarks, Buffalo, New York, April 20, 2004, https://georgewbush-whitehouse.archives.gov/news/releases/2004/04/20040420-2.html. For an analysis of Bush's approach to the war on terror and executive power, see Julian Zelizer, "How Conservatives Learned to Stop Worrying and Love Presidential Power" (chapter 2), and Timothy Naftali, "George W. Bush and the 'War on Terror'" (chapter 4), in *The Presidency of George W. Bush: A First Historical Assessment*, ed. Julian Zelizer (Princeton, NJ: Princeton University Press, 2010).

17. Tom Rosentiel and Scott Keeter, "Trends in Public Opinion about the War in Iraq, 2003-2007," Pew Research Center, March 15 2007, www.pewresearch.org/2007/03/15/trends-in-public-opinion-about-the-war-in-iraq-20032007/; "President Bush's Second Inaugural Address," transcript, National Public Radio, January 20, 2005, www.npr.org/templates/story/story.php?storyId=4460172.

18. Charles Creitz, "Tucker Carlson: Now is the Time to Pull Out of Iraq for Good," Fox News, January 8, 2020, www.foxnews.com/media/tucker-carlson-iraq-iran-donald-trump-leave-war; Glenn Beck, *Liars: How Progressives Exploit Our Fears for Power and Control* (New York: Simon and Schuster, 2016), 228; and remarks in Tulsa, Oklahoma, "Jerome R. Corsi: Impeach Bush," Youtube, October 1, 2007, www.youtube.com/watch?v=RJRYzuLehT8.

19. David M. Herszenhorn, Carl Hulse, and Sheryl Gay Stolberg, "Talks Implode During a Day of Chaos; Fate of Bailout Plan Remains Unresolved," *New York Times*, September 25, 2008, www.nytimes.com/2008/09/26/business/26bailout.html.

20. David M. Herszenhorn, "Bailout Plan Wins Approval; Democrats Vow Tighter Rules," *New York Times*, October 3, 2008, www.nytimes.com/2008/10/04/business/economy/04bailout.html; Martin Kady II, "GOP Slams Bush over Bailout," *Politico*, December 19, 2008, www.politico.com/story/2008/12/gop-slams-bush-over-bailout-016753.

21. Christopher Caldwell, "The Antiwar, Anti-Abortion, Anti-Drug-Enforcement-Administration, Anti-Medicare Candidacy of Dr. Ron Paul," *New York Times Magazine*, July 22, 2007, www.nytimes.com/2007/07/22/magazine/22Paul-t.html; Jim Rutenberg and Sergei Kovaleski, "Paul Disowns Extremists' Views but Doesn't Disavow the Support," *New York Times*, December 26, 2011.

22. akchuk, "Ron Paul's 2002 Speech Warning Against War in Iraq," US House of Representatives, video, YouTube, January 5, 2017, www.youtube.com/watch?v=a2IdTtQb7YA; Amy Gardner, "Ron Paul Forms GOP Presidential Exploratory Committee," *Washington Post*, April 26, 2011, www.washingtonpost.com/politics/ron-paul-forms-gop-presidential-exploratory-committee/2011/04/26/AFb5SntE_story.html; Juliet Eilperin, "What the 2002 use of force resolution against Iraq can tell us about the Syria vote," *Washington Post*, September 1, 2013;

W.W. 'Chip' Wood, "Ron Paul on 'End the Fed,'" *The New American*, March 3, 2010, thenewamerican.com/ron-paul-on-end-the-fed/; and Andrew Kreighbaum, "Bombs Away!," *Texas Tribune*, May 3, 2010, www.texastribune.org/2010/05/03/money-bombs-a-new-political-organizing-tool/.

23. David M. Halbfinger, "Ron Paul's Flinty Worldview Was Forged in Early Family Life," *New York Times*, February 5, 2012, www.nytimes.com/2012/02/06/us/politics/for-ron-paul-a-distinctive-worldview-of-long-standing.html; Morgan Little, "Ron Paul, Social Security Opponent, Acknowledges He Receives Benefits," *Los Angeles Times*, June 20, 2012, www.latimes.com/archives/la-xpm-2012-jun-20-la-pn-ron-paul-social-security-opponent-acknowledges-he-receives-benefits-20120620-story.html; and Rutenberg and Kovaleski, "Paul Disowns."

24. Ron Paul, "The Trouble with the '64 Civil Rights Act," transcript, LewRockwell.com, July 3, 2004, www.lewrockwell.com/2004/07/ron-paul/the-trouble-with-the-64-civil-rights-act/; Talking Points Memo, "Ron Paul: I Would *Not* Have Voted for the 1964 Civil Rights Act," May 13, 2011, https://talkingpointsmemo.com/dc/ron-paul-i-would-em-not-em-have-voted-for-the-1964-civil-rights-act-video; and ProPublica, "House Vote 374—On Passage," July 13, 2006, https://projects.propublica.org/represent/votes/109/house/2/374.

25. "The Republican Debate," transcript, *New York Times*, November 28, 2007, www.nytimes.com/2007/11/28/us/politics/28debate-transcript.html; Caldwell, "The Anti-War, Anti-Abortion, Anti-Drug Enforcement Administration;" Brendan Spiegel, "Ron Paul: How a Fringe Politician Took Over the Web," *Wired*, June 27, 2007, www.wired.com/2007/06/ron-paul/; ChooseRonPaul, "North American Union Question for Ron Paul," video, YouTube, December 1, 2007, www.youtube.com/watch?v=6Y30k3nkk54; and Ron Paul, "Excerpt: *The Revolution: A Manifesto*," *Talk of the Nation*, NPR, May 14, 2008, www.npr.org/templates/story/story.php?storyId=90438900.

26. Rutenberg and Kovaleski, "Paul Disowns"; Halbfinger, "Ron Paul's Flinty Worldview"; RonaldReaganVIDEO, "Ron Paul on Larry McDonald," video, YouTube, August 31, 2010, https://www.youtube.com/watch?v=lQQ--ju7Vxk. "More people died from the [flu] shot than they did who had gotten the flu," Paul told the John Birch Society, recalling his and McDonald's proud votes against flu-vaccine funding. Zach Dorfman, "The Congressman Who Created His Own Deep State. Really," *Politico*, December 2, 2018, www.politico.com/magazine/story/2018/12/02/larry-mcdonald-communists-deep-state-222726/.

27. "L Rockwell," n.d., handwritten note, "week of August 23d–27th"; Welch to Llewellyn H. Rockwell Jr., January 13, 1966, B: 5, F: 43, JBSR. Welch addressed him as "Rocky."

28. James Kirchick, "Angry White Man," *The New Republic*, January 8, 2008; Andy Kroll, "10 Extreme Claims in Ron Paul's Controversial Newsletters," *Mother Jones*, January 3, 2012, www.motherjones.com/politics/2012/01/ron-paul-newsletter-iowa-caucus-republican/; Brian Todd, "Ron Paul '90s Newsletters Rant Against Blacks, Gays," CNN, January 10, 2008, www.cnn.com/2008/POLITICS/01/10/paul.newsletters/; Jerry Markon and Alice Crites, "Ron Paul Signed Off on Racist 1990s Newsletters, Associates Say," *Washington Post*, January 27, 2012; Julian Sanchez and David Weigel, "Who Wrote Ron

Paul's Newsletters?," *Reason*, January 16, 2008, https://reason.com/2008/01/16/who-wrote-ron-pauls-newsletter.

29. Rutenberg and Kovaleski, "Paul Disowns"; Southern Poverty Law Center, "Stormfront," accessed July 25, 2022, www.splcenter.org/fighting-hate/extremist-files/group/stormfront. The SPLC called Stormfront "the first major hate site on the Internet."

30. Rutenberg and Kovaleski, "Paul Disowns."

31. Bennett, "Amero Conspiracy"; Berlet, "North American Union"; and John Harwood, "Libertarian Legion Stands Ready to Accept Torch from Paul," *New York Times*, August 25, 2012.

32. David Barstow, "McCain Confronts Christian Right, Citing Divisiveness," *New York Times*, February 29, 2000, https://archive.nytimes.com/www.nytimes.com/library/politics/camp/022900wh-gop-mccain.html; Jonathan Weisman, "N.H. Momentum Carries McCain to South Carolina; Bush Leads in Polls in Conservative State," *Baltimore Sun*, February 3, 2000, www.baltimoresun.com/news/bs-xpm-2000-02-03-0002030325-story.html.

33. Pew Research Center, "How the Faithful Voted," November 5, 2008, www.pewresearch.org/religion/2008/11/05/how-the-faithful-voted/; Dan Nowicki and Bill Muller, "John McCain Sheds Maverick 'Tag,' Goes Establishment for 2008 Election," *Arizona Republic*, April 2, 2018, www.azcentral.com/story/news/politics/arizona/2018/04/02/john-mccain-sheds-maverick-goes-establishment-2008-presidential-election-iraq-war-arizona-senator/537899001/.

34. Jennifer Steinhauer, "Confronting Ghosts of 2000 in South Carolina," *New York Times*, October 19, 2007, https://www.nytimes.com/2007/10/19/us/politics/19mccain.html; Cenk Uygur, "Not the Candidate He Used to Be," *Politico*, March 12, 2008, https://www.politico.com/story/2008/03/not-the-candidate-he-used-to-be-009000; and Nowicki and Muller, "McCain Sheds"; Sam Stein, "McCain Backer Hagee Said Hitler Was Fulfilling God's Will (Audio)," *Huffington Post*, May 29, 2008, www.huffpost.com/entry/mccain-backer-hagee-said_n_102892; Press Release, "Hagee Goes Off the Rails; McCain Must Act," Catholic League, March 4, 2008, www.catholicleague.org/hagee-goes-off-the-rails-mccain-must-act/; Reuters, "U.S. Pro-Israel Evangelical Leader Hagee Endorses McCain," *Haaretz*, February 28, 2008, www.haaretz.com/2008-02-28/ty-article/u-s-pro-israel-evangelical-leader-hagee-endorses-mccain/0000017f-f096-d223-a97f-fddf98f90000.

35. Lisa Marie Segarra, "Watch John McCain Strongly Defend Barack Obama During the 2008 Campaign," *Time*, July 20, 2017, https://time.com/4866404/john-mccain-barack-obama-arab-cancer/.

36. eminehart, "Palin's Excessive Use of 'Maverick' at the VP Debate," video, YouTube, October 5, 2008, www.youtube.com/watch?v=sBzXVHoF-pI.

37. *Saturday Night Live*, "Weekend Update: Sarah Palin Rap—SNL," video, YouTube, August 12, 2013, www.youtube.com/watch?v=dQlgkq_EW64.

38. Jo Becker, Peter S. Goodman, and Michael Powell, "Once Elected, Palin Hired Friends and Lashed Foes," *New York Times*, September 13, 2008, www.nytimes.com/2008/09/14/us/politics/14palin.html; Ben Smith, "What's On the Desk?," *Politico*, September 18, 2008, www.politico.com/blogs/ben-smith/2008/09/whats-on-the-desk-012015; David Neiwert and Max Blumenthal,

"Meet Sarah Palin's Radical Right-Wing Pals," *Salon*, October 10, 2008, www
.salon.com/2008/10/10/palin_chryson; and Robb Fulcher, "Tiny Alaska Independence Movement Slumbering—for Now," UPI, October 22, 1984, www.upi
.com/Archives/1984/10/22/Tiny-Alaska-independence-movement-slumbering
-for-now/9732467265600/.

39. "Bush's Address to the Republican National Convention," transcript,
New York Times, September 2, 2008, https://www.nytimes.com/elections/2008
/president/conventions/videos/transcripts/20080902_BUSH_SPEECH.html;
New Republic Staff, "Palin and Pegler," *New Republic*, September 13, 2008,
https://newrepublic.com/article/44391/palin-and-pegler; and David Mack, "Katie Couric Says Her 2008 Question to Sarah Palin About Newspapers Probably Wouldn't Have the Same Effect Today," *BuzzFeed News*, March 21, 2019,
https://www.buzzfeednews.com/article/davidmack/katie-couric-sarah-palin
-question.

40. Dana Milbank, "Unleashed, Palin Makes a Pit Bull Look Tame," *Washington Post*, October 7, 2008, www.washingtonpost.com/wp-dyn/content
/article/2008/10/06/AR2008100602935_pf.html; Ben Smith, "Palin's Source,"
Politico, September 10, 2008, www.politico.com/blogs/ben-smith/2008/09
/palins-source-011713; Ben Smith, "What's on the Desk?," *Politico*, September 18,
2008, www.politico.com/blogs/ben-smith/2008/09/whats-on-the-desk-012015;
New Republic Staff, "Palin and Pegler"; and Russell Goldman, "Is Negative Rhetoric a License to Taunt?," ABC News, October 8, 2008, https://abcnews.go.com
/Politics/Vote2008/story?id=5987004&page=1.

41. Suzanne Goldenberg, "US Election: Palin's Place in Republican Party Uncertain After Defeat," *The Guardian*, November 5, 2008, https://www.theguardian
.com/world/2008/nov/05/uselections2008-palin-republicans.

42. "Good Riddance, GOP Moderates," *The Rush Limbaugh Show*, October
24, 2008, https://www.rushlimbaugh.com/daily/2008/10/24/good_riddance_gop
_moderates/; Alex Seitz-Wald, "On Limbaugh's Show, Bush Acknowledges That
Limbaugh and His Comrades Killed Immigration Reform," *ThinkProgress*, November 10, 2010, https://archive.thinkprogress.org/on-limbaughs-show-bush
-acknowledges-that-limbaugh-and-his-comrades-killed-immigration-reform
-ec1a10fefbc4/.

43. Eliza Relman, "How a Public-Access Broadcaster from Austin, Texas, Became a Major Conspiracy Theorist and One of Trump's Most Vocal Supporters," *Business Insider*, June 19, 2017, www.businessinsider.com/alex-jones-bio
-conspiracy-trump-megyn-kelly-2017-6; Eric Boehlert, "Why Don't We Just Pre-
tend Rush Limbaugh Has 50 Million Listeners?," Media Matters for America,
March 9, 2009, www.mediamatters.org/rush-limbaugh/why-dont-we-just-pretend-
rush-limbaugh-has-50-million-listeners; Charlie Warzel, "Alex Jones Will Never
Stop Being Alex Jones," *BuzzFeed News*, May 3, 2017, www.buzzfeednews.com
/article/charliewarzel/alex-jones-will-never-stop-being-alex-jones#.mh28Vlbbv.
Emphasizing the centrality of right-wing talk radio in the rise of Trumpism, Brian
Rosenwald's *Talk Radio's America: How an Industry Took Over a Political Party That
Took Over the United States* (Cambridge, MA: Harvard University Press, 2019)
points to Rush Limbaugh's ascent as a national talk radio shock jock in 1988 as a
pivotal moment.

44. John Richardson, "Alex Jones: Father Knows Best, Updated for the Apocalypse," *Esquire*, December 2, 2015, www.esquire.com/news-politics/news/a24349/alex-jones-interview.

45. Richardson, "Alex Jones"; AP, "Stella Tremblay resigns: NH Lawmaker Said Government Was Behind Boston Marathon Bombings," *MassLive*, June 20, 2013, www.masslive.com/news/boston/2013/06/stella_tremblay_resigns_nh_law.html.

46. Nicholas Fandos, "Alex Jones Takes His Show to the Capitol, Even Tussling with a Senator," *New York Times*, September 5, 2018, www.nytimes.com/2018/09/05/us/politics/alex-jones-marco-rubio-inforwars.html; Elizabeth Williamson, "Alex Jones's Podcasting Hecklers Face Their Foil's Downward Slide," *New York Times*, April 18, 2021, www.nytimes.com/2021/04/18/us/politics/alex-jones.html; John Birch Society (@The_JBS), "Alex Jones is the latest victim of the #DeepState," Twitter, August 8, 2018, https://twitter.com/the_jbs/status/1027238099376631808?lang=en; Andy Cush, "The Invisible Empire of Alex Jones," *Spin*, October 26, 2016, www.spin.com/featured/the-invisible-empire-of-alex-jones/; and Mediamatters4America, "Trump Ally Alex Jones: Clinton, Obama Are Demons," video, YouTube, October 10, 2016, www.youtube.com/watch?v=M5KTiAcTEyc.

47. Alex Koppelman, "Glenn Beck Makes Nice with the John Birch Society," *Salon*, July 26, 2007, https://www.salon.com/2007/07/26/birch_beck/; David Folkenflik, "Glenn Beck's Show on Fox News to End," National Public Radio, April 6, 2011, www.npr.org/2011/04/06/135181398/glenn-beck-to-leave-daily-fox-news-show; and Sean Wilentz, "Confounding Fathers: The Tea Party's Cold War Roots," *New Yorker*, October 11, 2010.

48. Alexander Zaitchik, "Meet the Man Who Changed Glenn Beck's Life," *Salon*, September 16, 2009, www.salon.com/2009/09/16/beck_skousen/. Former Bush White House speechwriter David Frum once described Skousen as "one of the legendary cranks of the conservative world, a John Bircher, a grand fantasist of theories about secret conspiracies between capitalists and communists to impose a one-world government under the control of David Rockefeller." Jamison Foser, "David Frum: 'What the Hell Is Going on at Fox News?,'" Media Matters for America, March 18, 2009, www.mediamatters.org/fox-news/david-frum-what-hell-going-fox-news. Also see Sarah Posner, "Glenn Beck, the John Birch Society, and the Conservative Movement," *American Prospect*, March 18, 2009, https://prospect.org/article/glenn-beck-john-birch-society-conservative-movement./.

49. Wilentz, "Confounding Fathers"; Dana Milbank, "Why Glenn Beck Lost It," *Washington Post*, April 6, 2011; Dana Milbank, "Glenn Beck vs. the Rabbis," *Washington Post*, January 28, 2011; and RonPaulFriends, "Glenn Beck and G. Edward Griffin Talk About the FED," video, YouTube, March 27, 2011, www.youtube.com/watch?v=ZmW3ytfhZ9M. Media Matters and other liberal critics assailed Beck's decision to air Griffin's ideas.

50. TheSmokingArgus, "Rick Santelli calls for Tea party on floor of Chicago Board of Trade," Youtube, www.bing.com/videos/search?q=rick+santelli+tea+party+rant&view=detail&mid=38E49B84E3149A53FBE338E49B84E3149A53FBE3&FORM=VIRE; Newsweek staff, "Tea Party Movement Is Full of Conspiracy Theories," *Newsweek*, February 8, 2010, www.newsweek.com/tea-party-movement-full-conspiracy-theories-75153.

51. Theda Skocpol, *The Tea Party and the Remaking of Republican Conservatism* (New York: Oxford University Press, 2012); and Melissa Deckman, *Tea Party Women: Mama Grizzlies, Grassroots Leaders, and the Changing Face of the American Right* (New York: New York University Press, 2016). These political scientists stress the evolution of the Republican conservative movement, arguing that the Tea Party meaningfully changed the tone, ideas, and outlook of the GOP.

52. David Barstow, "Tea Party Lights a Fuse for Rebellion on the Right," *New York Times*, February 15, 2010. Timothy McVeigh wore a T-shirt bearing the "tree of liberty" motto on the day he bombed the Oklahoma City federal building. Steve Bryant, "Armed Men Attend Obama Speech," NBC Chicago, August 17, 2009, www.nbcchicago.com/news/politics/man-with-assault-rifle-attends-obama-rally/1859764/. See Andrew Cohen, "Tyranny, from Tim McVeigh to Ginni Thomas," *The Atlantic*, March 18, 2010, www.theatlantic.com/national/archive/2010/03/tyranny-from-tim-mcveigh-to-ginny-thomas/37637/.

53. Editorial, "In Two Cities, Facts Beat Fluoride Fantasies," *Tampa Bay Times*, September 16, 2012, www.tampabay.com/archive/2012/09/16/in-2-cities-facts-beat-fluoride-fantasies/; Kate Zernike, "In New Jersey, a Battle over a Fluoridation Bill, and the Facts," *New York Times*, March 3, 2012; Lizette Alvarez, "Looking to Save Money, More Places Decide to Stop Fluoridating the Water," *New York Times*, October 14, 2011. During the Great Recession, towns and cities were also looking for ways to cut budgets, and reports of fluorosis—yellow spots on teeth due to over-consumption of fluoride—led to renewed efforts to stop fluoridating the drinking water.

54. Bryan Gervais and Irwin Morris, "Reading the Tea Leaves: Understanding Tea Party Caucus Membership in the US House of Representatives," *PS: Political Science and Politics* 45, no. 2 (2012): 245–250, www.jstor.org/stable/41433688; Bryan Gervais and Irwin Morris, *Reactionary Republicanism: How the Tea Party in the House Paved the Way for Trump's Victory* (New York: Oxford University Press, 2018), chapter 1.

55. "Laura Ingraham: Cantor Loss 'Massive Wake-up Call' for GOP on Amnesty," *Breitbart*, June 10, 2014, www.breitbart.com/politics/2014/06/10/laura-ingraham-cantor-loss-massive-wakeup-call-for-gop-on-amnesty/; Emily Stephenson, "Meet Dave Brat—The Tea Party Challenger Who Beat Eric Cantor in a Stunning Upset," *Business Insider*, June 11, 2014, www.businessinsider.com/dave-brat-2014-6; and Kiran Dhillon, "Before Cantor: Seven Other Tea Party Upsets," *Time*, June 12, 2014, https://time.com/2864303/before-cantor-seven-other-tea-party-upsets/. A few Tea Party candidates were so toxic that they lost otherwise winnable general elections—Missouri's Todd Aiken, Nevada's Sharron Angle, Indiana's Richard Mourdock.

56. Michael Grunwald, "Mick the Knife," *Politico Magazine*, September/October 2017, www.politico.com/magazine/story/2017/09/01/mick-mulvaney-omb-trump-budget-profile-feature-215546/; Matthew Yglesias, "Trump's Budget Director Has Some Obviously Strange Ideas About Economic Policy," *Vox*, December 21, 2016, www.vox.com/policy-and-politics/2016/12/21/14033896/mick-mulvaney-debt-ceiling; and Pema Levy, "Trump's Budget Director Pick Spoke at a John Birch Society Event," *Mother Jones*, December 19, 2016, www.motherjones.com/politics/2016/12/trump-mulvaney-john-birch-society/.

57. Jennifer Rubin, "Palling Around with Birchers," *Washington Post*, February 7, 2014, www.washingtonpost.com/blogs/right-turn/wp/2014/02/07 /palling-around-with-birchers/; Betsy Woodruff, "Bevin Facebook Post: 'Enjoying Time with the John Birch Society in Union, Ky.,'" *National Review*, February 7, 2014, www.nationalreview.com/corner/bevin-facebook-post-enjoying -time-john-birch-society-union-ky-betsy-woodruff/.

58. ElectionsInfo.com, "Michele Bachmann 2012 Presidential Campaign Launch," accessed September 5, 2022, http://electionsinfo.com/Michele _Bachmann_2012_Presidential_Campaign_Launch; Spring Chenoa Cooper, "Michele Bachmann and Vaccines: If Only We Could Vaccinate Against HPV Rumors," *The Conversation*, October 4, 2011, https://theconversation.com/michele -bachmann-and-vaccines-if-only-we-could-vaccinate-against-hpv-rumours-3608; Benjy Sarlin, "Michele Bachmann's Radical Reading List," *Talking Points Memo*, August 8, 2011, https://talkingpointsmemo.com/dc/michele-bachmann-s -radical-reading-list; Gervais and Morris, "Reading the Tea Leaves"; and Gervais and Morris, *Reactionary Republicanism*, chapter 1. The authors argue that the Tea Party reached the height of its power in 2011, when an estimated 30 percent of Americans said they supported the movement.

59. Frank Rich, "The Axis of the Obsessed and Deranged," *New York Times*, February 27, 2010; Eric Black, "Pawlenty, CPAC, and the John Birch Society," *Minnesota Post*, January 8, 2010, www.minnpost.com/eric-black-ink/2010/01 /pawlenty-cpac-and-john-birch-society/; Governor Ronald Reagan, "We Will Be a City Upon a Hill," transcript of remarks to the First Annual Conservative Political Action Committee Conference, January 25, 1974, www.cfif.org/htdocs /freedomline/current/america/governor_ronald_reagan.htm; and Adam Nagourney and Kate Zernike, "Conservatives of All Stripes Gather, Emboldened but Far from Unanimous," *New York Times*, February 18, 2010.

60. Lymari Morales, "Obama's Birth Certificate Convinces Some, but Not All, Skeptics," Gallup, May 13, 2011, https://news.gallup.com/poll/147530 /obama-birth-certificate-convinces-not-skeptics.aspx. Still, in 1965, according to one poll, a plurality of Americans thought that communists had infiltrated civil rights groups. See Roper Center for Public Opinion Research, "Public Opinion on Civil Rights: Reflections on the Civil Rights Act of 1964," accessed August 17, 2022, https://ropercenter.cornell.edu/public-opinion-civil-rights-reflections -civil-rights-act-1964; Dana Blanton, "Fox News Poll: 24 Percent Believe Obama Not Born in U.S.," Fox News, December 23, 2015, www.foxnews.com/politics /fox-news-poll-24-percent-believe-obama-not-born-in-u-s.

61. Neil Genzlinger, "John Stormer, 'None Dare Call It Treason' Author, Dies at 90," *New York Times*, July 17, 2008; Kyle Cheney, "No, Clinton Didn't Start the Birther Thing. This Guy Did," *Politico*, September 16, 2016, www.politico.com /story/2016/09/birther-movement-founder-trump-clinton-228304; Trumprulezdot com, "Donald Trump on the View; Trump Wants to See Obama's Birth Certificate," video, YouTube, March 25, 2011, www.youtube.com/watch?v=emkDpm_vQDg.

62. Newsweek staff, "Tea Party Movement"; Ashley Parker and Steve Eder, "Inside the Six Weeks Donald Trump Was a Nonstop 'Birther,'" *New York Times*, July 2, 2016; and Glenn Kessler, "More 'Birther' Nonsense from Donald Trump and Sarah Palin," *Washington Post*, April 12, 2011, www.washingtonpost.com

/blogs/fact-checker/post/more-birther-nonsense-from-donald-trump-and-sarah
-palin/2011/04/11/AFrme2MD_blog.html.

63. Matt Negrin, "Trump's Birther Claim Eclipses Romney," ABC News, May 29, 2012, abcnews.go.com/Politics/OTUS/trump-birther-theory-mitt-romney-accepts -support/story?id=16452474; John Bohrer, "Making Mitt: The Myth of George Romney," *BuzzFeed News*, October 15, 2012, www.buzzfeednews.com/article/john rbohrer/making-mitt-the-myth-of-george-romney; Reid Epstein, "Trump Endorses Mitt," *Politico*, February 2, 2012, www.politico.com/story/2012/02/trump -to-endorse-mitt-072365.

64. Wilentz, "Confounding Fathers"; Jamelle Bouie, "'Stop the Steal' Didn't Start with Trump," *New York Times*, January 15, 2021.

65. *Republican National Committee's Growth and Opportunity Project Report*, March 18, 2013, reprinted in the *Washington Post*, apps.washingtonpost.com/g /documents/politics/republican-national-committees-growth-and-opportunity -project-report/380/?itid=lk_inline_manual_1.

Chapter 12. Radicalization

1. Albin Krebs and Robert McG. Thomas Jr., "Notes on People: Roy Cohn Joins Board of Anti-Communist Group," *New York Times*, May 15, 1982, www .nytimes.com/1982/05/15/nyregion/notes-on-people-roy-cohn-joins-board-of-anti -communist-group.html.

2. Tim Perone, "Obama Mocks Trump at White House Correspondents' Dinner," *New York Post*, May 1, 2011, https://nypost.com/2011/05/01/obama -mocks-trump-at-white-house-correspondents-dinner/.

3. Callum Borchers, "The Wrongest Media Predictions About Donald Trump," *Washington Post*, November 9, 2016, www.washingtonpost.com/news/the-fix /wp/2016/11/09/the-wrongest-media-predictions-about-donald-trump/; Dana Milbank, "Trump Will Lose, or I Will Eat This Column," *Washington Post*, October 2, 2015, www.washingtonpost.com/opinions/trump-will-lose-or-i-will-eat-this -column/2015/10/02/1fd5c94a-6906-11e5-9ef3-fde182507eac_story.html.

4. Reuters Staff, "What Trump Has Said About the United Nations," *Reuters*, September 17, 2017, www.reuters.com/article/us-un-assembly-trump-comments -factbox-idUSKCN1BS0UO; Meg Wagner and Brian Ries, "Trump Gives Remarks on U.S.-Mexico-Canada Deal," CNN, October 1, 2018, www.cnn.com/politics /live-news/trump-us-mexico-canada-remarks-oct-18/h_2c0a8c6bad4dc7a2f98 acda7c57ea454; and Amber Phillips, "'They're Rapists.' President Trump's Campaign Launch Speech Two Years Later, Annotated," *Washington Post*, June 16, 2017, www.washingtonpost.com/news/the-fix/wp/2017/06/16/theyre-rapists-presidents -trump-campaign-launch-speech-two-years-later-annotated/.

5. Nolan D. McCaskill, "Trump Accuses Cruz's Father of Helping JFK's Assassin," *Politico*, May 3, 2016, www.politico.com/blogs/2016-gop-primary-live -updates-and-results/2016/05/trump-ted-cruz-father-222730; Dierdre Shesgreen, "Donald Trump, Russia and Ukraine: Five Conspiracy Theories Debunked," *USA Today*, December 10, 2019, www.usatoday.com/story/news/politics/2019/12/09 /president-donald-trump-russia-ukraine-conspiracy-theories-fbi-witch-hunt -campaign-spy-election/2612331001/; Dareh Gregorian, "Meet Meuller's Team:

The Best Prosecutors in the Business or 'Angry Democrats'?," NBC News, March 23, 2019, www.nbcnews.com/politics/donald-trump/meet-mueller -s-team-best-prosecutors-business-or-angry-democrats-n976226; Dylan Matthews, "The Conspiracy Theories About the Clintons and Jeffrey Epstein's Death, Explained," *Vox*, November 14, 2012, www.vox.com/2019/8/10/20800195/clinton bodycount-conspiracy-theory-jeffrey-epstein; Adam Goldman, Mark Mazzetti, and Matthew Rosenberg, "F.B.I. Used Informant to Investigate Russia Ties to Trump Campaign, Not to Spy, as Trump Claims," *New York Times*, May 18, 2018, www .nytimescom/2018/05/18/us/politics/trump-fbi-informant-russia-investigation. html; and Devlin Barrett, Matt Zapotosky, Karoun Demirijan, and Ellen Nakashima, "FBI Was Justified in Opening Trump Campaign Probe, but Case Plagued by 'Serous Failures,' Inspector General Finds," *Washington Post*, December 9, 2019, www.washingtonpost.com/national-security/inspector-general-report-trump -russia-investigation/2019/12/09/d5940d88-184c-11ea-a659-7d69641c6ff7 _story.html.

6. "Donald Trump's Argument for America," two-minute campaign ad, C-Span, November 4, 2016, www.c-span.org/video/?418167-101/trump-presidential -campaign-ad.

7. Bill Kristol (@BillKristol), "Trump has entered John Birch Society/Pat Buchanan territory," Twitter, December 7, 2015, https://twitter.com/BillKristol /status/673984214514204672.

8. Democracy Now!, "The Iraq War Was a Big, Fat Mistake," video, YouTube, February 15, 2016, https://www.youtube.com/watch?v=whX35NKthQw; Ben Shapiro, "Peak Trump: 'I Don't Need Anybody's Money,'" *Breitbart*, June 16, 2015, www.breitbart.com/politics/2015/06/16/peak-trump-i-dont-need-anybodys -money/; and Team Fix, "The CBS News Republican Debate Transcript, Annotated," *Washington Post*, February 13, 2016, www.washingtonpost.com/news /the-fix/wp/2016/02/13/the-cbs-republican-debate-transcript-annotated/.

9. Juliana Menasce Horowitz, Ruth Igielnik, and Rakesh Kochhar, "Trends in U.S. Income and Wealth Inequality," Pew Research Center, January 9, 2020, www.pewresearch.org/social-trends/2020/01/09/trends-in-income-and-wealth -inequality/; Chad Stone, Danilo Trisi, Arloc Sherman, and Jennifer Beltran, "A Guide to Statistics on Historical Trends in Income Inequality," Center for Budget and Policy Priorities, January 13, 2020, www.cbpp.org/research/poverty-and -inequality/a-guide-to-statistics-on-historical-trends-in-income-inequality; Federal Reserve Bank of St. Louis, "How Has Income Inequality Changed over the Years," *On the Economy Blog*, June 30, 2016, www.stlouisfed.org/on-the-economy/2016 /june/how-has-income-inequality-changed-years.

10. US Census Bureau, "1960 Census: Supplementary Reports: Race of the Population of the U.S. by States," September 7, 1961, accessed July 25, 2022, www .census.gov/library/publications/1961/dec/pc-s1-10.html; US Census Bureau, "2010 Census Shows America's Diversity," press release, March 24, 2011, www.census .gov/newsroom/releases/archives/2010_census/cb11-cn125.html.

11. Nicole Narea, "The demise of America's asylum system under Trump, explained," *Vox*, November 5, 2019, www.vox.com/2019/11/5/20947938/asylum -system-trump-demise-mexico-el-salvador-honduras-guatemala-immigration

-court-border-ice-cbp; Lulu Garcia-Navarro, "Stephen Miller and 'The Camp of the Saints,' a White Nationalist Reference," NPR, November 19, 2019, www.npr.org/2019/11/19/780552636/stephen-miller-and-the-camp-of-the -saints-a-white-nationalist-reference; Jean Raspail, *The Camp of the Saints* (Petoskey, MI: Social Contract Press, 1973).

12. CNBC, "President Donald Trump on Charlottesville: 'You Had Very Fine People on Both Sides,'" video, YouTube, August 15, 2017, www.youtube.com /watch?v=JmaZR8E12bs; ABC News, "'Stand Back and Stand By' Trump Said When Asked to Condemn White Supremacy," video, YouTube, September 30, 2020, www.youtube.com/watch?v=It-2Rsqb9pA; and Katie Rogers and Kevin Roose, "Trump Says QAnon Followers Are People Who 'Love Our Country,'" *New York Times*, August 19, 2020; Andrew O'Reilly, "Trump Addresses QAnon Conspiracy Theory for the First Time: 'I Heard That These Are People That Love Our Country,'" Fox News, August 19, 2020, www.foxnews.com/politics/trump -qanon-conspiracy-theory-first-time; and Will Rahn and Dan Patterson, "What Is the QAnon Conspiracy Theory?," CBS News, March 29, 2021, www.cbsnews.com /news/what-is-the-qanon-conspiracy-theory/.

13. Adam Serwer, "Jeff Sessions Still Hates the ACLU," *American Prospect*, December 22, 2010, https://prospect.org/article/jeff-sessions-still-hates-aclu./; Tina Nguyen, "Steve Bannon Has a Nazi Problem," *Vanity Fair*, September 12, 2017, www.vanityfair.com/news/2017/09/steve-bannon-has-a-nazi-problem; Mark Potok, "Revealed: Conway, Bannon Members of Secretive Group," Southern Poverty Law Center, August 31, 2016, www.splcenter.org/hatewatch/2016/08/31 /revealed-conway-bannon-members-secretive-group; Adam Edelman, "Trump Not Crazy Enough for You? Here Are Five Ideas Spread by Site Run by the Mogul's New Campaign CEO," *New York Daily News*, August 17, 2016, www.nydailynews .com/news/politics/5-breitbart-conspiracy-theories-head-spin-article-1.2755173; Eric Hananoki, "Breitbart Reporter Is a White Nationalist with a Long Trail of Racist and Anti-Muslim Twitter Posts," Media Matters for America, January 28, 2017, www.mediamatters.org/breitbart-news/breitbart-reporter-white-nationalist -long-trail-racist-and-anti-muslim-twitter-posts; Daniel Victor and Liam Stack, "Stephen Bannon and Breitbart News, in Their Own Words," *New York Times*, November 14, 2016, www.nytimes.com/2016/11/15/us/politics/stephen-bannon -breitbart-words.html; Elisabeth Sherman, "Ten Most Despicable Stories Breitbart Published Under Bannon," *Rolling Stone*, November 23, 2016, www.rollingstone.com /culture/culture-lists/10-most-despicable-stories-breitbart-published-under -bannon-115278/; Anti-Defamation League, "Steve Bannon: Five Things to Know," May 3, 2022, www.adl.org/resources/backgrounders/steve-bannon-five-things -to-know?ref=patrick.net; and Aiden Pink, "Steve Bannon's Five Most Controversial Moments at Breitbart," *The Forward*, January 9, 2018, https://forward .com/news/391784/steve-bannons-5-most-controversial-jewish-moments-at -breitbart/.

14. Benjamin Wermund and Kimberly Hefling, "Trump's Education Secretary Pick Supported Anti-gay Causes," *Politico*, November 25, 2016, www.politico.com /story/2016/11/betsy-devos-education-secretary-civil-rights-gay-transgender -students-231837; Milton Gaither, "Betsy DeVos and the History of

Homeschooling," *Process: A Blog for American History*, March 7, 2017, www .processhistory.org/devos-homeschooling/; Zack Stanton, "How Betsy De-Vos Used God and Amway to Take Over Michigan Politics," *Politico Magazine*, January 15, 2017, www.politico.com/magazine/story/2017/01/betsy-dick -devos-family-amway-michigan-politics-religion-214631/.

15. D'Angelo Gore, Eugene Kiely, Lori Robertson, and Rem Rieder, "Timeline of Trump's COVID-19 Comments," Factcheck.org, October 2, 2020; Media Matters staff, "Fox News Guest Claims the COVID Vaccine Is Killing 'Hundreds of Thousands' and Says It's 'the Most Dangerous Vaccine Ever Created,'" Media Matters for America, August 10, 2022, www.mediamatters.org/fox-news /fox-news-guest-claims-covid-vaccine-killing-hundreds-thousands-and-says-its -most-dangerous; Reuters Staff, "Fact Check: COVID-19 Is Not a Hoax to Eliminate Trump," *Reuters*, June 19, 2021, www.reuters.com/article/uk-factcheck-covid -hoax-eliminate-trump-idUSKBN27S31E; and Ron Filipkowski (@RonFilipkowski), "In a new interview, Michael Flynn says covid was intentionally introduced into the world by global elites," Twitter, January 29, 2022, https://twitter.com /RonFilipkowski/status/1487432929038983172?s=20&t=X_d_yXo10qwito O58uuXgg.

16. David Smith and Julie Carrie Wong, "Trump Tacitly Endorses Baseless QAnon Conspiracy Theory Linked to Violence," *The Guardian*, August 19, 2020, www.theguardian.com/us-news/2020/aug/19/trump-qanon-praise-conspiracy -theory-believers; Darlene Superville and Amanda Seitz, "Trump Defends Disproved COVID-19 Treatment," ABC News, July 28, 2020, https://abcnews.go.com /Health/wireStory/trump-pushes-unproven-drug-covid-19-treatment-72027409; and Caitlin Dickson, "Coronavirus Conspiracy Theories Make Fauci the Villain, Because Someone Has to Be," *Yahoo! News*, April 28, 2020, https://news .yahoo.com/coronavirus-conspiracy-theories-make-fauci-the-villain-because-some one-has-to-be-140013416.html?guccounter=1.

17. Jamelle Bouie, "'Stop the Steal' Didn't Start with Trump," *New York Times*, January 15, 2021; Suzanne Goldenberg, "US Election: Republican Claims Community Organization Commits Voter Fraud," *The Guardian*, October 14, 2008, www.theguardian.com/world/2008/oct/14/uselections2008-republicans-acorn; Jess Henig, "ACORN Accusations," Factcheck.org, October 18, 2008, www.fact check.org/2008/10/acorn-accusations/.

18. Laurence Swanson to Robert Welch, week of October 19, 1964, B: 1, F: 6, JBSR; "Irregularities Charged in Fluoride Issue in 3 Towns," n.d., unnamed newspaper article, B: 4, F: 23, ADLC.

19. Tom Hill to William Burke, January 22, 1973, B: 9, F: 2, JBSR. In 1973, Hill acknowledged that Rabbi Meir Kahane, leader of the violence-prone Jewish Defense League who was later convicted on charges related to bomb making, had been a Bircher in the mid-1960s, under the name Michael King; "Trump's Full Speech at D.C. Rally on Jan. 6," Wall Street Journal Video, February 7, 2021.

20. Ed Pilkington, "Incitement: A Timeline of Trump's Inflammatory Rhetoric Before the Capitol Riot," *The Guardian*, January 7, 2021, www.theguardian.com /us-news/2021/jan/07/trump-incitement-inflammatory-rhetoric-capitol-riot; *Bulletin*, November 30, 1959, B: 121, F: 6, HPP.

21. Jackie Salo, "Black Capitol Police officers say DC rioters repeatedly used N-word," *New York Post*, January 10, 2021; Robert Page, "21 Million Americans Say Biden Is 'Illegitimate' and Trump Should Be Restored by 'Violence,'" *The Conversation*, September 23, 2021, https://theconversation.com/21-million-americans-say-biden-is-illegitimate-and-trump-should-be-restored-by-violence-survey-finds-168359; Ed Pilkington, "What Is 'Great Replacement' Theory and How Did Its Racist Lies Spread in the US?," *The Guardian*, May 17, 2022, www.theguardian.com/us-news/2022/may/17/great-replacement-theory-explainer.

22. Aymann Ismail, "We Know Exactly Who the Capitol Rioters Were," *Slate*, January 4, 2022, https://slate.com/news-and-politics/2022/01/january-6-capitol-riot-arrests-research-profile.html; Mallory Simon and Sara Sidner, "Decoding the Extremist Symbols and Groups at the Capitol Insurrection," CNN, January 11, 2021, www.cnn.com/2021/01/09/us/capitol-hill-insurrection-extremist-flags-soh/index.html; Caitlin Dickson, "Poll: Two-Thirds of Republicans Still Think the 2020 Election Was Rigged," *Yahoo! News*, August 4, 2021, https://news.yahoo.com/poll-two-thirds-of-republicans-still-think-the-2020-election-was-rigged-165934695.html.

Conclusion

1. Brian Stelter, "Experts Warn About the Radicalizing Power of Right-Wing Media Network," CNN Business, December 21, 2020, www.cnn.com/2020/12/21/media/right-wing-radicalization-election-results/index.html; Caroline Fredrickson and Lisa Graves, "On Dark Money and the Right's Judicial Revival," *National Law Journal*, May 31, 2019; George Hawley, *Making Sense of the Alt-Right* (New York: Columbia University Press, 2017), chapter 3; John Huntington, *Far-Right Vanguard: The Radical Roots of Modern Conservatism* (Philadelphia: University of Pennsylvania Press, 2021); Public Citizen, "Public Citizen Supports Bipartisan Constitutional Amendment to Overturn Citizens United," press release, January 21, 2021, www.citizen.org/news/bipartisan-constitutional-amendment-to-overturn-citizens-united-introduced/; David Jackson, "Donald Trump, Power Broker: Primaries Show He Retains a Degree of Control over Republicans," *USA Today*, August 3, 2022, www.usatoday.com/story/news/politics/2022/08/03/donald-trump-primaries-control-gop/10222402002/?gnt-cfr=1; and Alec Tyson, "Tea Party Republicans Exert Stronger Influence in GOP Primaries," Pew Research Center, August 7, 2013, www.pewresearch.org/fact-tank/2013/08/07/tea-party-republicans-exert-stronger-influence-in-gop-primaries/.

2. For more on the history of conservatives who lost a debate or an election but achieved long-term victories, see Jeffrey K. Tulis and Nicole Mellow, *Legacies of Losing in American Politics* (Chicago: University of Chicago Press, 2018).

3. For an overview of the fractures that have shaped American life since Watergate, see Kevin Kruse and Julian Zelizer, *Fault Lines: A History of the United States Since 1974* (New York: W.W. Norton, 2019).

4. Reuters, "Fact Check: False Quote Attributed to Abraham Lincoln Is Distortion of an 1838 Speech," January 26, 2021, www.reuters.com/article/uk-factcheck-lincoln-quote-fake-idUSKBN29V2HH; Matthew Dallek, "Alan Brinkley and the

Revival of Political History," in *Alan Brinkley: A Life in History*, ed. David Greenberg, Moshe Temkin, and Mason Williams (New York: Columbia University Press, 2018), 85; and Judith N. Shklar, "The Liberalism of Fear," in *Liberalism and the Moral Life*, ed. Nancy L. Rosenblum (Cambridge, MA: Harvard University Press, 1989), 22–37.

INDEX

Western Front, 145–147
Western Goals Foundation, 271–272
Western Islands, 99
Westin, Alan, 71, 77, 137
Where's the Birth Certificate (Corsi),
   267–268
White, Walter, 146
White Citizens' Councils, 69, 154, 157,
   169, 194, 202, 279
White House Correspondents' Dinner,
   272
White House Labor-Management
   Committee, 64
white supremacy/white supremacists,
   99, 127, 145–147, 152–154, 157,
   169–170, 182–183, 199–201, 235,
   255–256, 277
white-power militias, 212
*Why the Philadelphia Police Advisory
   Board Should Be Abolished*, 119
Wicker, Tom, 217
Wilentz, Sean, 268
Will, George, 227
Williams, Harrison, 15
"Willie Horton" ad, 231, 246
Wilson, Jane, 80, 168
Wilson, Woodrow, 13, 23, 76
women
   acceptance of, 42, 162
   conservative beliefs of, 164–166
   devotion to cause and, 166–167
   education policies and, 167, 168,
     169–170

electoral politics and, 171
feminism and, 163–164
lack of in leadership positions,
   163–164
MMM office and, 172–176
see also individual women
Women of the Klan, 164
World Health Organization (WHO),
   241, 276
World War I, 23, 32, 38
World War II, 13–14, 23–24, 138,
   195, 220
WorldNetDaily.com, 267
Wright, Lloyd, 185

X, Malcolm, 169–170

Yabbacio, Jeri, 175
Yellen, Janet, 273
YMCA, 285
Young, Milton, 59, 66
Young, Stephen, 15, 77, 189
Young Americans for Freedom (YAF),
   45, 91, 200–201
Young Republican Club, 99
Young Republicans, 92, 93

Zack, Isadore, 136, 138–139, 140–145,
   148–150
Zetterberg, Eric, Jr., 131
Ziegler, Bea, 120
Ziegler, Ron, 198
Zika virus, 265

Sammy Sarathy Dallek

Matthew Dallek is a historian and professor of political management at George Washington University's College of Professional Studies. He is the author of *The Right Moment* and *Defenseless Under the Night*, and his writing has also appeared in the *New York Times*, the *Washington Post*, the *Los Angeles Times*, *Politico*, and other publications. He lives in Washington, DC.